CONNECTIONS
Writing
FOR
YOUR WORLD

Doris Humphrey, Ph.D.

Career Solutions Training Group

Robert Conklin, Ph.D.

DeVry University-Columbus

THOMSON

SOUTH-WESTERN

Australia · Canada · Mexico · Singapore · Spain · United Kingdom · United States

THOMSON
SOUTH-WESTERN

Connections: Writing for Your World
By Doris Humphrey and Robert Conklin

Vice President/ Editor-in-Chief
Dave Shaut

Senior Publisher
Karen Schmohe

Acquisition Editor
Joseph Vocca

Project Manager
Penny Shank

Production Manager
Tricia Matthews Boies

Production Editor
Alan Biondi

Marketing Manager
Lori Pegg

Marketing Coordinator
Georgianna Wright

Manufacturing Coordinator
Kevin Kluck

Design Project Manager
Stacy Jenkins Shirley

Cover Design
Lou Ann Thesing

Internal Design
Lou Ann Thesing

Compositor
Electro Publishing

Internal Cartoons
W. Grant Brownrigg

Printer
Edwards Brothers
Ann Arbor, MI

International Division List

ASIA (Including India):
Thomson Learning
60 Albert Street, #15-01
Albert Complex
Singapore 189969
Tel 65 336-6411
Fax 65 336-7411

LATIN AMERICA:
Thomson Learning
Seneca 53
Colonia Polanco
11560 Mexico, D.F. Mexico
Tel (525) 281-2906
Fax (525) 281-2656

UK/EUROPE/MIDDLE EAST/AFRICA:
Thomson Learning
Berkshire House
168-173 High Holborn
London WC1V 7AA
United Kingdom
Tel 44 (0)20 497-1422
Fax 44 (0)20 497-1426

AUSTRALIA/NEW ZEALAND:
Nelson
102 Dodds Street
South Melbourne
Victoria 3205
Australia
Tel 61 (0)3 9685-4111
Fax 61 (0)3 9685-4199

CANADA:
Nelson
1120 Birchmount Road
Toronto, Ontario
Canada M1K 5G4
Tel (416) 752-9100
Fax (416) 752-8102

SPAIN (includes Portugal):
Paraninfo
Calle Magallanes 25
28015 Madrid
España
Tel 34 (0)91 446-3350
Fax 34 (0)91 445-6218

Expect More
from South-Western with...

Basic English Review,

Schachter/Schneiter (0-538-72720-9)
The eighth edition of this popular text takes a unique and time-proven approach to understanding the fundamentals of English. This user-friendly text and CD package motivates learners with activities focused on grammar, punctuation, spelling, vocabulary, and writing skills.

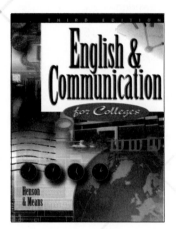

English & Communication for Colleges,

Henson/Means (0-538-72303-3)
This text is designed to build the critical communication skills valued by employers in the workplace today. A focus is placed on grammar and mechanics as the foundation skills for good writing and on the essential writing, speaking, and listening skills needed to excel in today's business environment.

Your Career: How to Make It Happen,

Levitt (0-538-72708-X)
This market leading text provides thorough coverage of the job search, interviewing, and career building activities and is rich with Internet links and activities. Packed with resources, this text will not only enhance learning, but will serve as a valuable reference in the future.

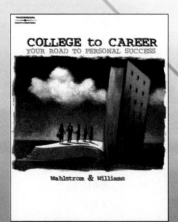

College to Career: Your Road to Personal Success,

Wahlstrom/Williams (0538726695)
Focused on career success skills and career development, an emphasis is placed on lifelong learning by connecting the skills mastered for college success with those needed for success and life on the job. Essential skills and strategies are presented concisely for busy users, and the text and supplements feature a highly interactive approach to learning.

Brief Contents

CONTENTS

Contents

CONTENTS

CONTENTS

CONTENTS

CONTENTS

Contents

 **CONTENTS OF DATA CD**

Readings and Writings with Activities

Worksheets for Applying Your Skills Activities

Files to Accompany Select Activities and Practices

PREFACE

Ask managers or supervisors to identify the top two or three skills employees need for career success, and the answer almost always includes *good communication*. Inquire about communication weaknesses, and these employers will tell you that being *unable to write well* is a major weakness of workers in all types of jobs at all levels of their careers. While most people can get words on paper, relatively few write well enough to get their message across effectively.

You are one of the fortunate students whose instructor or school has chosen a unique textbook to help you build your writing skills. *Connections: Writing for Your World* will provide you with the writing tools you need to be successful—starting with your first day of employment. The textbook will help you understand *why* you need to learn a specific writing skill and also *how* to apply that skill to the career of your choice.

This textbook was written with your future writing needs in mind. The authors have excellent insight into the writing demands of today's jobs. They have had successful careers as writing instructors, both in schools and in training programs for employees, and they have worked with employers to identify the writing weaknesses that employees must overcome.

Take advantage of what can be learned from *Connections: Writing for Your World*, and you will be one of the employees who stands out because of excellent writing ability. Keep in mind: Anyone can be a good writer. It just takes time and practice.

Organization of the Text

Connections: Writing for Your World is divided into two major sections: (1) twenty-five chapters of writing basics that are connected to activities and exercises, and (2) a Writer's Handbook that will build your skill in the fundamentals of grammar, word usage, spelling, and punctuation. These two sections are described below.

The Chapters

The twenty-five chapters of *Connections: Writing for Your World* are divided into three parts. Each part has a specific purpose that is described below.

Part I is introductory and will help you identify how you can become a better writer.

Part II focuses on writing paragraphs, the first building block to becoming an effective writer.

Part III focuses on writing essays—not only traditional essays like those you have written in school previously, but also business documents such as proposals, reports, summaries, and letters.

Writer's Handbook

The Writer's Handbook serves two purposes: (1) to teach you some of the most frequently used grammar, word usage, spelling, and punctuation guidelines and (2) to provide practice in troublesome areas.

Within the Chapters

To learn the most from a writing course, you should be able to enjoy the content of the textbook. *Connections: Writing for Your World* offers several interesting and motivating features that will add to your overall pleasure and success. Look for the following features in each chapter.

➤ Objectives

Every chapter includes a list of the chapter *Objectives*. A quick glance at these will tell you what you can expect to learn in the chapter.

➤ Career Pathways Chart

The uniqueness of this textbook is its approach to writing as a career skill. Therefore, each chapter begins by breaking careers down into the six general pathways that represent all jobs that exist today or will be created in the future.

The *Career Pathways* chart provides valuable information. It (1) identifies one sample career in each of the six pathways, (2) shows how the chapter's topic connects to the career, and (3) gives a career-related writing example related to the chapter's topic. (For example, the *Career Pathways* chart in Chapter 11 features *Narration*, which is the chapter's topic.)

➤ On The Job

Near the beginning of each chapter, *On The Job* introduces an employee who is writing for work and gives an example of the employee's writing. You will read about Kara, an administrative assistant in Chapter 1 who resists when her supervisor asks her to prepare a rough draft proposal; about Keola, a promotions manager in Chapter 5 who needs to write a publicity notice; and about Jasmine, a TV reporter in Chapter 21 who has to prepare a news story. In the remaining 22 chapters, you will learn about the concerns, questions, and need for writing guidance of other profiled employees.

➤ Self-Assessment

One important way to improve any skill is to analyze how well you are currently doing. The *Self-Assessment* provides a short checklist that allows you to evaluate your writing ability.

➤ Did You Ever?

To give a clearer picture of each chapter's topic, *did you ever?* suggests times when you previously might have used a technique covered in the chapter. For example, *Did you ever return from vacation and tell your friends how you spent your time?* appears as an example of illustration in Chapter 21.

➤ Ethics Connections

If you read newspapers or listen to the news, you are aware of the ethics violations that occur daily and often lead to embarrassment for companies and organizations. Because writing often includes facts and figures, research or quotes, an unethical writer can misuse data and mislead readers. The *Ethics Connections* feature will help you identify what is ethical and unethical and how to ensure that all your writings are ethical.

➤ Technology Connection

By using technology effectively, a writer can reduce or eliminate much of the time-consuming *do-over* work that writers experienced in the past. From giving tips about cutting and pasting to describing how charts and graphs can add value to a document, the *Technology Connection* provides shortcuts and helpful hints that make writing more efficient.

➤ Writing Workshop

Look for the *Writing Workshop* in each chapter to provide excellent additional information. For example, in Chapter 21 you will learn how to find the correct synonym to replace an overused word.

➤ Cartoon

You will enjoy the *Cartoon* that appears in most chapters. Each cartoon shows a visual image of an important writing concept.

➤ Activities

You will complete *Activities* that allow you to apply what you have learned. These activities are placed at intervals in the text, so you do not have to remember a great deal of information before having a chance to apply your knowledge.

➤ Practicing Your Skills

Near the end of each chapter, you will find either one or two *Practicing Your Skills* activities that require a higher level of skill. Often, these include paragraphs or essays for you to review before answering questions.

➤ Applying Your Skills

The *Applying Your Skills* section gives you an opportunity to create your own material in response to each chapter. In this section, you will be asked to write a paragraph or essay that is based on the concepts and techniques discussed in the chapter.

➤ Writing for Your Career

Each chapter begins with a career pathways chart and ends with career pathways writing. In *Writing for Your Career*, you are asked to choose your pathway preference and complete the writing assignment for that pathway. Often, you will be referred to web site links that provide additional information on the topic of the writing assignment. Pay special attention to your work in *Writing for Your Career*, as it closely matches the type of writing you can be expected to do in your chosen career field.

Within the Writer's Handbook

The *Writer's Handbook* is a snapshot of some of the important grammar, word usage, spelling, and punctuation guidelines that writers use. Examples are provided to help you understand the guidelines. The guidelines are followed by *On Your Own*, an important feature that allows you to practice your newly gained knowledge. You can use the Writer's Handbook in two ways: (1) as a reference tool when you are writing and don't remember a rule you learned in the past and (2) to test your knowledge of rules you have just learned.

Student Resources

Handy visual aids are present throughout *Connections: Writing for Your World*. Use these symbols to make your journey through this textbook more interesting and rewarding.

➤ Career Pathways Symbols

Notice the symbols that identify each career pathway in the chart at the beginning of each chapter. In addition to appearing in the chart, these symbols are conveniently placed anywhere an example of a pathway is given within the chapter. The same symbols are used in the *Writing for Your Career* section at the end of the chapters.

If you have an interest in a specific career pathway, therefore, you will want to take special note any time a symbol representing this pathway appears on a page.

An artist's palette represents Communication and the Arts

A medical symbol represents Health and Medicine

A team of coworkers represents Human, Personal, and Public Service

A graph represents Business and Marketing

A computer chip represents Science and Technology

A leaf represents Environment and Natural Resources

➤ Data CD

The Data CD is an-easy-to-use tool that expands the content of each chapter. Keep the Data CD in a convenient place so you can locate it quickly.

First, you will find one or more activities or practices from each chapter on the CD. You may choose your preferred method of performing these exercises—either in the book or electronically. Any time the Data CD symbol appears beside an activity in the text, you will know that the same or related material appears on the CD.

In addition, a form is given on the CD for your use in completing the Applying Your Skills section of each chapter. This is a standard form that takes you step by step through the Applying Your Skills activity.

Finally, several *Readings and Writings* related to each chapter are given on the Data CD. You will be asked to read these, answer the questions, and complete the writing assignments.

➤ Web Links

Many of the *Writing for Your Career* activities contain references to the textbook web site: http://humphrey.swlearning.com. By accessing the web site and clicking on the Links tab for any chapter, you will be able to locate additional helpful information.

➤ Instructor's Resource CD

While this CD is for your instructor's use, you will probably be asked to complete a variety of activities that your instructor provides from the CD. In addition, your instructor will have access to writing models, answers to activities, PowerPoint slides, exam questions, and other information that can expand the textbook.

Connections: Writing for Your World and its abundance of additional material can help you become an excellent writer. Remember, employers value strong workplace writers who can write clearly, accurately, and authoritatively.

Acknowledgements

Special thanks are given to the reviewers who provided important recommendations regarding the content and activities in this text. Their contributions enabled the authors to fine-tune the material so that it meets the writing requirements for both a successful education and a successful career.

Colleen Burke
Rasmussen College
St. Cloud, MN

Cheryl Carr
Mississippi ACTE
Madison, MS

Mike Courteau
The Art Institutes International Minnesota
Minneapolis, MN

Patricia Kato
Chattanooga State Technical Community College
Chattanooga, TN

Donna Kimmerling
Indiana Business College
Anderson, IN

Nancy Porretto
Katharine Gibbs School
New York, NY

Mark Ristroph
Augusta Technical College
Augusta, GA

Beverly Schellhaass
Lakeshore Technical College
Cleveland, WI

Candice Schiffer
Mercyhurst College
Erie, PA

Jeni Woessner
Heald College
Roseville, CA

PART 1

Anyone Can Write

1

Becoming a Writer

IN THIS CHAPTER YOU WILL LEARN TO:

- **Describe why writing is important.**

- **Value the ability to write well.**

- **Identify writing obstacles.**

- **Change how you think about writing.**

- **Write practice material.**

Career Path	Sample Career	Use for Career Writing	Example of Career Writing
Communication and the Arts	Graphic artist	Making recommendations for a catalog	Consider using an interesting full-color design on the front cover. The internal pages will be satisfactory in black and white. For the cover, use a paper stock that is heavier than the stock for the internal pages.
Health and Medicine	Hospice nurse	Writing in a patient's record	Mrs. Landow sleeps peacefully through most of the day and seems to accept her condition. She has the support of family and friends and sees visitors for about two hours each afternoon.
Human, Personal, and Public Service	Highway patrol officer	Describing an accident scene	A blue Buick LeSabre and a Lexus SUV were pulled into the median when I arrived on the scene. The driver of the LeSabre was seriously injured, and I immediately radioed for an emergency response team. The victims were transported to St. Mary's Hospital at 4:18 p.m.
Business and Marketing	Chef	Explaining to the servers the special on the evening's menu	The beef is marinated in a basil vinaigrette and served with a twice-baked, garlic-encrusted potato. A seafood garnish of clams, lobster, and minced crab lies atop the beef. Steamed, fresh, seasonal vegetables accompany the entrée.
Science and Technology	Software consultant	Asking a client to identify a problem	Please list the actions you take to enter the customer's account number. Then write the error message that appears in the dialog box.
Environment and Natural Resources	Nature preserve assistant	Requesting additional mulch for flowers and trees	The two tons of mulch we ordered covered the ground around most of the perennials and trees. However, in one area at the back of the preserve, about 15 trees and a bed of perennials did not receive a mulch application. Could you please order an extra ton of mulch?

3

ON THE JOB

Business Writing

As an administrative assistant to the director of a public relations firm, Kara doesn't think of herself as a writer, even though she writes e-mails, short memos, and occasional document attachments. She reserves the term *writer* for staff members whose primary job responsibility is writing.

When Rafael is hired as public relations director and Kara's new supervisor, he asks her to write a rough draft proposal to a client. Kara explains that she isn't a writer and wouldn't know where to start. She tells him that in the past the directors have written their own proposals, and she has only formatted and printed them.

Rafael says tactfully, "You can't escape your writing responsibilities, Kara, no matter what career path you choose. Everyone must write in his or her job. In the future, I'll expect you to do more writing, including letters, memos, instructions, reports, and proposals."

Later, when Kara tells her husband that she is worried about disappointing Rafael, he suggests that she write Rafael a brief note explaining her concerns. Today she starts her note. Notice the points she makes.

Dear Rafael:

It's a really nice compliment that you want me to do more writing. I think it's only fair for me to tell you again that I am not a good writer. I also don't have time to follow all of the rules of writing because I have so much other work to do. <u>My best skills are in the technical area</u>,[1] and you know how important that is to our work here. <u>Ask me to do computer work of almost any kind</u>,[1] and I am sure you will be pleased with the results. My <u>speed on the keyboard is fast</u>,[1] and <u>I make very few errors</u>.[1] In fact, although I am not a programmer, I have a <u>pretty good knack for developing short programs</u>.[1] <u>Writing is not something I have spent time on because I know the jobs I plan to do in the future will not need writing.</u>[2][3] <u>I didn't take writing courses in school</u>[2] because I was more interested in computers. That's why I did not apply for a job writing press releases when one came up last year.   Thanks, Kara.

Do Kara's comments suggest why she may be unsuccessful in writing? Perhaps she's afraid to write. Maybe she doesn't value writing enough. In this chapter, you will discover why writing is important. Then you'll review the obstacles that may be holding you back as a writer and learn how to get started writing documents that relate to your career.

Why Writing Is Important

Today's companies depend on information to maintain their competitive edge, and that means all employees must be able to **write** well. No longer do engineers only draw project designs and horticulturists only grow healthy plants. They also write a variety of business documents.

Employees in all careers fill out forms, request information, compose memos and letters, prepare reports, use e-mail, write proposals, develop status documents, give directions, prepare estimates, record telephone messages, and respond to customer requests. You, too, will be expected to write well enough to communicate clearly in work-related documents.

Consider these employees whose daily work requires good writing skills.

Magdeina, a physical therapy assistant, prepares reports about the treatments she provides and about each patient's response to the treatments. If she includes an incorrect fact or misrepresents a treatment, other therapists who read her notes may provide an improper treatment that injures the patient.

Ahmed, a legal assistant, approaches his manager with an idea for the firm's employee newsletter. He is asked to submit his idea in the form of a rough draft. Unless Ahmed is a skilled writer, he may be unable to explain his idea properly, resulting in it being rejected.

Kara obviously doesn't understand how her attitude about writing might be bad for her career. Use the numbered items in the On The Job story to analyze Kara's attitude about writing in her work.

1. Concentrating on technical skills
Technical skills alone will not lead to career success. When Kara speaks of her strengths, she names only the technical aspects of her job.

2. Lacking experience
Having avoided writing in school, Kara feels unprepared to do the writing her job demands. Instead of attempting to build her writing skills, she makes excuses for being unwilling to try.

3. Undervaluing writing
Kara underestimates the importance of writing in her career. She is unaware that lack of good writing skills may hold her back.

SELF-ASSESSMENT 1

When I think about writing for my career, I can:

	Usually	Sometimes	Never
Discuss why writing is important.	❏	❏	❏
Identify my writing obstacles.	❏	❏	❏
Overcome my writing fears.	❏	❏	❏
Get started with my writing.	❏	❏	❏
Set aside time for practicing and improving.	❏	❏	❏

If you checked "Sometimes" or "Never" for any of the items, this chapter will help you improve your writing skills. Even if you checked "Usually" in every instance, you will learn more about becoming a better writer.

Valuing the Ability to Write Well

According to a recent U.S. Department of Labor report, most jobs of the future will require good writing skills. Even though a job description may not list writing as a requirement, you cannot assume that you will not be writing.

In addition to government analysts, employers also name writing as one of the most important factors in an employee's success. A survey of employers identified writing as the most valued employment skill. Further, employers said that 80 percent of their employees at all levels need to improve their writing. Employers also stated that good writers stand out in the workplace because so many other employees write poorly.

How you write even routine documents has an impact on your success and on the workplace. For example, a poorly written resume may prevent a job seeker from getting a position. An e-mail full of errors makes a bad impression on coworkers and managers. Unclear instructions create confusion and can have serious consequences in terms of lost time, money, and worker safety.

On the other hand, effective writing can bring you many benefits, including the confidence of supervisors and advancement in your career. Well-written documents stand out. By giving some time and attention now to building your writing skills, you can guarantee yourself greater job success in the future.

The following employees value good writing because they have seen how it helps their career.

 Su-Jung, recently hired as an animal caretaker at the local zoo, was called for an interview because she effectively communicated her love of animals and her outstanding training in animal care.

 Nels, a claims adjuster for an insurance company, was recognized for his excellent claims reports and received an employee-of-the-month award.

did you ever?

- Put off writing a letter because you didn't know what to say or how to say it?

- Plan to write a report but wait so long that you didn't have enough time to do a good job?

- Delay writing a proposal because you had to research the topic?

In this chapter, you will learn techniques to overcome writing attitudes and obstacles that stand in the way of your career success.

Understanding Writing Obstacles

Writing is a skill that comes easily for some people but is more difficult for others. To become a better writer, you need to recognize some of the most common obstacles to success.

Fear of Failure

Like all phobias, fear of writing is a protective mechanism used by the mind to keep a person away from danger. A writing phobia is often triggered by an unpleasant writing event in the past. Perhaps an overly strict instructor filled your essays with red marks, or a supervisor was too critical.

The following techniques can help you overcome your writing fears.

(A) That Was Then; This Is Now	In every school course and new job, you get a fresh start. Remind yourself that all instructors and supervisors don't think alike, and if you had a bad writing experience with a teacher or boss in the past, the current one may take a different approach to writing.
(B) Recognize the Negative Association	Face up to what is scaring you about writing. Admitting a problem is the first step in correcting it.
(C) Do What Works	Some people need privacy when they write, or they may write best with soft music, a soda, or a snack. When possible, indulge your personal preferences if they help you write.

Lack of Formal Training

Lack of formal writing classes is an insufficient reason for delaying writing. Neither Mark Twain, William Shakespeare, nor Virginia Woolf finished high school, so their early writing training was limited. Yet, they are among the most successful writers of all time.

If you lack formal training, try some of these techniques to gain the skills you need.

- Read newspapers, magazines, textbooks, and the writing of others. Then analyze what makes some writing clear and easy to understand.
- Choose a subject you know well and practice writing about it. Revise your material until it sounds clear and interesting.
- Have a good friend or family member critique something you write. Ask the person to make suggestions about parts they don't understand. Then rewrite your sample and ask the same person to read it again. Continue the process until your meaning is clear to the reader.

If you are using this textbook, you are training to write. Whether you are enrolled in a formal educational setting or have decided to learn to write on your own, using the textbook as a guide will provide you with the tools you need to improve your writing skills. After completing this course, look for opportunities to continue your writing, either in school or at your workplace.

Poor Motivation

Motivation is affected to a large degree by how well you do something. Improving your writing skills will improve your motivation to write.

Here are other ideas to increase your motivation:

- Try establishing a writing schedule that offers small rewards. For example, you might set aside 15 minutes to concentrate on writing, followed by a break of 5 minutes to call a friend.
- Recognize that writing is essential to success in every career. Give writing the respect it deserves. Don't allow yourself to take the shortsighted view of those who ignore writing in favor of the technical side of their work.
- Allow plenty of time to write. Squeezing a big task into a small amount of time dooms any project to failure, including writing.

The best writers sometimes worry about whether they can write what they

ACTIVITY 1.1

want in a way that expresses their meaning. Think about your biggest writing fear and explain the problem in a few sentences.

My biggest writing fear:

_____

_____

_____

_____

_____

_____

_____

_____

_____

_____

_____

_____

_____

WRITING WORKSHOP

The Importance of Writing Accurately

Unclear, inaccurate, or incomplete workplace writing, such as e-mail messages, instructions, directions, or incident reports, can lead to misunderstandings. Sometimes the results can be embarrassing, frustrating, or, even, disastrous. What problem do you think is created when a human resource administrator writes this last line in a memo to employees about an upcoming holiday vacation?

(A) Unclear Message Enjoy your Thanksgiving vacation. I'll see everyone on Monday.

(B) Clear Message Enjoy a great Thanksgiving vacation. I will be taking the Friday off after Thanksgiving and will be back in the office on Monday.

In Example (A), the sentence implies that the Thanksgiving vacation goes from Thursday until Monday. In fact, employees only have Thanksgiving Day off.

ACTIVITY 1.2

Think about a bad academic or workplace writing experience you had in the past. How did it make you feel? What did you learn from the experience? What would you change if faced with the same situation in the future? Analyze your experience and describe it below.

My writing experience: _____

_____

The way my writing experience made me feel: _____

_____

What I learned from my writing experience: _____

_____

What I would do differently if faced with this situation in the future: _____

_____

Changing Your Thinking about Writing

You may have heard people say that they have a *mental block* about a particular thing—meaning they are blocked from doing what they want to do because of reasons they don't understand. Students are often blocked when they try to write because they bring baggage from the past to their current writing experience. You may be one of these students.

If you have negative issues from the past about writing, they may interfere with your ability to improve your writing in a current class. However, on the positive side, you can take action now to overcome past writing problems.

Here are a few examples of attitudes and experiences that can influence your ability to get the most from a writing course. Can you relate to any of these?

- Having a preference for visual communication
- Buying into society's emphasis on instant communication (e-mail, instant messaging)
- Thinking that putting words on paper is the same as writing
- Believing that you must be "creative" in order to write
- Thinking that writing is too hard or too much trouble
- Experiencing a teacher who was too strict
- Being critiqued too harshly by classmates
- Having too much class emphasis on grammar and punctuation
- Having too little class attention on generating ideas
- Lacking instruction in how to write correctly
- Lacking examples of effective and ineffective writing
- Considering writing or English as a throwaway course
- Procrastinating

Recognizing harmful attitudes and experiences that hinder your writing progress is the first step in overcoming them. Here are some simple and specific ways that can help you beat harmful past writing problems.

Identify	Write issues from the list above that create problems for you today. Add additional issues that you know influence your writing.
Eliminate	Cross off the issues that you cannot do anything about; for example "having had a teacher who was too strict." Mentally let go of those.

Prioritize	Prioritize the remaining items in order of importance to you. These are the ones you can do something about, for example, *having a preference for visual communication* and *procrastinating*.
Change	Beside each remaining issue, write what you can do to change. For example, beside *procrastinating*, you might write "Set a date for the first draft of my next essay. Finish first draft by the deadline."
Follow Through	Follow your own advice. Place the sheet you prepared in the front of your English book or attach it to your computer. Refer to it each time you write.

Practice Makes Perfect

In writing, as in any other skill, the more you practice, the better you get. Unfortunately, many beginning writers think their work should be perfect the first time, and they don't take time to practice.

For a moment, think about your favorite sports star or singer and answer these questions.

- Did this celebrity reach his or her current level of success with minimal practice, or did success take years of training or voice lessons?
- Did the celebrity stop practicing the skill after becoming successful?
- Does being successful require more or less practice in order to maintain the same or attain a higher level of skill?

What's blocking your path to being a good writer?

Now consider yourself as a beginning writer. If you are committed to becoming a skilled writer—one who can write business letters and proposals or poems and plays—you must spend time in training.

Many new writers think practice refers to starting an essay or a document, completing it, and beginning a different piece of writing. However, *practice* is a broad term that refers to many different things. For example, you practice when you do any of the following:

- Read what you have written to see if it will make sense to someone unfamiliar with the subject.
- Change words or phrases to substitute clearer, more descriptive ones.
- Move paragraphs around so your story or message is better organized and easier to follow.
- Delete words, phrases, or entire sections that do not add meaning to your message.
- Identify and remove distracting or irrelevant passages or paragraphs.
- Research your topic so you can write factual, interesting background information.
- Analyze facts, comments, and examples to determine whether they deliver the message you intended.
- Write a second, third, or fourth version of a document until the writing is as good as you can make it.
- Use your software to spell-check, grammar-check, and format your final version.

The upcoming chapters of this book can help you become an excellent writer. In Chapter 2, "The Writing Process and Your Career," you will learn more about some of the ideas discussed in this chapter. With each new chapter, you will learn one important writing concept and you will be given ample opportunity to practice. Keep in mind, however, that you must be committed to improving your writing skills.

ETHICS CONNECTION

Giving Credit

In school and at work, teams of writers often are assigned to large projects. Therefore, it is not always easy to identify which part of a final report each team member wrote. In a private conversation, is it ethical for one person to take sole credit for a report if other writers contributed?

Imagine that you, your supervisor, and several coworkers who were not involved in a writing project are having a private conversation and your supervisor makes the following statement: "That report you prepared on hazardous waste cleanup procedures was one of the best I have ever seen. Writing the report must have taken a great deal of time."

Whether the other writers on a collaborative writing project are or are not present, you are obligated to give them credit for their efforts. By taking full credit, you are being unethical. You also may be embarrassed and lose credibility if your supervisor learns that you were not the only person responsible for writing the report.

ACTIVITY 1.3   Maybe you have never thought about what you can do to make your writing situations more comfortable. If not, now is the time to analyze how to improve your writing environment, either for class or for work. First, consider your present writing space. Then think about things that would enhance your writing experience. In number 3, your personal preferences may be limited by the place you are writing. For example, at work or school, you may not be allowed to have music or sodas in the area where you write.

1. A place where I could write better than the place I currently use:

   _____

   _____

   _____

2. A better way to prepare my writing area and my writing tools (paper, pen, computer, printer, reference books):

   _____

   _____

   _____

3. The personal preferences (soda, music, other) that would make my writing a more comfortable process:

   _____

   _____

   _____

SUMMARY FOR CAREER WRITING

❑   Knowing why writing is important is the first step to becoming a better writer.

❑   Identifying writing obstacles is essential for improving your writing.

❑   Specific techniques can help you overcome a fear of writing.

❑   By recognizing negative experiences and attitudes that hinder your writing, you can overcome them.

❑   The best writers know they must continue practicing if they want to improve.

PRACTICING YOUR SKILLS

Now that you understand what you must do to become a better writer, put your knowledge to work in the following activities.

PRACTICE

This paragraph was written by Melanie Sharpe, a security officer at a large drug manufacturing firm. She is explaining an attempted break-in.

> On February 17, I made my half-hour rounds to check windows and doors in Building B. As I rounded the north corner, a light-colored truck with its headlights turned off drove through the parking lot, out the open gate, and onto Highway 419. I immediately checked the outside doors of Building B, but I saw no signs of forced entry. However, window 4 on the northeast side showed an attempted break-in. Three windowpanes were broken, and fresh bloodstains were visible on the woodwork. I checked Officer O'Brien's records from yesterday, and no windows were reported broken in his end-of shift report. The bloodstains on the glass indicate that the perpetrator received a cut during the attempted break-in. I recommend that we reconsider our policy of leaving the Highway 419 gate open at night. I have reported the broken window to the Maintenance Department, and it will be replaced today.

The Main Point
1. Underline the main point that Officer Sharpe is trying to make in her report?
2. Is the report clear? Does Officer Sharpe answer all of the important questions about the attempted break-in?

The Body
3. Underline the three most important details in Officer Sharpe's report in Practice 1.
4. Cross out any unnecessary words or sentences.
5. Do any follow-up actions need to be taken as a result of Officer Sharpe's report? If so, what are those actions.

 Importance to Career

6. Why is being able to write this report essential to Officer Sharpe's career?

APPLYING YOUR SKILLS

To overcome the attitudes and obstacles that may affect your writing, it is time to develop an action plan. For each of the obstacles listed below, write specific recommendations for how you can replace the obstacle with action. For example, if you said you fear getting a returned essay full of red marks, what actions can you take to guarantee that doesn't happen?

Obstacle 1:   I may get an essay returned that is full of red marks.

Action Plan: Before turning in my essay, I will review it carefully to make sure that it meets the criteria set by my instructor. I will take time to look for ways to improve my essay and then make any changes. I will check for spelling, grammar, and punctuation mistakes.

Obstacle 2:   I have no formal training in writing.

Action Plan: _____

_____

_____

_____

_____

Obstacle 3:   I just want to do the technical part of my work. I don't want to write.

Action Plan: _____

_____

_____

_____

_____

Obstacle 4:   I don't have time to write well because I have so many other things to do.

Action Plan: _____

_____

_____

_____

_____

WRITING FOR YOUR CAREER

This section presents writing obstacles that can get in the way of your success in each of the six career pathways. Choose one pathway that appeals to you and use your knowledge to analyze the obstacle and to make recommendations about overcoming it.

Communication and the Arts

Imagine that you are a newly employed graphic artist who has been given an assignment to design a brochure for an important client. Before you spend much time on the brochure, your supervisor wants a one-page description of your ideas. Because you have had excellent graphic arts training, you are confident that you can design a brochure that will sell the client's product. However, the thought of putting your ideas on paper for your supervisor is terrifying. You can't seem to get started, and you feel as though you have been keying and deleting lines for hours. List a few recommendations about how you can get started with your description.

Health and Medicine

You are a home health aide who performs personal services for your patients in addition to giving them medication and helping them with light exercises. One elderly patient tells you she is confused about the instructions for her new burglar alarm. In the past, her daughter set the alarm each evening when she came by to check on her mother, but this week the daughter is out of town on vacation. The elderly patient asks you to read the instructions and write them more simply so she can set the alarm after you leave. You know how nervous your patient gets when everything doesn't go right, and you are fearful that you will not be able to write simply enough for her to understand the directions. Make a list of things can you do to ensure that the instructions are clear and easy to understand.

Human, Personal, and Public Service

As one of only a few police officers in a small rural town, you resent the time you must spend writing reports. You believe you should be out patrolling the streets and handling investigations. Every time you start a report, you get distracted by something else you would rather be doing. Lately your supervisor criticized you twice for turning in reports with incomplete details. On your recent employee evaluation, you received low marks in the category of Follow-up Reports. Now you are concerned that your report-writing history will keep you from getting a promotion. Analyze your writing problems and list several recommendations for how you can overcome the bad marks you received for Follow-up.

Business and Marketing

As the pastry chef in an upscale restaurant, you have been asked by the head chef to prepare a description of your famous pastries for the new menus that will be printed soon. His instructions are to make the pastries sound so good that diners will be able to "taste the desserts" when they read your words. This is the first time you have been asked to describe your desserts on paper, and you don't think you have the writing background to do an effective job. You don't know where to start. What should you do? Write a few suggestions to help yourself get started.

Science and Technology

As a specialist in information technology, you feel good when coworkers turn to you for help with their technology problems. Recently, you were recognized as Specialist of the Year. With the honor came a promotion that requires you to write employee evaluations for the three people who now work for you. You have never cared much for writing, and you like it even less when it cuts down on time for troubleshooting technical problems. In addition, your worst grades in school involved writing. You don't like the thought of writing employee evaluations for human resources personnel to read. You worry that your prestige will suffer when people see your writing. What attitudes or obstacles must you overcome to improve your writing? Make a list that you can refer to later.

Environment and Natural Resources

As the expert on wildlife at a nature preserve, you have been asked by a local newspaper to write an article about the overpopulation of deer in the preserve. As part of the article, you are to describe what the preserve plans to do to reduce the deer population. You have some strong opinions on the subject, and you have no problem speaking to groups about the "deer problem." However, writing a newspaper article is the last thing you want to do. You get stuck every time you start the article. In fact, you can't even complete the first line. Analyze your problem and make recommendations about how you can overcome it.

2

The Writing Process and Your Career

IN THIS CHAPTER YOU WILL LEARN TO:

- Understand the writing process.

- Begin with prewriting.

- Ask open-ended questions.

- Narrow the focus.

- Write a series of drafts.

- Edit and proofread.

Using *the Writing Process* for Your Career

Career Path	Sample Career	Use for the Writing Process	Example of Career Writing
Communication and the Arts	Account executive	Preparing a proposal for a client	CarboBar enjoys a loyal following among fitness enthusiasts, but it is not well known to the general population. With a strong advertising campaign that combines television, radio, newspaper, magazines, and billboards, CarboBar can increase sales by 200 percent nationally in one year or less.
Health and Medicine	Nurse midwife	Submitting a freelance plan to a hospital	The nursing shortage in your maternity center and my skill as a nurse midwife are compelling reasons for us to work together. I can save the hospital money by serving as a contracted employee while performing the duties of a salaried nurse.
Human, Personal, and Public Service	Social services counselor	Reporting an incident in one of the on-campus cottages	At 10:07 P.M., I was called to Evergreen Cottage to intervene in a dispute between two residents. Rady Hudley and Mike Landstrum both claimed that it was his night to choose the 10 P.M. television show for the cottage.
Business and Marketing	Product development manager	Brainstorming which new products to develop	Here are descriptions of three products that we will consider for development next year. After you review these descriptions, list ideas for companion products that you think would appeal to the consumer.
Science and Technology	Science technician	Leading a large test group	On the morning of our half-day test to measure the effectiveness of sun blockers, you should arrive by 8 A.M. at Pier 3 on Altamo Beach. Refrain from using makeup, perfume, or any other substance that could interfere with the effectiveness of the blockers.
Environment and Natural Resources	Nature center director	Creating a survey to identify favorite visitor activities	By completing and returning this survey, you will help Forge Park identify the services and activities that you and your family enjoy most. We will take your information and compare it with other surveys to determine where we should place our attention.

Team Leader

Tashelia's sales team at Dyna-Tech, a software company, wins awards every year for the highest sales in retail stores. As a team leader with high energy, Tashelia possesses the ability to motivate others to excel. She has won a trip to Cancun, dinners at fine restaurants, and the Team Leader of the Month award three months in a row.

Tashelia looks forward to every workday, and she considers leading such a first-rate team a privilege. However, with regard to written communication, she has had to work hard to build her skills. Prior to this job, writing had not been a major part of her responsibilities. Now she often writes reports, proposals, action plans, and minutes of meetings.

Today as she begins to develop an action plan for promoting a new software product in retail stores, she plans to concentrate fully on the writing process. She knows that taking time to work thoughtfully through each step of the process will result in a better action plan—and a better action plan will mean more sales!

First, she thinks about what she will say in her plan—her main idea. Then she begins to narrow the topic. By adding several strong supporting ideas, ones that clarify and explain the main idea, she expects to eliminate any confusion the team may have about how the new software will be promoted and sold to customers.

> [1] Competition has never been stronger among software products sold in retail stores. [2] New tax software programs are introduced every day. Our team's challenge is [3] to develop such a creative, exciting promotion for *Easy TAX Planning*, our new program, that customers will rush in to see what we're offering. We must identify the features of the software that every customer wants and advise the advertising department to promote those features in radio, television, newspaper, and billboard ads. If we can convince customers that *Easy TAX Planning* will make April 15 (tax time) less stressful, the software should fly off the shelves. At our next team meeting, let's brainstorm what features to highlight in the promotion and how to make the features come alive in the customer's mind.

Did Tashelia begin with a main idea and develop it in the remainder of her paragraph? If she did, her prewriting was successful. In this chapter, you will learn about the writing process, including prewriting.

Understanding the Writing Process

Whether developing a paragraph, an essay, or a business report, you may be tempted to jump into the first draft immediately, beginning with the first sentence. However, such a strategy can be frustrating and may lead to hours of revision.

Professional writers know that the more time they devote to each stage of the **writing process**, the easier the overall task of developing a document will be. If you think of the writing process as a pyramid containing several levels, you can make the act of writing more productive and enjoyable. Just think of each level of the pyramid as becoming progressively narrower.

Each step serves a valuable purpose that, if followed, can improve the effectiveness of your writing.

Prewriting: Developing the main idea, narrowing the topic, and selecting supporting ideas occur during this stage.

Outlining: Preparing a structure for your document is the next step. With a well-planned outline, your writing will go faster and more smoothly.

Developing a first draft: The first draft is exactly what it sounds like—your first attempt to get words on paper. Every word does not need to be perfect.

Revising: Every good writer goes through several drafts before achieving the right mix of words. This stage should not be overlooked.

Editing: Your document is not finished until you check facts, remove un-necessary words, adjust the text, and make other minor changes.

Proofreading: Examining your writing for misspellings, grammar and punctuation mistakes, and typographical errors is your final step. An otherwise perfectly written paragraph or document becomes tarnished when it contains errors.

SELF-ASSESSMENT 2

When I need to write, I must:

	Usually	Sometimes	Never
Develop the main idea.	❑	❑	❑
Narrow the topic.	❑	❑	❑
Select supporting ideas.	❑	❑	❑
Prepare an outline.	❑	❑	❑
Develop a first draft.	❑	❑	❑
Revise the document.	❑	❑	❑
Edit the document.	❑	❑	❑
Proofread carefully.	❑	❑	❑

If you checked "Sometimes" or "Never" for any of the items, this chapter will help you use the writing process. Even if you checked "Usually" in every instance, you will learn more about the process of writing.

In the paragraph on the previous page, Tashelia followed these important stages of the writing process. First, she began her paragraph by giving a main idea— (1) Competition has never been stronger. Then she narrowed her idea to discuss the type of competition— (2) New tax software programs. Finally, she identified the challenge— (3) to develop a creative exciting promotion for EasyTAX planning. After writing a first draft and revising and editing her work, Tashelia makes her point effectively in the finished paragraph.

Beginning with Prewriting

Prewriting is the basic level of writing. In prewriting, your focus is on taking the first steps that will lead to a well-developed, finished document. The primary goal of prewriting is to come up with a number of ideas and then to select one workable topic for a report or an essay.

Developing main ideas becomes easier the more you do it. By copying some of the successful prewriting methods used by experts, you also can generate main ideas. Here are some methods that will help you arrive at interesting ideas for a report or an essay.

Listing Ideas, or Brainstorming

To brainstorm effectively, list on a notepad or computer page whatever ideas occur to you. Let one idea flow naturally into another. Don't try to evaluate or sort your ideas at this time. That comes later. This is your chance to be creative.

Here are some ideas on the subject of computers that might be generated during a listing, or brainstorming, session:

- computer problems
- the Internet
- World Wide Web
- chat rooms
- e-mail
- word processing versus pen/paper
- viruses/worms
- spam mail
- Internet dating
- server breakdowns
- company intranets
- ethernet
- hard-drive capacity

Using Free Association

Free association involves thinking of as many ideas as you can that are related to a topic. Start with a topic and write down any thoughts about it that come to mind. For instance, you may begin with the topic of pets and, through the process of free association, generate the following series: grooming, care, appetite, types, temperament, discipline, medical problems, and life span. Continue the free association process until you are satisfied with the ideas you have generated.

Here is how the free association technique might be used to develop ideas about the subject of e-mail.

E-mail: spam mail → special offers → like telemarketing → unwanted → unsolicited → send to "trash" → ways to block spam

Freewriting

This method works best when you give yourself a time limit, say, 15 minutes. Begin writing, by hand or on a computer keyboard, without pausing to think or revise. If you get stuck, write a series of nonsense words or write about another topic, such as your car or the weather. Eventually you should return to the topic and continue writing about it.

>   I enjoy surfing the World Wide Web for all kinds of information. Normally when I log on to my home computer, the first thing I do is go to my favorite web site. What are some things I look for? Well, I like checking out the sports page, and I'm also very interested in world politics. In a lot of ways, I like reading up on current events on the Web much more than I do reading a regular newspaper. For one thing, it's free. Well, most web sites are free, anyway. For another thing, it's instantaneous . . . .

Clustering or Grouping

Clustering is another method of thinking of ideas. To use clustering, group all ideas that seem interrelated. Don't worry about whether your groups are perfect. You can add and delete later.

By applying the grouping or clustering method of generating ideas to computers, you might come up with these groups:

- Internet
  - Internet dating
  - World Wide Web
  - Browsers
  - Search engines
    - Yahoo
    - AltaVista
    - Google
- Chat rooms
  - way to meet new people
  - newsgroups/discussion groups
  - "flaming" (insults/put-downs)
  - good for shy people
- Word processing
  - special features
    - bold/italic/underline
    - columns
    - text boxes/borders
  - ability to edit/revise quickly
    - movement of words and sentences
    - spell checker and thesaurus
    - formatting changes

Asking Open-Ended Questions

Open-ended questions are ones that cannot be answered with a simple yes or no. They begin with who, what, when, where, and why. The answers to opened-ended questions often lead to interesting thoughts that can help produce material for the content or body of a document. Questions that can be answered with yes or no are not valuable.

Look at these open-ended questions about Internet chat rooms.

Who

- Who participates in Internet chat rooms?
- Who can you meet in Internet chat rooms?

What

- What types of chat rooms are there?
- What do people who join chat rooms talk about?

When

- When did chat rooms come about?
- When do people chat the most?

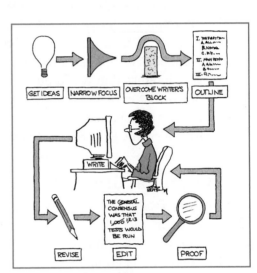

The writing process

Where

- Where can you access chat rooms?
- Where can you go to learn more about chat rooms?

Why

- Why do people like chatting?
- Why would people join a chat room?

How

- How do you access a chat room?
- How many people can participate in a chat room at one time?

ACTIVITY 2.1

Use the following prewriting techniques to develop the topic "hanging out with friends." Practice coming up with ideas based on the techniques you just learned. Then decide which technique works best for you.

1. brainstorming or listing

_____

_____

_____

_____

2. using free association

———————————————————————————————

———————————————————————————————

———————————————————————————————

———————————————————————————————

———————————————————————————————

———————————————————————————————

———————————————————————————————

3. clustering or grouping

———————————————————————————————

———————————————————————————————

———————————————————————————————

———————————————————————————————

———————————————————————————————

———————————————————————————————

———————————————————————————————

4. asking open ended questions

———————————————————————————————

———————————————————————————————

———————————————————————————————

———————————————————————————————

———————————————————————————————

———————————————————————————————

———————————————————————————————

5. freewriting

———————————————————————————————

———————————————————————————————

———————————————————————————————

———————————————————————————————

———————————————————————————————

———————————————————————————————

———————————————————————————————

Narrowing the Focus

Once you have settled on a topic and some ideas about it, a secondary goal is to narrow the topic until it is manageable. With a smaller topic, you can provide clear examples that clarify the topic and provide interesting details that engage the reader. Here is an example of a main idea that was narrowed to a more workable topic.

(A) Main Idea	A career needs to be motivating for me.
(B) Narrowed Focus	A career needs to offer fulfillment, variety, and challenge before I find it motivating.
(C) Narrower Focus	A career in health care that offers personal reward, some travel, and the opportunity to grow will be satisfying to me.

Example (C) is the best of these alternatives because it narrows the focus to specific features that the writer is seeking in a career. After beginning with sentence (C), the writer could continue by stating:

> In today's job market, consulting health care providers are in high demand. Building a career that meets my expectations is more likely now than ever before.

ACTIVITY 2.2   For the ideas listed below, narrow the topic twice, each time reducing it to a more focused subject.

1. dressing for success

    dressing appropriately for the job

    dressing in business casual

2. a day with my friends

    _____

    _____

3. a free vacation

    _____

    _____

4. pleasing the supervisor

    _____

    _____

WRITING WORKSHOP

Writer's Block

Not knowing what to say next in a paragraph, an essay, or a report is called writer's block, and it can occur at any stage of the writing process. Understanding what causes writer's block should help you find ways to overcome it. Here are some common causes, along with their possible cures.

Deadline pressure

Although some writers thrive on deadline pressure, others become blocked as a deadline approaches. Give yourself as much time as possible to complete a writing project. Mark a schedule on a calendar to indicate specific due dates for each stage of the writing process.

Concern about a critical reader

If you are thinking that your readers will pick apart your writing or toss it aside, you need to replace those negative mental images with positive ones. For a more positive approach, imagine someone you know well. Pretend that you are addressing this person as you write. You might prefer to imagine that you are actually talking, instead of writing, to the person.

Perfectionism

Perfectionists tend to become stalled in the writing process because they cannot bring themselves to move on unless they know that each comma is in the right place and every word is spelled correctly. Allow yourself to make mistakes in the early stages of the writing process.

Distractions

Sometimes you become blocked because you're distracted. Try to eliminate distractions that interfere with your concentration. For example, you can minimize interruptions by turning off your cell phone during the time you are writing a first draft of a document. Internal distractions, such as preoccupations and worries, are harder to ignore. If possible, put a problem on hold until you complete a stage of the writing process.

Blank slate

Sometimes your mind simply goes blank for no apparent reason. In these cases, your goal should be to power up your "right brain," the part of your brain that controls creative and imaginative thinking. Take a walk, watch a TV program, or call a friend. Then come back to the assignment. You might be amazed by what your unconscious mind thought of in the meantime.

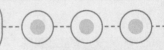
Keyboard Shortcuts

In writing, you can save a great deal of time by using keyboard shortcuts. For example, after coming up with main ideas using the listing method, copy one of your ideas onto a new page with the Copy command and begin the process of free association. Follow up by using Cut and Paste to cluster the ideas into related groups. Then under each cluster, ask who, what, when, and why and fill in the answers. Double-space and begin freewriting your essay. By using the keyboard effectively, you can reduce the frustration of rewriting by hand during each stage of brainstorming.

Outlining

If you have a creative personality, outlining a report or an essay may seem too restrictive, confining, or time-consuming. In general, though, most writers develop some type of an outline before beginning a first draft of a document.

Your outline can be as informal as you like—perhaps a series of handwritten notes. It also can be more formal. Keep in mind these few rules for outlining:

- For reader-friendly writing, begin with a main idea (topic sentence) and then add supporting material.
- Do not try to develop too many separate subtopics. Match the number of subtopics to the length of your document.
- Decide on an organization that works best for the document as a whole, for example, comparison-contrast or classification.
- Begin with your weakest point and end with your strongest. When you believe readers will read the entire document, build intensity by arranging the points so they lead to a climax.
- Begin with your strongest point or argument if you believe your audience will not read the entire document.

Here is an outline for an essay on tying knots.

Main idea: In today's technological world, it's still important to know how to tie a variety of knots for different purposes.

I. Stopper knots keep a rope from fraying at the end
    A. Overhand knots are good for sewing
    B. Stevedore's knot serves as a foothold for climbing
II. Binding knots are useful for common household tasks
    A. Packer's knot lets you pull a large package
    B. Lashing knots tie together poles
III. Hitches can be used when attaching or transporting material
    A. Clove hitch is perfect for tying a pet's leash in place
    B. Half hitches are great when tying objects to the top of a vehicle

ACTIVITY 2.3   Think of a hobby, a sport, or another pursuit that you enjoy. Imagine that someone you know is interested in this activity and wants more information about it. Develop an outline of three aspects of the topic that you think your reader should know. Then add at least two supporting details for each main point.

Activity: _____

I.   _____

    A. _____

    B. _____

II. _____

    A. _____

    B. _____

III. _____

    A. _____

    B. _____

ETHICS CONNECTION

Collaborative Writing

To what degree should all members of a team be able to contribute to a project? Assume that you are a member of a five-person accounting team that has been asked to make a recommendation about what accounting software the company should purchase.

After each team member turns in one section of the report for team review, you become concerned that parts of the report are poorly written. You go to the team leader and suggest that you and he take control of the project. The two of you meet on your own without other team members and rewrite the report. After the report is in order, you distribute it to the rest of the team.

Is merely informing the other team members that the report is being rewritten an appropriate action? What if the views expressed in the report do not accurately reflect what they believe? A better solution is for the team to work together to revise the report.

Writing a Series of Drafts

Once you have created an outline, the next step is to start writing your document. Undoubtedly you will go through a series of drafts before your document is final.

Developing a First Draft

The first step is to develop a first draft of your document. To write a first draft, you may decide to write slowly, building on your outline one sentence at a time. Or you may write swiftly, using your outline as a guide.

Revising Your Work

However you accomplish a first draft, the next question is how many additional drafts should you write. Unfortunately, there is no standard answer. It depends on how much time you have before your deadline, the overall importance of the document you are writing, your attention to detail, and your personal standards.

If you are writing a short memo to employees to remind them of the awards banquet tomorrow night, you may not devote much attention at all to the revision process. However, if you are writing a report to be submitted to your department manager recommending a compressed workweek, you may revise your writing several times before you are satisfied.

Revision includes major changes, such as relocating paragraphs to better positions within the document and changing the order of sentences within paragraphs. You also may add examples and details as they occur to you. Or you may wish to delete information if you think your written work is too long.

Here is an example of the revision process for a paragraph about security.

(A) First Draft	New security measures have helped stores. Sales are increased as people shop to fill idle downtime. Security measures are important in today's changing world. This is a particularly big issue in airports.
(B) Revised Draft	Security plays an important role. Especially in today's consumer driven world. New airline security measures, for instance. These have helped airport stores gain sales as travelers shop to fill idle time. People arrive early to check in for their flights, they make extra purchases of clothing food and magazines.

In Example (A), the writer is still struggling with the topic. The writing is too general, and the ideas are out of order. In Example (B), the writer has rearranged the ideas and added specific examples. The sentences, however, are choppy and incomplete, and there are several mistakes with grammar and punctuation.

Editing and Proofreading

Once you develop a nearly perfect draft, you can continue editing by fine-tuning the sentence structure and style. As you proofread your work, check your document one last time for mistakes. Look at the example from the preceding section. Here are the final stages of the writing process.

(A) Editing	Security can play a role in today's consumer driven world. For instance, new airline security measures—these have helped airport stores and shops gain sales as travelers shop to fill idle time. As people arrive early to check in for their flights. They are likely to make extra purchases of clothing food and magazines.
(B) Proofreading	In today's consumer-driven world, security can play an unexpected role. For instance, new airline security measures have helped airport stores and shops gain sales as travelers shop to fill idle time. Because people arrive early to check in for flights, they are likely to make purchases of clothing, food, and magazines.

In these final stages, in moving from (A) to (B), the writer smoothed out the flow of ideas and corrected problems with punctuation and grammar.

ACTIVITY 2.4 Revise the following writing sample by correcting each of the underlined groups of words. In some cases, the error is a simple problem with punctuation or grammar. In other cases, you may need to simplify the wording of a phrase or eliminate awkwardness.

One overlooked <u>consequence,</u> of a natural <u>catastrophe.</u> Such as tornadoes, hurricanes, or <u>an earthquake,</u> is <u>the seemingly inconsequential,</u> but <u>potentially devastating,</u> problem of missing street signs. For unsuspecting drivers, <u>a missing street signs</u> can mean wrong turns, lost time, and <u>it also can include</u> wasted fuel<u>.</u> <u>Not only that, but think about</u> the serious consequences of a stop sign that is <u>no longer there at an intersection to stop oncoming traffic at a crossroads.</u> As an insurance claims <u>adjuster trying</u> to find a specific address after one of these kinds of natural disasters can be a nightmare. After one series of devastating tornadoes in <u>the general vicinity of the Topeka, Kansas, area,</u> one agent worked 18-hour <u>days and evenings and nights.</u> Simply trying to locate insured homeowners so she could assist them in <u>processing, taking care of, sorting through, and generally handling</u> their claims.

Summary for the Writing Process

❏ A writing task can become less overwhelming if you think about writing as a process.

❏ The writing process can be divided into the following stages: prewriting, outlining, developing a first draft, revising, editing, and proofreading.

❏ Goals of prewriting include brainstorming for a topic, narrowing the topic you select, and generating additional ideas to support the topic.

❏ Brainstorming techniques include listing topics, using free association, freewriting, clustering or grouping, and asking open-ended questions.

❏ Understanding various causes of writer's block, such as being a perfectionist and imagining a critical reader, can help you cure the problem.

❏ Creating an outline makes the task of writing a first draft much easier. The outline can be informal or formal.

❏ Once you write a first draft, continue to revise, edit, and proofread your writing until you are satisfied.

PRACTICING YOUR SKILLS

The writing process is a simple, straightforward approach to creating documents for business settings or essays for school assignments. Now that you understand the process, sharpen your new skills by completing the following writing activities.

PRACTICE 1

Anita Hernez, an assistant manager in a company that services home mortgage loans, has been assigned by her supervisor to investigate the feasibility of hiring more temporary workers. To begin her assignment, she takes time to brainstorm the pros and cons of such a move.

Advantages	lower overhead costs
	additional personnel to handle higher call volume
	more flexible scheduling
Disadvantages	higher employee turnover rate
	need for extra training
	resentment among full-time employees

For her next step, Anita writes a first draft organizing and summarizing her initial thoughts.

A distinct advantage to hiring additional temporary workers at this time is the pressing need for more employees to handle an increased call volume. This is due to our recent acquisition of home mortgages. In addition, working with a temp agency makes it much easier to find workers to fill three different shifts, now that we have begun handling customer calls 24/7. These advantages are on top of the usual savings the company enjoys by not having to pay out benefits and insurance. On the other hand, we should keep in mind that we have experienced a significantly higher turnover rate among temp workers in the past in comparison with our full-time employees. Because of the high turnover rate, training sessions must be run continuously. Also, several full-time workers have expressed their resentment at having to keep introducing new temp workers to their job functions within the department. These employees have also expressed a general dissatisfaction with the abilities of temps who have been previously sent our way.

Main Idea

1. Now that Anita has finished a first draft, she realizes she has yet to state her main idea about whether to hire more temp workers. If you were Anita, what would you recommend? Write a statement expressing your viewpoint.

_____

_____

Revising

2. Imagine that you are Anita's assistant, and she has given you her document for review. Specifically she wants to know which of her statements require supporting data or evidence. Underline the sentences you identify.

Editing

3. Now Anita wants you to comment on her writing style. As you read over her document, circle phrases that seem too wordy or awkward. If new ideas for wording a point occur to you, write them above the phrase in question.

 # PRACTICE 2

Here is the opening paragraph written by a local government agency as the first draft of a study of historic neighborhoods.

> Several local neighborhoods that haven't been officially designated as historic sites are still considered historic by those who live there. However, a neighborhood valued by one group may be offensive to another. For example, no one questions that elegant, well-maintained Victorian houses should be preserved. But what about a neighborhood of rundown row houses from the 1930s? Or mobile homes used in the 1950s to house itinerant fruit pickers? As long as a group attaches some historic value to a neighborhood, it should receive equal consideration for funding.

Brainstorming

1. Assume that this paragraph is written about your hometown. Come up with an example of a neighborhood you believe is historic. Briefly describe it below.

Main Idea

2. Underline what you believe to be the main idea of the Practice 2 paragraph.

3. Explain whether you agree or disagree with the author's statement:

_____

_____

APPLYING YOUR SKILLS

Now that you understand the steps involved in the writing process, you can practice your writing. As you complete each stage of the writing process, save your work so you can return to it later. Then reflect on your writing experience as indicated below.

Prewriting

Use one or more of the strategies discussed in this chapter to develop a topic that is of interest to you, such as a hobby, sport, or field of study. Then narrow your topic and develop supporting points, ideas, and details.

Outlining

Create an outline that helps you understand the direction you want your writing to take. Try to come up with four or five complete sentences that could serve as the basis for a first draft. Arrange your sentences as you deem necessary. These sentences will serve as your first draft.

Revising, Editing, and Proofreading

Using the sentences from the preceding step, develop a second draft of your outline. Try rearranging the order of the sentences to see if you can make your point clearer and easier for the reader to understand. Also experiment with sentence structure and word choice. Sometimes just using a different descriptive word can create a mental picture for the reader that aids in understanding. As you modify your outline, consider reading your sentences aloud to identify awkward areas. Then revise these trouble spots as many times as necessary until your phrasing sounds more natural and conversational. If possible, ask a friend or colleague to review your written work and make suggestions for improvement.

Reflecting on Your Experience

Think about your writing experience by answering the following questions:

❑ Which brainstorming technique or techniques did you use?

❑ Which step of the writing process did you most enjoy? least enjoy?

❑ Which step gave you the most difficulty? Which seemed easiest?

❑ How many drafts did you produce during the revision process?

❑ What kind of changes did you make when editing your outline?

❑ How satisfied are you with the finished outline?

❑ If you were to continue working on this writing assignment, what features of your writing would you continue to change?

❑ Did you experience writer's block? If so, how did you overcome it?

WRITING FOR YOUR CAREER

CRITICAL THINKING

Further explore and develop your writing skills by completing one or more of the following workplace scenarios. Each assignment requires you to develop your response in stages. When the project description refers you to the textbook web site, go to http://humphrey.swlearning.com and look for Chapter 2 "Writing for Your Career." There you will find direct links to helpful web references.

Communication and the Arts

As a disk jockey, you enjoy a high-profile job at a major radio station in your town. In addition to introducing upcoming songs and announcing commercial breaks, you serve as a newsreader and interviewer. Now that several new stations are competing with you, the search for more listeners is intense. Your operations manager has scheduled a think-tank session for all disk jockeys to attend to brainstorm ideas for increasing the station's market share of listeners. She wants a list of specific ideas for making the station more appealing, especially during the morning and evening rush hour.

In response to your manager's request, brainstorm a list of ideas for special shows, segments, and features that you could host on the air. Take one of your ideas and narrow it to a more manageable idea that you might write about later.

Health and Medicine

As it considers various candidates for promotion to positions of higher responsibility, your company expects a certain amount of voluntary service to the community each year. To become eligible for promotion, you decide to volunteer for a hospice program. As a volunteer, you are assigned to visit a patient's home and spend three hours with her each week. For the most part, you are expected to provide companionship, relieving the patient's overburdened family members.

Now that you have spent several weeks interacting with the patient, you need to describe your volunteer activity. First, create an outline of the main points you wish to include. Then develop a few sentences describing your experience. For information that can help you with your narrative, go to the textbook web site and locate the link for Chapter 2, Health and Medicine.

Human, Personal, and Public Service

You are a postal worker who has recently experienced several problems on your route. In a single week, you were accused of stealing a customer's mail-order catalogs, delivering mail late to two separate customers, and taunting three customers' canines. Your supervisor has scheduled a one-on-one conference with you to discuss your past week's performance. However, he wants you to describe, in writing, the complaints from your point of view. First, use the freewriting method to develop your ideas. Then write a few sentences defending your actions. Revise as necessary.

Business and Marketing

Due to a recent economic downturn, your company has been forced to cut back on its operating costs. Unfortunately, yearly raises will not be given until the company rebounds. As a department manager, you know that your employees have come to expect a standard three percent cost-of-living increase and merit raises of one to four percent based on their performance. You have already heard grumbling about the new policy from your employees. Although you assured them that the cutbacks are only temporary, this decision has not boosted their morale.

To help reduce ill will on the part of your employees, you would like to reward continued good performance with special gifts and perks. Write a request to your superiors requesting funding for such rewards. First, develop a free association list of the types of items you have in mind to purchase. Then develop an outline of reasons why they are needed at this time. Finally, put your thoughts together in a few sentences.

Science and Technology

Genetically enhanced fruits, vegetables, and grains are slowly gaining visibility in grocery markets, where they are placed side by side with naturally grown food items. Still, many consumers remain skeptical about eating a genetically altered banana or peach or tomato. Imagine that you are a public relations representative for CWR-Gene Research, Inc., a biotech company that conducts genetic research to improve the yield and quality of food products. Write a draft to distribute to your department about the concerns that consumers are voicing about genetically altered food. For background information, log on to a search engine and enter the key words *genetically altered foods.*

Environment and Natural Resources

How many times have you thought about recycling just before you threw a plastic bottle or an aluminum can in the trash? Did you promise yourself you would start participating in your community's recycling program with the very next round of trash pickups?

Ramon, who works as a middle manager for R & R Waste Removal, Inc., a specialist in residential recycling, believes these questions run through the minds of potential customers each week. He has recently learned that upper management is concerned about a 15 percent drop in recycling during the past financial quarter. A meeting has been scheduled next week to brainstorm ways to encourage more residents of neighborhoods serviced by R & R to recycle. Imagine that you are in Ramon's position and develop a list of ideas to bring to the meeting. Use any method you prefer for arriving at ideas. Then write a sample draft based on your ideas. For information pertaining to your paragraph, go to the textbook web site and locate the link for Chapter 2, Environment and Natural Resources.

3

Four Strategies for Effective Writing

IN THIS CHAPTER YOU WILL LEARN TO:

- Understand your purpose and audience.

- Write clearly and coherently.

- Revise and edit your work thoroughly.

Using the *Four Strategies* in Writing for Your Career

Career Path	Sample Career	Use for Effective Writing	Example of Effective Writing
Communication and the Arts	Jeweler	Describing a piece of jewelry for sale over the Internet	This beaded necklace is both bold and delicate. The beads are small and subtle, but the colors are quite striking. Because each necklace is made lovingly by hand, no two are exactly alike.
Health and Medicine	Nutritionist	Recommending a diet for a patient with hypertension	You should eat large quantities of fresh fruits and vegetables—at least five servings every day. In addition, you should avoid salt and salty products, especially processed foods that may contain large amounts of hidden salt.
Human, Personal, and Public Service	Staffer for a state representative	Responding to a constituent's letter	Thank you for contacting Representative Frank about the need for smaller classes in your district's schools. Ms. Frank has introduced a bill that would increase school funding and provide for smaller classes across the state.
Business and Marketing	Market researcher	Reporting the results from a focus group	The majority of respondents claim that they purchase soft drinks at least once a week. Their choice of brands is based primarily on habit and taste. For example, respondents tend to have favorite brands that they buy regularly.
Science and Technology	Locksmith	Preparing an invoice and explaining charges	Because we were able to replace all locks at the same time, you will be charged for a single service call in addition to the price of the materials and labor.
Environment and Natural Resources	Park ranger	Explaining to visitors how to protect their food from bears	Do not leave food in your car. Bears are able to break windows to reach it. Instead, use the bearproof trash receptacles that are provided. When camping, store your food in a bag and hang it from a tree branch overnight.

39

ON THE JOB

Case Study

Tanya Carpenter is a social worker who works for Child Protection Services. Her job is to investigate cases in which families are having difficulty providing for their children's needs. She provides support and connects the families with available resources. She also meets with these families to assess their needs and make sure they know what services are available to help them.

To keep track of each child's progress, Tanya maintains detailed records of these visits and of the information she gathers about each case. Today Tanya has just met with the family of a nine-year-old girl named Sara, whose case Tanya has been working on for the past month.

When she sits down to write, Tanya is aware of her goal: She wants to maintain a detailed record of Sara's situation and of her own work with Sara and Sara's family. Tanya also keeps in mind who may be reading the paragraph. In addition to making notes for herself, she knows that her supervisor will read the file. It is also available to Sara's family if they request it. If the courts get involved, a judge may read the file. Because there are so many potential readers, Tanya knows she must write clearly and precisely.

Today's visit left me feeling very positive about Sara's progress. She seems much happier than she did two weeks ago, and she tells me that her grades are improving and she is making more friends at school. Her parents confirm this news. At first, Sara was having trouble adjusting to her mother's new job, which keeps her away three evenings a week. However, Sara seems to be adapting to the situation. Because her father also works evenings, Sara often was home alone when her mother was at work. However, her parents have since made contact with a neighboring family who have agreed to allow Sara to do her homework in their apartment until her mother gets home from work. In return, Sara helps with some of the household chores. This arrangement appears to be doubly beneficial, because helping with the chores gives Sara a sense of responsibility and makes her feel good about her contribution. I will visit Sara's teacher this week to talk about her progress in school, but for now, I believe she is doing well.

Does the paragraph give a clear explanation of Sara's progress? Is it appropriate for Tanya supervisor, Sara's family, and a judge to read? Is the subject clear and focused? Does the paragraph show attention to mechanical details (correct grammar, spelling, and punctuation)? If the answer to these questions is yes, then Taniesha's paragraph is effective.

Understanding the Strategies

Many strategies and skills can make your writing more effective. In this chapter, you will learn four basic guidelines that are easy to remember and can help with any writing.

The four guidelines are:

- Know your purpose.
- Know your audience.
- Be clear and coherent.
- Revise and edit.

Here is how the four guidelines aided Tanya in writing her paragraph. Relate the guidelines to the underlined words and phrases on page 40.

1. Main purpose of the paragraph: The paragraph documents the child's progress and becomes part of a permanent record of the case.

2. Intended audience: Tanya, her supervisor, Sara's family, and a judge (potentially) are the audience. Notice that the entire documents is directed to this audience; therefore, a (2) is not shown.

3. Clarity and coherence: Tanya's writing is clear. She makes her points simply and directly and avoids extra words and confusing statements. She keeps the paragraph coherent by remaining focused on the central issue (Sara's progress over the past two weeks).

4. Revising and editing: Good writing is rarely easy. In fact, experienced writers often spend more time revising and editing than inexperienced writers. Furthermore, effective revising and editing are invisible. If the reader is not distracted by sloppy language, misspelled words, and incorrect grammar, the writer has revised and edited well. A (4) is not shown in Tanya's record because her revisions and edits are invisible.

With experience, these guidelines become such a natural part of the writing process that writers follow them without thinking. As you work through this chapter, you will begin to develop the habits you need to make your writing clear and effective.

SELF-ASSESSMENT 3

When I compose a piece of writing, I ask myself:

	Usually	Sometimes	Never
What goal or goals do I want to achieve?	❑	❑	❑
Who is the intended audience?	❑	❑	❑
Is my writing clear and well organized?	❑	❑	❑
Have I revised carefully to make sure the writing reads easily and flows smoothly?	❑	❑	❑
Have I edited my writing for spelling, grammar, punctuation, and other mechanics?	❑	❑	❑

If you checked "Sometimes" or "Never" for any of the items, this chapter will help you improve your skills. Even if you checked "Usually" in every instance, you will learn more about techniques of effective writing.

Knowing Your Purpose

Writing can accomplish many things. It can tell a story, teach a skill, paint a mental picture, or persuade people to adopt a point of view. Each of these purposes—among many others—affects the style and content of the writing. Your finished product will be much more effective if you consider your purpose and keep it in mind as you write.

If you are writing a restaurant review for a local newspaper, you will write in a different tone than if you are presenting a business plan to a potential investor. Professional writing may be formal or informal, personal or impersonal, or light-hearted or serious, depending on the writer's goals.

Below are examples of writing styles that are appropriate for various purposes.

(A) Advertising

(PERSUASION)

The Kitty Castle will pamper your beloved pet while you are gone. You might even have trouble tearing Kitty away when you return from your vacation!

(B) Memo to Employees

(ILLUSTRATION)

Please note that our vacation policy has changed. For example, employees must request time off at least 30 days in advance. Thank you for your cooperation.

(C) Instructions

(HOW-TO)

First, make sure the CD-ROM drive is installed correctly. Next, replace the battery pack and memory card. (See Diagram 6-4.)

did you ever?

- Meet a friend's parents and talk to them differently than the way you talk to your friend?

- Try to persuade someone to see things from your point of view?

- Check your resume for spelling and grammatical mistakes before sending it out?

Each of these common uses of language involves one of the four guidelines. These techniques guide your communication every day. In this chapter, you will learn how to use them to improve your writing.

(D) Job Announcement

(DESCRIPTION)

The ideal candidate will be self-motivated, innovative, and able to work well with others. The position requires excellent organizational skills.

(E) Report

(NARRATION)

We arrived half an hour early for our site visit, which gave us time to see the layout of the office and meet several employees. At the appointed time, we met with a group of managers and presented our plan.

In each example, the style, tone, and content are appropriate to the writer's purpose. Because most jobs involve many different types of writing, being able to adapt your writing style to the specific task is important.

ACTIVITY 3.1 For each of the communication goals listed below, write a sentence or two that would be appropriate to the goal. The first one has been completed for you.

1. explaining to a customer why her order is late

   I'm very sorry, Ms. Washington. Unfortunately, the red blouse is out of stock and has been placed on back order. A shipment is due within three to four business days, and the blouse will be shipped to you immediately when received in our warehouse. We appreciate your patience.

2. persuading a friend to watch your favorite movie

   _____

   _____

   _____

3. advertising discount airline tickets to potential customers

   _____

   _____

   _____

4. explaining upgraded phone service to customers

   _____

   _____

   _____

5. explaining to a potential employer why you are right for the job

_____

_____

_____

6. describing a house to a potential buyer

_____

_____

_____

7. giving a client directions to your office

_____

_____

_____

8. telling a story about an experience that taught you an important lesson

_____

_____

_____

9. describing a sweater from a mail-order catalog

_____

_____

_____

10. explaining to a friend how to change a tire

_____

_____

_____

11. describing a customer's problem to your supervisor

_____

_____

_____

WRITING WORKSHOP

Avoiding Misplaced Modifiers

Many people, including experienced writers, sometimes confuse their readers by using misplaced modifiers. A misplaced modifier is a descriptive word or phrase that is located in the wrong part of the sentence. The words and phrases confuse the reader by making the meaning of the sentence unclear. Below are examples of two misplaced modifiers and two corrected sentences. Do you see that the sentence is clearer and easier to understand when the modifier is placed at its correct location?

Misplaced modifier	Fearing that it might rain, the party was moved indoors.
Misplaced modifier	The party was moved indoors, fearing it might rain.
Correct	Fearing that it might rain, the organizers moved the party indoors.
Correct	Because the forecast called for rain, the party was moved indoors.

The first sentence is confusing because it sounds as though the party was afraid of rain. Although the reader can probably figure out what the writer means, the sentence is awkward and grammatically incorrect. In the second sentence, the same problem exists even though the phrases are switched. The two corrected sentences show two different options. In both cases, the writer states clearly *who* thought it might rain. In the first corrected sentence, the organizers thought it might rain. In the second corrected sentence, the forecast called for rain.

Another common misplaced modifier is the word *hopefully*. In everyday speech, people often say things such as, "Hopefully, you'll be able to come to the party tomorrow." While this expression is fine for personal communication, it is not generally accepted in writing since it fails to indicate who is hoping. Instead of writing, "Hopefully, you will enjoy your stay in Dallas," you should write, "We at Budget Airlines hope you will enjoy your stay in Dallas."

Knowing Your Audience

Deciding who is your intended audience is one key to effective writing. Before you start writing, think about who will read your words. You will compose paragraphs differently depending on whether you are writing for adults, children, strangers, customers, employees, or your supervisor.

Here are examples of writings directed to different audiences.

A New Retiree	You've earned the right to relax and enjoy the vacation of your dreams.
Child	Bring your parents to the grand opening of Toy Farms. We will have clowns, free toys, and ice cream.
Supervisor	Do you have an opening on your calendar for a brief meeting next week?

In each example, the writer considered who would be reading the words and formed the sentences so they would be interesting and appealing. Although messages can be written in many different ways, they should always be appropriate to the audience.

ACTIVITY 3.2 In each of the following examples, imagine that the person has asked you to "tell me something about yourself." Write a sentence or two that is appropriate for each intended audience.

1. a prospective employer during a job interview

    _____

    _____

    _____

2. your new eight-year-old next-door neighbor

    _____

    _____

    _____

3. your fiancé's grandmother

    _____

    _____

    _____

4. a reporter who is interviewing residents of your neighborhood for a story about diversity in the community

_____

_____

_____

_____

5. a friend of a friend whom you have just met at a party

_____

_____

_____

_____

6. an online dating service

_____

_____

_____

_____

7. a workshop leader who wants to get to know the participants

_____

_____

_____

_____

8. a host on a call-in talk show

_____

_____

_____

_____

9. a stranger who sits beside you on a plane

_____

_____

_____

Being Clear and Coherent

Good writing is clear, direct, and well focused. You should make your point in a straightforward way and organize the rest of the paragraph so it supports the main idea. This means identifying your main point, stating it clearly, and backing it up with supportive details. To keep your writing clear, you should choose your details carefully to avoid cluttering the paragraph or document.

Sometimes writers try so hard to include all their ideas that their paragraphs ramble in many different directions. While you may be tempted to say everything that is on your mind, remember that your paragraph will be stronger if you keep it simple. Read the following examples of weather reports. The first is unclear or rambling while the second is clear and coherent.

Unclear	The longer term forecast at this point suggests that the weather early in the week may be partly cloudy and cool with scattered periods of sun. Later, we can expect a fairly good chance of warm days with possible intermittent precipitation.
Clear	The weather will likely be cool and partly cloudy early in the week. Later, we can expect warm days with a chance of scattered showers.

In the first example, the writer tried to include too much information and too many qualifiers (such as "may be" and "possible.") The result is wordy and confusing. The second example communicates the same information in a simple and straightforward way.

Below are further examples of clear and unclear writing. Notice how the clear writing is easier to read and understand.

Unclear	Because physical education courses constitute an important part of the university graduation requirement, students should fulfill the aforementioned requirement by registering for the courses of their choice that meet the requirement by following the guidelines elaborated in this pamphlet.
Clear	Students must register for physical education classes to fulfill the graduation requirement. Guidelines for registration are described in this pamphlet.

Again, clear writing is well focused and concise. Effective writers use as few words as possible and get right to the point.

Incoherent writing wanders from one topic to another instead of sticking to a single idea.

Incoherent	The weather is going to be beautiful this weekend. It looks as though the long cold spell may finally be over. Time to start thinking about summer. Lots of people like to go to the beach in the summer when the weather is nice.
Coherent	The weather will be beautiful this weekend. We can expect warm temperatures and sunny skies all the way through Sunday evening. The humidity will be low, and the chance of rain is almost zero.

In the first example, the writer rambles from one idea to the next. The paragraph is incoherent because it does not stick to a single main idea. The second paragraph makes a statement and then supports it with specific details.

Incoherent	First, I met with the supervisor of human resources. He was a very nice person. Then he introduced me to an interviewer who wanted to know about my background and told me a lot about the job. She was young and looked like she was just out of college. After she told me about the job, she gave me a tour of the building. Everyone was busy and looked like they enjoyed their work, although one person seemed frustrated and wanted to talk with someone about a problem.
Coherent	First, I met with the supervisor of human resources. Then he introduced me to the interviewer who reviewed my background and discussed the requirements for the job. Afterwards, the interviewer gave me a tour of the building.

To write clearly and coherently, a writer must identify the main idea, state it clearly, and include any details that will help the reader understand. Once the point has been made, the paragraph is complete.

ACTIVITY 3.3 Below are several examples of unclear writing. How can each be improved? Does the writer use too many words? Is the paragraph confusing? Does it ramble from one idea to another? Rewrite each paragraph to make it clearer, focused, and coherent.

1. Students need to master a variety of writing styles to succeed in most jobs. In today's economy, different kinds of jobs are being created all the time. You might end up with a job that doesn't even exist today.

    _____

    _____

    _____

    _____

2. Peanut butter can be a nutritious snack. However, many people are allergic to peanuts. People should read labels since many foods are produced on the same machinery as peanut-based foods and contain traces of peanuts.

    _____

    _____

    _____

    _____

3. The warranty covers all repairs for damages incurred during normal usage for a period of up to 12 months. In some cases, damage may be caused by usage that is not considered normal and to which this guarantee does not apply. Such damages are not covered by this warranty.

    _____

    _____

    _____

    _____

4. This memo is to inform all employees of the fact that the interoffice e-mail system will be under repair from 9 P.M. to 6 A.M. on Thursday and Friday. You should save all important messages before this time.

    _____

    _____

    _____

    _____

5. Today's numerous activities consist of a variety of gatherings, workshops, lectures, and other events designed to stimulate discussion regarding innovative strategies for articulating our visions regarding the direction in which this industry is moving and the ways in which we can all participate in that process.

   _____

   _____

   _____

   _____

6. When the police arrived on the scene, the first thing they did was to collect and record information regarding the specific events that had taken place. The events were certainly tragic and will not be forgotten any time soon.

   _____

   _____

   _____

   _____

7. When purchasing an automobile, the first thing one should do is determine the purpose for which one wishes to use the vehicle. It is very important to apply one's knowledge about the intended purpose when making decisions about what type of car to purchase.

   _____

   _____

   _____

   _____

8. The travel policy has been adjusted to deal with the problems associated with plane delays, long lines, and cost of traveling. Please be aware that we need your help in keeping expenses down. We still want your travel for the company to be a pleasant experience.

   _____

   _____

   _____

   _____

Revising and Editing

Do you think experienced writers get all their words and paragraphs right the first time? Think again! The famous novelist Ernest Hemingway once said, "Writing is one percent inspiration and 99% perspiration." Even for the best writers (or maybe *especially* for the best writers), choosing the clearest words and most effective construction is hard work that requires repeated revision, addition, and deletion.

After you have gotten your ideas down on paper in a rough draft, go back and reread the text. Look for places where the writing could be clearer, more precise, and more interesting or where it could just sound better. Do not be afraid to get rid of a phrase or a sentence—or even a whole paragraph—if it does not seem right. Although throwing out your hard work can be stressful, a good final draft is worth the sacrifice.

Here are some suggestions that may help you revise your work:

- Read your paragraph out loud.
- Read each sentence with the intent of eliminating any words that don't contribute to the meaning of the sentence.
- Look for words like *very, also, really, in order to, a lot.* Decide whether they seem awkward or out of place.
- Set your writing aside for a few hours (or a few days if you can) and then reread it with a fresh perspective.
- Ask a friend or colleague to read your document and provide feedback.
- Imagine that you are the intended audience and think about how the writing would sound to you.

Editing is the final step after you have revised your work completely and are happy with the wording. Go back and read everything again, but this time don't pay attention to the meaning. Instead, follow these guidelines:

- Check spelling, punctuation, grammar, and other mechanics.
- Run spell check and grammar check, but don't rely on them completely since these functions miss many obvious errors. (For example, if you write, "I red the newspaper this morning," your computer's spell check will not notice the mistake since *red* is an actual word.)
- Check that punctuation is consistent throughout the document. For example, if you are using bullets, do bulleted phrases always end with a period or never end with a period? Do you consistently use a comma before *and* in a series? Or do you never use a comma before *and*?

Four secrets of effective writing

Besides spelling mistakes, writers make several common mechanical errors in early drafts. With practice, you can train yourself to catch these errors during the editing process. Below are descriptions of common errors, along with suggestions for finding and correcting them.

- Run-on sentences: A run-on sentence is two or more complete sentences that are combined inappropriately. For example, "We went to the beach, it was really sunny and we lay on the sand all day." In this case, "We went to the beach" is a complete sentence and should stand alone. To catch run-on sentences, read your work out loud and listen for places where your voice pauses naturally. This is a good indication that you have reached the end of a sentence.
- Incorrect pronouns: Many people mix up subjective and objective cases when using two or more pronouns together. For example, "Dad bought a nice present for Manny and I" is incorrect because "Manny and I" is the object of the sentence. To check for correct usage, try the sentence with a single pronoun. You wouldn't say, "Dad bought a nice present for I." Instead, you would say, "Dad bought a nice present for me." Therefore, *me* is the correct pronoun.
- Inappropriate use of apostrophes: Do not use an apostrophe to indicate a plural. For example, "I have five pair's of shoes in my closet" is incorrect because *pairs* is a plural noun. No apostrophe is needed. Use apostrophes only when indicating a possessive: "My dog's leash is in the drawer."
- Incorrect conditionals: Do not write, "If I would have..." The correct formulation is, "If I had..."

A few other common errors:

- *A lot* is always two words.
- Contractions should be avoided in formal writing.
- Numbers less than 100 should be written out in formal writing. Instead of "We saw 17 dogs at the park," write, "We saw seventeen dogs at the park."
- Write "should have," "would have," and "could have," not "should of," "would of," or "could of."
- Watch out for homonyms such as *their*, *there*, and *they're* or *to*, *two*, and *too*.

Below are some suggestions that may help with editing.

- Read the finished work aloud—again.
- Read it again, backwards this time, to check for spelling errors.
- Take a break between revising and editing.

For most writing, you can usually do something to make it just a little better. However, at some point, you must decide that you are finished. If you have given yourself plenty of time to revise and edit—and if you keep in mind the guidelines you have learned in this chapter—you should be confident that your finished product represents your best work.

TECHNOLOGY CONNECTION

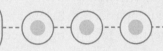

Grammar Check

These days most word processors have a grammar check function. Grammar check identifies everything from mechanical errors (such as too many spaces between words) to more complicated constructions (such as the use of passive verbs).

Although grammar check can be very helpful, you should not let it rule your writing. The program responds automatically to certain word formations without understanding the meaning of the whole sentence or paragraph. Before making a change simply to satisfy the word processor, be sure the change is one you really want to make. If you don't know what is wrong (or what the computer suggests is wrong), ask someone else for a second opinion. Remember, you are the writer, and you must make the final decision about your work.

On the other hand, don't completely ignore the grammar check function. It may suggest some ways to make your writing stronger.

SUMMARY FOR USING THE FOUR STRATEGIES

❑ Four strategies for effective writing are knowing your purpose, knowing your audience, being clear and coherent, and revising and editing.

❑ Your paragraph should have a clear purpose and should be designed to achieve the purpose as effectively as possible.

❑ A misplaced modifier is a descriptive word or phrase that is confusing because of its position in the sentence.

❑ You should be aware of your intended audience and make sure that your tone, style, and vocabulary are appropriate for the audience.

❑ Make your points simply and directly.

❑ Take time to revise and edit your work carefully. If possible, set it aside for a while to get a fresh perspective.

PRACTICING YOUR SKILLS

Now that you have learned about the four guidelines of effective writing, practice using those guidelines in the following activities.

PRACTICE 1

Read this paragraph and answer the questions that follow.

Children should learn good dental hygiene habits at an early age. Once these habits are established, they will become second nature and will remain with the child throughout his or her life. As the parent or primary caregiver, your role in establishing your child's dental hygiene habits is crucial. First, you can demonstrate the importance of good dental hygiene through example: Let your child see you brushing and flossing on a regular basis. Second, show your child how to use a toothbrush properly. Don't simply assume that proper use will come naturally. Explain how to brush gently from the gums outward and show how to reach all sides of the teeth. Third, provide healthful (not sugary!) snacks that won't promote cavities. Finally, ensure that your child has the necessary personal items: a new toothbrush every four to six weeks, good toothpaste, and plenty of dental floss. Before long, your child's dental care habits will be well established and he or she will maintain a healthy mouth without a second thought.

Knowing Your Purpose

1. What do you think is the writer's main goal?

_____

2. How can you tell?

_____

_____

Knowing Your Audience

3. Who is the intended audience?

_____

4. How does the writer tailor the paragraph to the intended audience?

_____

_____

PRACTICE 2

Below is the rough draft of a paragraph written by Tonia Meyers, the manager of a florist shop. On the lines below, choose three sentences that need revising and rewrite the sentences to make them clearer and more coherent.

 Knowing that Mother's Day is one of our busiest times of the year, with the other busiest times being Valentine's Day and the June wedding season, our most valued customers will be offered special incentives at this particular time. Mother's Day is a perfect opportunity to use a fresh bouquet of flowers to tell your mother (or other special woman in your life) how much you love and appreciate her. Our bouquets come in a wide variety of colors, scents, and combinations. Many special deals are available at this time, including discounted floral arrangements and free or partially discounted delivery with certain purchases, depending on the type of arrangement ordered. We hope you will stop by Main Street Florist to check out some of our great Mother's Day deals.

First Sentence:

_____

_____

_____

_____

_____

Second Sentence:

_____

_____

_____

_____

_____

Third Sentence:

_____

_____

_____

_____

APPLYING YOUR SKILLS

Now that you have studied and practiced the four guidelines, you will apply them in a paragraph of your own. During the prewriting stage, you will consider your purpose and intended audience and think about how those considerations will shape your paragraph. Use a separate sheet of paper or a word processing file for writing. Label and save each stage of your writing.

Prewriting

(a) Begin by selecting a topic for your paragraph. Here are some suggestions.

The most recent movie you have seen

A place you would like to visit

Your extended family

A job you would like to have

Your favorite food

What a good supervisor is like

Your favorite holiday

Your favorite movie

The perfect mate

The best time of the year

(b) Once you have chosen a topic, identify the purpose of your paragraph. For example, if you have chosen to write about your family, your purpose might be to share secrets of successful family relationships or to explain your family's unique traditions to a guest who is coming for a holiday dinner.

Purpose of Paragraph _____

_____

_____

_____

_____

_____

(c) Now that you have decided on the topic and purpose of your paragraph, consider the intended audience. Who will read this paragraph? Remember, when you construct the paragraph, you must keep the audience in mind to help you in choosing appropriate vocabulary, tone, and format.

Intended Audience _____

_____

_____

_____

_____

_____

(d) To ensure that your paragraph will be clear and coherent, write a sentence that sums up the main point of the paragraph. When you write the paragraph, you can use this sentence as a guide to help you stick to the central point.

Main Point _____

_____

_____

_____

_____

_____

Writing

Now write the first draft of your paragraph. As you write, keep in mind the purpose, audience, and main point that you identified previously. Remember to remain focused on your purpose and include only the details that are necessary to make your point clearly and effectively.

Revising

Read through your first draft. You may want to use some of the techniques listed on page 52 to help you revise. In addition, use the checklist below to make sure you have thought about the important points.

❑ Did you write the paragraph with a clear purpose in mind? Does the writing stick to that purpose?

❑ Is this paragraph written to a specific audience? Are the tone, style, and vocabulary appropriate to the intended audience?

❑ Is the writing clear, simple, and straightforward? Are there any unnecessary words or phrases that could be eliminated?

❑ Is the paragraph coherent? In other words, does it identify a specific topic and then remain focused on that topic?

When you think you have revised thoroughly, write a second draft. Label it *Draft 2*. If you are writing on paper, use a clean sheet. If you are writing on a computer, retype the paragraph from the beginning.

Follow the same process with your second draft. If possible, set the draft aside for awhile so you can come back to it with a fresh perspective. If you do not have time for this, you might try reading something else in order to shift gears for a few moments.

When you believe your content and presentation are as good as you can make them, move on to the editing stage. You are almost finished.

Editing

In this final stage, you will check your paragraph for mechanical errors. Closely examine the grammar, spelling, word use, punctuation, and capitalization. Review the descriptions of common errors in the Revising and Editing section of this chapter. You may want to try the suggested techniques for checking your work.

If you are using a word processor, run the spell checker and grammar checker, but do not count on these to find every error. Also, as the writer, make final decisions about what sounds best and ignore the computer's suggestions if you believe they are inappropriate.

After you have polished your writing, make a new copy in the format your instructor specifies. Proofread your paragraph one final time for the small, easily overlooked errors that often slip by when you are concentrating on larger matters.

WRITING FOR YOUR CAREER

CRITICAL THINKING

This section presents a writing project for each of the six career pathways. Choose one that appeals to you and use your new skills to write a paragraph on the subject.

When the project description refers you to the textbook web site, go to http://humphrey.swlearning.com/ and click on the Links tab. Look for Chapter 3, "Writing for Your Career." There you will find direct links to helpful web references.

Communication and the Arts

Imagine you are a wedding photographer. Last weekend you photographed a wedding and now you have developed the proofs. The next step is to send the proofs to the client, along with a brochure explaining the different options for ordering photos (sizes, shapes, books, and frames).

Along with the proofs and brochure, you want to include a brief but clear cover letter that explains what is enclosed, encourages the clients to purchase the photographs, thanks the couple for their business, and congratulates them on their new marriage.

Keeping in mind your purpose and your audience, write a clear and coherent paragraph for your cover letter. When you have completed the first draft, revise and edit your work until it is polished and ready to send. Read the paragraph a second time. Then revise and edit once more.

Health and Medicine

As a pharmacist at a neighborhood drug store, you have just filled a prescription for the pain reliever Celebrex®. You need to write a paragraph explaining the warnings and instructions to the consumer. Although the patient has already been instructed by his doctor about the proper use and risks of the medication, he should have a summary of this information in writing so he can refer to all of the risks. Consider your audience before writing the paragraph and choose the best approach to deliver a clear and coherent message. Be simple, yet direct and thorough, in your instructions.

To learn about Celebrex®, go to the textbook web site and select the link for Chapter 3, Health and Medicine. After you have studied the background information, compose a paragraph for the specific purpose of informing your 68-year-old male customer of the risks and proper use of the drug.

Human, Personal, and Public Service

As the budget director for a small not-for-profit organization that runs after-school programs for urban children, you need to compose a letter for your organization's annual fundraising drive. You will send the letter to those who have supported your organization in the past, as well as anyone who has asked for information or expressed an interest in your work over the past year.

In the opening paragraph of your letter, thank the readers for their past support or interest, and tell them something about the projects that their donations have made possible.

Business and Marketing

As the owner of a small coffee shop, you have just decided to start offering sandwiches for lunch, in addition to the bagels, pastries, and specialty coffee drinks that you already serve. Write a paragraph for the menu that introduces the new lunchtime offerings and describes two or three of the sandwiches you will be serving.

Science and Technology

Imagine you are an architect who has been working on the design for a family home. Throughout the process, you have been working closely with the clients to ensure that their vision is incorporated into your design. You have nearly completed the initial blueprint, but you want to ask your clients a question about the layout of the kitchen and dining room: Do they want a standard-sized door between the two rooms, or do they prefer a wider door that will allow them to easily carry large items back and forth?

You will send the query in an e-mail, and because you have been communicating extensively with these clients for quite some time, your tone can be fairly casual. Write a paragraph that describes the two options and asks your clients which doorway they prefer.

Environment and Natural Resources

You are a professional horticulturalist who writes a weekly gardening column for your local paper. The column is entitled, "Ask Randy," and it includes answers to readers' questions related to gardening. Write a paragraph responding to the following question. For information, go to the textbook web site and check out the information for Chapter 3, Environment and Natural Resources.

Dear Randy:
I'm interested in growing hydroponic tomatoes, but I'm not sure how. Can you give me some advice about how to do this?

PART I SUMMARY FOR CAREER WRITING

❑ Knowing why writing is important is the first step to becoming a better writer.

❑ Identifying your writing obstacles is essential for improving your writing.

❑ Specific techniques can help you overcome a fear of writing.

❑ By recognizing negative experiences and attitudes that hinder your writing, you can overcome them.

❑ The best writers know they have to continue practicing if they want to improve.

❑ A writing task can become less overwhelming if you think about writing as a process.

❑ The writing process can be divided into the following stages: prewriting, writing, revising, editing, and proofreading.

❑ Goals of prewriting include brainstorming for a topic, narrowing the topic you select, and generating additional ideas to support the topic.

❑ Brainstorming techniques include listing topics, using free association, freewriting, clustering or grouping, and asking open-ended questions.

❑ Understanding various causes of writer's block, such as being a perfectionist and imagining a critical reader, can help you cure the problem.

❑ Creating an outline makes the task of writing a first draft much easier. The outline can be informal or formal.

❑ Once you write a first draft, continue to revise, edit, and proofread your writing until you are satisfied.

❑ Four strategies for effective writing are: knowing your purpose, knowing your audience, being clear and coherent, and revising and editing.

❑ Your paragraph should have a clear purpose and should be designed to achieve the purpose as effectively as possible.

❑ A misplaced modifier is a descriptive word or phrase that is confusing because of its position in the sentence.

❑ You should be aware of your intended audience and make sure that your tone, style, and vocabulary are appropriate for the audience.

❑ Make your points simply and directly.

❑ Take time to revise and edit your work carefully. If possible, set it aside for a while to get a fresh perspective.

The Paragraph: Where All Your Writing Starts

4

How Does
a Paragraph
Work?

**IN THIS CHAPTER YOU WILL
LEARN TO:**

• **Develop a purpose
for a paragraph.**

• **Create a topic
sentence.**

• **Write supporting
sentences.**

• **Improve the unity
and coherence of
paragraphs.**

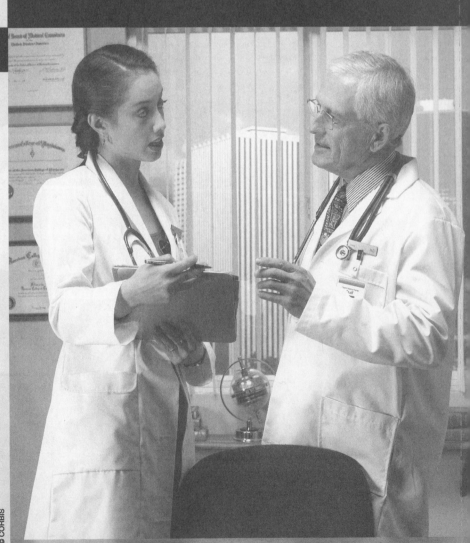

Using *Paragraphs* in Writing for Your Career

Career Path	Sample Career	Use for Paragraph Writing	Example of Paragraph Writing
Communication and the Arts	Advertising copywriter	Developing the body copy for a major car manufacturer's ad	Test-drive a Grand Cobra now! With a 3.8-liter, 240-horsepower, V-6 engine, you're in for a memorable ride. The revolutionary shock design will ensure that your ride is a smooth one.
Health and Medicine	Physician assistant	Explaining the diagnosis of a patient's condition	Mr. Morrow's X-rays have confirmed the doctor's diagnosis of a hiatal hernia. Symptoms at this stage indicate that the hernia is minor. However, surgery may be required if the diaphragm strangulates the hernia.
Human, Personal, and Public Service	Park ranger	Detailing in a park brochure the objectives of a night hike	Our October Owl Hike will begin in the parking lot at 9 P.M. While in search of the Great Horned Owl, we may come across other nocturnal animals. Bring your flashlights.
Business and Marketing	Computer instructor	Outlining the components of a middle-school introductory course in computers	In this course, you will learn basic operating functions of an IBM-compatible computer. The first lesson will teach you how to move and click the mouse. You will also create a short word document and learn how to locate filenames on the computer.
Science and Technology	Safety officer	Reporting on a safety hazard in the workplace	Our newly purchased forklifts are causing several problems in the warehouse. Delayed braking action has produced damage to inventory. So far, no employees have been injured.
Environment and Natural Resources	Hazardous waste manager	Indicating the extent of irresponsible waste disposal by a major company	Brand Corporation's waste disposal equipment has leaked a number of contaminants into ponds and streams. The health of residents in adjacent communities has been affected. Ignitable waste products and contamination of well water also need to be investigated.

Drunk Driving

ive drunk-driving accidents in one month caused alarm all across the state. For Reggie Thomas, a lobbyist who represents an anti-drunk driving organization, the issue is important. As a part of his job, he must try to influence new laws about drunk driving. His first task is to put together a statement of purpose in paragraph form. This paragraph is the beginning of a report that he will send to state legislators for review.

Reggie's purpose will shape what he writes in his paragraph. As someone who argues for the passage of new laws, his purpose is to persuade legislators.

First, Reggie discusses the issue of drunk driving with his organization's leaders. Next, he devises a main point, or topic sentence. He uses this sentence to begin his paragraph. Then he comes up with reasons in support of his argument. Lastly, he writes a closing sentence that emphasizes the importance of this issue.

> The state government must pass legislation seeking harder-hitting penalties for drunk drivers. There are several reasons for this. First, current laws have been ineffective in reducing the number of alcoholics on our roads. In fact, the number of repeat offenders arrested for drunk driving has increased 17 percent. Secondly, the current law allows first-time offenders to keep their driver's license. This means that drunk drivers retain their driving privileges while on probation. Automatic suspension of an offender's driver's license would send a stronger message: Drunk driving will not be tolerated. Finally, intoxicated drivers receive a mere slap on the wrist. Consequently, the victims of drunk-driving accidents suffer unjustly. Any person who recklessly chooses to drive drunk should be required to compensate the people injured or the families of victims killed in an accident they cause. Overall, tougher legislation would act as a deterrent to irresponsible drivers. Thus, fewer drivers would consider driving while intoxicated, a condition that can cause harm to the driver, to passengers in the car, to other motorists, and to pedestrians.

If you were a legislator in Reggie's state, would you agree that drunk-driving laws need to be changed? If so, Reggie has created an effective paragraph. Notice the way he uses a series of reasons to structure his paragraph. Also consider how his transitions—*first, secondly, finally, consequently, overall,* and *thus*—improve the flow of the paragraph.

In this chapter, like Reggie, you will practice writing high-quality paragraphs. You will learn to express a single point of view in a topic sentence. You will also find ways to support your viewpoint with evidence. In addition, you will take steps to improve the unity and coherence of a paragraph.

Writing Paragraphs

Paragraphs are building blocks in longer documents. They usually contain two to five sentences. In special cases, a paragraph can be as short as one sentence. In other situations, a paragraph may comprise a half page. At times, a paragraph stands on its own, for example, in a summary or synopsis.

The traditional model of a paragraph includes:

1. A main idea or point. This is expressed as a topic sentence.
2. Material that supports the topic sentence. This includes facts, statistics, examples, and illustrations. It can also comprise scenarios, comparisons, and contrasts. Many instructors refer to this kind of material as "specific details."
3. A final sentence recaps the content. This sentence may also provide a transition to the next paragraph.

Reggie's paragraph about the need for stronger drunk-driving laws reflects this format. Here is the pattern of his paragraph.

First, he introduces his topic sentence. He calls on the state legislature to create tougher drunk-driving laws. Because his goal is to persuade, the body of his paragraph presents three reasons why legislators should take action.

Reason: Current laws do not do a good job of deterring repeat offenders.

Reason: The penalty for first-time lawbreakers is too mild.

Reason: Existing legislation does not compensate the victims of drunk-driving accidents.

After presenting his major reasons, Reggie adds a closing statement that stresses the importance of this issue.

In this chapter, you will practice writing paragraphs using this model. You will also learn about approaches that differ from this method. In addition, you will learn to avoid common mistakes in paragraph writing.

As you discovered in Chapter 2, it is useful to approach a writing project in stages. In this chapter, you will start by thinking about your purpose. Then you will fine-tune the writing style of your paragraph.

SELF-ASSESSMENT 4

When I express a viewpoint in writing or conversation, I can:

	Usually	Sometimes	Never
Sum up my main idea in a single sentence.	❑	❑	❑
Predict my readers' or listeners' questions.	❑	❑	❑
Draw on my own experience to illustrate a point.	❑	❑	❑
Keep my focus on one point.	❑	❑	❑
Recap my central idea or sum up my thoughts.	❑	❑	❑

If you checked "Sometimes" or "Never" for any of the items, this chapter will help you improve your skills. Even if you checked "Usually" in every instance, you will learn more about writing paragraphs using an accepted format.

Identifying the Topic

A paragraph is similar to a box used for moving. An organized packer tapes a label to the box to identify the contents. For example, entertainment items and cooking utensils go in separate boxes. In the same way, an organized writer develops a label for a paragraph. The label is a topic sentence that states the main idea of a paragraph.

Coming up with a topic sentence for a paragraph is more difficult than slapping a label on a box. Imagine that you are an environmentalist reporting on a threat to the nation's wetlands. Here are five different topic sentences on this subject.

(A) Too Broad or Abstract	Our nation's wetlands are in big trouble.
(B) Too Narrow or Factual	Two out of three wetlands are polluted.
(C) Too Personal or Opinionated	My family and I are angry that wetland habitats are being destroyed by waste.
(D) Too Complicated	Wetlands can be subdivided into three types, and each type is threatened by suburban development.
(E) Suitable Topic Sentence	Industrial runoff is a major threat to U.S. wetlands.

Examples A through D illustrate common problems with topic sentences. Example A would work better as the topic of a longer document. Example B offers a simple statistic. Example C expresses a personal attitude. Example D deals with two separate topics. Each statement could be revised to produce a more effective topic sentence. Only Example E specifies a problem. Now the problem can be illustrated in a paragraph with supporting examples.

did you ever?

- Write a journal entry describing a life event, such as a new relationship or a new job?

- Explain to a friend how to access his or her e-mail account or how to open a new computer program?

- Give a "thumbs up" or "thumbs down" review of a movie you've seen, commenting on the acting or the special effects?

Situations like these ask you to focus on a single topic and add details that explain or describe the situation. This is what a paragraph does as well.

ACTIVITY 4.1 For each of the following exercises, three different topic sentences are presented. Select the most effective sentence by labeling it "Correct." For the other sentences, identify their weaknesses using the following key:

TB = Too Broad   TN = Too Narrow   TP = Too Personal   TC = Too Complicated

1. electronic books

   ____TN____ The online version of *Robinson Crusoe* is an electronic book.
   __Correct__ Electronic books are easier to access than library books.
   ____TP____ I would rather read an electronic book than a book from the library.

2. sports

   _____ Major league baseball has undergone a series of financial losses; also, baseball is in danger of losing its reputation as the national pastime.
   _____ In many nations, soccer is better known by the term *football*.
   _____ Soccer deserves more coverage on broadcast networks.

3. immigration

   _____ Illegal immigrants should have the right to be taught in U.S. public schools.
   _____ More than 7 million Mexicans immigrate to the United States each year.
   _____ Immigrants leave their country of origin for many reasons.

4. genealogy

   _____ I think genealogical research is worthwhile.
   _____ Several Internet sites provide useful information about Native-American families.
   _____ Research on adopted children can be complicated, and several genealogical CD programs fail to address the issue of remarriage.

5. careers

   _____ Some careers require advanced degrees.
   _____ I like the career field I have chosen in electrical engineering technology.
   _____ The career outlook for IT professionals remains promising.

6. astronomy

   _____ The brightest stars are not always the closest.
   _____ Astronomers are trying to understand the makeup of dark matter in the universe, as well as the nature of black holes.
   _____ The largest earthbound reflecting telescope is in Hawaii.

Developing the Body Sentences

If you think of a paragraph as a box for packing and the topic sentence as the label, the body of a paragraph is similar to the contents of the box. Body sentences should supply the contents—the evidence that explains the main idea in detail. When moving, you do not transport an empty box from one house or apartment to another. Likewise, you do not want to write an underdeveloped paragraph body.

Supporting evidence can take several forms. You can build a paragraph with facts and statistics. You can provide details that appeal to the senses. You can also give examples from real-life situations. More informally, you can illustrate your topic sentence by telling a short story or an anecdote. Still another method involves quoting experts. Finally, you might build a series of reasons, causes, or effects. The kind of evidence you choose will depend on your topic.

Below are sentences taken from the body of different paragraphs. The first sentence is vague because it lacks specifics. The second sentence goes into more detail.

(A) Vague Sentence	Master chefs prepare a wide range of dishes.
Detailed Sentence	Master chefs prepare dishes ranging from old-fashioned family favorites to gourmet vegetarian meals.
(B) Vague Sentence	Criminologists use many new techniques to prevent crime.
Detailed Sentence	Body search scanners, radar guns, and digital fingerprinting are three new techniques criminologists use to prevent crime.
(C) Vague Sentence	Viruses can damage computer systems.
Detailed Sentence	Many computer viruses maliciously invade computer systems, erasing hard drives, deleting files, and reformatting floppy disks.
(D) Vague Sentence	A paralegal is an indispensable aide to many attorneys.
Detailed Sentence	Many attorneys rely on paralegals to retrieve and file documents, as well as to draft briefs and index computer databases.

As you write the body sentences of a paragraph, be as detailed as possible. Detail is a main ingredient in developing reader-friendly paragraphs, and it keeps the reader from having to second-guess the writer's meaning.

ACTIVITY 4.2 Write three body sentences that support each of the following topic sentences. In each case, try to use a variety of evidence. For instance, you may use reasons, examples, or facts to support one topic. For the next, you might rely on sensory details, anecdotes, or statistics.

1. Video-game addiction impairs an addict's social life.

   _____

   _____

   _____

2. Spam mail amuses some readers and annoys others.

   _____

   _____

   _____

3. Internet search engines produce interesting results.

   _____

   _____

   _____

4. Drivers should avoid road rage.

   _____

   _____

   _____

5. One of my friends deserves a Nobel Prize for inventiveness.

   _____

   _____

   _____

6. Many college students rarely eat a balanced diet.

   _____

   _____

   _____

Unifying the Content

All of the body sentences in a paragraph should connect with the topic. This is a concept known as unity. When packing a box labeled "cookware," you probably would not toss in a baseball mitt or a pocket calculator. When writing a paragraph on a specific topic, you should delete unrelated sentences. For example, when writing about soil erosion, do not go off on a tangent that describes depletion of the ozone layer.

Take a look at the following paragraph about aerobic exercise. Which supporting statement does not relate to the topic sentence?

Topic Sentence   You should choose an aerobic exercise that best matches your lifestyle.

Supporting Sentences   (a) Going on a fast-paced walk around the block would take only 20 minutes of your time right before or just after your workday.

                            (b) Stretching can help loosen tight muscles, and you should stretch immediately before and after a workout to prevent wear and tear.

                            (c) Riding a stationary bicycle would be a good workout for anyone living in an area without opportunities for outdoor exercise.

                            (d) If you want to exercise and maintain your social life at the same time, join an aerobics class.

Example (b) offers good advice, but it doesn't explain how an aerobic exercise matches a person's lifestyle. Additional information is needed to make an effective supportive statement.

Here are additional tips for improving the unity of a paragraph:

- Avoid stating too many main ideas in a row.
- Avoid reciting a series of facts about a topic without stating a main idea.
- Avoid a rambling effect. Too many body sentences can weaken a paragraph.

Building an effective paragraph

ACTIVITY 4.3   Improve the unity of the following paragraph written by a food safety expert for a brochure. First, underline the topic sentence. Then strike out sentences that do not support the topic sentence.

Spoilage bacteria cause food to deteriorate and develop unpleasant odors, tastes, and textures. Some spoilage bacteria grow at low temperatures in the refrigerator or freezer. Others grow at room temperature. Believe it or not, these one-celled organisms, too small to be seen with the naked eye, are responsible for fruits, such as oranges and cantaloupe, getting mushy. Under the right conditions, spoilage bacteria reproduce rapidly and their populations can grow quite large. In some cases, they double their numbers in as little as 30 minutes. Over time, they give many vegetables a slimy surface. Spoilage bacteria grow anywhere they have access to water and nutrients. The worst thing about spoilage bacteria is that they can cause illness. Finally, many meats, when left out of the refrigerator for long periods, develop a rancid odor. Food that is left too long at unsafe temperatures may be dangerous to eat.

ETHICS CONNECTION

Avoiding Generalizations

When a writer underdevelops the body of a paragraph, the result may be an overgeneralization. For example, when words such as *all* or *every* are used incorrectly, they may label a group improperly, as in "All engineering majors are analytical-minded." A different claim, which uses the words *none or no one*, is also an overgeneralization: "No one takes politics seriously."

Writers commit a similar error when they make hasty generalizations or exaggerated claims about a group based on limited information. For instance, if two student athletes state that they value English composition classes more than physical education, you should not claim that all student athletes value academics more than athletics.

Readers distrust writers who make misleading overgeneralizations. One way to avoid this error is to qualify your statements by using the words *most, several, many,* or *a majority.* Avoiding hasty generalizations, on the other hand, requires the collection of additional data.

Achieving Coherence

Try to use a clear pattern when writing the body sentences of a paragraph. This is known as being coherent. One way to achieve coherence is by using transitions—words or phrases that tie the sentences together. Here are some transitions and the reason for each.

- *furthermore, in addition, meanwhile:* to indicate continuity of thought
- *however, on the other hand, instead:* to express a change of thought
- *for example, for instance, such as:* to introduce new material
- *first, next, therefore, thus, finally, last:* to show a sequence of thought
- *similarly, likewise, in comparison:* to reveal a comparison

The last sentence of a paragraph can also improve coherence by recapping the main idea. In addition, it can provide a transition to the next paragraph of a longer document.

Still another way to make a paragraph more coherent is by using subordinating conjunctions. These words show relationships between separate parts of a complex sentence. For example, in the following sentence, *whenever* is a subordinating conjunction: "*Whenever* I shop online, I try to protect the privacy of my transactions." Other examples of subordinating conjunctions include *although, because, before, since, unless,* and *when*.

Below are two versions of a recipe written in paragraph form. The first lacks coherence. The second uses transitions and subordinating conjunctions to improve coherence. These words have been italicized so you can see the improvements.

Poor Coherence

Cooking a parsley frittata takes little preparation. Beat together two tablespoons of milk, two eggs, one tablespoon of parsley, and a crushed garlic clove. Add a pinch of dried chili flakes. Add salt and pepper. Heat one tablespoon of olive oil in a pan. Pour in the mixture. Cook for three minutes. Slide the frittata onto a plate. Turn the pan over the plate. Carefully flip the pan and plate over. Cook the other side of the frittata. Sprinkle one tablespoon of Parmesan cheese on the frittata. Cook for several more minutes. The cheese should melt, and the underside should appear golden.

Improved Coherence

Cooking a parsley frittata takes little preparation. *First,* beat together two tablespoons of milk, two eggs, one tablespoon of chopped parsley, and a crushed garlic clove. *Then* add a pinch of dried chili flakes *in addition to* salt and pepper. *After* heating one tablespoon of olive oil in a frying pan, pour in the mixture. Cook for three minutes. *Afterward,* slide the frittata onto a plate. *Once* you turn the pan over the plate, carefully flip the pan and plate over. *Next,* cook the other side of the frittata. *Lastly,* sprinkle one tablespoon of Parmesan cheese on the frittata and cook for several more minutes *until* the cheese melts and the underside appears golden.

ACTIVITY 4.4 The following letter was submitted to a law firm that handles cases where a product caused damage or injury. Improve the coherence of the letter by adding one of the following transitions wherever there is a blank: *in fact, in conclusion, recently, for example, thus, unfortunately, as a result, in my opinion, clearly, consequently, as well*. Use each transition only once.

_____, I purchased the Hi-Fidelity exercise treadmill at L&L Athletic Equipment. _____, the product has not performed well. _____, my ten-year-old son was thrown against a concrete wall as he used the treadmill at its highest setting. _____, he acquired a slight concussion. _____, the directions for operating and using the treadmill fail to ensure safe operation. _____, I feel the product was delivered in an unsafe condition. Adults have experienced difficulty staying on the treadmill, _____. _____, my sister-in-law, who is a trainer at an area gym, could not maintain her balance at the highest setting. _____, she had to shut off the machine or risk being thrown from it, as had happened with my son. _____ , the instructions should have included a warning about using the treadmill at high speeds. _____, I would appreciate your legal services on behalf of my son.

ACTIVITY 4.5 The following writing sample is the first draft of a paragraph written by a telecommunications specialist. Improve the unity and the coherence of the paragraph.

Teleworkers use the Internet to work from their homes. Teleworkers may use dial-up 56K modems to connect to the workplace. There are two basic categories of teleworkers. Local teleworkers live in the same vicinity as the company facility. Instead of driving to work each day, they simply log on to the Internet. A high-speed DSL or wireless hookup may also be used. A good example of a teleworker is a single parent who enjoys working from home to be with his or her preschool children. Long-distance teleworkers use the Internet to conduct business overseas or in other states. *Telecommuting* is another term for *teleworking*. Disabled employees can also benefit from telecommuting.

_____

_____

_____

_____

_____

_____

_____

_____

Placing the Topic Sentence

So far, you have looked at paragraphs that begin with a topic sentence. This is called direct placement. With this pattern, paragraphs start on a strong note so the reader knows what the paragraph is about. Most routine business writing uses direct placement. The fast pace of business demands writing that is clear and concise. However, you may wish to use two other patterns instead.

The indirect pattern places the topic sentence at the end of the paragraph. This method is used in persuasive or sales writing. In this case, the writer leads in with a series of reasons or benefits before asking the reader to do or buy something. This pattern is also useful for increasing reader interest. Additionally, it can create mystery or suspense. Consider the following example from a senior living brochure.

Lead-in Sentences	(a) Quality care is delivered by a concerned team of professionals in a quiet setting.
	(b) Residents may choose from five different activities a day, including swimming and dancing.
	(c) Best of all, residents retain a sense of dignity and wellness as they interact freely with family and friends.
Topic Sentence	All in all, assisted living not only meets the needs of today's seniors, it also makes them feel right at home.

Another strategy places the topic sentence in the middle of a paragraph. In this case, the topic sentence balances the opening and closing content. For instance, imagine that you review a new restaurant for a community newsletter. After dining, you produce this paragraph.

Opening Sentence	Most fast-food restaurants boast friendly customer service. At the counter, cashiers greet each person with a smile and provide prompt service.
Topic Sentence	If you're looking for the same kind of gracious service at Arnold's Cuisine on Route 67, you may come away disappointed.
Closing Sentence	This new restaurant produced a server who was the epitome of rudeness. Who knows what she was doing for a half hour while we waited for her to take our order?

ACTIVITY 4.6 Reorder the sentences in each of the following paragraphs so the result makes more sense. First, write what you believe to be the topic sentence at the beginning of each exercise. Then place the numerals 1 through 4 in the blanks to indicate the correct order of sentences.

1. Topic sentence: _____

_____   I watched the paramecium hit an object and recoil.

_____   The idea that a paramecium is robotic, similar to a computer program, isn't a fair parallel.

_____   Although its movements looked random, in reality, it was reacting "intelligently" to invisible substances on the slide.

_____   One day as I was watching a paramecium on a microscope slide, I saw something unusual.

2. Topic sentence: _____

_____   These thieves are then able to make calls of their own or sell the phone numbers they stole.

_____   "Shoulder surfers" use binoculars or video cameras to record the calling-card numbers of unaware victims using cell phones in public.

_____   Identity theft is one of the fastest-growing types of fraud.

_____   "Internet burglars" can easily find an unsuspecting customer's social security number, which they use as a key to unlock personal financial data.

3. Topic sentence: _____

_____   Having a "crush" still means being infatuated with a member of the opposite sex, and "gyp" still means to cheat someone out of money.

_____   "Banana oil" was a phrase meaning complete nonsense.

_____   In the Jazz Age of the 1920s, many new words and expressions were invented that are still being used today. However, other expressions have not been so long-lived.

_____   If you really liked someone, you might have thought of him or her as the "bee's knees."

4. Topic sentence: _____

_____   Finally, drive with courtesy by using your turn signal as you change lanes.

_____   Also make sure that you keep a safe distance between your car and the car ahead of you so it doesn't appear that you're tailgating.

_____   If you stop trying to race the clock, you'll be amazed at how relaxed you feel behind the wheel.

_____   These are just a few tips recommended by AAA for avoiding the dreaded driving hazard of road rage.

5. Topic sentence: _____

_____ E-mail viruses have been a problem at our company for some time.

_____ This causes your monitor to pop up the alert, "This contains a virus!"

_____ Even though we update the virus software on a daily basis, some viruses manage to bypass the detection software.

_____ With luck, you hit the delete key and the infected attachment is removed.

6. Topic sentence: _____

_____ Other observers have reported that dunes sound like propeller aircraft or buzzing telegraph wires.

_____ Researchers do not agree on why, under certain conditions, the sand sings.

_____ Listeners have compared the sound that these "booming" dunes make to bells, pipe organs, trumpets, foghorns, cannon fire, and thunder.

_____ At least 30 "booming" sand dunes have been found in deserts and on beaches, intriguing listeners and baffling researchers.

TECHNOLOGY CONNECTION

Netiquette

Because it is so informal, e-mail has been cited for causing a breakdown in communication. For instance, many writers of e-mail messages tend to use abbreviations, acronyms, and lower case. In a business setting, you should make your e-mail paragraphs sound professional. To achieve a professional style, keep a few simple rules of Internet etiquette, or netiquette, in mind:

- Do not overuse punctuation marks to reinforce a point. For instance, avoid multiple exclamation points!!! Worse are combinations of exclamation points and question marks?!!?

- Do not use smileys (smiley faces) and emoticons (emotional icons). Although emoticons help convey your mood, they are too childish and distracting for business writing.

- Do not write in ALL CAPITAL LETTERS. This is known as SHOUTING, which can be interpreted as rude. Another act of courtesy is keeping your e-mail short and to the point.

- Acronyms or abbreviations are fine for personal use, but avoid them in business writing. Not everyone in a business will understand what you mean by BBFN (bye-bye for now), LOL (laughing out loud), or TIA (thanks in advance). Follow standard rules for punctuation and grammar as well.

WRITING WORKSHOP

Varying Your Sentences

To enhance the variety of your paragraphs, experiment with three types of sentences: simple, compound, and complex.

(A) Simple Sentences

Generation Xers have grown up to become the industrial and service workers of the 21st century. Employers have unfairly stereotyped these new workers as bored and apathetic.

(B) Compound Sentence

Generation Xers have grown up to become the industrial and service workers of the 21st century, and employers have unfairly stereotyped them as bored and apathetic.

(C) Complex Sentence

As Generation Xers have grown up to become the industrial and service workers of the 21st century, employers have unfairly stereotyped these new workers as bored and apathetic.

In Example (A), each sentence is straightforward and direct. Example (B) uses the conjunction *and* to join the two sentences together. Example (C) ties the two sentences together by turning the first into a dependent clause with the word *as*.

SUMMARY FOR WRITING PARAGRAPHS

❏ A traditional paragraph contains a topic sentence, a body, and a concluding sentence.

❏ A suitable topic sentence should state a single idea about a specific topic.

❏ Body sentences should support the main idea of a paragraph with specific evidence.

❏ Paragraph unity means that all sentences in a paragraph connect with a single topic.

❏ Coherence can be achieved through the use of transitional expressions such as *in addition*, *however*, or *therefore*.

PRACTICING YOUR SKILLS

Now that you understand how to use paragraphs effectively, put your knowledge to work in the following activities.

PRACTICE 1

An insurance claims representative wrote the following paragraph. It begins clearly enough. However, the supporting points are too abstract. Follow the directions below to analyze the paragraph.

 _____ One overlooked road hazard is the seemingly trivial but potentially devastating problem of missing street signs. _____ There are several reasons why street signs end up missing. _____ For unsuspecting drivers, missing street signs can cause several problems. _____ Something needs to be done to make sure missing street signs are replaced as soon as possible, before serious consequences occur.

Paragraph Structure

1. Place a *T* in the blank before the sentence you think is the topic sentence.

2. Which sentence does the best job of supporting the topic sentence? Identify this sentence by placing an *S* in the blank before it.

3. Which sentence seems unrelated to the topic sentence? Write the letter *U* in the blank before this sentence.

4. Write a *C* in the blank before the sentence that works best as a concluding sentence.

Supporting Evidence

5. For the sentence you labeled with an *S*, think of three specific examples that would help the reader better understand the issue. Brainstorm your ideas below.

   (a) _____

   _____

   _____

   (b) _____

   _____

   _____

   (c) _____

   _____

   _____

PRACTICE 2

Here is a paragraph taken from a report about whistle-blowers in business and industry.

   The term *whistle-blower* has negative connotations. Whistle-blowers have been stigmatized and even ostracized by the very firms whose business practices they are trying to "clean up." Furthermore, whistle-blowing is difficult. In fact, a whistle-blower may be viewed in an unfavorable light as someone seeking to undermine the productivity of a business enterprise. In one well-publicized case, a whistle-blower received numerous death threats from coworkers because she had gone to the media about an illegal accounting procedure. In due course, she gave up her position with the company, even though she had been a model employee for 25 years.

Topic Sentence

1. Underline the sentence that functions as the topic sentence.

Supporting Evidence

2. List the subpoints that support the topic sentence. As much as possible, rephrase the supporting sentences in your own words.

   (a) _____

   _____

   (b) _____

   _____

   (c) _____

   _____

   _____

   (d) _____

   _____

Response

3. What is your own attitude about whistle-blowers? Do you view them in a positive or negative light? Sum up your thoughts in a short paragraph.

_____

_____

_____

_____

_____

APPLYING YOUR SKILLS

Write a paragraph about a topic of your choice. Develop your paragraph in stages, as described below. Begin by choosing a topic. Next, narrow the topic so that it focuses on one idea. Then develop a topic sentence that clearly expresses your main idea. Start your writing with a rough draft that includes examples to support your topic sentence. After thorough revising and editing, your paragraph should deliver the message you intended.

Generating Ideas

Brainstorm one or more of the following areas for a topic. Use the prewriting techniques discussed in Chapter 2 to come up with a variety of ideas. Then select one topic that seems most promising.

(a) **Current events:** Page through a couple of magazines at your school library or surf some news sites on the Web. What is currently being presented or debated in the news?

(b) **Historical events:** If you enjoy history, select a past event. A creative way of thinking about the past is to come up with an alternate history. This involves changing a single event and asking "What if?" For instance, "What if the *Titanic* hadn't sunk when it hit an iceberg?"

(c) **Natural objects:** Just as artists carry a sketch pad, you, as a writer, should bring along a notebook on your next nature hike or walk around campus. When you see something interesting, take a moment to describe it.

(d) **Technological objects:** What machines fascinate you? What machines frighten you? On what machines are you dependent? Focus on a technological item as a starting point for your paragraph. Maybe you want to discuss how you would redesign the object if you were the engineer in charge.

(e) **People:** Think about someone you admire or someone you would like to emulate. This person could be someone famous or someone closer to home. Or focus on a person who has had a great deal of influence on your development.

(f) **Workplace issues:** What are some of the major issues you are facing in your place of employment? Are there problems with morale? What about technology or training? Brainstorm ways to solve this workplace problem.

Narrowing Your Topic

Once you have selected a topic, make sure it is focused enough for the length of the assignment. For instance, if you are writing about a person, you may only need to write about his or her personality. You might write about the one personality trait you most admire. Narrowing your topic even further, you might reflect on a single episode where you saw this trait in action.

Developing a Topic Sentence

Remember to avoid topic sentences that are too broad or too factual. You should also avoid topic sentences that are too opinionated or too complicated. As you prepare to write about your topic, try coming up with three different sentences that express a main idea. Then choose the sentence you like best.

Writing a Rough Draft

Try one of the following methods for composing a first draft of your paragraph. If you are feeling ambitious, write two versions of your paragraph, using each method, and compare the results.

(a) **Freewriting:** When freewriting about your topic, let your thoughts flow freely. Whether handwriting or typing, give yourself a time limit. Ten or fifteen minutes should be fine. Then try to keep writing until the time limit is reached. Don't pause to correct your mistakes. Try not to think about your word choices. Doing so will only slow you down. Once you have completed your freewrite, you can go on to the next stage: revising.

(b) **Outlining:** If you choose to outline your paragraph, you must organize your thoughts from start to finish. At first, your outline may be an informal series of keywords or phrases. In fact, you may find that you need to rearrange the order of your ideas. Once you are satisfied, begin turning keywords into phrases and phrases into complete sentences. Continue building your outline until you have turned it into an actual paragraph.

Revising

Now that you have a first draft of your paragraph, you may begin revising it. Use the following checklist as a guideline.

- ❑ Does the topic sentence express a single idea?
- ❑ Have you placed the topic sentence in the most effective position: beginning, middle, or end?
- ❑ Do you have enough supporting evidence to explain the main idea?
- ❑ Could you add extra supporting evidence to make the paragraph more specific?
- ❑ Is your paragraph too wordy or bulky? Can some sentences be deleted without sacrificing your meaning?
- ❑ Does the paragraph flow smoothly from start to finish? What can you do to improve the sequence of thoughts?

Editing

As you continue to fine-tune your paragraph, begin with a grammar and spell check. Vary your writing style by combining simple sentences into compound or complex sentences. Finally, read your paragraph aloud so you can easily hear any remaining rough spots.

WRITING FOR YOUR CAREER

CRITICAL THINKING

This section presents a writing project for each of the six career pathways. Choose one or more of the following writing activities. Then develop a paragraph in response. In some cases, you may want to conduct research on the Internet. When the project description refers you to the textbook web site, go to http://humphrey.swlearning.com and click on the Links tab. Look for Chapter 4, "Writing for Your Career." There you will find direct links to helpful web references.

Communication and the Arts

Imagine that you are a freelance interior designer. Your specialty is working on commercial properties. Recently, you acquired a new hotel chain as a major client. In meetings with the hotel's managers, you learned that they hope to market their hotel rooms to businesspeople and vacationers. You realize that each group has different expectations about superior hotel service.

Write a paragraph that describes an ideal hotel room that can accommodate both groups. Explain the amenities you plan to add that the hotel chain can offer to its various groups of guests. Be as detailed as possible with your descriptions.

Health and Medicine

As a recreational therapist for a retirement community, you are responsible for planning social activities three times a week. These activities must appeal to the senior residents of the community. Part of the challenge is coming up with one activity that can benefit all of the residents. Various residents have different interests. Many also have special needs. Some are wheelchair bound.

Think about an activity that would meet the needs of the greatest number of residents. Describe the activity in a paragraph to be included in a flyer. Try to make the activity sound as appealing as possible by including compelling descriptions. Your writing should be motivational in tone.

Human, Personal, and Public Service

As a personal image consultant, you help clients prepare for interviews with employers. Many of your clients are highly skilled technical specialists. For instance, you deal with many engineers, computer programmers, medical assistants, graphic artists, criminal justice aspirants, and hazardous waste professionals. However, some of these new graduates feel intimidated by the interview process and have trouble motivating themselves for interviews. For the most part, their experience has been limited to entry-level jobs. These types of jobs required a brief screening interview at best.

Write a paragraph that you can distribute to your clients in the form of a pamphlet. Your paragraph should give advice on interviewing at a professional level.

Business and Marketing

Have you ever hung up on a telemarketer? Have you wrangled your way out of a telemarketer's sales pitch? For a change, try looking at the situation from a telemarketer's point of view. Think of a product or service you could sell over the phone. Then develop a surefire paragraph that would keep a prospect from hanging up. Or think of an objection a customer might make to your offer and write a paragraph rebuttal.

Science and Technology

As an industrial designer, you enjoy creating 3-D representations of products for everyday use. Some clients request scale models, while others are satisfied with computerized images. In either case, your design is accompanied by a paragraph description.

Recently, a furniture manufacturer, who became aware of your award-winning designs, approached you. The manufacturer commissioned you to design a chair for apartment dwellers. Potential users of the chair have limited space and lead active lifestyles. As part of the brainstorming process, think about the kinds of special features a chair of this sort might offer. Then write a detailed paragraph that describes your concept for such a chair. You should seek to explain why your chair design is unique.

Environment and Natural Resources

One of the duties you enjoy as a hazardous waste manager is visiting area schools. During your lectures to students, you point out the dangerous materials that may be found in students' homes. Although hazardous waste is associated with heavy industry, many households contain similar harmful products. If flushed down a drain or poured into the ground, these products can damage the environment. Some household products can even cause serious illness or threaten human life. Poisons, toxic substances, flammable liquids, paint strippers, drain cleaners, pesticides—all of these materials are considered hazardous waste.

One point you try to communicate to younger audiences is that homeowners should strive to reduce the amount of household waste. If nothing else, homeowners can purchase fewer hazardous products or participate in a recycling program.

Write a paragraph to distribute as a handout during your presentation. Your paragraph should describe the kinds of hazardous waste found in ordinary households. It might also explain how families can best dispose of such waste. Research this topic on the Internet using http://www.google.com or another search engine.

5

Illustration: Paragraphs That Give Examples

IN THIS CHAPTER YOU WILL LEARN TO:

- Write sharp, effective examples to illustrate a point.

- Write focused topic sentences.

- Guide your reader with transitional expressions.

USING *ILLUSTRATION* IN WRITING FOR YOUR CAREER

Career Path	Sample Career	Use for Illustrative Writing	Example of Illustrative Writing
Communication and the Arts	Webmaster (manager of a web site)	Informing clients how to prepare files for uploading	Before submitting picture files for the web site, please save them in a compressed format. The most common compressed format is JPEG, which produces especially compact image files. Another example, the GIF format, works best for simple pieces of artwork.
Health and Medicine	Art therapist	Reporting on a patient's progress	Suzanne Mulrooney is making rapid progress. Yesterday, for example, she drew a picture of herself walking with crutches. This was the first time she did not depict herself in a wheelchair.
Human, Personal, and Public Service	Career counselor	Explaining what a particular career involves	A journalist has a tremendous responsibility for getting the news right. For one thing, he or she must check all facts carefully.
Business and Marketing	Bank officer	Detailing the benefits of a savings account	Every customer should take advantage of the benefits that our savings accounts offer. First, our interest rates rank in the top 5 percent nationwide. Second, we require only a $100 minimum in the account.
Science and Technology	Quality inspector	Justifying a decision to reject a product	McNamara Corporation's order of drinking straws was delayed because the products failed inspection. Almost 40 percent of the straws had creases in the plastic. Another 10 percent were shorter than the customer required.
Environment and Natural Resources	Landscape architect	Explaining advantages of using a certain plant	English ivy is an excellent plant for solving landscaping dilemmas. Often, ivy helps to prevent soil erosion on a riverbank. It can also serve as ground cover on a barren patch in a yard or garden.

ON THE JOB

Film Distribution

In his own opinion, Keola Burns has the best job in the world. As the promotions manager for IndyFlicks, a small distributor of international films, he has the opportunity to watch new movies from around the globe. He then helps convince movie theaters and film festivals to screen these films.

Today Keola viewed an exciting new work by a young Latin American woman. Her film tells the story of three generations of an extended family, the Selgados, from the 1940s to the present. Keola thinks this film will appeal to a wide audience, and his task is to write a short publicity notice.

He wants to focus on the film's depiction of the major changes that occur over time in the life of the family. As part of his prewriting, he lists examples he might use to demonstrate these changes. Soon he has written down 15 examples, far more than he can use, so he selects the most important and most vivid ones.

Next, Keola writes an outline, then a rough draft. After revising and editing, his publicity release includes the following key paragraph. Notice the three examples he uses to make his point.

In this compelling saga of three generations, the Selgado family undergoes dramatic changes. <u>In economic terms,[1] for instance, the family rides a roller coaster.</u> Beginning in poverty, the grandparents establish a furniture store that becomes so successful that their children move to a ritzy neighborhood in the capital. Then, in a surprising reversal, the grandchildren lose the store—and most of their money—in a business catastrophe. <u>In the family's cultural life,[2] too, we witness a remarkable evolution.</u> The grandparents are conservatives who cling to established customs, as laid down by the church and by family tradition. Their rebellious children shun the church and immerse themselves in rock music and popular literature. Then the third generation brings another twist, as the youngest Selgados become disillusioned with the modern world and return to traditional ways. <u>Finally, the family shows a[3] steadily rising political-consciousness.</u> The grandparents seem to be indifferent to the government, perhaps even unaware of what is happening in their country. Their children and grandchildren, though, become increasingly active in politics, to the point that young Ricardo Selgado runs for mayor of the town.

Do you agree that this family went through dramatic changes over the generations? If so, Keola chose good examples.

In this chapter, you will learn how to build a paragraph that uses examples to illustrate a point clearly and effectively.

Understanding Illustration

In writing, **illustration** means the action of giving examples to explain or clarify a point. This is the technique used in Keola's paragraph. Illustration is a simple, useful way to make your point clear and convincing for the reader.

To write an illustration paragraph, use this basic format:

- The topic sentence states your main point.
- Follow-up sentences provide examples that support the main point.
- Transitional expressions help carry the reader from one example to the next.

Can you see how Keola's paragraph about the film follows this pattern? Below is Keola's outline for the paragraph. Compare the outline to the numbered examples in his actual paragraph.

Main point for topic sentence: The family in the film goes through dramatic changes over three generations.

Example 1: Economic changes
- Family begins in poverty
- Family rises to wealth
- Family's fortunes decline when business collapses

Example 2: Cultural changes
- First generation's traditionalism
- Second generation's rebellion, interest in modern culture
- Third generation's return to tradition

Example 3: Political changes
- Indifference of grandparents to government
- Rising interest of second and third generations
- Ricardo's campaign for mayor

As you can see from this outline, Keola illustrated the family's changes by naming three kinds of change. Then he explained each of these changes.

By looking back at the paragraph, you can also see that Keola used transitional terms—*for instance, too,* and *finally*—to show when he was moving from one example to another.

SELF-ASSESSMENT 5

When I need to give examples to support a general point, I can:

	Usually	Sometimes	Never
State the main point clearly.	☐	☐	☐
Think of several examples to support the point.	☐	☐	☐
Choose words that state the examples clearly.	☐	☐	☐
Eliminate examples that do not support the point.	☐	☐	☐
Use transitional expressions to move from one example to another.	☐	☐	☐

If you checked "Sometimes" or "Never" for any of the items, this chapter will help you improve your skills. Even if you checked "Usually" in every instance, you will learn more about writing paragraphs that use sharp, effective examples.

Stating the Main Point

As you learned in Chapter 4, the topic sentence of a paragraph should state just one main point. The sentence should also be focused enough so the rest of the paragraph can support or develop the point.

You may think that the topic sentence of an illustration paragraph would be simple to write. But it is surprisingly easy to get off on the wrong foot. Say you are a bank officer, and you are writing an illustration paragraph to show a potential customer the benefits of the savings accounts your bank offers. Look at these variations of the topic sentence.

(A) Too Generalized First National's savings accounts are an excellent way to save money for a rainy day.

(B) More Than One Main Point First National's savings accounts are safe because they are federally insured, and they pay a higher rate of interest than checking accounts.

(C) Good First National offers consistently high interest rates on personal savings accounts.

Example (C) is the best of the three alternatives because it states just one main point and it is focused on a specific subject. After beginning with sentence (C), you could continue with examples such as these:

For the past seven years, First National's interest rates have ranked in the top 10 percent nationally.

The rate on the Gold Star account is the best currently available in the city.

did you ever?

- Say that you like a certain type of food—for instance, spicy Mexican food—and then offer examples of specific dishes?

- Argue that an actor you like is really great and then cite specific film roles to support your point?

- Explain that a particular person often gets on your nerves and then give examples of annoying things that he or she does?

All of these uses of language involve illustration, a technique you use every day. With practice, you can apply the same skill to your writing.

ACTIVITY 5.1 For each of the subjects in the following list, write a focused, interesting topic sentence that can lead readily into examples that illustrate the topic. After the topic sentence, in parentheses, jot down some of the examples you might use. The first item has been completed for you.

1. my daily diet

    On school days, I stoke up on carbohydrates (cereal, pasta, pizza).

2. my parents

    _____

    _____

    _____

3. my experiences in high school

    _____

    _____

    _____

4. the job I would most like to have

    _____

    _____

    _____

5. my favorite actor or actress

    _____

    _____

    _____

6. a quality (or qualities) I look for in a friend

    _____

    _____

    _____

    _____

WRITING WORKSHOP

Avoiding Sentence Fragments

In paragraphs that provide examples, it is easy to make the mistake of writing sentence fragments. A sentence fragment is a sentence that is incomplete because it lacks a subject or a verb. Look at the following examples.

(A) Complete Sentences	Kateryna's report gave a detailed analysis of quality problems at the toy manufacturing plant.
	For example, she listed all of the different types of flaws that had been reported.
(B) Sentence and Fragment	Kateryna's report gave a detailed analysis of quality problems at the toy manufacturing plant.
	For example, all of the different types of flaws.

In Example B, the first sentence is complete. The second sentence, however, has no verb. So it is a fragment rather than a complete sentence.

In your prewriting for an illustration paragraph, you will make a list of possible examples to use. When you move on to your first draft, be sure that each example translates into one or more full sentences.

Finding Examples

After identifying the main point, the next step is to think of possible examples to illustrate the point. The best examples are not necessarily the ones that come immediately to mind. This is a time to be creative! Let your mind roam over the subject and use the brainstorming techniques described in Chapter 2 to come up with as many ideas as possible. The more good alternatives you have to choose from, the better your paragraph will be. Activity 5.2 will help you practice your creativity.

ACTIVITY 5.2 For each of the following topic sentences, think of one interesting, clear, memorable example. On the blank lines, write your example in one or two full sentences.

1. Great athletes are made, not born.

    _____

    _____

    _____

2. In my family, everyone enjoys holidays.

    _____

    _____

    _____

3. One cheerful person makes a huge difference in any group.

    _____

    _____

    _____

4. Life seems to move faster in the city than in the country.

    _____

    _____

    _____

5. In spite of national television and radio networks, North Americans still speak with diverse accents.

    _____

    _____

    _____

6. When we watch television, my friend Jaime is really impatient with shows that annoy her.

    _____

    _____

    _____

Selecting Your Best Examples

When is an example inappropriate for the subject? Look at the following outline for a paragraph. Do you see anything wrong with the examples listed?

Topic Sentence	A debit card is a handy thing to carry in your wallet.
Examples	(a) It is as easy to use as a credit card.
	(b) Many stores now accept debit cards.
	(c) You can use a debit card to withdraw cash from a bank machine.
	(d) You can overdraw your account if you aren't careful.

Example (d), although true, does not support the topic sentence. In fact, it undermines the topic sentence. Instead of explaining why debit cards are handy, it gives the reader a reason to be wary of debit cards.

Another problem occurs when an example is too vague to be helpful.

Topic Sentence	A debit card is a handy thing to carry in your wallet.
Vague Example	You will find plenty of occasions to use it.

The vague example says nothing new. Such useless padding may bore the reader.

Finally, examples can confuse the reader if they are irrelevant to the main point.

Topic Sentence	A debit card is a handy thing to carry in your wallet.
Irrelevant Example	Some cards come in attractive designer colors.

An irrelevant example can derail your paragraph by taking the reader off in a new direction.

In summary, a good example should be:

- *Relevant* to the topic of the paragraph.
- *Specific* rather than vague.
- *Supportive* of the main point.

Without good examples, your readers can get very confused.

ETHICS CONNECTION

Honest Examples

If you know your main point is true, may you use examples that are not completely accurate? Imagine that you are asked to write a report on the business climate in a country run by a repressive dictator. You want to make the point that some businesses are thriving despite the regime's political oppression. In a section describing the nation's social and educational characteristics, you begin a paragraph this way.

> The country's educational system has improved greatly in the past decade. As one indicator, the adult literacy rate rose from 73 percent in the mid-1990s to 88 percent today.

In this case, the example seems to support the topic sentence, but what if the figure of "88 percent" comes from a government agency that often issues inflated statistics designed to make the dictator look good? If you know the figure may be inaccurate, you are misleading your readers.

When a supposed fact is untrustworthy, you should not use it as an example, even if the main point it illustrates is true. An ethical writer can find an honest way to support the point.

ACTIVITY 5.3 In each of the numbered items, the topic sentence is followed by examples that are supposed to illustrate it. In every case, one example is not as good as the others. Identify the weak example and use one of the following abbreviations to indicate why it is weak:

I = Irrelevant   V = Vague   U = Unsupportive of the main point

1. In addition to technical knowledge about the product, a quality control inspector should possess excellent computer skills.

_____ The images from the inspection equipment are displayed on a computer screen.

_____ If a computer image shows a flaw, the inspector needs to access several different screens to pinpoint the exact nature of the problem.

_____ Inspectors must use the computer to enter data on each item they examine.

_____ The software that inspectors use is easy to learn, requiring no more than two hours of training time.

2. People in my office have remarkable business talents.

_____   Albert writes the clearest, most precise instructions I have ever read.

_____   Raisa is so friendly that I liked her immediately.

_____   Nykesha can fix almost any software problem in a matter of minutes.

_____   Terry manages a dozen complicated projects and keeps them all on schedule.

3. After taking just one course, my roommate, Marisa, has mastered Mexican cooking.

_____   When she cooks her special burritos, the aroma makes everyone in the building hungry.

_____   Last week she made an excellent Mexican dish.

_____   Our neighbor, who comes from Mexico City, says that Marisa's mole sauce is the best he has ever tasted.

_____   At the church potluck, Marisa's chile rellenos disappeared faster than any other dish.

4. My career counselor says that I have the skills and temperament for a career in financial services.

_____   My average in math classes has always been between 90 and 95 percent.

_____   I enjoy working with all kinds of people, both coworkers and customers.

_____   Because financial services are becoming more global, the job may involve travel.

_____   I need a career that makes me feel socially useful, and financial services would do that.

5. At my college, interest in national politics has been increasing.

_____   More than 20 percent of the students say they never vote because both major parties ignore or oversimplify the important issues.

_____   More than 65 percent of the students voted in the last congressional election, compared to only 53 percent six years ago.

_____   Political speakers now draw big crowds on the campus, often filling our 300-seat auditorium.

_____   A recent campus survey showed that 9 percent of the students plan a career in a politically related field. Five years ago the figure from a similar survey was only 3 percent.

6. In recent years, U.S. business leaders have become deeply concerned about the writing skills of their employees.

_____ Large companies, such as Ford Motor Company and Boston Scientific, have set up their own writing classes.

_____ Corporate training firms report that they are often asked to conduct workshops on basic composition skills.

_____ According to statistics from the U.S. Department of Labor, writing skills rank high on the list of traits that managers look for in their employees.

_____ Many executives worry that their employees cannot write as well as they should.

TECHNOLOGY CONNECTION

Collaborative Writing

In the workplace, much of your writing may take place in collaboration as part of a team project. In collaborative writing, various team members draft sections of the document. Then they edit and revise each other's work.

Often, in writing illustrative material, several team members contribute possible examples, and they exchange comments about which examples best support the main point the team wants to make.

Most word processors have features that support this type of collaborative writing:

- Track Changes or Review modes allow you to mark insertions and deletions with color, underlining, strikethrough, and other easy-to-spot cues.

- Comment commands or buttons permit you to add a comment to a particular spot in the text, tagged with an identifier that shows your name or initials.

- Highlighting buttons help you use color to highlight a word, a phrase, or an entire section.

These tools are essential when an electronic document must go through multiple revisions by various people. For instance, if you have a great idea for a new example, you can insert a comment suggesting it to the original author. Or you can draft the example yourself and display it with the Track Changes feature or with highlighting.

Be sure to learn how to use these word processing features, as well as any other collaborative tools provided by your employer.

Using Transitional Expressions

In writing, any movement from one point or subject to another is called a transition. **Transitional expressions** help you signal such movement so your readers understand where you are going.

In an illustration paragraph, a transitional expression can clarify your intentions early on. You can lead in to the first example with a phrase such as *for example* or *for instance*.

> Many kinds of birds stay in our town all winter. <u>For example</u>, in January, the river is crowded with Canada geese.

Later in the paragraph, transitional expressions can indicate that one example is ending and another is beginning.

> <u>Other</u> river birds we see in winter include seagulls and mallards.

The transitional expression does not always need to appear at the beginning of a sentence. Sometimes, in fact, the sentence reads more smoothly when you work the transitional expression in later.

> Many kinds of birds stay in our town all winter. In January, <u>for example</u>, the river is crowded with Canada geese.

 ACTIVITY 5.4   In the following paragraph, improve the clarity and flow by inserting transitional expressions at appropriate places. (*Hint:* The paragraph has four examples. See the Writing Workshop on the next page for a list of transitional terms.)

 Rashawn's new position as webmaster makes him responsible for keeping the company's web site up to date and free of trouble. The Marketing Department sends him bulletins about new offers, and he must figure out how to incorporate this material into the site. He must keep the antivirus software current so computer viruses cannot infect the network. Last year a virus attack cost the company over $1 million. Rashawn is responsible for taking extra security measures when hackers try to break in to the company's protected data. He fields e-mail queries from customers and staff members who are having difficulty with the site, and he advises them on how to solve their problems.

WRITING WORKSHOP

Transitional Techniques

Here are some common transitional expressions that can help you move from one example to another within a paragraph.

- for example
- for instance
- other
- one example, another example
- first, second, third
- also

- too
- as well
- in addition
- furthermore
- finally

Another way of creating transitions is to use a sequence of parallel expressions, such as similar terms that appear in similar positions in their sentences. Look at the underlined words in the following paragraph.

> The new corporate home page on the Web offers an easy-to-use guide to information about our company. For customers, the page includes a list of products as well as a link to our online store. Investors can access our annual report and data about company performance. Employees can use the home page to connect to information about insurance benefits and personnel policies. Finally, job applicants will find lists of available positions in each of our locations.

The underlined terms specify types of people who would use the web site. Each of these words appears near the beginning of a sentence, introducing a new example. This parallel structure helps carry the reader along.

SUMMARY FOR ILLUSTRATIVE WRITING

❑ Illustration is the action of giving examples to explain or clarify a point.

❑ Examples should be specific, relevant, and supportive of the main point.

❑ Transitional expressions such as *for example* and *finally* signal movement so readers understand where a paragraph is going.

PRACTICING YOUR SKILLS

Now that you understand the elements of a good illustration paragraph, put your knowledge to work in the following activities.

PRACTICE 1

This paragraph was written by Danielle Zoeller, an art therapist. She is explaining the potential benefits of art therapy.

Art therapy offers an excellent way for patients to resolve emotional conflicts and to come to terms with their conditions. First, the process of creating art is therapeutic. People feel better when given a chance to express their inner thoughts and feelings through art. Many patients, particularly children, use drawings and paintings to convey painful emotions they cannot put into words. Second, the accomplishment of creating the art increases patients' pride and self-esteem. People who take art therapy often discover an artistic talent they never knew they had, and this makes them feel better about themselves. Finally, art therapy can help patients reach a better understanding of their own condition. If a patient draws a self-portrait with a huge head and practically no mouth, he or she may begin to wonder what the drawing means. In such situations, by suggesting interpretations for the artwork, the therapist can guide the patient to greater insights.

The Main Point

1. Find the topic sentence, which states the main point of the paragraph, and underline it.

The Examples

2. Danielle's paragraph offers three examples to support the main point. Write the numbers 1, 2, and 3 above the sentences that introduce these examples.

The Transitional Expressions

3. Circle the words or phrases that create a transition from one example to the next.

PRACTICE 2

Here is an illustration paragraph written by Michelle Stevens, a quality inspector at LectroPlate Steel, to explain why steel plates failed to pass inspection.

In the past week, the high failure rate at the tin plate mill resulted from a variety of defects. Some of these involved discrepancies in the gauge, or thickness, of the plate. In one order, for example, the customer specified a maximum gauge variation of 3 percent from front to back, but three sheets varied 5 percent in gauge. Other flaws occurred at the edges of the plate, where the most common problems were cracks and dents. Still other quality failures arose from defects in the tin coating. Three sheets had oil spots on the coating, and two showed serious blisters.

The Main Point

1. Underline the topic sentence.

The Examples

2. To illustrate the "variety of defects," Michelle gives examples of three main types of problems. Then, for each of these general types, she provides more specific instances. To understand the structure of Michelle's paragraph, fill in the following outline. The first lines have been completed for you.

Problem type (A)	gauge discrepancies
	Specific instance: 5 percent gauge variation
Problem type (B)	
	Two specific instances:
Problem type (C)	
	Two specific instances:

The Transitional Expressions

3. Circle the words or phrases that Michelle used to create a transition from one example to the next.

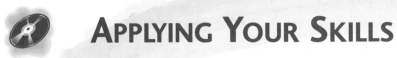

APPLYING YOUR SKILLS

Now you will write an illustration paragraph of your own. To do this, work through the stages of the writing process that you learned in Chapter 2: prewriting, writing, revising, and editing. Use a separate sheet of paper or a word processing file. Label and save each stage of your writing.

Prewriting

(a) Begin by selecting a general subject for your paragraph. Here are some samples to choose from.

Subject	Types of Examples to Use
advances in technology during my lifetime	examples of technological change
my taste in music	examples of musicians and recordings that you like
my friend's best qualities	examples of a friend's character and behavior
great athletes I have seen	examples of athletes you have seen perform, either live or on TV

(b) Once you have identified your topic, brainstorm about it. On your paper or with your word processor, list ideas for examples. Let one idea feed the next. Do not worry if some of your ideas seem weak. You can weed those out at the next stage.

Also write down possible ideas for your topic sentence. Remember that the topic sentence of a paragraph should be focused enough so the rest of the paragraph can support it. "I like music" is not a good topic sentence because it gives little direction to the paragraph. A better choice would be "My favorite musicians are experimental jazz artists."

(c) When you have a list of ideas for topic sentences and examples, sort through them. Find the best choice for your topic sentence and the best examples to illustrate that sentence. Make sure you have at least three examples that are clearly supportive, relevant, and specific.

(d) Construct a simple outline for your paragraph in a form similar to this:

Topic Sentence _____

Example 1 _____

Example 2 _____

Example 3 _____

Writing

Now write the first draft of your actual paragraph. Word the topic sentence as precisely as you can and develop each example clearly. Link the examples with appropriate transitional expressions.

Revising

Read through your first draft. Use the following checklist of questions to make sure you have revised thoroughly.

- ❏ Does the topic sentence state just one main point?

- ❏ Is the topic sentence focused? That is, does it make the point specific enough so the rest of the paragraph can readily support or develop that point?

- ❏ Are there enough examples to establish the main point? (You should have at least three examples.)

- ❏ Do all of the examples support the main point? (For this and the next two questions, review what you learned in Activity 5.3.)

- ❏ Are all of the examples relevant to the point?

- ❏ Is every example specific rather than vague?

- ❏ Are the transitions smooth enough so the reader understands where one example ends and the next begins? Are more transitional expressions needed?

When you think you have revised thoroughly, write a second draft. Label it *Draft 2*. If you are writing on paper, use a clean sheet. If you are writing on a computer, retype the paragraph from the beginning.

Follow the same process with your second draft. Critique and revise it thoroughly. If necessary, write a third draft.

When you believe your content and presentation are as good as you can make them, move on to the editing stage.

Editing

In this final stage, check your paragraph for mechanical errors. Closely examine grammar, spelling, word use, punctuation, and capitalization. Be sure, for example, that all of your statements are complete sentences, not fragments.

If you are using a word processor, run the spell checker and grammar checker, but do not count on these tools to find every error. If you accidentally wrote "On the soccer field, my friend is the absolute beast," the computer will not know that you meant to write "the absolute best"! Use a dictionary to check any spellings about which you are unsure.

After you have polished your writing, make a new copy in the format your instructor specifies. Proofread your paragraph one final time for the small, easily overlooked errors that often slip by when you are concentrating on larger matters.

WRITING FOR YOUR CAREER

This section presents a writing project for each of the six career pathways. Choose one that appeals to you and use your new skills to write a paragraph on the subject.

When the project description refers you to the textbook web site, go to http://humphrey.swlearning.com and click on the Links tab. Look for Chapter 5, "Writing for Your Career." There you will find direct links to helpful web references.

Communication and the Arts

Pretend you are the leader of a team of web designers. Your team is redesigning the web site for Toy Time, a nationwide company with stores in 50 cities. Toy Time's current web site is outdated, unattractive, and difficult to use. You decide to write a short paper to explain to your team members how you think the design of the site can be improved.

Write a paragraph in which the topic sentence describes the look you think is best. Add supporting sentences that give examples of specific web sites that illustrate your point.

To write this paragraph, you need to do research on the Internet. First, go to the textbook web site and use the web link provided, which will take you to a web style guide. In the guide, locate one or more sections about design principles and read the material. After thinking about the recommendations, decide what design technique you want to stress in your paragraph.

Next, choose some sites to use as examples for your paragraph. You may already know of sites that support the point you want to make. If not, browse the Web to locate examples. Remember to discuss how each site supports your point.

Health and Medicine

You are a nutritionist at General Hospital. A patient with a heart condition is about to be discharged, and the cardiologist has asked you to write instructions for a heart-healthy diet. In your topic sentence, include a main point about a proper diet. In the rest of the paragraph, give examples that explain what you mean.

For information on diets that promote a healthy heart, you can search the Web by entering "heart+diet" in a search engine. To begin, you may want to check the sites recommended on the textbook web site.

Human, Personal, and Public Service

Think of a friend or relative whose talents are clearly suited for a certain career. Now imagine that you are a career counselor and you are advising this person. Write a paragraph that uses examples to show why the person is well qualified for the career you have in mind. If you need background on career requirements, you can find many resources online. You can begin at the textbook web site, which provides a direct link to a career information center.

Business and Marketing

You have recently opened a bicycle shop, where you sell and repair bikes and riding gear. Today you are preparing a brochure to promote your business. You want customers to believe your business is not just any bike shop, but something special. Write a paragraph for the brochure that offers examples of the kinds of services you offer.

Make your topic sentence focused. Saying that you provide "complete sales and service" will not help the reader much. Think about how your shop is different from others, try to convey that uniqueness in your topic sentence, and back up your statement with strong examples.

If you need background information about bicycles and related gear, check an online store or the web site of a major manufacturer. The textbook web site provides a direct link to get you started.

Science and Technology

Imagine that you are a carpenter who specializes in creating custom furniture. This week you are preparing plans for a new customer who has given you a free hand in design but wants a detailed description before you begin.

For the purpose of this project, choose a type of furniture that you will build, such as a coffee table or an entertainment center. Write a paragraph in which you lay out one main feature of the design and then give examples of how that feature will be realized.

Here are three sample topic sentences you might use for a paragraph about an entertainment center.

(a) Throughout the entertainment center, I will use fine woods that blend together harmoniously.

(b) All equipment in the entertainment center will be easy to access.

(c) In designing the entertainment center, I have considered the needs of the entire family.

You can use one of these sentences if you like or you can write your own.

Environment and Natural Resources

Here is a topic sentence for you:

The accomplishments of landscape architects are visible all around us.

Write a paragraph giving examples to support this sentence. You can find material for your paragraph in a library, and the textbook web site provides a link to a useful online source.

Description: Paragraphs That Appeal to the Senses

IN THIS CHAPTER YOU WILL LEARN TO:

- **Choose words that draw mental pictures.**

- **Write simply and smoothly.**

- **Find fitting words for a description.**

- **Describe specific details.**

Career Path	Sample Career	Use for Descriptive Writing	Example of Descriptive Writing
Communication and the Arts	Museum curator	Describing the layout of a new exhibit	A life-sized diorama recreates a nineteenth-century sod house interior. The floor is packed earth with three rag rugs, and fabric covers the ceiling to catch falling dirt and bugs. Furniture is sparse and functional: a bed, a table, four chairs, and a stove. Though cramped, the house appears spotless. It is an almost perfect representation of life in the early nineteenth century.
Health and Medicine	School nurse	Helping teachers identify a health condition that requires treatment	Symptoms show up in a variety of forms. They usually include dull or throbbing pain in the ear combined with a low fever. The child's face will look flushed and feel hot to the touch. Fever is often accompanied by head and/or body aches. The child may be irritable and sleepy or clingy and despondent, often wanting to go home or to call a parent to come to the school.
Human, Personal, and Public Service	Counseling psychologist	Referring a patient to a specialist	The patient shows clear and prominent signs of bipolar disorder. Lethargic and despairing at one visit, he can hardly contain his energy the next time we meet. To the unsuspecting bystander, he can, at moments, appear to be very happy. Yet he breaks into tears without provocation.
Business and Marketing	Sales representative for a sporting goods supplier	Persuading retailers to stock your new line of fleece jackets	With an extra-tight weave, this new fleece resists wind and rain, yet weighs less than similar jackets. This soft, easy-to-wear fabric caresses the skin while providing warmth, style, and breathability.
Science and Technology	Boilermaker	Describing a flaw in a pressure vessel that needs to be fixed	The seams of the pressure vessel join improperly, thus weakening the entire structure and causing grave danger to anyone who works on it. Because of faulty welding during construction, the plates are not aligned properly and the entire structure is unstable.
Environment and Natural Resources	Water department engineer	Explaining why water use should be limited	As we enter our fifth week without rain, drought conditions increase every day. Lawns show large brown patches; cracks split the dry soil; and small young plants struggle to survive. The harsh heat shows no signs of abating.

ON THE JOB

Vegetarian Specialties

As the co-owner of a small catering business, Ramona is in charge of marketing and customer relations. Her job involves talking to potential customers to find out what they want and trying to persuade them to hire the company. She must know what dishes are offered, how to combine dishes, and how to communicate with customers to make sure their needs are met.

This morning Ramona received a call from a woman who is planning her wedding. Several of the guests are vegetarians, and the caller wants to know what vegetarian dishes are available. Ramona offers to write a description of hors d'oevres, soups, and main courses without meat. She decides to save the descriptions to use for a brochure that will be sent to other customers.

First, Ramona chooses three dishes that she can describe vividly. Next, she jots down some words and phrases that come to mind for each dish. Finally, she selects the best descriptors and drafts a paragraph for each dish. After reviewing the paragraphs, she revises and edits her work and includes it in a letter to the caller.

With <u>puffs of flaky pastry</u>[1] surrounding a <u>creamy center</u>, the mushroom canapés provide an <u>elegant</u> predinner nibble. <u>Tender mushrooms</u> sautéed in garlic and olive oil are stirred into a <u>rich cream sauce</u> <u>spiced with pepper</u> and a <u>hint of thyme</u>. Then this creamy center is <u>enfolded</u> in a <u>pastry dome</u> and baked to <u>a golden glow</u>.

Pumpkin ginger soup is the perfect start to a <u>midautumn feast</u>. Picked at the <u>peak of sweetness</u>[2], the golden pumpkin makes a <u>thick, rich base</u>, while the ginger adds a <u>spicy surprise</u>[3]. A <u>blend</u> of herbs and a <u>dollop of fresh cream</u> provide just the right <u>balance of flavors</u>. Served <u>steaming hot</u> and garnished with a <u>sprig of rosemary</u>, this soup <u>brings a splash of bright color</u>[4] to any table.

Our pasta primavera is a <u>festival of tender seasonal vegetables</u> sautéed just to the <u>point of crispness</u> and served in a <u>light red-wine</u> sauce over <u>house-made angel-hair pasta</u>. With a <u>tomato base</u> and <u>generous fresh basil</u>, the sauce sets off the <u>multiple flavors</u> of our locally grown and <u>hand-picked vegetables</u>. <u>Topped with fresh Parmesan cheese</u>[5] and <u>calamati olives</u>, this dish is both <u>light and satisfying</u>.

Are you ready to run to the nearest restaurant? If so, Ramona chose her words and phrases well. In this chapter, you will describe clear and vivid pictures.

Understanding Description

In writing, **description** means choosing words and phrases that make your reader experience sights, sounds, and smells as realistically as possible. You can think of this technique as drawing a picture with words. In the previous paragraphs, Ramona used descriptive language to illustrate taste.

Description appeals to the reader's senses. Good descriptive writing makes the reader see (or feel, taste, smell, or hear) what the writer is describing. When writing a descriptive paragraph, follow these guidelines:

1. Use words and phrases that are simple and direct (*flaky pastry*).
2. Choose interesting words and avoid clichés (*peak of sweetness*).
3. Appeal to as many different senses as possible (*spicy surprise*).
4. Use active verbs instead of passive words (*brings a splash*).
5. Be specific (*topped with fresh Parmesan cheese and calamati olives*).

Can you see how Ramona's paragraphs about her dishes follow these guidelines? Ramona made sure that the opening sentence of each paragraph mentioned the dish she was describing and that it gave enough detail to draw a clear picture in the reader's mind. Ramona kept in mind three different senses in her prewriting notes.

S E L F - A S S E S S M E N T 6

When I need to describe something in writing, I can:

	Usually	Sometimes	Never
Use simple and straightforward language.	❑	❑	❑
Use my own words.	❑	❑	❑
Include a topic sentence.	❑	❑	❑
Appeal to two or more. senses	❑	❑	❑
Be specific.	❑	❑	❑
Be concise.	❑	❑	❑

If you checked "Sometimes" or "Never" for any of the items, this chapter will help you improve your skills. Even if you checked "Usually" in every instance, you will learn more about writing paragraphs that use examples.

Mushroom canapés
- Taste: creamy, garlic
- Appearance: golden, dome
- Texture/touch: flaky, tender

Pumpkin soup
- Taste: rich, spicy, sweet
- Appearance: bright color, garnished with green
- Texture/touch: thick, hot

Pasta primavera
- Taste: basil, many fresh vegetable flavors
- Appearance: red sauce, cheese and olive topping
- Texture/touch: crisp, light

Using Simple and Direct Words

When writing descriptive paragraphs, you may be tempted to use long, fancy, or uncommon words. There is nothing wrong with using a lengthy or unusual word if it fits, but your words should flow so easily and smoothly that the reader notices what you are saying, not how you are saying it.

Another common mistake in descriptive writing is to use too many adjectives and adverbs. Remember that nouns and verbs can be descriptive too. Using colorful nouns and verbs can help you draw clear mental pictures without long, boring lists of descriptive words. Here are some examples of overdone and appropriate descriptions.

(A) Too Complicated   The entrée to the sequestered hot tubs at Whispering Pines Spa is achieved via a peripatetic ascent that rewards the excursionist with halcyon tranquility.

(B) Too Many Words   The long, narrow, winding paths to the private, secluded hot tubs will help you feel calm, relaxed, and tranquil as you leave the busy, hectic world behind.

(C)   Good   The private hot tubs at Whispering Pines Spa can be reached by a winding footpath. The secluded location provides a calming atmosphere for guests.

Example (C) is the best of the three alternatives because it draws a picture of the path to the hot tubs through use of clear and simple language. The reader is not distracted by complex vocabulary or long lists of unnecessary words.

did you ever?

- Send a postcard or an e-mail message while you were on vacation and try to make your reader picture what the place was like?

- Describe your favorite band or musician to someone who listens to a different type of music?

- Try to get a friend to remember someone you both met by giving details of the person's appearance, voice, mannerisms, or personality?

All of these situations involve descriptive language. You describe things frequently without thinking about what you are doing. In this chapter, you will learn how to use description in your writing.

ACTIVITY 6.1 For each of the sentences below, write a description that illustrates the same subject with simpler and more direct language. Use a dictionary to look up the meanings of words you do not understand. Feel free to rearrange the order of the sentence or break it up into two parts if that helps. The first example has been completed for you.

1. The incandescent, resplendent sun issued from the horizon and thus commenced another torrid day.

    The bright sun appeared on the horizon, promising another scorching

    day.

2. A tall, statuesque, willowy woman entered the room suddenly and unexpectedly, startling all of the guests.

    _____

    _____

3. Dessert was a toothsome confection bedecked with a corona of luscious carmine berries.

    _____

    _____

4. The oversized pickup is a burly, stalwart 2.3 tons of steel constructed to endure a multitude of years and a plethora of weather conditions.

    _____

    _____

5. The day was nascent, and my plans were inchoate, so I loitered idly at the breakfast table as I cogitated on the upcoming day.

    _____

    _____

6. Beneath the sparkling lunar orb, the sea glistened brilliantly and the adamantine rocks appeared radiant in the moonlight.

    _____

    _____

WRITING WORKSHOP

Eliminating Unnecessary Words

Good writing is concise. While long sentences or long words may be necessary occasionally, every word should have a purpose. Otherwise, the point you are making may get lost.

One way to cut down on extra words is to eliminate redundant expressions or sentences that restate an idea you have already covered. For example, *each and every* is a redundant expression because *each* and *every* mean the same thing. Choose one and eliminate the other.

An expression can also be redundant when it uses an unnecessary adjective. For example, *free gift* is redundant because if it's a gift it's obviously free.

Below are examples of wordy writing followed by concise writing. Notice how the concise writing gets the point across more effectively and makes the writer sound more authoritative.

Wordy	Our new and improved cleaning solution will get the tough, stubborn stains out of carpets, car seats, and many other common household surfaces.
Concise	Our improved cleaning solution gets tough stains out of carpets, car seats, and many other surfaces.
Wordy	A group of several young children at a local neighborhood daycare center are the first unfortunate victims of this year's annual flu epidemic.
Concise	Several children at a local daycare center are the first victims of this year's flu.

In these cases, many words can be eliminated because they are implied or redundant. For example, nothing is added by calling a stain *tough* and *stubborn*, since both words mean more or less the same thing. By eliminating unnecessary words, the writer keeps the reader's attention and communicates the meaning more effectively.

ETHICS CONNECTION

Exaggeration

When you describe something to a friend, you may occasionally exaggerate in order to make a point. For example, if you saw a limousine that was really long, you might say, "That limo was longer than my driveway!" You and your friend both know that your comparison is not literally true, but you make the point that the limo was very long.

Sometimes exaggeration is not as obvious. For example, if you are designing the web site for a limousine company, you may be tempted to add comments to your writing about a few extra inches of legroom or about special features that show how luxurious the limousines are. As long as your overall point is true—the limos really are luxurious—does it hurt to exaggerate slightly to get the point across?

In this situation, exaggerating the details of the car is unethical and illegal, as it is a form of false advertising. Customers looking at the web site will be misinformed and might order a limousine based on false information. Make your details colorful, but stick to the facts.

Using Your Own Words

Expressions or descriptions repeated too often become meaningless. Have you heard someone say, "I slept like a baby" or "It's raining cats and dogs"? These clichés are fine in casual conversation, but they should be avoided in writing. They are so overused that they no longer create vivid mental pictures.

For more powerful writing, describe things in your own words. Find just the right adjective or adverb or make comparisons that enable the reader to picture your subject in a new way. Or just keep it simple—sometimes "I slept well" or "It's raining hard!" is fine.

Cliche	That baby is cute as a button.
Clear Description	That baby has a big smile and adorable dimples.
Cliche	My uncle's dog is as mean as the day is long.
Writer's Own Words	My uncle's dog is as mean as a hornet trapped in a jelly jar.

ACTIVITY 6.2 For each of the following overused expressions, or clichés, think of a more original—or a simpler and more straightforward—way of expressing what you want to say. Write your own description on the lines below each example.

1. He's so cheerful he's like a breath of fresh air.

   _____

   _____

   _____

2. I'm so hungry I could eat a horse.

   _____

   _____

   _____

3. Those two sisters are as different as night and day.

   _____

   _____

   _____

4. Andrew talks a mile a minute.

   _____

   _____

   _____

5. My niece is growing like a beanstalk.

   _____

   _____

   _____

6. We were having so much fun that the time just flew by.

   _____

   _____

   _____

Being Specific

In a casual conversation, you may use some of the same descriptive words over and over—words such as *nice, cool,* and *nasty.* Your friends know what you mean, but with readers, you need to write more specifically to get your point across.

Using specific nouns and verbs makes your writing more vivid and cuts down on extra words that can distract the reader. For example, instead of writing "Ling came into the room quickly," write "Ling rushed into the room." Look at these examples.

Unclear	That pecan pie was really good.
More Specific	That pecan pie was rich and packed with nuts.
Less Precise	"Stop interrupting me," she said angrily.
More Specific	"Stop interrupting me," she snapped.
Unclear	"He is a really interesting person."
More Specific	"His hobbies include hang gliding and gourmet cooking."

In the first example, the writer removed the word *good,* which is vague, and replaced it with strong details that show the reader exactly what was good about the pie. In the second example, the writer used the word *snapped* in place of *said angrily* because it creates a clearer, more interesting, and more precise picture. In the third example, the writer replaced a general word with specific types of hobbies enjoyed by the person being described.

In all three of these examples, without having to take the writer's word for it, the reader can figure out that the pie was good, the speaker was angry, and the person was interesting. This is sometimes called the "show, don't tell" rule. Use this rule for clear and specific writing. Here are some further examples of the difference between telling and showing.

Telling	It was a very cold day.
Showing	After being outside for ten minutes, my toes were numb and my teeth were rattling.
Telling	The customer was happy with his new voicemail service.
Showing	The customer called to say how much the voicemail service had helped his business.

ACTIVITY 6.3   Each of the sentences below includes a description that is unclear or unspecific. On the lines below the sentence, rewrite the description using more specific language. Try to show instead of tell.

1. A weekend in Las Vegas can be a lot of fun!

    _____

    _____

    _____

2. This food processor is very convenient.

    _____

    _____

    _____

3. The heroine of the movie *Battle Creek* is extremely brave.

    _____

    _____

    _____

4. George walked up behind Elisa very quietly, startling her.

    _____

    _____

    _____

5. If you sign up now, you can get excellent deals on long-distance service.

    _____

    _____

    _____

6. The lawn care company did a great job on our yard.

    _____

    _____

    _____

TECHNOLOGY CONNECTION

Using the Thesaurus

You have probably used a printed thesaurus to locate just the right synonym to make a point or to complete a phrase. Here are a few important tips to keep in mind when using a thesaurus.

- Stick with words you already know and can use comfortably. A thesaurus should remind you of words you know, not teach you new vocabulary. (While you should be learning new words, you shouldn't use a word in your writing until you have a good understanding of its meaning and connotations.)

- Keep in mind the intended audience and choose words that are appropriate for the specific reader.

- Don't overdo it! If you use a thesaurus too often, your writing may end up sounding unnatural or pretentious.

Create a clear and vivid picture in the reader's mind.

Writing the Topic Sentence

In this chapter, you have learned about various techniques writers use to describe. But how do all of those techniques come together to form a complete paragraph?

A descriptive paragraph, like other paragraphs, includes a topic sentence and details that support or elaborate on the topic. While the topic sentence usually comes at the beginning of a paragraph, with a descriptive paragraph, you have greater flexibility in where to place the topic sentence. As long as your subject is clear, you can be creative in the way you present it.

In the paragraph below, notice how the topic sentence is the first sentence. It makes clear what is being described, and the next three sentences provide supporting details that flesh out the description. The last sentence ties all of the sentences together in an interesting way.

 Once you drive our new sport wagon, you will wonder how you ever got along without it. The spacious rear compartment has plenty of room for all of your weekend gear, and the roof rack provides extra storage for bikes and skis. Optional four-wheel drive gives you power in tough conditions, but the handling is so smooth that you'll feel as though you're driving on air. Finally, the compact size means slick maneuverability and gas mileage that rivals a midsize sedan. This car is custom made for the practical adventurer.

Notice the underlined topic sentence. The topic sentence does not say, "Here is a description of our new sport wagon." However, it does contain words that identify the topic as a sport wagon. As long as the subject of the paragraph is mentioned clearly, the reader will know what is being described.

Placing the topic sentence at the end of a paragraph creates a slightly different effect. This format allows the writer to create a mood or draw the reader into the paragraph with interesting details before stating the subject of the paragraph. This strategy is most useful in informal writing when the reader has time to enjoy the process of reading the description. If a writer needs to grab the reader's attention immediately, the topic sentence should be placed at the beginning.

In the paragraph below, the writer sets a mood and *teases* the reader by presenting details before identifying the topic. Note the difference in effect.

 An incredibly compact size and light weight mean you can take it anywhere at any time for any purpose. At the same time, the high power and large memory capacity give you the versatility of a larger unit. High-resolution video and audio capabilities make this a state-of-the-art model. From video editing to desktop publishing to gaming, this computer meets the needs of professionals, students, and personal users alike. The Centrum XE laptop is the ideal personal computer for anyone who needs high performance on the go.

ACTIVITY 6.4 For each of the subjects in the following list, use one or more of the details provided to compose a topic sentence. The topic sentence should tell the reader what the paragraph is describing.

After writing your sentence, evaluate it to determine whether other words would draw a clearer picture in the reader's mind. Substitute better words, if possible—ones that are more specific and imaginative. Have fun and try to be creative.

1. allergy symptoms   itchy nose
    constant sneezing
    red and watery eyes

_____

_____

_____

2. a room in a luxury hotel   spacious, airy, sunny
    a fully stocked minifridge
    luxury mattresses
    views of city landmarks

_____

_____

_____

3. sportswear fabric   lightweight, breathable
    retards moisture, dries quickly
    warm in winter, cool in summer

_____

_____

_____

4. gourmet coffee   dark roast
    rich, smoky flavor
    shade-grown

_____

_____

_____

5. a floral bouquet   a variety of shapes and sizes
                              spring colors
                              sweet fragrance

   _____

   _____

   _____

6. a white wine   a light, fruity flavor with a hint of cedar
                              a smooth finish
                              perfect with fish or a light chicken dish
                              a popular California chardonnay

   _____

   _____

   _____

7. a digital camera   lightweight and easy to transport
                              high-resolution, high-quality pictures
                              easy to use
                              interfaces with most home computers

   _____

   _____

   _____

SUMMARY FOR DESCRIPTIVE WRITING

❑   Description means creating a clear and vivid picture in the reader's mind.

❑   Details should be specific and should appeal to as many senses as possible.

❑   The language should be simple and direct.

❑   The words should be the writer's own, not overused expressions that have lost their meaning or are boring.

❑   The writing should be concise.

❑   A topic sentence identifies for the reader what is being described.

PRACTICING YOUR SKILLS

Practice your descriptive writing skills in the following activities. Be creative.

PRACTICE 1

Below is a paragraph composed by Jermaine Collins, a counseling psychologist. He has written a description of a patient's progress for that patient's file.

 I have been rendezvousing with Mr. White on a weekly basis for four months. When we commenced therapy, he was suffering from depression, which manifested itself in attenuation of appetite, insomnia, and withdrawal from social interaction. He was eating like a bird and sleeping only three to four hours a night. He looked bad. Now after discussing the underlying causation of his depression, he has begun to eat better and to interact more with friends and family. He still has trouble sleeping, but that problem seems to have been mitigated as well.

Simple and Direct Words

1. List the words in Jermaine's paragraph that sound elaborate and could be distracting. Then write another word that says the same thing more simply.

_____

_____

Using Your Own Words

2. On the lines below, identify a cliché in Jermaine's paragraph. Write an alternative description that is not a cliché.

_____

_____

Being Specific

3. Find the words that are too vague or that do not create a clear picture in your mind. Write each word or expression and suggest a more specific alternative.

_____

_____

_____

Topic Sentence

4. Underline the topic sentence in Jermaine's paragraph.

Description: Paragraphs That Appeal to the Senses

PRACTICE 2

Kim Rivera, a sales representative for a sporting goods supplier, wrote the following descriptive paragraph. She is describing a new mountain bike model.

Imagine that you are cruising down a rocky mountain trail with dust flying around you as your eyes scan the rocks ahead. Your hands are clenched on the rubber-lined handles that are ribbed for an improved grip. Your feet are clipped to the pedals with quick-release Stoni clips, ready to snap free in case of a sudden spill. Though your path is rocky and bumpy, you hardly feel a thing because of the cool state-of-the-art ReFlex shock absorbers. You and this bike are a match made in heaven. With all of the above features and more, the Bradley 400 is the best new mountain bike of the year.

The Topic Sentence

1. Underline the topic sentence in the paragraph.

2. What is the effect of Kim's placing the topic sentence where she did?

_____

Clear, Direct, Effective Language

3. Keeping in mind all of the techniques discussed in this chapter, circle and number three places in the paragraph where Kim's writing could be improved. Write the reason for each change (vague, redundant, cliché, or other) and your suggestion for improvement.

Reason for Change   **Suggested Improvement**

1. _____

   _____

   _____

   _____

2. _____

   _____

   _____

3. _____

   _____

   _____

APPLYING YOUR SKILLS

Now you are ready to write a descriptive paragraph of your own using the techniques you have studied in this chapter. You will follow the stages of the writing process.

Prewriting

First, choose a subject you can describe vividly. After selecting a topic, write details that describe it, including ones that appeal to two or more senses and that create a clear picture in your reader's mind. Here are suggested subjects:

- An item I bought recently
- An unusual person I know
- My bedroom
- My dream house

Writing

Now write the first draft of your paragraph. Be sure to include a topic sentence that tells the reader what you are describing.

Revising

Read through your first draft and revise thoroughly. The following checklist will help.

- ❑ Is the language simple and straightforward?

- ❑ Are the words original (not clichés)?

- ❑ Are the words and details specific?

- ❑ Is every word necessary?

- ❑ Does the description appeal to two or more senses?

- ❑ Does the topic sentence clearly state what is being described?

When you have revised thoroughly, write a second draft. Label it *Draft 2*. Review and revise it, using the same process as Draft 1. After you believe your content and presentation are as good as you can make them, go on to the editing stage.

Editing

In this final stage, check your paragraph for mechanical errors. Closely examine grammar, spelling, word use, punctuation, and capitalization. Check for sentence fragments and run-ons, wordiness, and clichés. After editing your work, make a final copy and proofread the final draft one last time.

WRITING FOR YOUR CAREER

This section presents a writing project for each of the six career pathways. Choose one that appeals to you and use your new skills to write a paragraph on the subject.

When the project description refers you to the textbook web site, go to http://humphrey.swlearning.com and click on the Links tab. Look for Chapter 6, "Writing for Your Career."

Communication and the Arts

As a feature story writer for a local newspaper, you write weekly profiles of interesting people in the community. This week you have interviewed Joe Barclay, an 83-year-old retired cabinetmaker who has lived in this town his entire life. Besides keeping up his famous woodworking, Joe has been actively involved in his community, leading efforts to clean up a nearby river and serving for several years on the town council.

You want your readers to see Joe as you see him so they can appreciate what a fascinating character he is. Creating the details you need, write a paragraph that introduces Joe: how he looks, how he sounds, and what his personality is like and other details you think are important. Remember to include a topic sentence that tells the reader who Joe is.

Health and Medicine

You are a nurse practitioner specializing in obstetrics. One of your patients has just become pregnant for the first time at the age of 39. She is nervous about the possible complications of a late-life pregnancy. To reassure her, you write out a brief description of the signs of a normal pregnancy during the first trimester. This way your patient will know what to expect and whether her experiences are normal.

Write a paragraph describing how a pregnancy looks and feels during the first trimester. For information to help with your writing, go to the textbook web site and locate the instructions for Chapter 6, Health and Medicine. Access the web site provided and read about pregnancy. Organize your thoughts and use clear, strong details in your descriptive paragraph.

Human, Personal, and Public Service

As a group psychologist specializing in work-related situations, you have been hired to conduct a stress-relief workshop with the employees of a large company. In one session, you will ask the participants to close their eyes and picture themselves in a beautiful and peaceful setting that you describe. Write the paragraph you will use with the participants. Include descriptions that appeal to at least three senses.

Business and Marketing

Imagine that you have just opened a Brazilian restaurant in your neighborhood. In the press release that you will send to local papers to announce your store's opening, you want to include a paragraph that describes the food in detail. Your descriptions should be sharp and should engage the readers' senses. Use words that will enable readers to visualize the appearance of the food. Try to tantalize their senses of smell and taste using terms that describe texture, spices, and preparation techniques.

Compose the paragraph. For information about Brazilian food, go to the textbook web site and locate the instructions for Chapter 6, Business. Access the web site recommended and read about Brazilian food to find descriptions to include in your paragraph. Or choose another kind of food with which you are familiar.

Science and Technology

A client calls your metalsmith shop to ask if you can build an ornamental ironwork gate to add to his fenced front yard. Imagine that you have made ironwork gates from several different designs in the past and that you will choose one of these to recommend. Write a paragraph describing your design. Use words that describe the beauty and uniqueness of the design. For information on ironworking and sample designs, go to the textbook web site and locate the instructions for Chapter 6, Science and Technology. Access the web site provided and choose a design you find appealing. Develop descriptions that you can use in your paragraph.

Environment and Natural Resources

Imagine that you are a landscaper who works in a very dry area of the country. At the landscape architect firm where you work, you specialize in designing landscapes that require only a small amount of water to flourish. A customer calls to ask about the types of plants that are suitable for your area's dry climate. Write a paragraph describing a few of the most interesting trees, bushes, and flowers. Include words that will help the customer visualize the foliage and the blooms. For information about low-water landscaping, or xeriscaping, go to the textbook web site and locate the instructions for Chapter 6, Environment and Natural Resources. Access the web site provided and write your descriptive paragraph.

7

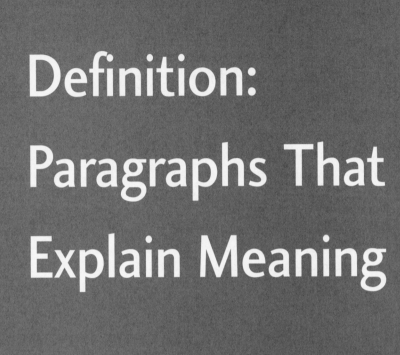

Definition:
Paragraphs That
Explain Meaning

IN THIS CHAPTER YOU WILL LEARN TO:

- Write accurate, clear, and vivid definitions.

- Give appropriate synonyms.

- Define terms by using categories and details.

- Define a term by saying what it does *not* mean.

Using *Definition* in Writing for Your Career

Career Path	Sample Career	Use for Definition	Example of Definition
Communication and the Arts	Video technician	Explaining a special effect	The term *wipe* refers to a transition in which a new image gradually moves across the original image, "wiping" it off the screen.
Health and Medicine	Physician assistant	Writing an information sheet for patients	An electrocardiogram (EKG) graphs the heart's electrical action.
Human, Personal, and Public Service	Cosmetologist	Explaining a skin treatment to customers	The glycolic peel treatment uses glycolic acid to exfoliate the skin, gently removing the dry top layer to create a healthier, more youthful look.
Business and Marketing	Caterer	Informing a customer about a particular dish	Black Forest cake is a chocolate layer cake with a creamy cherry filling.
Science and Technology	Cable TV installer	Defining a technical term	A ground rod is a copper-clad or galvanized steel rod used for electrical grounding. It is usually about 8 feet long and $5/8$ inch in diameter.
Environment and Natural Resources	Agricultural extension agent	Explaining a type of insect pest	The Colorado potato beetle, a small beetle with yellow and black stripes, causes serious harm to potato crops.

ON THE JOB

Exercise Program

At the Pikestown Fitness Center, where he manages the exercise programs, Guillermo Osorio is studying the sign-up sheets with a puzzled expression. The sessions in low-impact aerobics, advanced aerobics, yoga, and strength training all have long waiting lists. Yet the new Pilates program has attracted only six participants.

Later that morning he asks his colleague Melissa why she thinks the fitness center's clients have shown little interest in Pilates. "I know some celebrities have tried it," Melissa says, "but not many people here know what it is."

Guillermo decides to test Melissa's theory by chatting with a few people in the weight room. "Quick question: Have you ever thought of trying Pilates?" he asks a woman he recognizes as a regular. She ponders a while and answers, "I think my Greek grandmother used to cook that. Does it have spinach in it?"

After similar responses from other members, Guillermo realizes he must explain the new program to the gym's customers. He decides to do a one-paragraph write-up on Pilates and post it on the bulletin board next to the class schedules. His task, he realizes, is essentially *definition*—telling people what the term *Pilates* means in language they can readily grasp.

Using the computer in his office, he brainstorms by typing in a number of different phrases and examples. Then he writes the following first draft.

What Is Pilates?

Pilates is an <u>exercise program aimed at complete body conditioning,</u> [1] <u>balancing strength with flexibility and coordination. Developed in the 1920s by physical trainer Joseph Pilates,</u> it first became popular with professional dancers in Europe and New York City. Today not only dancers, but also actors and athletes, extol its benefits. Rather than building muscle bulk, <u>the Pilates method works toward a lean [2] type of strength and a harmony between body and mind, so movements become natural and graceful.</u> <u>"Everything should be [3] smooth, like a cat,"</u> Joseph Pilates said. Instead of demanding dozens of repetitions, the <u>technique emphasizes fewer, more</u> [3] <u>precise movements.</u> Our Pilates class, taught by a certified instructor, begins with floor exercises and progresses to the use of spring-resistance equipment that increases mobility and power without placing undue stress on muscles and joints.

What do you think of Guillermo's explanation of Pilates? Does he define the term well enough so people who have not heard of the method will understand its basic principles?

Qualities of a Good Definition

Definition is saying what a term means. You are familiar with the kinds of definitions found in dictionaries: a word followed by a list of the different meanings it may have. You will probably never write a dictionary, but definition as a technique can help you in many other writing situations.

Like Guillermo when he realized the fitness center's customers did not understand Pilates, you often must give your readers a brief introduction to a term's basic meaning. Maybe the term is a technical one that your readers have not seen before, or perhaps it is a term used in a special way by the company or organization for which you work.

A good definition should meet three criteria (see the numbered passages in Guillermo's paragaph):

1. *Accuracy:* The definition should state exactly what the term means, with no mistakes or misleading phrases. In Guillermo's definition of Pilates, all of the details must be correct. If Pilates actually began in the 1940s instead of the 1920s, the definition is not accurate.

2. *Clarity:* The definition should be clear enough for the intended audience to understand. If you are defining a technical term, for instance, you should use common words, not another technical term. If Guillermo had defined Pilates by mentioning tai chi (another exercise system), he would have likely confused his audience.

3. *Vividness:* Whenever possible, the definition should be vivid, with strong descriptive details that help the reader remember the term's meaning. This is why Guillermo's paragraph about the Pilates method included the quotation "Everything should be smooth, like a cat."

In the following sections, you will look at three common techniques for writing a definition: giving a synonym, putting the term in a category, and defining by difference.

SELF-ASSESSMENT 7

When I need to define an unusual term for readers, I can:

	Usually	Sometimes	Never
Define the term accurately.	❑	❑	❑
Define the term clearly.	❑	❑	❑
Choose words that make my definition vivid.	❑	❑	❑
Find a good synonym.	❑	❑	❑
Define the term by putting it in a category, then adding details.	❑	❑	❑
Define the term by telling readers what it does *not* mean.	❑	❑	❑

If you checked "Sometimes" or "Never" for any of the items, this chapter will help you improve your skills. Even if you checked "Usually" in every instance, you will learn more about writing paragraphs that use effective definitions.

Defining with Synonyms

The simplest way to define a term is to supply another term that means the same thing—a **synonym.** Sometimes with a synonym, you can accomplish your definition in a single sentence.

Say you work for a garden center, and you are preparing a list of tree varieties currently in stock. Since the list will be given out to customers, you include synonyms for tree names that may be unfamiliar to some people.

Serviceberry (Juneberry)

Sycamore (buttonwood, buttonball)

Tulip poplar (tulip tree)

Putting the synonym in parentheses is often a quick, convenient way to work it into your text. You can also use other methods such as these:

Modifying Phrase	The sycamore, also known as a buttonwood or buttonball, is a popular shade tree.
Full Sentence	In some regions of the country, the sycamore tree is known as a buttonwood or buttonball.

The more technical your subject, the more important it is to include simple synonyms. Imagine that you are a physician assistant preparing an information sheet for expectant mothers. To avoid bewildering your audience, you want to clarify your technical words with common synonyms.

Technical Term	More Common Term
varicella	chickenpox
varicosis	varicose veins

did you ever?

- Use a slang term that your parents didn't understand so that they had to ask you for a translation?

- Say that a movie you saw was "a total disaster," only to have a friend ask what you meant by "disaster"?

- Mention a new cultural phenomenon that your best friend had never heard of so that he or she had to ask, "What's that?"

In all of these common situations, you use definition to explain what you mean. This chapter will help you apply the same technique to your writing.

ACTIVITY 7.1 For each term in the following list, supply two synonyms. Make sure your synonyms are common words that most people understand. The first item is completed for you.

1. fetters

   shackles, chains
   _____

2. wedlock

   _____

   _____

3. brawl (as in "The hockey game turned into a brawl.")

   _____

   _____

4. elevate

   _____

   _____

5. abode

   _____

   _____

6. absolute

   _____

   _____

TECHNOLOGY CONNECTION

Using an Electronic Thesaurus

The most common place to find synonyms is in a thesaurus, a dictionary of synonyms. Conventionally these collections come in book form, but a typical word processor also has an electronic thesaurus built in. If you need a synonym for *dictionary*, for example, the click of a mouse or the touch of a pair of keys will produce alternatives such as *lexicon, vocabulary,* and *word list.*

For even more word choices, you can visit a web site that offers a searchable online thesaurus.

Defining by Category and Details

Some terms cannot be defined with simple synonyms, so you must offer a more elaborate type of definition. The most common way to elaborate involves two steps:

- *Category:* Name a larger category to which the term belongs.
- *Details:* Add details to separate the term from other items in the same category.

In other words, first you tell the reader the general kind of thing you are talking about and then you narrow the meaning with specifics. As an example, look at this paragraph written by a caterer to a potential customer.

> For dessert at your party, we recommend Black Forest cake. Black Forest is a chocolate layer cake with a creamy cherry filling. The filling is composed of heavy cream and whole cherries and is flavored with vanilla extract and cherry liqueur. On the top, we sprinkle semisweet chocolate curls.

In this paragraph, the basic category is "cake" or "layer cake." The writer immediately supplies two types of detail ("chocolate" and "creamy cherry filling") and then goes on to describe further mouth-watering ways in which the Black Forest cake differs from other cakes. This paragraph is a good example of using details to make a definition vivid.

WRITING WORKSHOP

Parallelism in Definitions

A good definition uses language that is parallel to the term being defined. You cannot define a chef as "cooking food" because *chef* is a noun and *cooking* is a verb. Instead, you can say that a chef is a *person* who cooks food. As another example, look at the following two definitions written by cable television installers.

(A) Nonparallel   The *drop* is <u>where</u> you connect the line to the customer.

(B) Parallel   The *drop* is the <u>connection</u> between the main cable and the customer's building.

A drop cannot be called a *where* because *where* is a different part of speech. For that reason, the second definition is clearer.

ACTIVITY 7.2   For each of the following items, use the category-detail method to write one or two sentences that provide a useful and accurate definition. A sample is provided for you. The general category does not need to be the first word in your definition (in the sample below, the category is "mammal"), but it should come early, before most of the details.

1. horse

   A horse is a plant-eating mammal with four legs, hooves, and a long tail. Domesticated long ago by humans, the horse serves as a draft animal and as a means of transportation.

2. dolphin

   _____

   _____

   _____

3. word processor

   _____

   _____

   _____

4. suitcase

   _____

   _____

   _____

5. fork (as in knife, fork, spoon)

   _____

   _____

   _____

6. skyscraper

   _____

   _____

   _____

Defining by Difference

Another way to define a term is to begin by telling your reader what it does *not* mean. Right away you establish a distinction between the item you are defining and something else. This technique is especially useful when you think your audience may have mistaken ideas about the subject.

A botanist writing for students might define a lichen in these terms:

> Contrary to popular impression, a lichen is not a type of moss. Scientifically speaking, it is not even a plant. A lichen is made up of a fungus that grows together with algae.

Notice how this definition begins by setting up two differences. The lichen is *not* a moss, and it is *not* even a plant. Of course, these negatives by themselves do not make a full definition. The botanist must go on to make a positive statement about what a lichen really is.

Here is a longer example written by an agricultural extension agent to warn about gypsy moth infestation.

Recipe for an effective definition

Everyone has heard of gypsy moths, but can you identify them? In spite of their notoriety, gypsy moths do not look at all spectacular. Unlike cecropia moths, for example, gypsies do not startle people with their huge size and bright color. The adult male gypsy moth is only about an inch long, and its color is a dull brownish-gray. The female is a bit larger and whitish, with black markings. The caterpillars, although extremely hairy, are dark and hard to spot against a tree's bark. You may walk by a tree infested with gypsy moths without noticing them.

Nevertheless, the gypsy moth caterpillar, with its enormous appetite, has become one of the most destructive pests of North American hardwoods. Each tiny caterpillar alone can consume as many as 35 leaves. In heavily infested areas, the caterpillars strip entire trees of their leaves, an attack that makes the trees susceptible to drought and disease.

Realizing that people may have trouble identifying gypsy moths, the agent began by contrasting the gypsy moth with a larger, more conspicuous type. Then, to complete the definition, the agent offered specifics about the gypsy moth. Notice, too, that the agent tailored the paragraph for a general audience. Rather than just mentioning cecropia moths as a contrasting variety, the agent explained exactly *why* the two types are different.

ACTIVITY 7.3 For each term listed below, write a short paragraph that begins with the defining-by-difference technique. Say what the term is *not* and continue with sentences that define what the term *is*. The first item has been completed for you.

1. ant lion

   Despite its name, the ant lion is not a kind of lion. Nor is it an ant, although it does belong to the same overall class as ants, namely, the insects. In its adult stage, the ant lion resembles a dragonfly. In its larval stage, about half an inch long, it hides in a burrow in sandy soil with its big jaws sticking up—ready to devour other insects, such as ants, that fall in.

2. rock music

   _____

   _____

   _____

   _____

   _____

   _____

3. margarine

   _____

   _____

   _____

   _____

   _____

   _____

4. liberty

   _____

   _____

   _____

   _____

ETHICS CONNECTION

Emotionally Slanted Definitions

The more abstract the term, the more leeway you have in defining it. Sometimes unscrupulous writers turn this fact to their advantage by slanting a definition to suit their own purposes. Look at the following paragraph, which begins by defining the word *traitor.*

> A traitor is anyone who betrays our trust. Senator Finch voted to raise the tax rate even though he campaigned against high taxes. Therefore, Senator Finch is a traitor!

By using a very broad definition of *traitor,* the writer sets up an accusation against someone who may not deserve such name-calling. It is fine to argue a point, but it is unethical to trick or deceive the reader by slanting a definition.

Using Multiple Techniques

The three definition techniques described in this chapter—defining with synonyms, by category and details, and by difference—are not mutually exclusive. Often you will use more than one technique in a single paragraph to give your readers a full sense of the term you are defining.

Below is a paragraph written by a marketing manager for an agricultural association. It uses all three definition techniques. Can you identify each one?

[1]The chickpea is not what Americans call a pea, but it belongs to the same family, the legumes. [2]Also known as a garbanzo bean or gram, the plant grows in temperate climates around the world. [3]Its round seeds, larger than peas, are high in protein, and they form a vital part of the diet in many cultures. [4]They are the chief component of Middle Eastern hummus and Indian dhal.

In sentence 1, the author defines by difference (the chickpea is not a regular pea) and also names a general category (legumes). Sentence 2 offers two synonyms (garbanzo bean, gram), and sentences 3 and 4 supply details that differentiate the chickpea from other legumes.

The author could have begun this paragraph with a formal dictionary-style definition: "The chickpea is an edible legume grown in temperate climates." As you can see, that kind of formality is not always necessary. However, your topic sentence should focus on the term in such a way that the reader knows you intend to explain its meaning.

ACTIVITY 7.4   For each of the following terms, write a definition paragraph that combines at least two of the techniques you have used in this chapter: defining with synonyms, by category and details, and by difference.

1. motorcycle

_____

_____

_____

_____

_____

_____

2. dictator

_____

_____

_____

_____

_____

_____

_____

SUMMARY FOR
DEFINITION WRITING

❏   Definition is saying what a term means.

❏   A definition should be accurate, clear, and vivid.

❏   One way of defining a term is to give a synonym—another term with the same meaning. To find good synonyms, you can consult a thesaurus.

❏   Many definitions begin with a name of the general category to which the term belongs, followed by details that separate the term from others in the category.

❏   Defining by difference—telling what a term is *not*—is another useful technique.

PRACTICING YOUR SKILLS

Now that you understand how to write a good definition paragraph, practice your skills by completing the following activities.

PRACTICE 1

The following first draft was written by Dan Yoblanski of the Minton Youth Center. By posting this paragraph on the center's web site, he hopes to convince people to sign up for the Teen Club. Can you help Dan improve the paragraph?

The Teen Club is an after-school program. Eligible students are between the ages of 13 and 17. The members do community service projects. In the past year, the Teen Club has begun a sidewalk-improvement project to help revitalize Minton's downtown. The Center's staff supervise, but students choose and plan their own activities, so this is not an adult-dominated group. Through their efforts, Teen Club members develop leadership skills and help to make a real difference in our community.

Analyzing the Beginning

1. The paragraph opens in a choppy way with several short sentences that each explain a tiny amount. Circle sentences you think could be merged into one.

Defining by Difference

2. Underline the passage that uses definition by difference.

Rewriting to Improve

3. Now rewrite the paragraph to eliminate the choppiness. Bring the definition by difference closer to the beginning. Make each sentence lead smoothly to the next.

_____

_____

_____

_____

_____

_____

PRACTICE 2

Industrial designer Jill Stanton has helped develop a new line of office partition panels covered with a fabric called olefin. Since olefin is an advance over older fabrics, Jill has been asked to write a definition of the material that explains its unique features. She has been struggling to organize her thoughts. Here is her first draft.

Olefin is a synthetic fiber. As a covering for office panels, it is a high-quality, practical solution. Compared to other synthetics, olefin is lightweight and highly resistant to scuffs, dirt, and stains. It is not the same as polyester, although it is manufactured in a similar way. Olefin is made of polypropylene or polyethylene. It can be cleaned with soap and water, and it dries quickly. Although the finished fiber is hard to dye, vivid, long-lasting colors can be added during manufacturing. It is also called P2.

Analyzing the Organization

1. To help Jill improve the paragraph's organization, underline the phrases that explain olefin's basic composition. Circle the phrases that describe its good qualities as a fabric. Double-underline the passage that defines olefin by what it is not. Put brackets around the synonym.

Rewriting to Improve

2. With what you have learned by marking up the paragraph, rewrite it to improve the organization and to make the definition clearer.

_____

_____

_____

_____

_____

_____

_____

_____

_____

_____

APPLYING YOUR SKILLS

It is time to apply your skills by writing a longer definition paragraph. The following sections will guide you through the stages of the writing process as you brainstorm, plan, and build your paragraph. Use a separate sheet of paper or a word processing file. Label and save each stage of your writing.

Prewriting

(a) Begin by selecting a term to define. Here are some general topics that may interest you:

the Information Age	conservatism
exercise	peace
religion	justice
abundance	wealth
love	selfishness
loyalty	sport utility vehicle (SUV)
middle age	youth

(b) Some of the terms listed above are so broad that you could devote an entire book to defining them! For your paragraph, therefore, narrow the topic. If you are writing about peace, for example, do you mean peace between nations, an individual's feeling of peacefulness, or something else? If you select religion, are you going to define your own religion, your notion of what true religion should be, or the qualities that all religions share? If you select one of the more abstract topics, be sure you are comfortable with the terminology you must use to define it.

(c) Once you have narrowed your topic, brainstorm about it. On your paper or with your word processor, list ideas that can help you define the term. Make note of examples that may help explain what you mean. List synonyms as well as antonyms (terms that mean the opposite of the one you have chosen). Use a thesaurus if necessary.

(d) Think about whether your term fits into a larger category. What names might you give that category? How does your term differ from other items in that category?

(e) Once you have a collection of notes, read them over and select the best ideas. Decide which techniques you will use in your definition. Will you use synonyms? Will you fit your term into a category? Will you contrast your term with other terms? How should you frame your topic sentence?

(f) Write an outline for your paragraph.

Writing

Now write the first draft of your paragraph. Word the topic sentence so it conveys to the reader your intention to define the term. Use as many of the techniques described in this chapter as seem appropriate. Work toward the three characteristics described at the opening of this chapter: accuracy, clarity, and vividness in your definition.

Revising

Read through your first draft and revise it as necessary. Use the following checklist of questions to make sure you revise thoroughly.

❑ Does the topic sentence name the term you are writing about and alert the reader to the fact that the paragraph will define that term?

❑ Have you included appropriate synonyms? If you have introduced a word as a synonym, is it really a good match for the term you are defining? If your paragraph lacks synonyms, is that because no good ones exist?

❑ If you used synonyms, did you work them smoothly into your text with modifying phrases, parentheses, or full sentences?

❑ Did you establish a general category for your term and then differentiate it from other terms in that category?

❑ Does your language avoid nonparallel constructions?

❑ Did you take advantage of opportunities to clarify your term by saying what it does *not* mean?

❑ Is your definition free from emotional slant and bias?

❑ Overall, is your definition accurate?

❑ Is your definition clear so the reader will know just what you mean?

❑ Is the definition as vivid as you can make it?

When you think you have revised thoroughly, write a second draft. Label it *Draft 2*. If you are writing on paper, use a clean sheet. If you are writing on a computer, retype the paragraph from the beginning.

Then follow the same process with your second draft. Critique and revise it thoroughly. If necessary, write a third draft.

When you believe your content and presentation are as good as you can make them, move on to the editing stage.

Editing

As a final step, check your paragraph for mechanical errors. Study the grammar, spelling, word use, punctuation, and capitalization. Watch for instances of nonparallelism in particular.

If you are using a word processor, run the spell checker and grammar checker, but do not assume that they will save you from all embarrassments.

After you have finished polishing your writing, make a new copy in the format your instructor specifies. Proofread your paragraph one final time for small errors that can escape your notice when you are focusing on larger matters.

WRITING FOR YOUR CAREER

CRITICAL THINKING

This section presents a writing project for each of the six career pathways. Choose one that appeals to you and use your new skills to write a paragraph on the subject.

When the project description refers you to the textbook web site, go to http://humphrey.swlearning.com and click on the Links tab. Look for Chapter 7, "Writing for Your Career." There you will find direct links to helpful web sites.

Communication and the Arts

As a news desk assistant at a television station, you often do background research to help the reporters and news anchors prepare stories. Today you are working with reporter Amy Kramer on a profile of a local scientist who has made important new discoveries concerning coelacanths. You and Amy know that a coelacanth is a fish; otherwise, you know little about the creature. Do some research, take notes, make an outline, and write a paragraph defining *coelacanth* in a way that will help Amy prepare her story for a general audience. Many online sites can help with your research. You will find a starting point at the textbook web site.

Health and Medicine

"What exactly is an EMG?" You are an assistant in a neurologist's office, where you often hear this question from worried patients who have been told they need such a test. You decide to prepare an information sheet that you can hand out. For this sheet, write a paragraph that defines an EMG by saying what the acronym stands for, what the test involves, how long it takes, and what kind of medical information it yields. Remember that your readers have little technical knowledge and that you want to be both straightforward and reassuring. For useful web links, see the textbook web site. (*Hint:* EMG stands for electromyography.)

Human, Personal, and Public Service

You work as a cosmetology consultant at BodyCare Spa, Ltd., where the services range from hair coloring to complete makeovers. This month BodyCare has added a treatment known as the Bahamian Complete Facial, and you are preparing a description sheet to explain it to customers. Here are the facts:

Cost: $240 for 5 treatments

Services included: skin analysis, deep pore cleansing with enzyme mask, steaming, exfoliation with glycolic acid, mineral mask, massage, moisturization with aloe vera and algae extracts

Using this information, write a paragraph to define the term *Bahamian Complete Facial* for your customers.

Business and Marketing

On the menu of your catering service, you list pastitsio as one of your most popular items, but many customers are not familiar with the dish. To supplement the menu, write a paragraph defining *pastitsio*.

Include information about the ingredients and how the dish is prepared. You also may want to explain the dish's cultural history. Your audience consists of anyone who hires a catering service: people getting married, families planning a reunion, and so on.

If you do not already enjoy pastitsio yourself, consult a cookbook or do a web search for the term. For useful web links, see the suggestions provided on the textbook web site.

Science and Technology

In the catalog for your air conditioning business, you list the Btu rating for each unit you stock. This rating is an important indicator of an air conditioner's ability to cool a given area, and it helps determine the unit's energy efficiency.

Some of your customers, however, do not understand the term *Btu*, so they do not know how to use the Btu rating to evaluate an air conditioner. To help these customers, write a paragraph defining *Btu* for the opening page of your catalog.

As part of your research, do a web search for information about air conditioners. The web site for this textbook has a helpful link. Encyclopedias are another good source for basic explanations.

(*Hint: Btu* stands for British thermal unit, and you can find the term in a dictionary. But a dictionary definition by itself will not be much help for your audience. Define the term in a practical way that will help your customers make decisions about which air conditioner to buy.)

Environment and Natural Resources

The pond at Stone Valley Nature Center is a popular spot for nature programs, especially on late spring evenings when the leopard frogs are active and noisy. Pretend that you are a staff member preparing a handout for visitors. Define this type of frog in a paragraph that children as well as adults can understand.

Your task is to answer these questions:

- What exactly is a leopard frog?
- How will visitors know when they find one?

(*Hint:* The frog's scientific name is *Rana pipiens*. Nature guides can tell you about this common frog. You can also find information online by entering the scientific name in a search engine.)

8

Comparison and Contrast: Paragraphs about Similarities and Differences

© Getty Images/PhotoDisc

IN THIS CHAPTER YOU WILL LEARN TO:

- Identify key points of comparison and contrast.

- Write a point-by-point comparison or contrast.

- Write a one-side-at-a-time comparison or contrast.

- Combine comparison and contrast in a single paragraph.

Using *Comparison and Contrast* in Writing for Your Career

Career Path	Sample Career	Use for Comparison or Contrast	Example of Comparison or Contrast
Communication and the Arts	Jeweler	Contrasting two gemstones	Because it is harder, sapphire cracks less often than other blue stones.
Health and Medicine	Pharmacist	Comparing two medicines	The generic drug reduces fever just as well as the name brand.
Human, Personal, and Public Service	City planner	Contrasting two development proposals	The Payne proposal includes retail stores, unlike the Groffman design, which focuses on an entertainment center.
Business and Marketing	Purchasing agent for a courier service	Contrasting new uniform jackets	The trekker-style jacket offers a hood, but the flight jacket does not.
Science and Technology	Research engineer	Comparing two printer models	The X850 is designed to print as many pages per minute as the more expensive T4900.
Environment and Natural Resources	Fish hatchery manager	Comparing and contrasting two species of fish	The largemouth and smallmouth bass both have sizable mouths and forked tail fins, but the largemouth's jaw is longer.

ON THE JOB

Minivans and SUVs

Leona Bryant is the assistant fleet manager of an appliance-repair business. The "fleet" is the company's collection of cars and vans that the technicians use on their service calls. This year the company will replace a quarter of the fleet, and Leona's department has a decision to make. Should the company buy minivans, like the ones the technicians use now, or switch to sport utility vehicles (SUVs)?

The fleet manager has asked Leona to do the research. Now she is writing a report on her findings and she realizes that her task involves *comparison and contrast*. She must tell how the two vehicles are similar and different. Since her audience already knows the basic facts about minivans and SUVs and since the purpose of her report is to help people choose one vehicle or the other, she decides to stress the differences. She studies her research data and makes a list of differences:

SUV	Minivan
4-wheel drive	2-wheel drive
240 horsepower	195 horsepower
165-cubic-feet cargo area	210-cubic-feet cargo area
four regular doors	two regular doors, two sliding doors
18 miles per gallon	24 miles per gallon
$33,000	$23,000

In her final report, Leona will have a full section for each of these contrasts. In her introduction to preview the content, she writes this paragraph.

> Although similar in size and weight, the SUV and minivan are very different vehicles. The SUV boasts four-wheel drive, which would help keep our service representatives from getting stuck in the snow. It also has a more powerful engine than the minivan. Fashionable and popular, the SUV suggests that the owner—in this case, our company—is in tune with contemporary style. By contrast, the minivan is a more sedate vehicle, associated with soccer moms and family picnics. Yet the minivan offers greater cargo capacity, along with convenient sliding side doors, which our service reps find handy when unloading parts and tools. The minivan gets better gas mileage than the SUV, and perhaps most important, its purchase price is 30 percent lower. Except for service calls in winter weather, then, the minivan may be a more practical vehicle.

What do you think of Leona's paragraph? Does it clearly show the main differences between the two kinds of vehicles?

Understanding Comparison and Contrast

Comparison and contrast are common techniques in speaking and in writing. In fact, they are basic to the way you think about the world. Whenever you think, talk, or write about how two objects or people are like each other, you are using **comparison.** When you discuss differences, you are using **contrast.**

| Comparison | Like fruit bars, cookies are a tasty snack. |
| Contrast | Cookies tend to have more calories and a higher fat content than fruit bars. |

In common use, the word *comparison* often includes contrast as well. For instance, if a friend asks how your college compares with another, you would probably talk about differences as well as similarities.

Leona Bryant's paragraph in the "On the Job" scenario illustrates a key feature of effective comparison and contrast. She can compare and contrast SUVs and minivans because the two types of vehicle are relatively similar (1). You have probably heard people talk about the need to "compare apples with apples." Or perhaps you have heard someone criticize a comparison by saying, "That's like comparing apples with oranges." The point is that comparisons and contrasts are meaningless unless the two subjects are similar.

For example, you could do a detailed comparison and contrast between an airplane and a raspberry soda, but that would prove a waste of time. No one can drink an airplane or fly a soda.

Leona's paragraph also illustrates a common technique for organizing comparison and contrast: the one-side-at-a-time format (2). First, she discusses SUVs, which are one side of her comparison. Then she discusses minivans, the other side. In the next section, we will look at this format in detail, along with another option, the point-by-point arrangement.

SELF-ASSESSMENT 8

When I need to compare or contrast items in my writing, I can:

	Usually	Sometimes	Never
List the key points of comparison or contrast.	❑	❑	❑
Construct a point-by-point comparison or contrast.	❑	❑	❑
Construct a one-side-at-a-time comparison or contrast.	❑	❑	❑
Combine comparison and contrast as necessary.	❑	❑	❑
Use appropriate transitions.	❑	❑	❑

If you checked "Sometimes" or "Never" for any of the items, this chapter will help you improve your skills. Even if you checked "Usually" in every instance, you will learn more about writing paragraphs that use comparison and contrast.

Organizing Comparison and Contrast

To understand how to organize comparison and contrast, imagine that you are a preschool teacher who is talking to a child about two toy blocks on a table in front of you. Your goal is to help the child see the similarities and differences as clearly as you do.

One approach is to touch the block on the right and name all of its important qualities: "This block is red, square, and small." Then you touch the block on the left and name all of its important qualities: "This one is different. It is blue, rectangular, and larger." To make the similarities and differences clear, you choose the same kinds of qualities for each block. If you mention that the block on the right has dents in it, you also discuss whether the block on the left is dented. This method is the one-side-at-a-time format you have already seen in Leona Bryant's writing.

Another choice is to concentrate on individual points of comparison, going back and forth between the two blocks. As you touch the block on the right, you say, "This one is red." Then you touch the block on the left and say, "This one is blue, a different color." Next, you focus on another quality, such as shape. "The block on the right is a square. The one on the left is a rectangle." This is the point-by-point format.

In summary:

- *To use the one-side-at-a-time format,* discuss all of the relevant qualities of one subject. Then switch to the other subject, focusing on the same kinds of qualities.
- *To use the point-by-point format,* begin with one similarity or difference between the two subjects. Then discuss a second point of comparison, and then a third, and so on until you have covered all of the important points.

You should remember one other tip about these formats: Whichever format you choose, stick with it. Do not switch suddenly from one to another. Switching techniques can confuse your reader and damage the effectiveness of your writing.

did you ever?

- Tell a friend how one movie differed from another?

- Discuss the approaches of two instructors, describing their similarities and their differences?

- Explain what two of your favorite writers have in common?

In these everyday situations, you use comparison, contrast, or both to convey your meaning. This chapter will help you apply the same techniques to your writing.

Writing Comparison Paragraphs

For a deeper understanding of comparison and contrast, you'll begin with comparison paragraphs. By now, you can guess that these paragraphs, like other types you have learned about, begin with a topic sentence.

Assume that you are a research scientist for a company that makes printers and other electronic equipment. You are drafting a memo describing progress in developing a new laser printer. Here is your topic sentence:

> Although it is designed to be inexpensive, the Model X850 shares many features of our top-of-the-line printer, the T4900.

The topic sentence states the two subjects to be compared—two printer models. It also announces the focus of the comparison, showing that you will be discussing "features," not marketing plans or manufacturing costs.

After the topic sentence, you go on to your comparison. Suppose you decide to use the point-by-point format. You take each relevant quality of the X850 printer and compare it to the more expensive model. The separate points are underlined so you can identify them.

> The X850 prints 23 <u>pages per minute</u>, not far below the T4900's mark of 25 ppm. The X850 also equals the T4900 in <u>resolution</u> (1200 dots per inch), in <u>memory size</u> (32 megabytes standard, expandable to 192 MB), and in the <u>size of the input paper tray</u> (250 sheets). Its <u>maximum recommended duty cycle</u>, 60,000 pages per month, approaches the sturdy T4900's 65,000 pages.

Finally, you can add a concluding sentence that wraps up the paragraph.

> With all of these remarkable qualities packed into a trim, economical machine, the X850 promises to be a great addition to our laser printer line.

If you decided to use the one-side-at-a-time format instead, the paragraph would cover the same qualities, but its organization would be different. Here the phrases introducing the two sides are underlined.

> Although inexpensive in its design, the Model X850 has many features of our top-of-the-line printer, the T4900. <u>The X850</u> has a resolution of 1200 dots per inch, a memory of 32 megabytes (expandable to 192 MB), a resolution of 1200 dots per inch, and an input paper tray that holds 250 sheets. It prints 23 pages per minute and has a maximum recommended duty cycle of 60,000 pages per month. <u>The T4900</u> has identical numbers in all but the last two of these categories, and even there its figures are similar (25 ppm and a 65,000-page duty cycle). Overall, the X850, with its many similarities to the more expensive model, promises to be a great addition to our laser printer line.

ACTIVITY 8.1 For each pair of items in the following list, supply three points of similarity that could be used in a comparison paragraph. The first example has been completed for you.

1. *Aladdin* and *The Little Mermaid*

   animated TV cartoons   highly popular   based on Disney movies

2. newspapers and popular magazines

   _____   _____   _____

3. guitar and banjo

   _____   _____   _____

4. radishes and onions

   _____   _____   _____

5. Thanksgiving and the Fourth of July

   _____   _____   _____

6. basketball and soccer

   _____   _____   _____

7. coffee and tea

   _____   _____   _____

8. lettuce and spinach

   _____   _____   _____

9. steel and aluminum

   _____   _____   _____

10. electric fans and air conditioners

   _____   _____   _____

11. doctors and dentists

   _____   _____   _____

ACTIVITY 8.2

Choose one pair of items from Activity 8.1 and write a short comparison paragraph about them. Decide whether you want to use the point-by-point or the one-side-at-a-time format. Begin with a topic sentence. Then cover your points of similarity with appropriate details. Add a concluding sentence to wrap up the paragraph.

_____

_____

_____

_____

_____

_____

_____

_____

_____

_____

_____

_____

_____

_____

_____

_____

_____

TECHNOLOGY CONNECTION

Using Tables for Comparisons and Contrasts

When you are brainstorming similarities or differences, you may find it useful to create a two-column list like the one in the "On the Job" scenario at the beginning of this chapter. If you are using a computer, you can separate the columns with tabs. Often, however, the most convenient way to type two columns is to set up a table with your word processor's table function. In a table, items that are supposed to be opposite each other will stay aligned even if one of them runs longer than one line.

Writing Contrast Paragraphs

In writing, contrasts are even more common than comparisons. Contrasts follow the same two basic formats: point by point or one side at a time. You choose whichever format seems most useful for the overall meaning you want to convey.

Comparing apples and oranges

Look at a paragraph written by an independent jeweler. He wants to explain to his customers why he works mostly with sapphire instead of the popular gem tanzanite. For this purpose, he decides to write a contrast paragraph to include in a handout describing his choices and methods. He begins with a topic sentence naming the two subjects that the paragraph will contrast.

> Although <u>tanzanite</u> is very popular among lovers of blue gems, I prefer working with <u>sapphire</u>, which, for my purposes, is a better stone.

Next, the jeweler supports the topic sentence with a point-by-point contrast.

> Sapphire is a <u>hard</u> gem, reaching 9 on the Mohs scale of hardness, second only to diamond. Tanzanite, by contrast, has a Mohs ranking of 6 to 7, meaning that it is prone to chipping and scratching. Worse, if you forget you are wearing your tanzanite ring and dip your hand in hot dishwater, you may crack the stone. This does not happen with sapphire, which is much <u>less sensitive to changes in temperature</u>. Tanzanite is famous for its lovely hues, but its color tends to change in different lights or against different backgrounds. Sapphire <u>maintains its color</u> no matter where you put it—an advantage, in my view, for someone who is wearing it.

Notice that the jeweler covers three separate points of contrast: hardness, temperature sensitivity, and steadiness of color.

Finally, he adds a concluding sentence to sum up his main idea.

> Sapphire may be less flashy, but I find it more appropriate for long-lasting pieces.

After such a strong contrast, customers may be embarrassed to ask him for tanzanite—and this is exactly the outcome he wants. As this example shows, contrasts can make your writing very effective.

ACTIVITY 8.3

Rewrite the jeweler's paragraph using the one-side-at-a-time format. (*Hint:* Talk about each of the good qualities of sapphire first and then show how tanzanite is not as good in each respect.) The topic sentence has been supplied for you.

Although tanzanite is very popular among lovers of blue gems, I prefer working with sapphire, which, for my purposes, is a better stone.

_____

_____

_____

_____

_____

_____

_____

_____

_____

_____

_____

_____

_____

_____

ETHICS CONNECTION

Fair Contrasts

Imagine that a friend of yours recently took up golf. At the end of a round, you ask his playing partner, "How is he doing?" The partner answers, "Well, he doesn't look like Tiger Woods out there." If it were said seriously, this comment would be a terribly unfair contrast.

The same principle applies to your writing. You can easily make a person look bad by contrasting him or her with someone who has more expertise. You can make a product look bad by contrasting it with a more expensive or more professional model. But that is not ethical writing. Remember that there is a good reason for not comparing "apples" with "oranges." When you do, you are usually being unfair to one or the other.

Combining Comparison and Contrast

Although comparison and contrast may seem to be opposites, writers often combine them. You may find yourself writing about two items that are similar in some ways and different in other ways. This is easy to do if you organize your paragraph well and keep your purpose and audience firmly in mind.

Suppose you work in a city planner's office. You are analyzing two proposals for developing a parcel of land along the river. You decide to write a paragraph that begins by pointing out the similarities of the proposals and then turns to their differences. Study the way this paragraph is organized.

Topic Sentence: Introduces similarities and differences

Comparisons

Transition to Contrast

Point-by-Point Contrast: Size of spaces, number of stories, use of river view

Concluding Sentence

Although the proposals by the Glendora Group and the Palmer Corporation are similar in approach, they offer startlingly different visions of the riverfront's future. Both allow for a mix of retail and entertainment, such as restaurants, a fashion shop, a movie theater, and a fitness center. In the Palmer proposal, these are all small to midsize spaces, the largest being the four-screen theater. In contrast, the Glendora Group has the complex anchored by a big-box retailer such as Garden Gallery or Orion. To allow enough room for other tenants, Glendora would create a four-story mall around the anchor space, complete with an atrium and fountains. Palmer's more modest design requires only two stories on the riverfront and one story at the street. Most important, these two proposals treat the river in radically different ways. Palmer imagines large windows on the riverfront so diners and shoppers can enjoy a view across the water. Glendora's design turns its back on the river, allowing only small, high windows facing the water. On the whole, although both proposals are billed as retail-entertainment blends, the Glendora Group offers a large mall that might exist anywhere, whereas the Palmer Corporation has given some thought to the unique riverside setting.

WRITING WORKSHOP

Comparative Modifiers

When comparing or contrasting two things, you often use modifier words (technically, adjectives or adverbs) such as *better, longer, widest,* and *youngest.*

> Abby is <u>younger</u> than Pablo.
> I took a <u>longer</u> route home so I could stop at the market.

You are probably so familiar with modifiers that you use them without giving them any thought. One problem, though, is that you may use the wrong endings. Grammatically, an *-er* ending means that you are comparing just two things. An *-est* ending implies that you are comparing more than two things.

Two (*-er*)	More Than Two (*-est*)
better	best
finer	finest
longer	longest
wider	widest
younger	youngest
harder	hardest

ACTIVITY 8.4

For each pair, list two or three similarities and differences.

	Similarities	Differences
1. a lamb and a calf	_____	_____
	_____	_____
	_____	_____
2. politics and theater	_____	_____
	_____	_____
	_____	_____

	Similarities	Differences
3. sandals and sneakers	_____	_____
	_____	_____
	_____	_____
4. sun and moon	_____	_____
	_____	_____
	_____	_____
5. college and high school	_____	_____
	_____	_____
	_____	_____

ACTIVITY 8.5 Choose one of the pairs from Activity 8.4 and write a brief paragraph combining comparison and contrast.

_____

_____

_____

_____

_____

_____

_____

_____

_____

_____

_____

_____

_____

_____

_____

_____

_____

_____

_____

WRITING WORKSHOP

Transitional Terms for Comparison and Contrast

Like any other kind of paragraph, comparison and contrast paragraphs need good transitions from one idea to the next. Here are some transitional expressions that occur frequently in comparison and contrast paragraphs.

Comparison	Contrast
similarly	unlike
in the same way	in contrast, by contrast
likewise	conversely
just as	however
also	rather than
both	while, whereas

SUMMARY FOR COMPARISON AND CONTRAST WRITING

❑ Comparison means writing about similarities or likenesses. Contrast means writing about differences.

❑ In a comparison and contrast paragraph, the topic sentence should introduce the two subjects to be discussed. The topic sentence should also indicate the general focus of the comparison or contrast.

❑ The body of the paragraph should use a point-by-point format or a one-side-at-a-time format.

❑ The point-by-point method deals with one similarity or difference, then the next, and so on.

❑ The one-side-at-a-time method discusses all of the relevant qualities of one subject and then the corresponding qualities of the other subject.

❑ The ending -er on a modifier (better, longer, wider) indicates that two subjects are being contrasted. Use the ending -est (best, longest, widest) only when talking about three or more subjects.

PRACTICING YOUR SKILLS

Now that you understand how to write comparisons and contrasts, you can practice your skills in the following activities.

PRACTICE 1

Marty Chen, a purchasing agent for Sampson Couriers, is ordering new uniforms for the firm's drivers. In a memo to his supervisor, he explains his choice of jackets.

 For the uniform jacket, we have considered a traditional flight-jacket style, like the ones the drivers now wear, and a new "trekker" style with a microfiber shell. The trekker jacket offers better weather protection since the microfiber repels water. Though just as warm, it is lighter in weight than the flight jacket. It has elastic cuffs, two outer pockets, and a hood that can be stowed inside the polyester collar when not in use. The flight jacket, in contrast, has no hood, and it does not repel water. It does have the advantage of four outer pockets, as well as a zippered inner pocket where drivers can keep important papers. Most important, the flight jacket's classic military styling, with button cuffs and a leather collar, better reflects the image we want our drivers to present to the public.

Type of Paragraph

1. Does Marty's paragraph offer a comparison, a contrast, or both?

2. Does the paragraph use a point-by-point or one-side-at-a-time format?

Identifying Individual Points

3. Make a two-column list of individual points that Marty compares or contrasts.

repels water   does not repel water

_____   _____

_____   _____

_____   _____

_____   _____

_____   _____

Identifying Transitions and Comparison/Contrast Terms

4. Circle the transitional terms that Marty uses in his paragraph.

5. Underline the *-er* modifiers that Marty uses.

Overall Effect of the Paragraph

6. Which jacket do you think Marty plans to order? Why?

PRACTICE 2

Joy Polansky, a fish hatchery manager, wrote the following paragraph to post on the state fish commission's web site. Here she uses some of her expertise to clear up a puzzling identification matter.

> Many new anglers have difficulty distinguishing the smallmouth bass from the largemouth. The two fish resemble each other closely. They belong to the same genus, and it is possible for them to interbreed. Both have dark green bars on their cheeks and olive-colored sides with bars or stripes. Both have a slightly forked tail, and both like clear-water lakes and streams. But there are differences if you observe carefully. The largemouth, true to its name, has a lengthy jaw that typically extends past the eye; the smallmouth's jaw is a bit shorter. The notch between the dorsal (top) fins is deeper on the largemouth. The smallmouth prefers cooler waters, no more than 70 degrees, while the largemouth does well at temperatures up to 82 degrees. Of course, both are excellent sport fish and are tasty on the dinner table.

Type of Paragraph

1. Does the paragraph use a point-by-point or one-side-at-a-time format?

Identifying Individual Points

2. Write numbers (1, 2, 3) above points of similarity. Write letters (A, B, C) above points of difference.

Identifying Transitions and Comparison/Contrast Terms

3. Underline the *-er* modifiers that Joy uses to distinguish between the two fish.

4. Circle the transitional terms.

APPLYING YOUR SKILLS

To apply the skills you have developed in this chapter, write a substantial paragraph of your own using comparison, contrast, or both. The following sections will guide you through the stages of the writing process.

Use a separate sheet of paper or a word processing file. Label and save each stage of your writing.

Prewriting

(a) Begin by selecting a pair of items to discuss. Here are some pairs that offer good opportunities for comparison and contrast:

dogs and cats	lemonade and cola
trains and airplanes	TV reality shows and game shows
e-mail and online chat	Mexican food and Indian food
movies and television	the beach and the mountains (vacation spots)

(b) Decide on the focus of your paragraph. Are you going to emphasize similarities, differences, or a combination of the two? What main point do you want to make?

(c) Once you have narrowed your focus, brainstorm about the subject. On your paper or with your word processor, make a two-column list showing points of comparison or contrast. Do not worry if some points seem weaker than others. During the brainstorming phase, you want to list as many ideas as possible.

(d) Go back and review the points you listed in the preceding step. Which points are strongest? Which will be easiest to explain to your reader? Which will best support your overall message? Choose a minimum of three points to use in your paragraph.

(e) Decide whether a point-by-point or a one-side-at-a-time format suits your needs. The point-by-point method often makes the individual comparisons or contrasts clearer. The one-side-at-a-time method gives a more complete view of each subject. Whichever method you choose, remember to stick with it through the entire paragraph.

(f) Write an outline for your paragraph. The outline should show the order in which you intend to raise your points. If you are doing both comparison and contrast, your outline should also indicate which comes first.

Writing

Now write the first draft of your paragraph. In your topic sentence, introduce the two subjects and state the general focus of your comparison or contrast. In the body of the paragraph, make the details as clear and vivid as you can.

Use appropriate transitional terms to move from one point to another. Since you are comparing just two subjects, remember to use *-er* rather than *-est* modifiers.

If your overall message is not obvious by the end of the paragraph, add a concluding sentence that reinforces the main idea.

Revising

Read through your first draft and revise it as necessary. Use the following checklist of questions to make sure you revise thoroughly.

- ❑ Does the topic sentence introduce the two subjects and show that you will be comparing or contrasting them? Does it indicate the general focus of your comparison or contrast?
- ❑ Have you included at least three points of comparison or contrast?
- ❑ Do all of the points you introduce support the paragraph's overall message?
- ❑ Does your paragraph follow either the point-by-point or the one-side-at-a-time format consistently?
- ❑ Do your comparative modifiers use the proper *-er*, not *-est*, ending?
- ❑ Do you use appropriate transitional expressions to signal movement from one point to the next or from one subject to the other?
- ❑ Is your overall comparison or contrast a fair one? That is, do you focus on aspects of the two subjects that can reasonably be compared?
- ❑ Are your details as vivid and precise as you can make them?
- ❑ Did you include a concluding sentence, if needed, to wrap up the paragraph and reinforce the main idea?

When you think you have revised thoroughly, write a second draft. Label it *Draft 2*. If you are writing on paper, use a clean sheet. If you are writing on a computer, retype the paragraph from the beginning. Then follow the same process with your second draft, critiquing and revising thoroughly and asking yourself the questions listed above. If necessary, write a third draft.

When you believe your content and presentation are as good as you can make them, move on to the editing stage.

Editing

Check your paragraph for mechanical errors. Study the grammar, spelling, word use, punctuation, and capitalization. Look again at your uses of *-er* and *-est* endings. If you are using a word processor, run the spell checker and grammar checker, but do not expect them to catch all of your mistakes.

After you have finished polishing your writing, make a new copy in the format your instructor specifies. Proofread one final time for small errors.

WRITING FOR YOUR CAREER
CRITICAL THINKING

This section presents a writing project for each of the six career pathways. Choose one that appeals to you and use your new skills to write a paragraph on the subject.

When the project description refers you to the textbook web site, go to http://humphrey.swlearning.com and look for the "Writing for Your Career" section of Chapter 8. There you will find direct links to helpful web references.

Communication and the Arts

You work for HiLite Photography Studio, which specializes in wedding photographs. For years, the studio's photographers have used lightweight traditional cameras, but you think it is time to upgrade to digital cameras. With digital cameras, the staff will be able to load images directly into the studio's computers for touch-up and cropping.

After doing some research online or in photography magazines, write a comparison or contrast paragraph analyzing two models. To find online reviews of digital cameras, try entering "digital camera review" in a search engine. Remember that the camera will be used at weddings, so it should be lightweight and portable. High resolution and large storage capacity are also important.

Health and Medicine

As an admissions officer at a health-sciences college, you advise incoming students about career fields. You find that many students are confused about the distinction between occupational therapy and physical therapy, especially since many of the requirements are the same. Write a paragraph that spells out the differences.

For this activity, you can begin your research with the U.S. Department of Labor's *Occupational Outlook Handbook*. (See the link on the textbook web site.) Remember that the audience for your paragraph is students who are deciding which path to pursue.

Human, Personal, and Public Service

As a communications specialist in the Food Safety Division of your state's Agriculture Department, you help educate the public about food safety issues. Lately you find that people have been increasingly worried about *E. coli* and *Salmonella*, but they remain confused about how these bacteria get into food and what illnesses they can cause.

Write a comparison/contrast paragraph in which you discuss the similarities and differences between these types of bacteria. By entering "food safety" in a search engine, you can find many online sources of information. Be sure to discuss:

- Ways the bacteria contaminate people's food.
- Symptoms of infection with these bacteria.

Business and Marketing

Pretend that you are Leona Bryant from the "On the Job" scenario at the beginning of this chapter. Leona, as you may remember, was researching new vehicles for her company's appliance-repair technicians. She was deciding between minivans and SUVs.

Assume that Leona has narrowed her search to two minivans.

Playing the part of Leona, choose two models to compare and contrast. Then select one of these two to recommend to your supervisor. Write a comparison/contrast paragraph to justify your choice.

(*Hint:* Many online sites offer information about new vehicles, and some even offer comparative analyses. See the links on the textbook web site.)

Science and Technology

Your company, Advanced Optics, specializes in polycarbonate lenses for eyeglasses. As part of a brochure for your products, you need to distinguish between polycarbonate and more traditional types of plastic. Write a paragraph contrasting the two materials.

For your research, try entering "polycarbonate + eyeglass" in a search engine. Look for the key qualities that make this material different from and superior to ordinary plastics.

Environment and Natural Resources

A customer at your tree farm in Massachusetts wants to plant six trees at the edge of her property along a busy highway. She expects the trees to provide a privacy screen in summer and to enhance the property's appearance.

When she comes to you for advice, she says she is considering two trees:

- Sugar maples (scientific name *Acer saccharum*)
- Red oaks (scientific name *Quercus rubra*)

Your job is to advise her about the suitability of these trees and recommend one of them.

Write a paragraph comparing and contrasting the two species. Many tree books and online sources can provide research information. Remember, though, to focus on your customer's particular needs.

(*Hint:* Notice that the customer plans to put the trees by a highway. In the winter in Massachusetts, the roads are salted. Which type of tree better tolerates road salt? On the Web, search for each of the scientific names with the word *salt*.)

If these trees are not common to your region of the country, you may choose two other varieties and change the customer's specifications as necessary.

9

Classification: Paragraphs that Assign Subjects to Categories

IN THIS CHAPTER YOU WILL LEARN TO:

- **Break down complicated material into units.**

- **Define classification subgroups.**

- **Decide when a classification paragraph is needed.**

- **Use transitional expressions and details.**

Using *Classification* in Your Writing

Career Path	Sample Career	Use for Classification Writing	Example of Writing That Uses Classification
Communication and the Arts	Art director	Telling designers which fonts are acceptable to use	Designers may choose from several types of fonts, depending on the media in which they are working: For print, use a sans serif or serif font no smaller in size than 9 point; for the Web, use sans serif only. It should be no smaller than 10 point. For presentations, use sans serif no smaller than 12 point.
Health and Medicine	Nurse manager	Instructing nurses on preparing a patient for an invasive procedure	The amount of prep differs and is based on the patient's age: Allow 10 minutes for prepping an adult, 15 minutes for prepping a child or an adolescent, and 30 minutes for prepping a toddler.
Human, Personal, and Public Service	Police officer	Drafting an incident report	The incident involved boys in three age groups: two are under 16; four are between 16 and 18; and two are over the age of 18. I telephoned the parents of the minors. I then took statements from the 18-year-olds.
Business and Marketing	Music merchandiser	Instructing a distributor about how to contact company reps	The new staff is organized by music style. For new rock releases, contact Rich Masio. For new classical releases, contact John Richards. For children's music, contact Julie Lawrence. For jazz and all other genres, contact me personally.
Science and Technology	Design engineer	Requesting more time for research and development	Test results varied based on the subject's mechanical knowledge and skills: While test subjects with advanced mechanical abilities had little difficulty with the assembly, intermediate users had great difficulty; and all of the beginners gave up in frustration.
Environment and Natural Resources	Farm manager	Detailing the problems with an order that arrived from a supplier	Three types of feed were missing from the order: ten 50-pound bags of goat feed, two 50-pound bags of rabbit chow, and one 50-pound bag of pig feed. Everything else arrived safely.

ON THE JOB

Health Benefits

Until recently, Human Resources Manager Bob Bond believed that the new health benefits at Carroll Park Marketing would improve retention and attract talented job candidates. But the new programs—including a weight-loss class, a smoking cessation program, a workshop on managing high blood pressure, and an "Ask a Registered Nurse" hotline—have drawn little interest.

To learn why so few employees were taking advantage of the new benefits, Bob put together an informal focus group of several people. Surprisingly, he discovered that most workers didn't know about the benefits because the information was buried in the 100-page booklet outlining the company's health plan.

Employees described the booklet as "overwhelming" and "impossible to read." So Bob decided to develop a short, easy-to-read brochure that would outline the new programs and describe the benefits to employees.

<u>Employees can be classified according to their health</u>[1]: Some are in excellent health; others require frequent medical care because of chronic health conditions; and others are of average health. Depending on which group you are in, you could save up to $2,000 this year by taking advantage of the new health programs.

<u>Employees in excellent health: Did you know that you are entitled to health-club reimbursement?</u>[2] This is an excellent benefit, especially for our healthy employees, 25 percent of whom work out at a gym three times a week. In addition, <u>we offer a variety of healthy living clinics</u>[2].

<u>Employees with chronic medical issues</u>[3]: Are you aware that <u>each week we post a price list from several local pharmacies</u> of the most commonly prescribed drugs? Our employees with chronic medical problems—those who are most likely to take advantage of their prescription drug benefits—can save up to 35 percent on drug purchases by checking the list before refilling a prescription.

<u>Employees of average health: We also sponsor smoking cessation clinics, weight-loss classes, disease management seminars, a nursing hotline, and nutrition courses</u>[4]. These programs work, but only when people participate.

For information on how the new benefits can save you money and improve your life, contact Bob Bond at extension 0882.

By dividing the benefits into three sections, Bob clarified the information for his readers. In this chapter, you will learn how to organize lengthy paragraph information into relevant units your readers will understand.

Understanding Classification

Classification means to arrange topics—items, places, ideas, or people—into categories. That is what Bob did in his introductory paragraph when he arranged employees into groups. By dividing employees into three groups based on their health, he was able to communicate clearly and effectively about his company's benefits.

Classification paragraphs usually divide topics into more than two categories. That distinguishes them from compare-and-contrast paragraphs, which divide items into two categories, as you learned in Chapter 8.

In this chapter, you will use the terms *categories* and *classifications* interchangeably. In a classification paragraph:

- The topic sentence states two things: what you will classify and how you will classify it, also known as the "organizing principle."
- Subgroups and examples help define your categories.
- Transitional expressions guide the reader from category to category.
- Follow-up sentences express an opinion or make a recommendation about what you classified.

Can you see how Bob's paragraph about his company's benefits follows this pattern? Below is Bob's outline for the paragraph. Compare the outline to his actual paragraph.

1. Main communication points
Employees can be divided into groups based on their health. Each group has different needs. All employees can lower their medical expenses this year by taking advantage of the new health benefit programs. There's something for everyone.

2. Employees in excellent health
- Health-club reimbursement
- Healthy living clinics

3. Employees with chronic medical issues
- Pharmacy price list posting each week
- Prescription savings up to 35%

4. Employees of average health
- Smoking cessation clinics
- Weight loss classes
- Disease management classes
- Nursing hotline
- Nutrition courses

SELF-ASSESSMENT 9

When I need to break down complicated material into categories so that it is easily understood, I can:

	Usually	Sometimes	Never
Describe what I'm going to classify.	❑	❑	❑
State how I'll classify it.	❑	❑	❑
Use transitional expressions to help writing flow.	❑	❑	❑
Select appropriate subgroups and relevent examples	❑	❑	❑
Follow up with a strong conclusion, recommendation, or position.	❑	❑	❑

If you checked "Sometimes" or "Never" for any of the items, this chapter will help you improve your skills. Even if you checked "Usually" in every instance, you will learn more about writing paragraphs that use classification.

The Topic Sentence

As you have learned, a topic sentence should state one main point. However, in a classification paragraph, the topic sentence says two things: (1) who or what you are going to classify and (2) how you are going to classify it (your organizing principle).

Certain words and phrases often appear in topic sentences for classification paragraphs. These words and phrases include *categories, divisions, groups, kinds, numbers, according to, classified as,* and *others include.* Consider the following topic sentences.

(A) Incomplete	The white clothing and the light and dark clothing get washed separately.
(B) Weak	Laundry gets sorted into piles; then it gets washed in hot, warm, or cold water according to color.
(C) Good	Laundry should be sorted into three piles according to color: Whites will be washed in hot water; light colors will be washed in warm water, and dark colors will be washed separately in warm water.

Example (C) is the best alternative because it begins by stating what will be classified (laundry) and how it will be classified (according to color). It also uses the word *sorted* to indicate that a classification is coming up.

- Example (A) doesn't indicate a classification.
- Example (B) says what will be classified, but it doesn't explain how it will be classified.

did you ever ?

- Say that you enjoy all types of music except for two or three? "I listen to everything except country and classical."

- Visit a museum where the objects are arranged in specific ways, such as eighteenth-century European painting, abstract expressionism, or Asian art?

- Ask a server what kinds of pies were available?

Each of these examples involves classification—breaking things down into smaller units. With a little practice, you'll be able to write concise, easy-to-understand classification paragraphs.

ACTIVITY 9.1 For each of the topics in the following list, write a topic sentence that communicates what people, places, or things you will classify. The first item has been completed for you.

1. physical fitness

   <u>Most people who exercise can be divided into three groups according</u>
   <u>to the reason they give for exercising: Some want to build muscles;</u>
   <u>some want to lose weight; and some want to improve their</u>
   <u>cardiovascular health.</u>

2. my favorite pets

   _____

   _____

   _____

3. classes I liked and disliked in high school

   _____

   _____

   _____

4. the kinds of movies that are made in Hollywood

   _____

   _____

   _____

5. restaurants in my neighborhood

   _____

   _____

   _____

6. people and their hobbies

   _____

   _____

   _____

WRITING WORKSHOP

When to Use a Colon

Often, the topic sentence of a classification paragraph contains a colon [:] to signal that more is to come. A colon is also used to introduce the classification categories. Any time a colon is used, it may be followed by a complete sentence or by a phrase. The first word after a colon should be capitalized if it begins a complete sentence. The first word should not be capitalized if it is part of a phrase.

(A) Complete Sentence   At Blaise Containers, Inc., we offer three types of leave of absence: Employees may elect medical, personal, or educational leaves.

(B) Phrase   At the factory, we watched the workers manufacture three kinds of vehicles: trucks, cars, and vans.

Defining Subgroups

After stating what you will be classifying and how you will be classifying it, you should name the subgroups you have chosen for classification. By identifying the subgroups, you give the reader a clear indication of what to expect in the material ahead. In essence, you are saying to the reader, "Here is what I am going to be writing about, so watch for it in the sentences you are about to read."

Subgroups may be classified in any way that will make sense to the reader. Before beginning to classify, take a few minutes to think of the category names that will help the reader understand what you are writing.

Here is an example.

Three types of automobiles are on the market today based on how the car is manufactured: <u>American-made by a U.S. manufacturer, imported from a foreign manufacturer, or made in the United States by a foreign manufacturer.</u>

ACTIVITY 9.2   For each of the following topic sentences, write a sentence or phrase that introduces the categories you will use to break down your topic. The first example has been completed for you.

1. People of different religions celebrate different holidays:

   Christians celebrate Christmas. Other holidays on the Christian calandar are Easter and the Epiphany. In Judaism, Rosh Hashananh is an important holiday. Other Jewish holidays include Chanukah and Passover. For Muslims, Ramadan is a major holiday. Other Muslim holidays are Hijrah and Eid.

2. Students who completed the course received one of three letter grades, depending on their scores:

   _____

   _____

   _____

3. There are three ways to recruit new customer service representatives, depending on how much money we want to spend on the search:

   _____

   _____

   _____

4. Almost all of the employees who elected to use the company's health insurance plan fall into one of three age groups:

   _____

   _____

   _____

5. Students can be classified by how many years they have been attending college:

   _____

   _____

When to Use a Classification Paragraph

When should you write a paragraph that breaks down information into easy-to-grasp classification units? When should you supply examples and illustrations, comparisons, and other writing techniques instead? Consider the examples below from a training manual for entry-level bank employees.

(A) Not Classified

Young adults (age 20-30), middle-aged people (age 40-50), and senior individuals (age 60 +) have different attitudes about saving money, making investments, paying into a retirement account, and managing consumer debt. Low-interest credit cards, home equity lines of credit, investment opportunities, and student loans are available to all.

(B) Classified

Banking needs often change according to a person's age group: People in their twenties and thirties often seek loans and credit cards. Those in their forties, fifties, and sixties tend to make investments, use home equity lines of credit, and save for retirement. Others, those in their seventies, and eighties, tend to save their money in case they need it unexpectedly.

Example (A) is grammatically correct, and it does contain information about categories. But the writer fails to classify the information into an easy-to-understand paragraph. Example (B), on the other hand, states what will be classified (banking needs) and how it will be classified (by customer age group). Bank employees reading these paragraphs would find that Example (B) helps them understand more about the bank's customers.

In summary, a classification paragraph communicates by dividing something big into smaller units. You should write a classification paragraph when the best way to convey your message is to break down the subject matter into several categories or subgroups.

The units can be divided in any way that will make the reader understand more clearly what the writer is trying to say. "Will this make sense to the reader?" is a good measurement to use when deciding on categories.

Classifying items into easy-to-understand units will give readers a clear understanding of the material.

ACTIVITY 9.3 Each of the examples below contains information for a classification paragraph and a specific reader. On the blank lines, write an appropriate topic sentence. The first example has been completed for you.

1. Without a classification system, it would be nearly impossible for a customer to find a particular nonfiction title in a bookstore. (customer)

   <u>Nonfiction may be classified according to topics such as history,</u>
   <u>religion and spirituality, cooking, art, geography, psychology, and</u>
   <u>business.</u>

2. The Powell Park Bank offers credit cards to college students. Each student's credit limit will depend on how much money the student places in a Powell Park checking account. For every $100 in the account, the student gets $1,000 in credit. The minimum credit limit on this type of card is $1,000. The maximum is $5,000. (college students)

   _____

   _____

   _____

   _____

   _____

3. Beverage manufacturers have three ways of processing fruit juice so it is fresh when it reaches the consumer's home. One process enables manufacturers to can or bottle fresh juice in an airtight container. Juice can also be frozen as a concentrate, or it can be freeze-dried to achieve a longer life. (consumer)

   _____

   _____

   _____

   _____

   _____

4. If you are shopping for a pet dog, the first thing you should know is that dogs come in three sizes. (potential dog owners)

   _____

   _____

   _____

   _____

Providing Examples

After stating what you will classify and how you will classify it, you may want to give a concrete example to help the reader better understand an idea. Consider the sentences below about music on the radio.

> Rock music may be divided three ways, based on the style of music: classic rock, modern rock, and alternative rock.

Next is a transitional sentence that narrows the classifications and provides a concrete example.

> If you like The Beatles, the Beach Boys, or ZZ Top, you'll like the local classic rock station.

Finally, the writer includes a follow-up—an opinion about the items that have been classified.

> This way of looking at local radio stations helps me recommend stations based on my friends' tastes in music.

ACTIVITY 9.4   The paragraph below from an employee handbook shows how a customer service department is broken down by job categories. You should be able to recognize the topic sentence, the categories, the subgroups, the supporting examples, and the follow-up sentence. After you read the paragraph, answer questions 1 through 4.

> The Customer Service Department at Global Initiatives has five salary ranges, depending on the job title: Customer Service Representative (CSR) Trainees are entry-level employees. Entry-level employees start at minimum wage. CSR Level I employees are at the next salary level. Typically, a Trainee will obtain a CSR I designation after completing three weeks of training. The next level is CSR II. The CSR II's earn a higher salary level than the CSR I's. They also help train new employees. Finally, CSR Supervisors I and CSR Supervisors II are at the highest and second highest salary levels. They are responsible for training, scheduling, and monitoring CSRs. This method of organizing salary scales provides a clearer understanding of pay ranges for both employees and managers.

1. Name the categories in the paragraph. (*Hint:* There are four.)

   _____

   _____

   _____

   _____

   _____

   _____

2. List an example for each category. Describe why the example is relevant.

   _____

   _____

   _____

   _____

   _____

   _____

   _____

3. Name the subgroups of supervisors. What is the purpose of a subgroup in this paragraph?

   _____

   _____

   _____

   _____

   _____

   _____

4. Does the writer include a follow-up sentence in the paragraph? If so, what is it and why is it there?

   _____

   _____

   _____

   _____

   _____

WRITING WORKSHOP

Classification and "Flow"

Good writing for classification seems to flow naturally and makes reading easy. To assure that your classification writing flows, you need to do some planning.

Good writers put their categories in a logical order. In Activity 9.4, for example, the jobs are listed from entry level to supervisor—from the bottom up. The writer might have chosen another way to introduce the jobs: from the top down. But most writers wouldn't begin with CSR Supervisors I and II, then CSR II and I, and then CSR Trainee.

A classification system should be clear and consistent. In Activity 9.4, each job title is described so the reader will understand the difference between one category and another. Another classification is shown below.

Poor Classification System

At the museum, paintings by Renoir are in the main gallery with the Monets and Cezannes. The six side galleries house other artists.

Good Classification System

The museum has a main gallery and six side galleries: The main gallery has paintings by Renoir, Monet, and Cezanne. The side galleries feature works by other artists.

The first example, although grammatically correct, doesn't show a clear plan for classifying the art galleries. In the second example, the classification system describes the galleries. The topics flow from general to specific in a logical sequence: *Museum → Galleries → Paintings*.

Transitional words and phrases should be used to move from one category to another. Common transitional expressions in classification paragraphs include these:

the first type	more types of
another type	depending on
a second kind	other kinds of
a third category	more genres include
in addition	what's more

SUMMARY FOR CAREER WRITING

❏ Classification means breaking things down into categories and sorting them into groups.

❏ In a classification paragraph, the topic sentence states two things: who or what you are going to classify and how you are going to classify it.

❏ Subgroups and examples are used to help define and narrow the categories.

❏ Categories and subgroups should be relevant to your readers. There may be several ways to classify a topic. The categories, subgroups, and examples you choose should be based on what you believe you need to know.

❏ Transitional expressions help you get from one category to the next and improve the flow of your writing.

❏ Follow-up sentences generally state a recommendation, an opinion, or a conclusion.

Practicing Your Skills

Now that you understand what a classification paragraph is, here's an opportunity to put your knowledge to the test.

Practice 1

The following paragraph was written by a career counselor. She is describing three styles of resumes used by job applicants.

 Three basic styles of professional resumes are popular: chronological, functional, and a combination of each. The style you use for your resume will depend on your profession and experience. For example, if you are an experienced manager seeking a position, you should use a chronological resume. A chronological resume highlights your work experience, starting with your current job. However, if you haven't worked for a while or your current job doesn't show management experience, you should consider using a functional resume. A functional resume highlights your capabilities, not your most recent experience. Futher, a functional resume presents your strengths, such as computer knowledge or excellent communication skills. Finally, a combination resume combines the chronological and functional approaches. It highlights both the skill set of a job candidate and past work experience. Start by determining what will sell you—your experience or your capabilities. When you decide which style of resume to use, you will have passed one hurdle of job shopping.

The Topic Sentence

1. Underline the topic sentence in this paragraph.

Examples

2. What is your opinion of the categories: chronological resume, functional resume, and combination resume?

_____

_____

Transitional Phrases and Flow

3. Circle the words or phrases that help the writing flow. They also may link categories to opinions or ideas in a way that makes the paragraph easy to read.

PRACTICE 2

The next classification paragraph was written for a retail store's company handbook. It describes the various ways the store has of communicating with its hundreds of customers.

Jim Brown Shoes has three ways of communicating with customers about in-store promotions based on how much money a customer spent at Jim Brown in the past year: Customers who spent more than $1,000 receive a monthly phone call from a personal shopper. The personal shopper tells the customer about new clothing lines available, fashion trends of interest, and special deals. In addition, the personal shopper makes a special recommendation based on the customer's buying habits and tastes. Because we at Jim Brown value our highest-spending customers, we offer them the most personalized service. Of course, this service is optional for the customer. Not all customers want us to contact them by telephone. The next level of communication is for customers who spent $500 to $999 at Jim Brown in the past year. These customers receive a bimonthly newsletter dedicated to fashion ideas, store events, and promotions. Sometimes the newsletters include coupons for store discounts. Finally, customers who spent less than $500 in the past year receive a bimonthly postcard notifying them of sales and promotions. No matter how much money customers spend, they will receive a communication about in-store promotions.

The Topic Sentence

1. What is being classified? How is it being classified?

_____

Categories

2. Why does the writer divide customers by how much they spend? Why not by their age, gender, geographical location, or by some other factor?

_____

_____

_____

Transitional Phrases and Flow

3. What transitions does the writer use to make the paragraph flow? Identify the transitional words, phrases, and sentences in the paragraph by circling each.

_____

APPLYING YOUR SKILLS

Now you will write a classification paragraph of your own. To do this, you must work through the stages of the writing process that you learned in Chapter 2: prewriting, writing, revising, and editing. Remember to use a separate sheet of paper or a word processing file at each stage. Save every version of your writing.

Prewriting

Begin by selecting a topic and deciding how you will organize your paragraph. Here are some examples.

Topic	Organizing Principle
sports	men's and women's pro sports
cooking	basic food groups
cash	denominations of paper money

Once you have identified your topic and your organizing principle, think about what categories you should use. If you want to classify music, how will you do it? By style? By time period? By composer? The classification will depend on what you want to communicate about music. Remember, the topic sentence of a classification paragraph should state what you will classify and how you will classify it.

If you are writing a paragraph about rock music, don't assume that your audience knows the difference between types of rock music, for example, classic rock and alternative rock. If that difference is important in conveying your idea, you should provide examples. If the difference between classic rock and alternative rock is *not* important in conveying your idea, you may have misclassified your subject.

When you know what you will be classifying and how you will be classifying it, think of a few good examples of your categories. You should have at least three examples that are clearly supportive, relevant, and specific. Now outline your paragraph in a form like this:

Topic Sentence _____

_____

category 1 _____

example 1 _____

category 2 _____

example 2 _____

category 3 _____

example 3 _____

Writing

Now it is time to write the first draft of your paragraph. Word your topic sentence precisely and develop your categories clearly. Does your topic sentence require a colon to introduce your categories? Should the first word after the colon be capitalized or written in lower case?

Use transitional expressions to get from one category to the next and to help make your paragraph flow. Include a follow-up sentence—a conclusion, an opinion, or a recommendation.

Revising

Read through your first draft. Use the following checklist of questions to make sure you have revised thoroughly.

❑ Does the topic sentence state what you will classify and how you will classify it?

❑ Did you break down the classifications into categories and subgroups?

❑ Are all of the categories and subgroups relevant to your main point?

❑ Do the transitional expressions help the paragraph flow from category to category?

❑ Do your examples support the topic sentence?

❑ Do your examples explain what the reader may not know about your categories?

After you have made revisions, put the draft away for a while and reread it when it is fresh. Then write a second draft. If you are writing on paper, use a clean sheet. If you are writing on a computer, retype the paragraph from the beginning.

Follow the same process with your second draft. Review and revise it thoroughly. If necessary, write a third draft. Does it flow? Does it sound right? Try reading your paragraph aloud.

Editing

Review your paragraph for errors in grammar, spelling, word use, punctuation, and capitalization. If you are using a computer, run the spell checker and grammar checker, but do not count on these to find every error.

Remember, if you mean to type "I like Sam" but by accident you type "I lake Sam," you won't see an error message. Spelling and grammar checks are useful tools, but they are no substitute for the human eye. After running your spelling and grammar checks, proofread your paragraph one final time.

If possible, put the draft away overnight. In the morning, approach your paragraph as though you were seeing it for the first time. You may be surprised by the small, easy-to-miss errors that slip by when you are thinking about bigger issues.

WRITING FOR YOUR CAREER

This section presents a writing project for each of the six career pathways. Choose one that appeals to you and use your new skills to write a classification paragraph on the subject.

When the project description refers you to the textbook web site, go to http://humphrey.swlearning.com and click on the Links tab. Look for Chapter 9, "Writing for Your Career." There you will find direct links to helpful web references.

Communication and the Arts

Imagine that you are the stage manager for a professional theater company. Your job is to make sure that the lights and curtain go up and down on cue and that all of the actors' props are in the proper place. You make sure that the changes to the set happen quickly during intermission and that the actors are in their proper place at show time. In short, you run the entire show from backstage.

Now imagine that you have been asked to participate in a college job fair. All attending theater majors will receive a small booklet about career opportunities in the theater.

You have been asked to contribute an essay about the responsibilities of a stage manager. Write a paragraph in which the topic sentence describes a stage manager's duties before, during, and after the show. To write this paragraph, you may need to do some research on the Internet. If you need some help online, go to the textbook web site and locate the instructions for Chapter 9, Communications and the Arts.

Health and Medicine

You are a nurse-manager at Rocky Beach Memorial Hospital. Not only is your hospital in the Sunbelt, but Rocky Beach is a college town. That means each spring you treat a lot of reckless, overly enthusiastic students for serious cases of sunburn and heatstroke.

This year the hospital and the university are working together to alert students to the dangers of overexposure to the sun. Your department has been asked to write a section of a pamphlet. Your assignment: Research all of the different methods of prevention and draft a summary to the full committee that is editing the pamphlet.

Write a classification paragraph that describes several methods of preventing overexposure to the sun. Examples to consider include using sunscreen, wearing proper clothing, wearing a cap or hat, and staying indoors during certain hours. For help with the content, go to the textbook web site and look for Chapter 9, Health and Medicine.

Human, Personal, and Public Service

Picture this: You are a Youth Services Worker who supervises 14 juvenile offenders at the Daniel Ferber Detention Center in Philadelphia. You write daily activity logs and incident reports. At the end of the week, you file a weekly summary.

Write a one-paragraph weekly summary that categorizes incidents based on degree of severity. (Coming home 20 minutes after curfew isn't as severe as getting into a fight. Showing disrespect to a staff member is somewhere in between.)

Business and Marketing

You own and operate a coffee shop. Early each morning you roast the beans so you have the freshest-tasting coffee in town. Write an introductory paragraph for your menu that introduces customers to your wonderful blends of coffees from around the world.

How should you categorize coffee? By region? By flavor? By price? By caffeine content? You decide. Remember, your readers are customers who enjoy coffee. Make your categories, subgroups, examples, and follow-up relevant to them.

For help with the content, go to the textbook web site and look for Chapter 9, Business and Marketing.

Science and Technology

As an industrial designer, you have been developing new packaging for Barry's Fresh Pasta Company products. Tomorrow your firm will be making a presentation to the client. Before Barry's CEO looks at the package designs, your manager wants you to explain the overall look and feel of the new pasta packaging.

Some of the sample boxes are bigger than others, although each holds one pound of pasta. The boxes are designed according to the shape of the pasta.

Write an introductory paragraph in which you classify pasta by size. For help with the content, go to the textbook web site and look for Chapter 9, Science and Technology.

Environment and Natural Resources

Imagine that you run a small family-owned farm and petting zoo. All of the animals at your zoo may be handled by children. Your animals are exotic, interesting, and safe.

You decide to write a letter to send to local elementary schools in your town. The letter will try to get teachers to bring their classes to the petting zoo. You want to impress the teachers with a description of the activities you offer to students. Write a classification paragraph describing the benefits of visiting your zoo. Create any details you need.

Process:

Paragraphs That Explain Steps in a Sequence

© Getty Images/PhotoDisc

© Getty Images/PhotoDisc

IN THIS CHAPTER YOU WILL LEARN TO:

- Develop paragraphs that explain a process.

- Create interest in a process topic.

- Describe the steps of a process in detail.

- Unify a process paragraph.

Explaining *Processes* in Writing for Your Career

Career Path	Sample Career	Use for Process Writing	Example of Process Writing
Communication and the Arts	Technical writer for a software company	Developing a user's manual for a new software program	Morphing software can blend together the faces of expectant parents so they can picture the face of their child. To use MorphVision 3.0, you first create a number of morphing layers. Then you superimpose these layers to achieve a desired effect. Finally, you manipulate a number of markers to edit the final image.
Health and Medicine	Hospital administrator	Planning an in-service training program for nurses	In this class, you will learn how to identify the stages of acute stress disorder a patient may undergo: (a) lack of emotional response, (b) reduced awareness of his or her environment, and (c) sense of unreality.
Human, Personal, and Public Service	Chef at a residential care facility	Instructing new chefs how to follow a recipe	Scrunchy Sweet & Sour Chicken is an easy-to-make meal that will add variety to your weekly menu. First, blend together two egg yolks, one tablespoon water, and two tablespoons cornstarch. Then toss cubes of skinless, boneless chicken into the cornstarch mixture. Finally, deep-fry the chicken in two inches of oil.
Business and Marketing	Audio sales representative	Designing a flyer to be distributed to customers explaining surround sound	Surround sound is produced by an A/V receiver that distributes audio signals to four to six separate speakers, depending on the format. Dolby Pro-Logic, for instance, uses two front speakers, two rear speakers, and one central speaker.
Science and Technology	Computer systems analyst	Informing a client how to create a new domain name	To establish a new domain, you must fill out a form with a company that handles domain names. An example of a company that does this is networksolutions.com. This company will then post an "under construction" page. Once the .com name server acknowledges the new IP address, web surfers will be able to access your new page.
Environment and Natural Resources	Oceanographer	Describing how a new sea-life center must set up a proper oceanarium for dolphins	First, you must ensure good water quality. Salt content of the oceanarium should approximate the 3.5 percent found in seawater. Next, the water must be kept clean through the installation of a water purification plant. Finally, you must add ocean chemicals, such as calcium, magnesium, and zinc.

ON THE JOB

Lasik Surgery

Laser eye surgery, known as Lasik, is becoming a common eye operation. Optometrist Adam Duvall hopes to ease his patients' fears about surgically tampering with their eyes with a brochure he has written. Here is the opening paragraph of the brochure.

> Nearly painless Lasik surgery should dramatically improve your eyesight. What can you expect before, during, and after Lasik surgery? First of all, you can leave your suitcase behind. As an outpatient procedure, Lasik lets you return home shortly after the operation. The actual surgery lasts only about a minute. You will be awake the whole time, after your eyes have been anesthetized with medicated drops. A restraining device will be placed over your eye to make sure your eyelids stay open. In addition, a suction ring will pressurize your eye so the surgeon can cut a flap in your cornea. This incision is made with a special instrument that cuts and folds back a thin, circular layer of the cornea. In fact, the flap is so thin that you won't even see it. Now the laser enters the picture. The surgeon will use a computer to adjust the laser for your prescription. You will be asked to look at a target light as the laser reshapes your cornea. A special tracking device follows your eye even if it moves. At this point, the laser will precisely and painlessly remove the corneal tissue. Although this sounds dangerous, the entire operation is routine. The original flap is then put back in place, covering the area where the corneal tissue was removed. After a short rest, you will be allowed to go home. However, someone else must drive you. You will be asked to relax and avoid strenuous activity for up to a week to avoid trauma to the eye. Medication will be prescribed for postoperative pain, but most patients feel only mild discomfort. As you can see, Lasik surgery is a safe, trauma-free procedure that will let you say good-bye to glasses and contact lenses.

Would Adam's paragraph help his patients feel more at ease with the operation? If so, he has achieved his purpose. In this chapter, like Adam, you will learn how to develop a process paragraph.

Explaining a Process

Process paragraphs come in two varieties: how-to and how-it-is-done. A how-to paragraph provides a series of hands-on steps that readers can carry out themselves. Examples of how-to topics include setting up a saltwater aquarium and compressing computer files. In contrast, a how-it-is-done paragraph deepens the readers' understanding of a process that they themselves may not carry out. How-it-is-done topics include how airline pilots navigate wind shear and how Alzheimer's progresses over time.

Adam Duvall's paragraph about Lasik eye surgery is a how-it-is-done paragraph. Here is how he organized his paragraph.

1. Topic sentence: Lasik surgery helps a patient achieve better eyesight.

2. Question: He asks a question to provide a transition and a preview. Now he is ready to explain the procedure using a chronological, or time-sequence, approach.

SELF-ASSESSMENT 10

When I need to write a process paragraph, I can:

	Usually	Sometimes	Never
Express the importance or value of a procedure.	☐	☐	☐
Organize the steps of a procedure in chronological order.	☐	☐	☐
Give extra information about the process or offer troubleshooting advice.	☐	☐	☐
Explain how and why a process unfolds.	☐	☐	☐
Assess the knowledge level of my readers regarding the process.	☐	☐	☐

If you checked "Sometimes" or "Never" for any of the items, this chapter will help you improve your skills. Even if you checked "Usually" in every instance, you will learn more about explaining a process.

3. Before surgery: The eye is anesthetized, a restraint is placed on the eye, and a suction ring pressurizes the eye. Then the surgeon folds back a flap of the cornea.

4. During surgery: The patient's eye focuses on a target light as the laser reshapes the cornea. A tracking device keeps eye movements in check.

5. After surgery: The patient undergoes a short rest, takes medication for mild pain, and returns home. The patient is encouraged to relax for a week.

To help move his reader through the paragraph more easily, Adam uses a series of transitions: *first of all, in addition, in fact, at this point, after,* and *as you can see.* He also provides enough details so the reader can easily comprehend each stage of the procedure.

Explaining a process is a common type of writing in business and industry. Procedural guidelines, operations manuals, and instruction booklets, for example, outline the series of steps employees need to follow to perform parts of their job.

In fact, this chapter presents a series of how-to lessons and activities to help you write your own process paragraphs. Key skills include developing a topic sentence and adding sufficient details so the reader develops a clear understanding of the process you are describing.

Developing a How-to Paragraph

As noted earlier, a how-to paragraph gives the readers a series of instructions for carrying out a procedure. The easiest way to structure a how-to paragraph is to use a step-by-step approach. Consider the following example from a travel agent's brochure.

You don't have to be Henry David Thoreau to enjoy a remote cabin with family or friends. To ensure a great outdoor experience, keep a few simple tips in mind. (1) <u>First, surf the Internet.</u> Keywords should include the desired state and area, as well as the name of the nearest state park or national forest. Plug in words such as *cabin, cottage,* or *bed and breakfast,* depending on the type of facility desired. Also, keep your eye out for cost-saving coupons. (2) <u>Next, call the facility before making a reservation.</u> Speak with someone in person. Have a checklist of questions about amenities and features. Do you need a hot tub or spa? Confirm the number of bedrooms. What appliances does the cabin have? Or will you really be roughing it? (3) <u>Finally, know the directions.</u> If driving, make sure you know the route. Nothing can slow down a weekend getaway more than rush-hour traffic or unanticipated detours. When you measure your vacation by days, not weeks, every hour counts. Just because a weekend getaway seems like a minimal vacation doesn't mean you should make minimal plans. A little extra preparation can make all the difference between a weekend to remember and another ordinary weekend.

In this paragraph, three separate steps are discussed. Each step has been numbered and underlined. Note that the paragraph begins with a topic sentence expressing the main idea about weekend excursions. Transitions are used to indicate the steps involved: *first, next,* and *finally.* The paragraph ends with a closing remark that recaps the main idea.

did you ever?

- Show a friend how to operate a technical device, such as a handheld organizer, scanner, or digital camera?

- Demonstrate how to cook a favorite easy-to-fix meal, beginning with the ingredients and ending with the garnishes?

- Describe how a combustion engine works or how a computer server provides data?

Each of these examples requires outlining the steps of a process to increase your listener's understanding. Explaining a process is a central purpose of everyday communication.

Writing a How-It-Is-Done Paragraph

A how-it-is-done paragraph explains how a process unfolds. The process may be something the reader cannot perform. Perhaps the procedure can be performed only by a specialist—for example, gene splicing. Or the process may be something that occurs in nature, such as the eruption of a volcano. Take a look at the following example.

Recent telescopic observations suggest that planets form more quickly than previously thought, perhaps in 3 million years, a mere heartbeat in cosmological terms. First, a vast cloud of interstellar dust and gas collapses due to gravity, which creates a new star. Then the dust forms a halo around the new star. As the halo begins to spin, it flattens into a thin disk. Uneven matter in the disk begins to clump together into ever-larger bodies called planetesimals or protoplanets. Close to the star, dense, rocky, metallic cores are formed, eventually becoming terrestrial-type planets, such as those found in our inner solar system. The colder, more remote outer planets retain icy cores that sweep up leftover gas, mainly hydrogen and helium. These become the giant gaseous planets, such as those found in our outer solar system. The disk continues to thin as material is gobbled up by the star and its planets. A hole forms in the disk near the star, much like that of a doughnut, and the newly formed planets circle the star within the hole. As the dust clears, a new solar system comes into view. So far, more than 100 solar systems with planets have been discovered in the past ten years, suggesting that planet formation is a common process in the universe at large.

Using a simple outline, here is how this paragraph is structured.

Topic Sentence	Planets form quickly around new stars.
Stage 1	A gas cloud collapses, forming a star.
Stage 2	The dust forms a halo around the star.
Stage 3	The halo flattens into a thin disk.
Stage 4	Matter within the disk clumps into protoplanets.
Stage 5	A hole forms in the disk within which the planets circle the star.
Closing Sentence	Planet formation is a common process in the universe.

Overall, this is a very time-consuming process! However, the goal of the paragraph is to enlighten the reader about a naturally occurring phenomenon. The reader should develop a basic understanding of forces that shaped our own planet Earth.

ACTIVITY 10.1 Think of a topic for a how-to paragraph. Select something specific, such as how to set up stereo speakers or how to design a personal web page. Use the template below to outline your paragraph as a series of steps. In each step, provide whatever detail you think is necessary. Remember that your goal for this paragraph is to help the reader perform a hands-on procedure.

Topic: _____

Step 1: _____

_____

_____

Step 2: _____

_____

_____

Step 3: _____

_____

_____

ACTIVITY 10.2 Now think of a topic for a how-it-is-done paragraph. Select a process that you already know. For instance, you may explain how U.S. Presidents are elected or how web links work. Depending on the topic, you may need to do some research. Use the template below to outline your paragraph as a series of stages. Your goal for this paragraph is to help the reader understand how a process unfolds.

Topic: _____

Stage 1:_____

_____

_____

Stage 2:_____

_____

_____

Stage 3:_____

_____

_____

Creating Interest in the Topic

The next time you visit a bookstore, note the large number of self-help books. The abundance of instructional manuals suggests that readers are eager to learn the hands-on procedures for a variety of topics. Popular how-to subjects range from computers and sports to hobbies and relationships.

When writing about a process, you must establish the importance or value of the topic. Typically, you do this at the start of a paragraph by writing a topic sentence. The sentence should attract readers who may have little initial interest in your topic. The sentence should also strengthen the positive attitude of readers desiring to learn more.

A good topic sentence of a process paragraph identifies the specific topic. In addition, it explains why a reader should learn the process in question. The topic sentence may also preview the sequence of steps involved. The complexity of the procedure may be indicated as well. Here are several pairs of topic sentences about the same subject. Each pair shows the difference between adequate and strong approaches.

Adequate	Presidents are chosen by the Electoral College.
Strong	The electoral process can overturn a popular vote for President.
Adequate	Tornadoes evolve from thunderstorms.
Strong	Updraft, vortex, and funnel cloud—how a thunderstorm produces a tornado is a simple but fascinating process.
Adequate	GPS receivers are useful devices.
Strong	GPS receivers rely on a combination of satellite hookups to pinpoint locations anywhere on Earth.

ACTIVITY 10.3 For each of the subjects below, write a specific topic sentence that expresses the significance or value of the procedure. Try creating interest by giving readers a reason to learn about the process.

1. how to perform an aerobic exercise workout

   _____

   _____

2. how to use a search engine

   _____

   _____

3. how to shop online

_____

_____

4. how the digestive system works

_____

_____

5. how electricity is generated

_____

_____

6. how to maintain a good credit rating

_____

_____

7. how to play a certain card game

_____

_____

8. how to refinish a wood surface

_____

_____

9. how advertisements lure buyers

_____

_____

10. how the heart pumps blood

_____

_____

Describing the Steps of a Process

How much detail should you go into when developing a process paragraph? If the reader already knows about the process, you can give minimal detail. A beginner, however, must be told each step in sufficient detail. Consider the following examples explaining how to create a PowerPoint® slide.

(A) Minimal Details

(1) Insert a blank slide from the drop-down menu.

(2) Add the following title: Sample Picture.

(3) Insert a .jpg file in the body of the slide.

(B) Sufficient Details

(1) Insert a blank slide into your presentation by selecting *New Slide* from the Insert menu. Then highlight the appropriate slide from the gray pop-up box and click *OK*.

(2) At the top of the slide where it says "Click to add title," left-click the mouse and type in the following: Sample Picture.

(3) Insert a .jpg file in the body of the slide by clicking *Insert*, scrolling to Picture, and choosing the From File option. Select a .jpg file from your Documents folder and click *Open*.

Example (A) is appropriate for a reader who knows PowerPoint. A beginning reader requires more information, as in Example (B). Compare the following examples from a rental car flyer explaining how to start a car in cold weather.

(C) Minimal Details

First, turn off all accessories. Then push down the accelerator pedal and hold it. Finally, turn the ignition key and ease up on the gas pedal.

(D) Sufficient Details

First, turn off all electrical accessories, such as the radio, to lessen the drain on the battery. Then depress the accelerator pedal halfway and keep it in place while starting the engine. Next, turn the ignition key for 15 seconds at a time until the engine starts. Finally, release the gas pedal gradually as the engine revs up.

The instructions in Example (C) would even be difficult for an expert driver. Example (D) does a better job of explaining each step in the sequence.

ACTIVITY 10.4 The following process paragraph is written with beginners in mind. Revise the paragraph for advanced readers by striking phrases or sentences expressing ideas that are too basic.

A tornado is a column of air rising into a thundercloud. In its early stages, a tornado may begin to form in the turbulent atmosphere near the squall line of a storm. A squall is a sudden, violent windstorm accompanied by rain, whereas, a squall line is a zone of severe weather resulting when a current of cold incoming air replaces a mass of warm air. As a column of warm air rises during a thunderstorm, it may become a vortex—technically speaking, a fluid flow of air forming a whirlpool about an invisible axis, much like an eddy in a stream of water. At first, this is seen as a funnel cloud descending out of a larger cloud. A funnel cloud is just that—a cloud shaped like a funnel, the kind you use to add oil to your car. At the center of the funnel's vortex is an area of low pressure. In general a low-pressure cell is formed if a mass of cold air surrounds a center of light, warm air. As air rushes into the low-pressure area, the inflow of winds can reach tornado strength. The cooling air within the vortex condenses into water vapor, allowing observers to trace the shape of the tornado. Water vapor is water diffused in the atmosphere. As the tornado sweeps up dirt and debris from the ground, it takes on an even more sinister and ominous appearance.

TECHNOLOGY CONNECTION

Instruction Manuals

In the workplace, you may be asked to assist with the development of an instruction manual for a special purpose. You can improve the manual's appearance by using the following Word features.

- Numbered Outline: When writing a procedure, use the numbered outline function from the Format menu. Alternate a series of numbers and letters to indicate steps and substeps.

- Manual Template: Download an instruction manual template for a greater range of formatting options, including specialized section breaks, subheads, and lists.

Unifying a Process Paragraph

Combining the relevant parts of a process paragraph is called *unifying*. To unify a paragraph, eliminate redundant or irrelevant sentences. For example, here is a sequence of steps explaining how to select a background picture for a computer monitor.

Step 1	Select *Settings* from the Start tab. Then go to the Control Panel.
Step 2	Double-click on the **Display** icon to open the Display Properties pop-up box.
Step 3	By surfing the Internet, you can find literally thousands of free background pictures.
Step 4	Click on the Background tab and select from the drop-down menu the wallpaper design that you wish to install.

In the above case, step 3 is a false step. It doesn't belong. Although it provides useful information, the sentence interrupts the sequence of steps in this procedure.

ETHICS CONNECTION

Acknowledging the Difficulty of a Procedure

Technical writers are hired to ensure that no important detail is left out when a company needs a procedure manual. However, in the writing of sales messages to customers, technical details are sometimes left out or oversimplified.

A car audio manufacturer knows that the installation of its audio system is difficult for the beginner. Yet to increase its mail-order and Internet-shopping accounts, it advertises that the system is "incredibly easy to install."

A diet plan promises astounding weight reduction in just ten days if customers drink a power aide three times a day. However, the ad fails to mention that this must be done in combination with a well-balanced diet and an exercise program. The ad also ignores research indicating that the results in test subjects are only short-term.

Businesses should be held responsible for honestly conveying information.

ACTIVITY 10.5 For each of the following paragraphs, cross out the sentence that does not explain an actual step in the process. Then arrange the remaining steps in order by writing the numerals 1 through 3 above them. In the blanks provided, rewrite the paragraph using your own writing style.

1. steps in a recipe

   Add two tablespoons of raw peanuts and continue frying for an additional 30 seconds. Stir-fry two slightly crushed cloves of garlic and two hot chili peppers for a maximum of 10 seconds. Cut down on cholesterol in your diet by cooking with vegetables. Heat a wok at a high setting for 30 seconds.

   _____

   _____

   _____

   _____

   _____

2. stages of glaucoma

   Glaucoma treatment includes pressure-lowering eye drops. High pressure eventually damages the optic nerve. Patients discover a reduction in their peripheral vision. Intraocular pressure increases to a dangerous level.

   _____

   _____

   _____

   _____

   _____

3. formation of a lightning bolt

   Electrical charges build up inside a cloud. An average lightning bolt carries an electrical current of 200 million volts. Oppositely charged particles overcome air resistance to connect and complete an electrical circuit. At the same time, particles with an opposite charge form on the ground.

   _____

   _____

   _____

   _____

   _____

WRITING WORKSHOP

Parallelism in a Series

When writing a process paragraph, you can improve the flow of your writing through parallelism. You can achieve parallelism by using the same kinds of words—nouns, verbs, or adjectives— to begin each item in the series. Here is an example of poor parallelism.

> To maintain a good credit rating, you should *pay* your bills by the deadline, *catch* up with late payments, *keep* in touch with your creditors, and *your credit report* can also be reviewed for a fee.

The first three tips begin with verbs: *pay, catch,* and *keep*. The last tip begins with a noun phrase: *your credit report*. To keep the series parallel, revise the last item so it also begins with a verb: *review*. Here is another example of a faulty series.

> You will need the following kitchen implements to prepare a pineapple-orange gelatin dessert: a *medium bowl*, an *electric mixer*, a *rubber spatula*, and *you will also need* to obtain a one-quart gelatin mold.

The first three items in the list are a series of adjectives and nouns. The final item in the list veers away from this pattern by adding a completely new sentence. To achieve parallelism, you should revise the list as follows: *medium bowl, electric mixer, rubber spatula, and one-quart gelatin mold*.

SUMMARY FOR PROCESS PARAGRAPHS

❑ There are two basic types of process paragraphs: how-to and how-it-is-done.

❑ When planning a process paragraph, use a time-sequence pattern to outline a series of steps.

❑ The topic sentence of a process paragraph should establish the value of the subject.

❑ Go into sufficient detail with your explanation of a process so your reader does not have any questions or is not confused.

PRACTICING YOUR SKILLS

Practice the skills you have learned about writing process paragraphs by completing the following activities.

PRACTICE 1

A loan officer of a bank wrote the following paragraph to help customers improve their credit rating.

 Many loan applicants don't realize that they can investigate their credit report to correct mistakes and to update the report. First, contact a credit bureau to request a copy of your report. The report will cost a minimal fee. However, if you have been denied credit, you can obtain a copy of your report for free within 30 days. Under the Fair Credit Reporting Act, a bureau is obliged to provide a written summary of your report. Most agencies, though, furnish the entire computer-generated printout that they supply to creditors. After receiving a copy of your report, you should question any item in your file that you believe is inaccurate. The burden is then placed on the credit bureau to remove an item that it cannot verify. At this point, the credit bureau must update your report to show that you are now current on payments that have been late in the past. Finally, you should request that the credit bureau send a revised copy to each of the creditors that received your report during the past six months.

Topic Sentence

1. Underline what you believe is the paragraph's topic sentence.

2. Explain the importance of this process. _____

_____

Sequence of Steps

3. Place brackets around those sentences that explain the steps of the actual procedure loan applicants can follow to correct their credit report.

4. Circle the sentences that provide extra information or insights but that do not reflect the hands-on procedure.

PRACTICE 2

The next paragraph was included in a flyer at an aquatic entertainment facility.

Clicker training uses a system of positive reinforcement to reward dolphins for carrying out a task. At first, the clicker is paired with a more tangible reward, such as a fish snack, as the dolphin performs a series of actions. The clicker method works well because dolphins, like other aquatic mammals, have a highly developed sense of hearing. Gradually the dolphin places its full attention on only those behaviors that result in a reward. Once a dolphin begins to perform an action repetitively, the trainer makes a distinctive clicking sound so the dolphin learns which action is desired. The auditory signal of the clicker tells the dolphin, "You're right!" Then the trainer combines smaller actions to get the dolphin to perform more complex and amazing tricks. Overall, what makes clicker training challenging is that trainers must take into account the individual personality of each dolphin.

Main Idea

1. Underline the statement that functions as the topic sentence of the paragraph.
2. Rephrase the topic sentence using your own words. _____
   _____

Transitions

3. Circle the transitions in the paragraph. Replace each word or phrase with a different transition of your own that works just as well. Write your choices above the original transitions.

Stages of the Process

4. Identify the steps needed to train a dolphin by writing the numbers 1 through 4 above the sentences that describe them.

Parallelism

5. Check the parallelism of the series of sentences you have marked 1 through 4. Which of the four sentences does not match the others in terms of its structure? In the space below, revise this sentence so it resembles the others.

_____

_____

_____

APPLYING YOUR SKILLS

You should now feel more prepared to write a process paragraph of your own. Develop your paragraph in stages, as follows.

Selecting a Topic

Begin with a procedure you know something about or a subject that holds your interest. For this assignment, you may write a how-to paragraph or a how-it-is-done paragraph. Note that how-it-is-done topics may require outside research. Consider the following subjects.

How-to Topics

- playing a musical instrument
- operating a technological device
- preparing for a job interview
- performing a dance step
- cooking a special recipe

How-It-Is-Done Topics

- celebration of a holiday
- formation of a hurricane
- rules for hockey or lacrosse
- development of a pearl
- manufacture of glass

Do not limit yourself to the above topics. These are provided only to give you an idea of suitable subjects for process paragraphs. If you select your own topic, make sure it is focused enough to require only a paragraph write-up. Be aware that some process topics, such as flying a jet airplane, require multiple paragraphs to inform the reader of the steps involved.

Prewriting

Once you have selected a topic, jot down as many steps of the process as occur to you. For each step, create a list of details to help the reader completely understand the process.

Consider the knowledge level of your audience. If you are writing for the beginner, you need to go into extra detail with your explanations. If addressing a more knowledgeable reader, you may wish to skip basic advice. Instead, you can offer advanced troubleshooting tips.

Outlining

The outline for a process paragraph should move through a series of steps in time-sequence order. Begin with a topic sentence that expresses the value or significance of the process. Then add the specific steps. Your outline may resemble the following format.

Topic Sentence _____

Step 1 _____

Step 2 _____

Step 3 _____

Writing

As you write the process paragraph, follow your outline as closely as possible. For a first draft, do not worry too much about punctuation and grammar. These issues can be addressed during the proofreading stage. Build the content of your paragraph while taking into account the needs of your audience. Often, you can develop a natural, conversational writing style by imagining that you are addressing a specific reader face to face.

Revising

After you complete your first draft, use the following checklist to revise your paragraph.

❑ Have you focused on a single process or procedure?

❑ Does your topic sentence express the importance of the process?

❑ Have you followed a time-sequence pattern of organization?

❑ Are there places where you backtrack or jump ahead? If so, how can you rearrange these parts of the paragraph more logically?

❑ Do you need to offer extra information in the form of precautions or advice? If so, where can this information be added without disturbing the flow of the paragraph?

❑ Can you improve the unity of your paragraph by eliminating irrelevant or redundant sentences?

❑ Is the series of steps parallel? If not, how can you adjust the structure of the series to achieve parallelism?

❑ Have you added appropriate and effective transitions?

❑ Have you checked your paragraph a final time for grammatical and punctuation problems?

Editing and Proofreading

Continue revising your process paragraph until the adjustments become more minor. Read the paragraph aloud to catch awkward or confusing spots. Put your paragraph through a final test by trying to complete the process yourself or give it to another person to read. See if he or she can perform or understand the process.

WRITING FOR YOUR CAREER

CRITICAL THINKING

Select one or more of the following scenarios and write a paragraph in response. Keep in mind the techniques for developing an effective process paragraph. For a given topic, you may wish to research relevant Internet sites. To do so, go to the web site http://humphrey.swlearning.com. Locate the instructions for Chapter 10, Writing for Your Career. Then access the web sites provided for additional information.

Communication and the Arts

Companies hire technical writers to translate technological concepts for the average reader. Often, these writers work closely with engineers, programmers, and other specialists to develop instruction manuals. Many manuals explain how to operate high-tech products, such as DVD players, A/V receivers, and cell phones.

To practice the art of technical writing, select one of the following topics:

(a) Think of a software program with which you are familiar. Write a paragraph explaining how to use the program to perform a basic function. Keep in mind the needs of a reader who has never used the software.

(b) Examine the instruction manual for a technological device you have purchased. Rewrite a section of the manual in paragraph form. Strive for a person-to-person writing style.

Health and Medicine

As an optometrist, you must know how the eye processes information. In addition, you must understand how diseases of the eye occur and progress. One disagreeable part of your job is informing a patient that he or she has contracted an eye disease. You wish to provide handouts for your patients about common eye diseases and disorders. Select one of the following eye problems: cataracts, macular degeneration, retinal detachment, or glaucoma. In a paragraph, explain how the disorder progresses over time or how the problem can be treated. To research information about eye problems, go to the textbook web site and locate the instructions for Chapter 10, Health and Medicine.

Human, Personal, and Public Service

Imagine that you are a hotel manager who oversees a chain of five hotels. Your basic duties include supervising staff and dealing with wholesalers. In addition, you must develop a system for handling customer complaints. Write a memo in paragraph form that outlines a procedure for front-desk clerks to follow in response to customer complaints. For example, you may want front-desk staff to acknowledge a complaint by repeating it to the customer. Then you may ask the clerks to write the complaint word for word. What should staff members do next? Add four additional steps that would result in a satisfied customer.

Business and Marketing

As a technical representative, you work in a department that provides information about your company's digital products. Many customers call your department with complaints about malfunctioning equipment. After talking with these customers, you realize that basic troubleshooting can solve most problems. Other customers wish to learn more about your company's product line. Mainly, they want to know how to operate a piece of equipment.

Keeping the concerns of technical representative in mind, choose one of the following:

(a) Select a digital product of your choice. For instance, think about a digital camera, DVD player, camcorder, or widescreen TV. Then write a troubleshooting guide in the form of a paragraph. You should explain how to correct common problems in the operation of the item.

(b) Select one of the items listed above and write a paragraph to be added to your company's web site. In this case, explain in detail how to operate one feature of the product.

Science and Technology

Television weather reporters explain weather patterns based on the research of meteorologists. The next time you watch the weather portion of the news, jot down a few notes about the development of the day's weather. You may want to choose a day when something unusual is building on the horizon. Maybe a thunderstorm is heading your way. Or perhaps a period of drought is lingering.

Write a paragraph summary of the weather forecast. Or write a paragraph explanation of a weather phenomenon, such as a thunderstorm or waterspout. In either case, focus on the stages of development. Be as detailed as possible. If you do outside research, make sure you define terms that a beginning reader might find difficult. To research information about weather, go to the textbook web site and locate the instructions for Chapter 10, Science and Technology.

Environment and Natural Resources

Everyone is bugged by at least one type of bug. Maybe mosquitoes or ticks cause you to panic. Or maybe cockroaches or hornets are the pests that bother you most. Entomologists take such bugging quite seriously. In fact, they have made a profession out of studying all types of insects. Take on the role of an entomologist by researching an insect of your choice. Then write a paragraph describing the stages of its life cycle. Make sure that you use a time-sequence method of organization. Use transitions to your readers' advantage. To research information about bugs, go to the textbook web site and locate the instructions for Chapter 10, Environment and Natural Resources.

11

Narration:
Paragraphs That
Tell a Story

IN THIS CHAPTER YOU WILL LEARN TO:

- **Understand the concept of narration.**

- **Identify significant events of a narrative.**

- **Develop supporting details.**

- **Use words that show sequence.**

Using *Narration* in Writing for Your Career

Career Path	Sample Career	Use for Narrative Writing	Example of Narrative Writing
Communication and the Arts	Radio deejay	Providing listeners with information about the origin of a song	This song was inspired by a near-death experience of one of the band members. He was driving his motorcycle on a mountain road late at night when another driver came around the corner toward him, driving in his lane. The band member swerved just in time and missed death by a few inches.
Health and Medicine	Nutritionist	Describing an experience in which a patient's health was improved through diet	When Mrs. Harlan began treatment, she was constantly tired and had difficulty meeting her daily responsibilities. I suggested she decrease consumption of heavy, fatty foods and eat more foods containing B vitamins. In just a few months, she said she felt ten years younger.
Human, Personal, and Public Service	Marriage counselor	Describing an example of successful conflict resolution	Neal and Mary frequently disagreed over financial matters. While Neal spends money as quickly as he earns it, Mary prefers to save her money. A major conflict erupted when Neal wanted to buy a new car.
Business and Marketing	Pet supplies retailer	Explaining a successful business strategy	When we first moved into the new space, business was slow. We started by redesigning the displays and placing novelty items in strategic locations where they would catch customers' attention.
Science and Technology	Spokesperson for a pharmaceutical producer	Describing the results of a drug that the company has produced	Prior to the introduction of this drug, the only allergy medicines on the market caused significant side effects, including drowsiness and headaches. When Santhrop first became available, doctors and the public were skeptical.
Environment and Natural Resources	Conservation biologist	Describing the changes produced in an ecosystem by the introduction of earthworms	Beginning in the early nineteenth century, settlers brought earthworms to the prairie, often unintentionally. At first, the earthworm population was too small to have any measurable impact.

ON THE JOB

Puppeteer

Martin Alexander is a puppeteer who performs with a traveling theater group. When the troupe is not traveling, Martin and his colleagues spend their time designing sets, building puppets, and writing plays that the puppets will perform.

This year one of the performances will be based on the traditional Greek story of Persephone, a story that explains the change in the seasons of the year. Persephone, daughter of Demeter, the goddess of the harvest, is kidnapped by Hades, king of the underworld. Persephone is forced to live with him for six months of every year. For those six months, Demeter makes the earth stop producing food, and humans experience winter. Martin's challenge is to adapt the story so it can be told by puppets to children in a lively and entertaining way.

Once he has identified this purpose, Martin outlines the story's most significant points. Next, he adds the supportive details that are necessary to make the characters and plot come alive. Finally, he eliminates unnecessary points to ensure that the story is coherent and focused. Here is Martin's summary of his story, which he will convert into the form of a play.

> On a warm and bright summer morning, the young Persephone sings to herself while picking flowers in a meadow. Suddenly, the ground rumbles and a huge crevice appears in the earth. <u>Hades, the god of the underworld, rides out from below the earth in his horse-drawn carriage. He kidnaps Persephone, disappears back into the earth, and makes her his wife and queen of the underworld.</u> When Persephone's mother, Demeter, goddess of the harvest, realizes that her daughter is gone, she <u>stops the crops from growing</u> and refuses to let them grow again until Persephone is returned. Finally, Demeter's brother <u>Zeus, the king of the gods, sends a messenger to convince Hades to let Persephone go</u>. Zeus says that Persephone cannot return if she has eaten anything while in the underworld. Because <u>Hades has tricked Persephone into eating six pomegranate seeds</u>, Zeus says she <u>must return to the underworld for half of every year</u>. While Persephone lives in Hades, Demeter grieves, and the people of the earth experience the cold and dark winter season when their crops will not grow.

Is the story interesting and well focused? Do the supporting details bring the plot alive? If so, Martin organized his narrative well, something you will learn to do in this chapter.

Understanding Narration

In writing, **narration** is the act of relating a sequence of events. A narrative may be fictional, like Martin's story, or it may tell of an actual incident.

In everyday life, many different things happen at the same time. When writers narrate, they choose the events and details that are relevant to the story they wish to tell. People do this when they tell stories about themselves. They know instinctively that some details should be included and others should not. In narrative writing, writers can be especially selective about choosing the best details and organizing them as effectively as possible. When writing a narrative paragraph, follow this process:

- Identify the purpose of your narrative.
- Note the significant events that must be included.
- Choose additional details as needed to make the story flow smoothly.
- Maintain coherence and ensure that all details are relevant and that they fit together in a way that addresses your purpose.

Can you see how Martin followed this procedure? Here are the steps he took in the process of composing his narrative about Persephone and Demeter. Compare his outline with the numbered items in the story. Note that the major events and supporting details are numbered.

Purpose of story

- To retell a traditional story
- To arrange the story in a way that it can be performed effectively with puppets
- To appeal to young children

1. Major events

- Hades kidnaps Persephone
- Demeter stops the crops from growing
- Persephone must return to the underworld for half of every year

2. Supporting details

- Hades rides out from below the earth
- Persephone eats six pomegranate seeds
- Zeus convinces Hades to let Persephone go

SELF-ASSESSMENT 11

When I tell a story in writing, I can:

	Usually	Sometimes	Never
Know my purpose and desired effect.	❏	❏	❏
Identify the events that are most relevant.	❏	❏	❏
Include appropriate supporting details.	❏	❏	❏
Be coherent.	❏	❏	❏
Include a beginning, a middle, and an end.	❏	❏	❏

If you checked "Sometimes" or "Never" for any of the items, this chapter will help you improve your skills. Even if you checked "Usually" in every instance, you will learn more about writing paragraphs that tell stories.

As the outline shows, Martin considered his purpose, noted the major events of the story and he included supporting details to add interest and coherence. The story is well organized and appropriate for a puppet show for children.

Identifying Significant Events

In this chapter, you will write narrative paragraphs by choosing only the most essential events needed to convey your story. For this reason, it is particularly important that you consider your paragraph's intended purpose.

Imagine that you are a technical support associate for a computer hardware company. After each interaction with a customer, you must file a brief report relating what happened during the call. Following the steps below will help you produce a paragraph that is concise, accurate, and appropriate to your goal.

Purpose	Create a record of the customer's problems and the technician's assistance.
Main Events	(1) Customer was unable to turn system on.
	(2) Technician instructed customer to unplug system, then remove battery.
	(3) Customer successfully turned system on.

Main events are those that are essential to the paragraph's purpose. In this case, the purpose is to create a record of the interaction between the customer and the technician. Therefore, the paragraph must identify the initial problem that caused the customer to need a technician, explain the action or actions taken by the technician, and note the result.

In addition to the main events, the writer must include a topic sentence that informs the reader of the paragraph's central point. For example, in the above scenario, the paragraph's topic sentence informs the reader that the paragraph is about the customer and technician interaction. The reader then knows what events the paragraph is describing and why.

did you ever?

- See a movie and tell a friend very briefly what the movie was about? Did you mention the movie's major events?

- Arrive late to work or school, explaining to coworkers or instructors what happened on the way that made you late?

- Try to make someone laugh by telling an embarrassing story about yourself?

All of these situations involve narration. You tell stories all the time, instinctively choosing the most significant events to include. In this chapter, you will learn to apply the same skill to writing narrative paragraphs.

ACTIVITY 11.1   Each numbered item below describes a situation in which a narrative paragraph is required. Based on the situation and the paragraph's purpose, identify three main events that will form the basis of the paragraph. Because the descriptions are incomplete, you must create the main events to finish each story.

1. You are a high school chemistry teacher. Today in class, one of your students was extremely disruptive. After several warnings, you gave the student a detention. You thought the punishment was necessary because the student behaved badly and because unruly behavior in the chemistry lab can result in an unsafe situation. The school requires that teachers write an explanation of the behavior that led to the detention.

    Paragraph's purpose _____

    _____

    _____

    First event _____

    _____

    Second event _____

    _____

    Third event _____

    _____

2. As a customer claims representative at an automobile insurance agency, your job includes talking with customers who have been involved in collisions. Based on each conversation, you must submit a report that will be evaluated to determine who was at fault. You have just finished speaking with Ms. Saunders, who was stopped at a red light when another car hit her from behind.

    Paragraph's purpose _____

    _____

    _____

    First event _____

    _____

    Second event _____

    _____

    Third event _____

    _____

3. You work for the local police department. One of your responsibilities is to respond to residents' calls, investigate the reported problems, and document what was done to address the problems. Today you received a call from a woman who reported that her purse was lost or stolen. She was in the park with her children and left her purse on a bench while she ran to help a child who had fallen. When she returned to the bench several minutes later, her purse was gone. After asking the woman several follow-up questions to get the details of her story straight, you file a report about the missing purse.

    Paragraph's purpose _____

    _____

    _____

    First event_____

    _____

    Second event _____

    _____

    Third event _____

    _____

4. As the owner of a small bed-and-breakfast, you have decided to advertise online in order to attract more customers to your business. The B&B houses guests in a 150-year-old schoolhouse that has been converted into a cottage with four separate bedrooms. To highlight the building's historic charm, you include in your advertisement the story of the original schoolhouse. The story includes how the community scraped together the money to build the schoolhouse and how they persuaded a teacher who lived 20 miles away to move to the village and teach their children. Tell the story of the schoolhouse in a way that will appeal to your guests' imaginations.

    Paragraph's purpose _____

    _____

    _____

    First event_____

    _____

    Second event _____

    _____

    Third event _____

    _____

WRITING WORKSHOP

Varying Sentence Structure

Read the following paragraph and note the rhythm of the sentences.

> My alarm went off at 6:30 this morning. I got up and went into the kitchen. Then I made some coffee and toasted some bread. Then I ate my breakfast. Then I took a shower and got dressed. Then I made the bed and cleaned up the kitchen. Then I read the newspaper for a few minutes. Then I went outside and waited for the bus. Then I caught the bus and arrived at work on time.

In this paragraph, every sentence is short and begins in the same way. To add interest, the writer can vary the length by combining sentences.

Two Short Sentences	Then I ate my breakfast. Then I took a shower and got dressed.
Combined Sentence	After eating my breakfast, I took a shower and got dressed.

Another way to create variety is to change the structure of the sentences. Instead of beginning every sentence the same way, the writer can change the order of the phrases.

Conventional Order	I read the newspaper for a few minutes.
Changed Order	For a few minutes, I sat down at the kitchen table to read the newspaper.

In the first example, the writer combined two events by using an introductory phrase. In the second example, the writer reversed the order of the sentence and added an additional detail to make the sentence clearer and more appealing.

> When my alarm went off at 6:30 this morning, I got up and went into the kitchen, where I brewed coffee and toasted some bread. After eating my breakfast, I took a shower and got dressed. Then I made the bed and cleaned up the kitchen. For a few minutes, I sat down at the kitchen table to read the newspaper before going outside to wait for the bus. I caught the bus and arrived at work on time.

Supporting Details

Once you have outlined the significant events to include in your paragraph, you should develop additional details. These details provide context for the story, make the paragraph smooth and coherent, and create a more interesting narrative.

In the example below, the technical support associate outlined the most important aspects of the conversation with the customer. These events formed the basic structure of the narrative paragraph. The writer then added supporting details.

Main Events

(1) Customer was unable to turn system on.

(2) Technician instructed customer to turn the system off, unplug it, plug it back in, and turn it on again.

(3) Technician instructed customer to remove battery from CPU body.

(4) Customer successfully turned system on.

Supporting Details

(1a) Customer had tried several times.

(1b) This had not been a problem in the past.

(2) This technique was unsuccessful.

(3) Customer had not checked battery for several months.

The writer's choice of supporting details depends on the paragraph's purpose. In this case, the technical support specialist's goal is to create a thorough and accurate record of the customer's problem and the steps that were taken to solve it. This information will be useful in assisting other customers in the future. Therefore, the technician must include information about all steps taken to fix the computer. The final paragraph might look like this.

> Mr. Ting called to say that he was unable to turn his system on after several attempts. This had not been a problem for him in the past. I asked him to turn the system off, unplug it, plug it back in, and turn it back on. The system still did not boot. Next, I suggested that he remove the battery and try again. This attempt proved successful, so I advised him to replace the battery—which he had not checked in several months—since it appeared to be dead and was likely to continue causing problems with the operation of the system.

When choosing supporting details, include only the most important ones. Too many details or irrelevant information can make the paragraph awkward and confusing. For example, the reader in the previous scenario does not need to know that the customer sneezed several times while removing the battery from his computer or that the technician switched to a speaker phone in the middle of the conversation. These details are not relevant to the writer's purpose, which is to record the customer's problem and the technician's solution. Because these bits of information are distracting, they should not be included.

Paragraphs that tell a story use various devices to create a good narrative.

To avoid cluttering a paragraph with irrelevant details, consider the purpose of the paragraph before you begin writing. List any details that you think are important. Then reread each one and ask yourself whether it is appropriate to your goals in writing the paragraph. If not, leave it out. Too much information can be just as confusing as too little information.

ETHICS CONNECTION

Implying Cause and Effect

In narrative writing, you relate events in the order they happened. In most situations, this is very simple and straightforward. Occasionally, however, describing a sequence can be tricky. Indicating a sequence may imply a cause-and-effect relationship that is not accurate.

For example, imagine that you work for a moving company and have just helped a family move its furniture across town into a new house. Most of the moving went smoothly. Unfortunately, after the moving was finished, you noticed a large dent in the wall near the front door. This might have happened when you wedged the couch through the door, or it could have happened later when the homeowner pushed a table through the same doorway. You are not sure what caused the dent.

When relating the story to your supervisor, you could say, "The homeowner pushed a huge table through the doorway, and then we noticed a big dent in the wall." This sequence may be accurate, in the sense that you noticed the dent after the customer moved the table. However, presenting it this way creates the impression that the homeowner caused the dent. Although this is possible, you do not know for sure.

In this situation, the ethical narrative would mention both large objects that went through the door, noting that the writer did not know what caused the dent. Being an ethical writer often starts with identifying the right thing to do.

ACTIVITY 11.2   Each numbered item below identifies the main events of a situation. For each item, create three supporting details that provide context, add interest, and tie the paragraph together smoothly.

1. Situation: Submitting an advertisement to a newspaper

    Main events:

    (a) I called the paper to inquire about ad prices.

    (b) I chose an appropriate size and designed an ad to fit it.

    (c) I submitted the ad to the newspaper.

    Supporting details:

    (a) _____

    (b) _____

    (c) _____

2. Situation: Planning a party

    Main events:

    (a) I invited all of my friends.

    (b) I went shopping for food.

    (c) I cleaned the house.

    Supporting details:

    (a) _____

    (b) _____

    (c) _____

3. Situation: Registering for classes

    Main events:

    (a) I spoke with my adviser.

    (b) I decided on the list of classes I will take this semester.

    (c) I registered using the online registration system.

    Supporting details:

    (a) _____

    (b) _____

    (c) _____

4. Situation: Finding a solution to a work problem

    Main events:

    (a) I called a team meeting.

    (b) I identified the problem.

    (c) I asked for suggestions.

    Supporting details:

    (a) _____

    (b) _____

    (c) _____

Words That Show Sequence

Since narrative writing describes events that happen sequentially, writers use sequence words to indicate to the reader in what order the events occurred. For example, if you write a paragraph describing a trip to the beach, you might begin by saying, "First, we packed the car with towels, sunscreen, and a picnic lunch." The following sentence might begin with transitional words or phrases such as *next* or *second* or *after that*.

Writers use two main types of transitional sequence words. The first type is ordinal transitions. Ordinal transitions are words such as *first, second* or *secondly, thirdly,* and so on. The second type of transition is time sequence words. These are words such as *then, afterwards, next, subsequently, previously, yesterday, later,* and *soon.* Any word that indicates when an event took place is a time sequence word.

Sequence Word	Sample Usage
next	Next, the conductor closed the door, and the train left the station.
after	After everyone had finished the main course, the server brought out the dessert.
before	Before getting on the bus, I checked to make sure I had all of my papers with me.
finally	Finally, I finished studying for the test and was able to sleep for a few hours.

These and other sequencing words help indicate the order of events. They also make the paragraph more readable by providing smooth transitions between events.

TECHNOLOGY CONNECTION

Ordinal Numbers

An ordinal number is a number that indicates sequence to the reader. Many word processors include functions that automatically change ordinal numbers to superscript as you key the words. For example, if you write, "That was my 2nd piece of pie," the program will automatically change 2nd to 2nd.

To turn this function on and off, look at the AutoFormat or AutoCorrect options on the Tools menu of most word processors. Note that in formal writing, it is more appropriate to write the complete word than the numeral. In a formal document, the sentence would read "That was my second piece of pie." Your purpose and intended audience will determine whether you use words or numerals.

ACTIVITY 11.3 Rewrite each set of sentences using transitional words that indicate sequence to the reader. You may combine events into a single sentence or leave them as separate sentences. Use a variety of transitional words that will make the writing more interesting. The first example has been completed for you.

1. Nieca bought a nice birthday present for her father. She wrapped the birthday present and made a card to go with it. She gave it to her father. Her father was delighted.

    Nieca bought a nice birthday present for her father. Later she wrapped the birthday present and made a card to go with it. The next day when she gave it to her father, he was delighted.

2. The doctor wrote a prescription. The patient took the prescription to the pharmacy. The pharmacist filled the prescription. The patient picked it up.

    _____

    _____

    _____

    _____

    _____

    _____

3. The server took the customers' orders. The server went into the kitchen and gave the orders to the cooks. The server brought the food to the customers.

---

4. I went to the store. I tried on several pairs of pants. I bought a pair of brown corduroys. I took them home and showed them to my roommate.

---

5. Chris made coffee. He made an omelet with onions and green peppers. He served breakfast to his family. Everybody sat down and ate together.

---

6. Annalis searched the classified ads for a job. She told her friends and family what kind of job she wanted. Her cousin gave her the number of a friend whose company was hiring. Annalis called the friend and got information about the job. She applied for the job. The employer called her for an interview.

Summary for Narrative Writing

- ❑ Narration is the act of structuring events and supporting details to tell a story.

- ❑ The writer chooses the most significant events to form the basis of the narrative.

- ❑ Ethical narratives avoid making inaccurate implications about cause and effect.

- ❑ Sentence structure and length are varied to make the paragraph flow smoothly and to avoid monotony.

- ❑ Additional details make the story clearer and more interesting.

- ❑ All details are relevant, and they fit together in a way that addresses the purpose.

- ❑ Transitional terms indicate sequence.

PRACTICING YOUR SKILLS

Now that you understand how to construct a good narrative paragraph, practice your skills in the following activities.

PRACTICE 1

Hannah Markowitz is a nurse at Central Hospital. To make sure patients get consistent care, nurses pass on essential information about their patients at the end of each shift. In some cases, this information may be a record of medicines administered, or it may be a detailed description of the patient's progress and interactions with the hospital staff. Below is a paragraph Hannah wrote about one of her patients, Mr. Smith, who is recovering from heart surgery.

When I first came in at 7 A.M., Mr. Smith was wide awake and in good spirits. Later in the morning, I changed his IV as usual and had a pleasant chat with him about his daughter's wedding. Suddenly, around noon, he buzzed me and was in a state of panic when I arrived. When getting up to use the restroom, he had knocked over the IV pole, which jerked the needle out of his arm and caused some bleeding. I helped him back into bed, calmed him down, and reinserted the needle. Afterward, I brought him some food from the cafeteria and tried to make him as comfortable as possible. Finally, after eating half a bowl of tomato soup, he went back to sleep and remained sleeping for the rest of my shift.

Paragraph's Purpose

1. What is Hannah's purpose in writing this narrative paragraph?

   _____

   _____

   _____

Main Events

2. Identify the sentences or phrases that you think represent the most significant elements of the story. Outline them below.

   (a) _____

   (b) _____

   (c) _____

   (d) _____

Supporting Details

3. On the lines below, list three supporting details that add coherence to the story.

   (a) _____

   (b) _____

   (c) _____

Transitional Terms

4. Underline the words and phrases in the paragraph that act as transitions and indicate sequence.

PRACTICE 2

The paragraph below is made up of many sentences with similar structures. After reading the paragraph, suggest three changes that would make the writing smoother and more varied. Underline and number the original sentences that you intend to revise. Write your suggested revisions on the lines below.

The customer came in just before closing. He said he was just looking around at office supplies. He walked up and down the aisles very slowly. Next, he asked if we had any toner. I said yes and told him where it was. Next, he walked over to the toner section. Then he asked if we had any plain white labels. I said yes and told him where they were. Next, he went over to the label section. Then I told him that we were closed. He said he would be leaving in a minute. Then he asked for something else. I told him that we had to close out the registers. Then he left without buying anything.

Suggested Variations

First revision: _____

_____

_____

Second revision: _____

_____

_____

Third revision: _____

_____

_____

APPLYING YOUR SKILLS

Now you can put your skills to work by writing your own narrative paragraph.

Prewriting

(a) First, choose a story that you can tell in several sentences. Here are a few suggestions:

- My most embarrassing moment
- An experience I once had on the job
- A current event in the news

(b) Second, identify your purpose in telling the story. Do you want to make someone laugh? Feel sorry for you? Be shocked? Your purpose will guide your writing.

(c) Next, write three or four of the most essential events in your story.

(c) Finally, list three or four additional details that will provide context, make your story more interesting, and allow it to flow smoothly.

Writing

Now write the first draft of your paragraph. The main events will create structure. The additional details will provide context. Use transitional words to show the sequence.

Revising

Reread your first draft. Use the checklist to make sure you have revised thoroughly.

❑ Are the wording and structure consistent with my purpose?

❑ Have I built the paragraph around the most significant events?

❑ Have I included additional details to provide context and to make the paragraph flow?

❑ Did I use transitional words to show the sequence of events?

❑ Did I vary the sentence structures and sentence lengths?

When you have revised thoroughly, write a second draft. Review and revise it carefully. If necessary, write a third draft. When you believe your content and presentation are as good as you can make them, go on to the editing stage.

Editing

In this final stage, check your paragraph for mechanical errors. Closely examine grammar, spelling, word use, punctuation, and capitalization. Check for sentence fragments and run-ons. Make a final copy and proofread it one last time.

WRITING FOR YOUR CAREER

CRITICAL THINKING

This section presents a writing project for each of the six career pathways. Choose one that appeals to you and use your new skills to write a narrative paragraph on the subject.

When the project description refers you to the textbook web site, go to http://humphrey.swlearning.com and click on the Links tab. Look for Chapter 11, "Writing for Your Career." There you will find direct links to helpful web references.

Communication and the Arts

You are a promoter for a musical band. As a part of your responsibilities, you publicize the band's tours by sending press releases to media outlets in the cities the band visits. To interest your readers, you include personal information about the band, including how the group met, how their music has evolved, why they have become so popular with fans, and how they work together. Write a paragraph about the band's history or tell a story about the band that will be interesting to potential audiences. Base your writing on any band that you find enjoyable, making up whatever details you need to write the paragraph.

Health and Medicine

As a family doctor, you emphasize preventative health care. You talk to your patients about the benefits of a balanced diet, pure water, regular sleep, and plenty of exercise. Over the years, you have determined that your patients have become healthier, both as a group and individually. One way to illustrate the importance of these habits is to tell stories about patients who have improved their overall health by changing their lifestyles. Write a paragraph telling the story of someone you know or have heard about who has improved his or her health by making a lifestyle change. For example, you may choose a person who has lost a great deal of weight or someone who has begun an exercise and fitness program that includes working out, walking, or engaging in some other form of exercise.

Human, Personal, and Public Service

As the director of a public shelter for homeless families, you spend a lot of time trying to increase funding for the many organizations that provide assistance to individuals and families in transition. You find that personal stories are more effective than statistics in helping people understand the reality of homelessness. Write a paragraph telling one family's story about how they lost their apartment and ended up at the shelter. Make up any details that you believe will add to your story. For additional information on this topic, access the textbook web site for Chapter 11, Human, Personal, and Public Service.

Business and Marketing

You work for a small coffee roaster that specializes in coffee from family farms. Because you know that many coffee drinkers are interested in the source of their coffee, on each package of beans that you sell, you include a story about one of the families. Write the story of one coffee-growing family, describing how the tradition has been passed on through the generations For help with this topic, access the textbook web site for Chapter 11, Business and Marketing.

Science and Technology

Many scientific discoveries and inventions are made by accident. One such lucky accident was the creation of nylon, which occurred when several chemists were working in a lab with a sample of polyester. While trying to see how far they could stretch the polyester, they found that they had created a new and much stronger material. Read about the origin of nylon at the web site for Chapter 11, Science and Technology. Write a paragraph telling how nylon was created.

Environment and Natural Resources

You work for a nonprofit organization that raises awareness about endangered species in your region. You are currently working on a project to protect and restore the bald eagle population. To alert people to the problems these animals face, you tell them about how the situation has changed over the past two centuries. Write a brief paragraph describing changes in the bald eagle population and the dangers eagles face today. You can find information at the web site for Chapter 11, Environment and Natural Resources.

Cause and Effect: Paragraphs That Explain Reasons and Results

IN THIS CHAPTER YOU WILL LEARN TO:

- Write paragraphs that explain causes and effects.

- Write a cause-and-effect topic sentence.

- Identify cause-and-effect events.

- Provide supporting details.

Using *Cause and Effect* in Writing for Your Career

Career Path	Sample Career	Use for Cause-and-effect Writing	Example of Cause-and-Effect Writing
Communication and the Arts	Newspaper editor	Explaining the importance of journalistic integrity	Fabricating newspaper stories results in public mistrust. If people don't trust a newspaper, they won't pay to read it or to advertise in it. If the public quits buying, we will all be out of work.
Health and Medicine	Physician assistant	Reporting on a drug's side effects	The patient, Nawal Farish, suffered several side effects after taking 10 mg. of sleep medication according to the prescription. Ms. Farish reported episodes of memory loss. She also indicated periods of daytime drowsiness.
Human, Personal, and Public Service	School vice principal	Explaining the school's new bullying policy	There are consequences for bullying anywhere on school property. After a first-time offense, parents will be notified. If bullying occurs again, it will result in an in-school suspension. A third offense will result in an out-of-school suspension.
Business and Marketing	Bicycle shop owner	Describing the benefits of daily cycling	By your second week of cycling, you will begin to see results. Typically you will have lost at least five pounds of body weight. Cycling has other benefits as well. For example, you will appreciate the beauty of your surroundings.
Science and Technology	Project manager	Defending a hiring decision	Our production schedule changed as a result of the decision to hire new staff. For one thing, the launch date for the new diabetes project was moved up by two months. Also, over the summer, we picked up two new clients. In addition, two arthritis research assignments have been announced.
Environment and Natural Resources	Park ranger	Explaining rules for activities in the park	Mountain biking has caused considerable damage to park grounds over the past decade and a half. On many of the park's trails, mountain biking is prohibited. On other trails, it is limited to certain seasons.

Boxed Lunches

Cary Penkower manages a gourmet sandwich shop, the Luke & Cary Sandwich Company. L&C bakes its own breads, smokes many of its own meats, uses the freshest toppings, and—according to the local food critics—makes the finest sandwiches in the entire region.

Today the sandwich shop is facing a potential crisis. L&C is located on the ground floor of an office building in the suburbs. The building's biggest occupant, a video production company called Lotus Productions, went out of business last spring. Lotus laid off its employees and shut its doors. In its place today is a warehouse that employs just a handful of individuals. Since L&C lost Lotus's lunch business, sales have been dismal.

But Cary has an idea: start an L&C catering service that will deliver boxed lunches to surrounding office complexes. By adding catering services, Cary thinks L&C can make more money than before.

Cary sat down and began to draft a business plan for the new venture. His goal was to show that the loss of Lotus created an opportunity to tap a new source of business.

> When <u>Lotus Productions closed its doors</u>[2] last spring, <u>it caused many changes at the L&C Sandwich Company</u>[1]. Lotus employed approximately 100 individuals, and <u>nearly one-third of them ate lunch at L&C every day</u>[3]. With Lotus out of the building, being replaced by a company with only six employees, <u>L&C's revenues took a huge hit</u>[3]. But there is a solution! Lotus's departure presents <u>an opportunity for L&C to branch out into catering</u>[3]. If we invest in a catering operation and market our lunch services to surrounding office complexes, we can rebuild—and even grow—our business. After all, many former Lotus employees are now working at other companies in neighboring office complexes. In other words, <u>they can tell their coworkers about us</u>[3]!

In Cary's opening paragraph, he wanted to write about the effects of Lotus's closing. The closing resulted in lost sales. Also, it resulted in Cary's idea for a new business plan.

In this chapter, you will learn how to draft a paragraph that uses cause and effect to tell why things happen, to examine the results of events, and to predict future events based on past experience. Cause and effect is a powerful writing technique that guides readers in understanding what writers mean.

Understanding Cause and Effect

Normally a **cause-and-effect paragraph** addresses either a cause or an effect. Review the examples of cause-and-effect writing in the Career Pathways chart on page 225. Note that each example is about a cause or an effect, but not both.

Think about some examples of cause and effect that you experience every day: You eat because you are hungry. You sleep because you are tired. Those examples explain cause. They are about why you eat and why you sleep. Say you stay up all night studying for an exam. Now you are sleep-deprived. Your current state is an effect of having too little sleep.

A cause-and-effect paragraph uses this basic format.

- The topic statement identifies the subject and says whether cause or effect will be discussed.
- Transitional expressions introduce new causes and effects, show their degree of importance, or tell which cause or effect came first.
- Supporting details show how one event caused another.

Can you see how Cary's paragraph follows this pattern? Compare the numbered points to the examples in the paragraph.

1. Main point for topic statement
The loss of Lotus's lunch business caused changes.

2. Cause
Lotus Productions went out of business.

3. Effects
- L&C has fewer lunchtime customers.
- L&C experienced lost revenue.
- L&C can branch out into catering.
- Former L&C customers may spread the word at their new jobs about L&C sandwiches.

Cary wanted to show that a new business opportunity existed. One event (the Lotus closing) caused another event (lost business), which caused another event (an opportunity). The writer's job is to explain so readers will understand why things happen the way they do.

SELF-ASSESSMENT 12

When I need to show cause and effect, I can:

	Usually	Sometimes	Never
Write a topic sentence that states either cause or effect.	❑	❑	❑
Explain how the cause and effect are related.	❑	❑	❑
Choose details that support my topic sentence.	❑	❑	❑
Eliminate details that do not support my topic sentence.	❑	❑	❑
Use transitional expressions to introduce the next set of cause and effect, to show importance, or to indicate time sequence.	❑	❑	❑

If you checked "Sometimes" or "Never" for any of the items, this chapter will improve your cause-and-effect writing skills. Even if you checked "Usually" in every instance, you'll learn more about writing paragraphs that show cause and effect.

The Topic Sentence

In Chapter 4, you learned that the topic sentence of a paragraph should state one main point. The sentence should be clear enough so that the rest of the paragraph can support the point that is made.

In a cause-and-effect paragraph, the topic sentence usually mentions both cause and effect. The topic sentence then signals what the rest of the paragraph will be about: either causes or effect. Here are three examples of a topic sentence for a cause-and-effect paragraph. Which one do you think works best?

(A)   On the first day of the state fair, it was pouring rain, and we did not go.

(B)   Because it rained on the first day of the state fair, we stayed home until the second day.

(C)   We stayed home today instead of going to the state fair.

Example (B) is the best of the three alternatives because it states a cause (rain) and an effect (a specific change in travel plans). In this sentence, the rain is the *causal event*. Example (A) is a weak cause-and-effect topic sentence because the reader may not understand that the two events are causally related. Example (C) does not work as a cause-and-effect topic sentence because it lacks both cause and effect. After beginning with Example (B), the writer could continue writing about effects with examples such as these:

When it's too wet to walk around the fairgrounds, many of the exhibits we enjoy are closed.

That's why when you called, we were still at home and hadn't left on our trip yet.

did you ever?

- Know someone who broke out in a rash every time he or she ate a certain type of food?

- Bounce a check because you didn't have enough money in your bank account?

- Read or hear about a terrific new movie and rush out to see it as soon as it opened at a nearby theater?

All of these examples involve cause and effect. You use cause and effect every day to help understand the world around you. With practice, you can apply the same technique to your writing.

ACTIVITY 12.1   For each of the subjects in the following list, write a cause-and-effect topic sentence. Identify whether your paragraph will be about cause or effect. The first two examples have been completed for you.

1. popular music

   Several developments in technology have changed the way music is

   sold. (Developments in technology = the *cause*)

   _____

2. my bicycle

   Riding a bicycle to work has resulted in several health and financial

   benefits. (Health and financial benefits = the *effect*)

   _____

3. getting into college

   _____

   _____

   _____

4. getting a raise at work

   _____

   _____

   _____

5. eating right

   _____

   _____

   _____

6. my grandparents

   _____

   _____

   _____

Providing Supporting Details

After identifying causal events, the next step is to provide details that support your main point. The best supporting details are not necessarily the first ones that you come up with. Often, they occur as a result of a prior thought or an idea that someone else suggests. So be prepared to have some fun brainstorming. For brainstorming, use the techniques described in Chapter 2.

Be sure you come up with more ideas than you will need. Good writers know that a key part of rewriting is throwing away details that are weak, unparallel, or confusing. If the details you think of do not support your topic sentence, keep brainstorming for details until you are satisfied that you have found the best ones.

Here are some examples of cause-and-effect topic sentences and their supporting details.

The team effort resulted in a successful project for our company. Every department played a valuable role. Engineering and Product Management employees, especially, contributed considerable time and talent to the effort. Additionally, Customer Service staff came in early and stayed late each day so they could finish every task.

Because of the high volume of holiday sales, Elgee Toys hires extra sales personnel every November. Elgee advertises for seasonal help in newspapers. Working for Elgee is a good way for a student to earn extra cash. Students like the employee discount they get during the holiday season.

Toyomi earned a four-day weekend by putting in extra hours on the new product launch. She plans to take a trip to the beach. On the way home, she may visit her sister. She thinks visiting her family is a good reward for the extra work.

The layoff announcement caused fear among employees. No one knew who would be terminated. There had been no warning. People believed they had been misled by their managers. The experience showed me why managers need to communicate with employees.

The high-volume ticket sales were a result of the radio airplay the band received in Los Angeles. People were lined up around the block the day tickets went on sale. I hadn't seen such a commotion since the Rolling Stones played here.

Supporting details add clarity and interest to a cause-and-effect paragraph. Readers appreciate the details when they are clear and helpful.

ACTIVITY 12.2   For each of the following topic sentences, think of one or two supporting details. Write your supporting details below the events. The first example has been completed for you.

1. Ron was running toward the house because it was raining, and he did not want to get wet.

   He hadn't brought a change of clothes, and he wanted to stay dry.

   After all, sitting around in wet clothes wouldn't be much fun.

   _____

2. Flora was not in attendance because T. J. had forgotten to tell her about the meeting.

   _____

   _____

   _____

3. Silvio cut his finger, which led to a trip to the emergency room.

   _____

   _____

   _____

4. Kate bought a bus ticket to visit Matt because she missed him.

   _____

   _____

   _____

5. When interest rates go up, the result is that bond prices go down.

   _____

   _____

   _____

6. Due to last month's $500,000 order, we need to rent additional warehouse space.

   _____

   _____

   _____

Selecting Supporting Details

Supporting details are appropriate for the subject when they are clear and relevant. Look at the following outline for a paragraph. Do you see anything wrong with the details listed?

Topic Sentence	Because the general manager wants the Banderston project completed by Friday, many people are working late every night this week.
Supporting Details	(a) All ten project managers are working an average of 60 hours per week.
	(b) Tariq and Heather have cancelled their travel plans so they can be at the office.
	(c) I generally arrive at work by 7 A.M.
	(d) Some managers are buying pizza for their late-night workers. They want to show their appreciation.
	(e) Success requires a team effort.

Example (c) may be accurate and grammatically correct, but it is not relevant to the topic sentence. In fact, Example (c) weakens the topic sentence because it does not explain or elaborate on it.

If supporting details are irrelevant to the topic sentence, they may confuse the reader.

Topic Sentence	Because the general manager wants the Banderston project completed by Friday, many people are working late every night this week.
Irrelevant Detail	I don't like to work late.

Another problem occurs when a supporting detail is vague.

Topic Sentence	Because the general manager wants the Banderston project completed by Friday, many people are having to work late every night this week.
Vague Detail	That's why you see people coming in and out of the building.

Good writers eliminate irrelevant or vague supporting details as part of their rewriting process and replace them with clear ones.

When you rewrite, pay careful attention to each detail you use to support your topic sentence. Ask yourself, "Does the detail add meaning to the paragraph? Is it clear? Is it relevant?" The details you provide should be:

- Supportive of the topic sentence.
- Clear, not vague.
- Strong and relevant.

The first step is to decide whether to write about the cause or the effect.

ETHICS CONNECTION

Truth in Cause and Effect

Some people who eat ice cream also swim often. However, ice cream doesn't cause people to want to swim. In paragraphs that indicate cause and effect, it is important to show that one event happened because another event happened. Consider this sentence: "Zachary ate Jean's pie, and the next day he was sick." A reader could reasonably conclude that Jean's pie made Zachary sick. A supporting detail such as "But six others who ate the same pie didn't get sick" clears up any misunderstanding. If the writer knows that six pie eaters remained healthy and one got sick, he or she has an ethical obligation to communicate that supporting detail. Otherwise, readers will be misled about Jean's baking skills.

ACTIVITY 12.3   A cause-and-effect topic sentence should be followed by details to support it. In the sentences below, one example is not as good as the others. Identify the poor one, and use one of the abbreviations below to show why it is not effective.

U = Unsupportive   N = Nonspecific   I = Irrelevant

1. Tedson, Inc., hired a web developer because of a steady rise in business.

_____   The Tedson team could not do the job without an extra person.

_____   A new web developer was just what the company needed.

_____   The project wouldn't begin for another month, but management wanted the new person to start as soon as possible.

2. The third time Elliott was late for work it resulted in a written warning from the human resources department.

_____   If Elliott has another unexcused lateness, his job could be in jeopardy.

_____   He went to his supervisor immediately and complained that the warning was discriminatory.

_____   A written warning is a clear signal that Elliott has a problem.

3. Lou's health improved because he started to ride his bicycle to work every day.

_____   Lou's brother, Nadine's father, and Quincy's sister also have bikes.

_____   His weight dropped several pounds in the first week.

_____   After a few weeks, he began to build muscles in his legs and abdomen.

4. Rosa's classified advertisement for a new assistant resulted in 100 job applications.

_____   She believed she had a big enough pool of candidates from which to choose.

_____   On the day the classified advertisement ran, it was partly sunny, but it did not rain.

_____   Rosa sent the three most impressive resumes to Human Resources.

5. I telephoned Anna because I missed class yesterday.

_____   She takes better notes than anyone else in class, and I thought I could rely on her.

_____   The telephone really is an amazing invention.

_____   Without excellent notes, I may not be able to catch up in this tough course.

6. Fernando performed a quick inspection of the plant because he heard that the CEO would be stopping by for a visit.

_____   It was good that he did because his inspection turned up two safety violations.

_____   During the inspection, Fernando reviewed the plant, the machinery, and the inventory in the stockroom.

_____   After the hour-long inspection, he commended the plant supervisors and requested a few minor modifications to the second shift's cleanup procedures.

TECHNOLOGY CONNECTION

Back Up Your Writing

The following cause-and-effect paragraph about saving data describes a common problem experienced by computer users. After the paragraph, advice is given for overcoming the problem.

> When our firm's main server crashed, a significant amount of data was permanently lost. Three of our seven project managers stored their data exclusively on the main server, instead of keeping backup copies on the server and other copies on their hard drives and on storage disks. This breach of protocol resulted in approximately three weeks of lost work time. That means we will lose a number of incentive rewards for completing projects ahead of schedule.

If you use a computer for writing, you should save more than one version of your daily work. The best recommendation is to save and store your daily writing in at least two places. That way, if your hard drive crashes or your disk gets damaged, you won't lose your work. Here's a relatively easy system for keeping backups of your writing:

- Save to your hard drive once every 15 or 20 minutes while you are writing. Some writers get in the habit of saving their file every time they take a break. In case of a sudden power outage, you will not lose your work.

- Once a day copy your file to a second drive, such as a CD, Zip®, or floppy drive. To be on the safe side, store your backup disk separately from your computer.

- Once a week back up your files to another disk. Also, store this disk in a safe place, preferably in a separate building or, if your company permits, in your home.

This method, which requires only a few minutes each week, could be your lifeline in the event of a system crash, a computer virus, a natural disaster, or an accident.

This advice may seem obvious, but you would be surprised by how many term papers, graduate dissertations, and book manuscripts perish each year due to flames, floods, and inquiring puppies.

Writers at every level of the profession are guilty of keeping only "one true version" of their work—and that is a mistake. Whenever you work on a writing assignment, keep multiple copies in multiple locations.

Using Transitional Expressions

In Chapter 5, you learned that in writing, any movement from one point or subject to another is called a transition. Transitional expressions help you signal movements so your readers understand where you are going.

In a cause-and-effect paragraph, a transitional word, phrase, or sentence helps the writer navigate from one idea to another. Transitional expressions also make paragraphs more readable and interesting, often motivating a reader to continue when he or she might otherwise stop.

Transitional expressions can show cause; for example, *first, the reason for that was . . . , because,* and *the results are in.* Transitional expressions can show effect too. Examples include *another result, consequently, one possible outcome,* and *therefore.*

You can introduce a supporting detail with a phrase such as *for example* or *in other words.*

> The traffic patterns in our neighborhood change according to the local college's calendar. *For example,* when students are home for the holidays, traffic is considerably lighter.

Later in the paragraph, transitional expressions can indicate that one supporting detail is ending and another is beginning.

> *Additionally,* when classes are out at night, it is much easier to find a parking space downtown.

ACTIVITY 12.4 In the following cause-and-effect paragraph, try to improve the quality of the writing by inserting transitional expressions in at least four places. (See the Writer's Workshop on page 237 for transitional expressions.)

> The Jimmy Joe Blues Band concert was marred by electrical problems resulting from a thunderstorm. The technicians couldn't manage to keep the stage lights on. The rain shorted out the sound board. The amplifiers got wet and wouldn't work. The backup singers were afraid they would be electrocuted by their microphones. The stage manager, after surveying the situation, decided to hold the show for 20 minutes while the road manager and her crew dried off the equipment and the stage. Just when everyone thought the show was about to start, the storm got worse, and the rain pounded down on fans.

WRITING WORKSHOP

Transitional Expressions for Cause and Effect

To Show Cause	To Show Effect
The carpet is wet <u>because</u> of the rain.	I think, <u>therefore,</u> I am.
<u>Another reason</u> Eve lost the race was weariness.	<u>One outcome of</u> repeated failure is permanent bitterness.
The hair on Craig's sofa <u>is the result of</u> his dog Smokey sleeping there.	Dr. Barnes became rich <u>as a result of</u> his invention.
The pipe is clogged <u>due to the fact that</u> no one has cleaned it in a year.	The mess you see is <u>caused by</u> several months of neglect.
My high blood pressure was <u>brought on by</u> stress, lack of exercise, and poor diet.	<u>Consequently,</u> everything Meredith thought about became interesting.

Earlier you learned that a cause-and-effect paragraph is usually about cause or effect, but not both. Paragraphs that bounce back and forth between cause and effect can confuse readers. Read the example below.

> Reading Luisa's long technical report caused me to feel tired and drowsy. First, it made my eyelids droopy and heavy. Finally, I fell asleep.

A better idea is to set up a cause-and-effect paragraph so the causes, the supporting details, and the transitional expressions are parallel. Writers call this "flow." The paragraph below has been rewritten to "flow" better. Observe how the transitional expressions help make the writing more readable and more interesting

> Reading Luisa's long, technical report caused me to feel tired and drowsy. First, it made my eyelids droopy and heavy. Then it put me to sleep.

SUMMARY FOR CAUSE-AND-EFFECT WRITING

❑   Paragraphs should be about cause or effect, but not both.

❑   The topic sentence of a cause-and-effect paragraph should state what the paragraph is about.

❑   Just because two events occur near one another in time does not mean that the first event caused the second event.

❑   Use transitional expressions such as *for example* and *finally* to help readers understand the sequence, or order, of importance of events.

❑   You should develop more supporting ideas than you need and discard the ones that are weak, irrelevant, or vague.

PRACTICING YOUR SKILLS

Now that you understand the elements of a clear cause-and-effect paragraph, it is time to apply your knowledge in the following activity. Read the paragraph in Practice 1 and follow the directions at the end.

PRACTICE

This paragraph is from a short story by Roosevelt Lewis, Jr. He is writing about the effects of poverty on criminality.

 Many factors contributed to Will's descent into criminal activities. For one thing, his father left the family when Will was just a year old. As you might imagine, that left Will's mother destitute. However, she was too proud to ask for public assistance. For years, she worked two jobs to support her children. Will came home to an empty house every day. Therefore, the young boy suffered from a lack of adult supervision. In the absence of such supervision, the call of the streets and peer pressure were too strong for Will to ignore. As a result, he succumbed to temptation. In some ways, Will's future could have been predicted at an early age.

The Topic Sentence

1. Underline the topic sentence—the main point of the paragraph. Is this paragraph about cause or effect? What specific words alert you to whether the paragraph is about cause or effect?

_____

_____

The Supporting Details

2. To show the effect of poverty on criminality, Roosevelt Lewis, Jr., provides a number of supporting details. Circle them.

The Transitional Expressions

3. Put brackets around the words or phrases that create a transition from one supporting detail to the next.

APPLYING YOUR SKILLS

Now you are ready to write a cause-and-effect paragraph of your own. To do this, you will work through the stages of the writing process: prewriting, writing, revising, and editing. Use a separate sheet of paper or a word processing file. Name and number each draft of your writing.

Prewriting

(a) Begin by selecting a general subject for your cause-and-effect paragraph. Here are some samples.

Subject	Examples of Cause and Effect
excelling in school	good study habits (cause) proper sleep (cause) scholarship opportunities (effect) sense of personal satisfaction (effect)
great cooking	learning from a world-class chef (cause) practice (cause) a job as a chef in a fine restaurant (effect) delicious meals (effect)
consumer spending	effective advertising (cause) sales and special offers (cause) consumer debt (effect) empty store shelves (effect)
traffic accidents	poor concentration (cause) fatigue (cause) collision (effect) injury (effect)

(b) Once you have identified your subject, decide whether you want to write a cause-or-effect paragraph. Remember, most cause-and-effect paragraphs are about cause or effect, but not both. Think about what you want to say. Do you want to discuss an event that caused another event, or do you want to discuss an event that was the effect of another event?

(c) Write possible ideas for your topic sentence. Remember that the topic sentence should be focused enough so the rest of the paragraph can support it.

(d) List ideas for supporting details. Find the best ones for your topic sentence. Make sure they are clearly supportive, specific, and relevant.

(e) Construct a simple outline for your paragraph in a form like the one shown below.

Topic Sentence _____

Detail 1 _____

Detail 2 _____

Detail 3 _____

Writing

Now write the first draft of your paragraph. Word the topic sentence as precisely as you can and develop each supporting detail clearly. Link the details with transitional expressions.

Revising

Read through your first draft. Use the checklist of questions that follow to make sure you have revised thoroughly. If you answer no to any question, revise and edit your paragraph until you are sure that it reads as you intend.

❑ Is your paragraph about cause or effect?

❑ Does the topic sentence state cause and effect?

❑ Are there enough supporting details to prove your topic sentence? (You should have at least three supporting details.)

❑ Are the details supportive of your main point?

❑ Are the details specific?

❑ Do the transitional expressions help explain order of importance, sequence, or other attributes of the cause-and-effect events? Are more transitional expressions needed?

After you revise your first draft, write a second draft, following the same process. Critique and revise the second draft thoroughly. Get another person's feedback, if possible. If you have enough time, write a third draft.

When you believe that your writing is the best it can be, edit your work.

Editing

In this final stage, check your paragraph for errors in grammar, spelling, word use, punctuation, and capitalization.

After you have polished your writing, make a new copy in the format your instructor specifies. If possible, put your draft away overnight. In the morning, proofread your paragraph one final time with your fresh eyes.

WRITING FOR YOUR CAREER

CRITICAL THINKING

This section presents a writing project for each of the six career pathways. Choose one that appeals to you and use your new skills to write a cause-and-effect paragraph on the subject.

When the project description refers you to the textbook web site, go to http://humphrey.swlearning.com and click on the Links tab. Look for Chapter 12 "Writing for Your Career." There you will find direct links to helpful web references.

Communication and the Arts

Imagine that you have an opportunity to create a tour of a natural history museum. The exhibits in the museum represent 10,000 years of the earth's history. Select one time period and write a paragraph that explains how that era ushered in the next era. Describe either a cause or an effect and show at least three supporting details.

Remember, just because Event A came before Event B does not mean that A caused B. Your job is to show the causal relationship between events.

If you need some help online, go to the textbook web site and locate the instructions for Chapter 12, Communication and the Arts.

Health and Medicine

Assume that you work at a health club as a personal trainer. Part of your job is to sell the health club and its services to the general public. Today you are writing the opening paragraph of a brochure that will introduce the benefits of physical fitness to prospective clients.

In this paragraph, you need to show how a healthy lifestyle, a sensible diet, and the right amount of exercise will result in better health. You also may want to explain how a loss of weight and a sense of well-being can be achieved through a total fitness regimen.

For help online, go to the textbook web site and locate the instructions for Chapter 12, Health and Medicine.

Human, Personal, and Public Service

Imagine that you work in the communications department of a large school district that is facing a major teacher shortage. Your manager has asked you to write a press release for distribution to the local newspapers and radio stations. The purpose of the press release is to encourage job seekers to apply.

Begin by composing a cause-and-effect paragraph about the teaching profession. For example, you could describe the feeling of satisfaction that results from teaching or you could describe the many benefits that result from one's decision to enter the profession.

If you need some help online, go to the textbook web site and locate the instructions for Chapter 12, Human, Personal, and Public Service.

Business and Marketing

Write a paragraph that explains how investing in advertising results in increased sales. You may write about any business and any kind of advertising that you wish.

For example, you might describe how mailing a catalog to more addresses results in increased sales. You also might explain how business grows as the result of a billboard on the side of the highway.

Science and Technology

Write a cause-and-effect paragraph that describes a natural weather phenomenon. It could be a hurricane, a tornado, thunder and lightening, a large snowstorm, a flood, or some other weather event. You may describe the cause of the weather event or its effect.

For information to help you with your paragraph, log on to an Internet search engine and enter the key words that identify your event, for example, *tornadoes* or *hurricanes*.

Environment and Natural Resources

Write a paragraph about the effect of offshore oil drilling. You may be in favor of offshore drilling, or you may be against it. Environmentalists could cite damaging effects on the environment. Proponents could take a favorable view of what drilling does for the economy. Do not describe the process of offshore drilling. Instead, write about its effect on the environment.

If you need some help online, go to the textbook web site and locate the instructions for Chapter 12, Environment and Natural Resources.

13

Persuasion: Paragraphs That Convince

© Getty Images/PhotoDisc

IN THIS CHAPTER YOU WILL LEARN TO:

- Use persuasion in writing.

- Present your argument.

- Support your argument with evidence.

- Appeal to readers' interests.

Using *Persuasive Writing* for Your Career

Career Path	Sample Career	Career Use for Persuasive Writing	Example of Persuasive Writing
Communication and the Arts	Independent record label promoter	Persuading musicians to sign with the label	The large recording labels complain of declining sales, yet the independent music industry continues to grow. In addition, musicians who work for independent labels can retain the rights to their own work, which means thousands, or even millions, of extra dollars for musical groups.
Health and Medicine	Public health official	Explaining the appropriate use of antibiotics	Antibiotic use should be limited to patients for whom they are absolutely necessary. When antibiotics are overused, bacteria develop resistance to them. As a result, the antibiotics lose their ability to fight disease.
Human, Personal, and Public Service	Peace Corps recruiter	Recruiting potential volunteers	Most volunteers return from their service saying, "The Peace Corps changed my life." Living and working in another country provides experiences you can gain in no other way.
Business and Marketing	Travel agent	Promoting midyear vacation packages	Escape your day-to-day drudgery and head for sunnier climates! Off-season prices offer the savvy traveler excellent vacation savings. As an added bonus, you won't be bothered by the hordes of tourists who travel at other times of the year.
Science and Technology	IT executive	Describing the benefits of e-training	Competition is intense in the information technology industry. To keep up with the changing environment, you must invest in e-training that upgrades your staff.
Environment and Natural Resources	Recycling advocate	Promoting local recycling programs	Do your part to protect the environment. Each time you take out your trash, spend five extra minutes to separate the recyclables. You personally will lower the amount of trash in the landfills, and you'll feel good about your contribution to the environment.

245

Water Conservation

Lea Wilson is manager of a hotel that is part of a national chain. She enjoys interacting with guests and tries to meet their needs smoothly and efficiently.

The housekeeping crew cleans each room every day. Recently, the chain requested that hotel managers conserve water by asking guests if they would like to use sheets and towels more than once. This will save money on water and cleaning costs and benefit the environment by conserving water.

As manager, Lea's job is to write a paragraph that will persuade guests to reuse their sheets and towels. However, they must not think they are being denied a service. Lea must convince them that they are being empowered to make a choice that will benefit themselves and their environment.

In preparation for writing, Lea decides on a central proposition. Using less water benefits guests. Next, she writes a few points to back up her proposition. Finally, she considers the readers' point of view and decides how to make her points appealing to her audience. Lea's first draft looks like this.

Valued Guest:

Here at Luxury Suites, we appreciate our natural environment, and we work hard to protect it. One way we do this is through our new water conservation program. With this program, <u>we offer you the opportunity to enjoy a comfortable stay at Luxury Suites while contributing to a healthier planet</u>[1]. As you know, <u>water is a precious resource</u>[2]. By using less water, we can <u>leave a greener and more vibrant planet for our children</u>[3]. In addition, reducing water consumption <u>helps to lower costs and to keep room rates affordable</u>[4] for our guests. Our water conservation program means that your housekeeper will provide clean sheets and towels to all new guests and allow long-term guests to continue using their sheets and towels for as long as they wish. As always, <u>our housekeeping staff will tidy your room at your convenience</u>[4]. <u>By participating in this program, you help conserve our region's water supply and contribute to the long-term</u>[5] health of the planet. We hope that you choose to be involved in this exciting new program and that you enjoy your stay at Luxury Suites.

Is Lea's paragraph effective in persuading guests that it is in their interest to reuse sheets and towels? What techniques does she use to achieve the desired result? In this chapter, you will learn strategies for supporting an argument or a point of view.

Understanding Persuasion

Writers use **persuasion** when they want to convince readers to do something specific or to agree with the writer's point of view on an issue. A persuasive paragraph consists of the following elements:

- A central proposition or argument
- Supporting points that demonstrate valid reasons for the proposition or argument
- An awareness of the audience and an appeal to the readers' interests
- A concluding sentence that reinforces the strongest argument of the writer's case

In Lea's paragraph about water conservation, the central (1) proposition appears in the third sentence: the hotel's conservation program allows guests to contribute to the health of the planet while enjoying a comfortable and pleasant stay.

Notice that Lea does not try to persuade guests to reuse towels and sheets by telling them that it will save money for the hotel. This is not likely to make much difference to guests. Guests are more likely to be persuaded by arguments that appeal to their self-interest. Therefore, by emphasizing the health of the environment, Lea is able to emphasize the program's benefits to everyone.

To support her central proposition, Lea includes these specific points that are underlined and numbered in the paragraph.

2. Water is a precious resource.

3. Reducing water consumption contributes to the long-term health of the planet.

4. Cutting water bills helps keep hotel room rates down.

In addition, Lea reassures guests that the service they expect will not be compromised: their rooms will be cleaned and tidied every day as usual (4). Finally, Lea restates her strongest point in the concluding sentence (5). This way, the idea of environmental health remains strongest in the readers' minds.

SELF-ASSESSMENT 13

When I need to write a paragraph that convinces someone of my point of view, I can:

	Usually	Sometimes	Never
Make a clear proposition statement.	❑	❑	❑
Support my proposition with strong arguments.	❑	❑	❑
Make factual arguments to support a debatable proposition.	❑	❑	❑
Appeal to the readers' interests.	❑	❑	❑
Represent opposing views fairly.	❑	❑	❑

If you checked "Sometimes" or "Never" for any of the items, this chapter will help you improve your skills. Even if you checked "Usually" in every instance, you will learn more about writing to persuade.

Stating Your Proposition

A persuasive paragraph is based on a central argument, or proposition, that is supported by logical reasons. The proposition may be a point of view or a proposed action. In either case, the writer provides evidence to support the main argument. The examples below demonstrate both kinds of propositions.

Point of View	Tax cuts are good for the economy.
Proposed Action	You should eat at least five servings of fresh fruits and vegetables every day.

An effective proposition must be clear, focused, and debatable. Being debatable means that there must be at least two sides to the argument, even though the persuasive paragraph presents only one side. A statement that is factually correct or incorrect is not appropriate for a persuasive essay because an opposing argument cannot be presented.

Debatable	Elementary schools should require students to wear uniforms.
Not Debatable	Schools that enforce uniform policies show higher achievement and fewer discipline problems than schools that do not require uniforms.

The first statement can be argued from the opposite point of view. The second statement is factually true, or it is simply false. Therefore, it can be proved or disproved, but not debated.

Finally, a proposition should not be merely a statement of opinion. To write persuasively, you must support your proposition statement with arguments, evidence, and logic. You must be able to offer reasons that support your point of view or proposed action.

did you ever ?

- Try to persuade someone to see a movie and give reasons why that person should go?

- Try to convince your parents when you were younger why you should be allowed to stay out late or get a pet?

- Express an opinion about a political issue and back it up with evidence?

In situations like these, you try to persuade people to do things or to agree with you. You can use the same techniques to develop arguments in writing.

ACTIVITY 13.1 Read each proposition statement below and determine whether it is appropriate for a persuasive essay. Ask yourself if the statement is debatable. If the statement can be argued from the opposite point of view, it is debatable and, therefore, appropriate. If the statement is factual—either factually correct or factually incorrect—it is not appropriate for a persuasive paragraph. In addition, the statement should not be merely an opinion.

1. The city should install more traffic lights at busy intersections.

    Appropriate?   Why or why not? _____

2. Chocolate cake is delicious.

    Appropriate?   Why or why not? _____

3. Working hard and getting good grades in school is important.

    Appropriate?   Why or why not? _____

4. This year's rainfall has been higher than average.

    Appropriate?   Why or why not? _____

5. The Honda Civic gets better gas mileage than the Subaru Outback.

    Appropriate?   Why or why not? _____

WRITING WORKSHOP

Citing Sources

Writers often refer to authoritative sources in their documents. What counts as an authoritative source?

Often, writers point to academic studies, quote public officials, and refer to media outlets such as newspapers, radio, and television networks. Writers also commonly cite researchers based at universities and think tanks. While none of these sources is infallible, most readers consider them to be fairly trustworthy. More importantly, citing them demonstrates to the reader that the writer has done serious research, which lends credibility to the argument.

Supporting Your Proposition with Arguments

Once you have composed an appropriate proposition statement, you must back up the point using arguments and evidence. Note that the word *argument* does not have a negative connotation in this context. *Argument* is the use of reasons to convince someone of something. While your proposition is debatable, the arguments that support it must be factual. They should be verifiable and specific.

In choosing supportive arguments, the writer must be aware of the paragraph's intended audience. Certain arguments will be more effective with some people than with others. For example, studies have shown that young men are more afraid of traffic tickets than traffic accidents, so public service announcements aimed at young men emphasize that those who are caught without seatbelts will be ticketed. Emphasizing the danger of being injured in an accident would be less effective with this target audience.

Gwen Lassiter is the manager of a theater that shows independent and foreign films. She is preparing an ad to be placed in the newspaper of a local school. Her central proposition is that readers should come to the theater. In preparation for writing, she writes several supporting arguments:

- The schedule features many prize-winning foreign and independent films.
- Many of the films are not available in other nearby theaters.
- The theater offers discounts for children and seniors.
- The theater is located in a central part of town, near the school.
- The adjacent cafe serves snacks, fresh juice, and coffee.
- Screenings are half price every Wednesday.

Looking over her list, Gwen verifies that each of her supporting arguments is factually accurate. Next, she considers her target audience: students. While most of the arguments listed above appeal to students, the discounts for senior citizens are not likely to appeal to a student group. Gwen crosses that argument off the list and composes a rough draft based on three or four of the other arguments. Her paragraph is below.

> Looking for something to do on the weekend or after school? The Orion Theater is the perfect place to relax, to meet friends, and to spend an evening watching interesting and unusual films. Conveniently located in the center of town, the Orion features many prize-winning foreign and independent films that are often unavailable at other theaters. The adjoining cafe serves coffee, snacks, and juice and provides a comfortable place to sit and discuss the show. Half-price Wednesdays are perfect for students' schedules and budgets. Don't miss out!

When making persuasive arguments, writers use various techniques. These techniques include stating factual evidence, citing authoritative sources, and rebutting opposing arguments. In the previous example, Gwen relies on factual points to support her argument that readers should come to the theater. Below are examples of other kinds of techniques that writers commonly use to support persuasive arguments.

Authoritative Sources	According to researchers, 64 percent of Americans receive calls from telemarketers in a given week.
Opposing Arguments	You might think a closet organizer would take up too much space, but customers report that it actually saves space by keeping odds and ends neat and organized.

Finally, a persuasive writer must gain the readers' trust by establishing credibility—that is, being reliable and believable. If a writer exaggerates or makes statements that are untrue, the reader will not take the rest of the writing seriously, even if some of the statements are factually accurate.

For example, if a restaurant owner promotes a popular restaurant by calling it "everybody's favorite restaurant," most readers will see this as an exaggeration. They will be less likely to believe statements made in the remainder of the paragraph. The writer should stick to factual statements, such as "In 2001, Charlie's Steak House won the annual Readers' Choice Award for Best Steaks in the City."

ACTIVITY 13.2 For each position statement below, list three supporting arguments. (You may disagree with the proposition!) All arguments should be specific, factual, and appropriate to the intended audience and purpose. Use a variety of techniques, including stating factual evidence, citing authoritative sources, and addressing opposing potential arguments. Establish credibility by making your arguments believable.

1. The city should pass a law requiring bicyclists to wear helmets.

a. _____

_____

_____

b. _____

_____

_____

c. _____

_____

_____

2. Advertisers have a right to send spam to reach potential customers.

    a. _____

    _____

    _____

    b. _____

    _____

    _____

    c. _____

    _____

    _____

3. Parents should not let their children watch a lot of television.

    a. _____

    _____

    _____

    b. _____

    _____

    _____

    c. _____

    _____

    _____

Appealing to Readers' Interests

Writers must consider their audiences when deciding which facts to include in a persuasive paragraph. In addition, they should present arguments in a way that appeals to the readers' interests.

For example, in the On the Job section, Lea could have told guests that they should reuse their sheets and towels because it will save the hotel money. While this statement is true, the argument will not persuade most guests because they are not concerned about the finances of the hotel. However, guests are interested in saving money, so Lea points out that lower water bills mean more affordable rooms.

Consider this example of an argument that does not appeal to the readers' interests, followed by one that does.

Not Appealing   You should hire me because this job would give me the experience I need.

Appealing   You should hire me because my education and past experience make me well qualified for this position.

The writer should also consider the readers' interests when writing a concluding sentence. This final sentence should tie the paragraph together and restate the strongest argument. This is an opportunity to leave a lasting impression in the readers' minds. Think about which argument is most persuasive to the reader and emphasize it in your closing statement.

Concluding Sentence   My experience, education, and enthusiasm match your requirements perfectly.

TECHNOLOGY CONNECTION

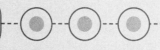

Using Bullets

When writing persuasive paragraphs or essays, writers often choose to emphasize their points using bullets. Bullets provide an effective way to highlight several key arguments so the reader can quickly see the factual information that supports the writer's proposition. Most word processing programs offer several types of bullets. The paragraph below uses bullets to emphasize the key points.

A Western Bank mortgage is ideal for first-time homebuyers for several reasons:

• Western Bank's mortgage counselors provide special guidance and advice for first-time buyers.

• Western Bank offers competitive interest rates.

• Western Bank offers a variety of packages to suit every homeowner's individual needs.

For details about our mortgage packages or to set up an appointment with a counselor, visit our web site or stop in at a nearby branch. We look forward to serving you!

ACTIVITY 13.3   Below are several examples of proposition statements for persuasive paragraphs. For each proposition, identify the target audience. Then write one argument that appeals to the readers' interests and one argument that does not.

1. Taking sick days when you aren't sick is acceptable.

    Target audience: _____

    Appealing argument: _____

    _____

    Unappealing argument: _____

    _____

2. You should use Silkie static cling remover.

    Target audience: _____

    Appealing argument: _____

    _____

    Unappealing argument: _____

    _____

3. You should come to the zoo this summer!

    Target audience: _____

    Appealing argument: _____

    _____

    Unappealing argument: _____

    _____

4. All employees should be allowed to dress casually on Fridays.

    Target audience: _____

    Appealing argument: _____

    _____

    Unappealing argument: _____

    _____

ETHICS CONNECTION

Arguing Fairly

In a persuasive paragraph, the writer is expressing an opinion. The writer is not expected to be objective and to present both sides of the debate. However, writers can express their points of view forcefully while still being fair to other perspectives. Besides helping establish credibility and strengthen the writer's case, it is the ethical way to approach persuasive writing.

For example, imagine that a candidate for governor thinks the state's clean-air laws are too strict and wants to loosen them. The candidate might say, "My opponent wants to destroy businesses in this state by creating impossible restrictions." While the candidate believes that clean-air laws harm businesses and wants to state the case as forcefully as possible, his claim that the other candidate *wants* to destroy businesses is probably not accurate.

A fair argument would be as follows: "My opponent believes that stricter pollution-control laws are necessary to protect public health. I believe they are not only unnecessary, but also harmful." The candidate should then present factual arguments to support this proposition.

SUMMARY FOR PERSUASIVE WRITING

- ❏ A persuasive paragraph attempts to convince the reader to do something or to agree with the writer's point of view.
- ❏ The paragraph's central proposition should be a statement that is debatable.
- ❏ The proposition statement should be backed up with valid arguments and evidence.
- ❏ While the central proposition is debatable, the supporting arguments are factual.
- ❏ When supporting your proposition, *argument* does not have a negative connotation.
- ❏ The writer should identify the intended audience.
- ❏ The arguments should appeal to the readers' own interests.
- ❏ A concluding sentence reinforces the strongest argument to make the writer's case.

PRACTICING YOUR SKILLS

In this chapter, you have learned several techniques for writing persuasively. Now you have the opportunity to practice those techniques with the following activities.

PRACTICE 1

Shawna Jacoby is a headhunter who serves companies in the technology sector. She has just interviewed a job seeker and believes this person is highly qualified for a position at a prominent IT company. Read the paragraph that Shawna has written to persuade the company to hire the applicant.

Justin Scalera would make an excellent addition to the team at Jefferson Systems. His educational background includes coursework in computer technology and business, with an emphasis on marketing. Since graduating from college, he has accumulated several years of experience in the Information Technology sector. In my interview with Mr. Scalera, I found him to be highly personable, confident, and articulate. In an industry where the ability to work well with others is an important asset, I believe Mr. Scalera has much to offer.

Main Proposition

1. What is Shawna's central point? What does she want to persuade her reader to do or agree on?

   _____

   _____

Supporting Arguments

2. On the lines below, list three factual statements that Shawna makes to support her main proposition.

   _____

   _____

   _____

Appealing to Readers' Interests

3. Shawna is aware that her argument will be most persuasive if she speaks to the readers' needs instead of her own or her client's. In Shawna's paragraph above, underline two sentences or phrases in which she frames her argument in terms of the readers' interests.

PRACTICE 2

Kyle McComb is the manager of a warehouse that distributes computer hardware. He just received an angry letter from a client whose order was late and incorrect. In the letter, the customer stated that she would no longer do business with Kyle's company. In response, Kyle composes a letter apologizing for the mistake and trying to persuade the customer to continue ordering parts from the warehouse.

Dear Ms. Llamas

I am very sorry about the mix-up with your most recent order. We were very short staffed last week due to a large number of illnesses. This kind of mistake is very unusual. We will send the correct order immediately, and there will be no shipping charge. You should continue to do business with us because we try very hard to meet customers' needs. Most of our customers are very happy with our performance. Furthermore, losing customers is very hard on our company. Finally, our dedicated and experienced staff is the best in the business. I hope you will accept your most recent order as our gift and that you will continue your relationship with our company.

Making Factual Arguments

1. In the letter, Kyle uses arguments that could be factual, but he does not offer evidence to back them up. Underline two sentences that could be true but for which there is not enough information to be sure.

Establishing Credibility

2. Claiming that his staff is "the best in the business" sounds like an exaggeration. They may be an excellent staff, but it is unlikely that Kyle has had the opportunity to compare them to all other workers in the business. This kind of exaggeration raises questions about his credibility. Rewrite the sentence about Kyle's staff so that he appears more credible.

_____

_____

_____

Concluding the Paragraph

3. Is Kyle's concluding sentence effective? Are any words overused? On the lines below, explain why it is or is not an appropriate conclusion.

_____

_____

_____

APPLYING YOUR SKILLS

Now that you have studied and practiced techniques of persuasive writing, you are ready to write a persuasive paragraph or essay of your own. This section takes you through the steps of the writing process. Label and save each stage of your writing.

Prewriting

(a) Begin by selecting a topic for your paragraph or essay. Remember that your topic should be debatable and should be a proposition that you can back up with reasons. It should not simply be your feeling about something. Here are some suggestions.

All students who want to attend college should (or should not) be allowed to attend for free.

Everyone should (or should not) exercise vigorously for at least one hour every day.

The government should (or should not) require car manufacturers to make more fuel-efficient cars.

Young children should (or should not) be allowed to dress in the style of current entertainers.

Employees should (or should not) be allowed to carry vacation over from one year to the next.

Politicians should (or should not) have limits on the amount of money they are allowed to raise for campaigning.

(b) Brainstorm several arguments that support your proposition. Record them as you think of them.

(c) Look at your list of arguments. Make sure they are factual, fair, and believable.

(d) Identify the audience for your paragraph or essay. Keeping the target audience in mind along with the central proposition you are presenting, read over your arguments and determine which ones are most appropriate to the audience. Consider how you can appeal to the readers' interests. Add more arguments if necessary.

Writing

Write a draft of your paragraph. Include your proposition statement, arguments, and a closing sentence that restates your strongest point or reason.

When writing, organize your paragraph in such a way that your arguments make the strongest possible impact on your reader.

Revising

Read through the first draft of your paragraph. Use the following checklist of questions to make sure you have revised thoroughly.

❑ Does your paragraph attempt to convince the reader to do something or to agree with your point of view?

❑ Is your proposition statement debatable?

❑ Are the proposition statements supported with reasons and clear supporting evidence?

❑ Are your arguments factual?

❑ Have you refrained from giving only an opinion?

❑ Have you argued fairly?

❑ Have you established credibility?

❑ Have you identified the reader?

❑ Do your arguments appeal to the readers' own interests?

❑ Have you refrained from using arguments in your own personal interest that the reader will find unappealing?

❑ Does your concluding sentence restate the strongest or most important point of the paragraph?

When you have revised thoroughly, write a second draft. Then follow the same process with your second draft. Critique and revise it thoroughly, using the checklist above.

When you believe your content and presentation are as good as you can make them, go on to the editing stage.

Editing

In this final stage, check your paragraph or essay for mechanical errors. Closely examine grammar, spelling, word use, punctuation, and capitalization. Run the spell checker and grammar checker, but do your own careful proofing as well. If time permits, put your essay aside overnight, and look at it with fresh eyes the next day.

After you have polished your writing, make a new copy. Proofread your paragraph one final time for small errors. Reading aloud will help.

WRITING FOR YOUR CAREER

CRITICAL THINKING

This section presents a writing project for each of the six career pathways. Choose one that appeals to you and write a persuasive essay on the subject.

When the project description refers you to the textbook web site, go to http://humphrey.swlearning.com and click on the Links tab. Look for Chapter 13, "Writing for Your Career." There you will find direct links to helpful web references.

Communication and the Arts

As the promoter of a new record label, your job includes identifying up-and-coming artists and attracting them to your label. To draw them in, you must persuade them that it is in their interest to sign with you. You are a small independent company that provides both advantages and disadvantages compared to large established labels. Your job is to emphasize the advantages. Write a paragraph in which you argue that musicians should choose your company. For background about the recording industry, go the textbook web site and locate the instructions for Chapter 13, Communication and the Arts. Follow the links for information about independent labels.

Health and Medicine

You are a public health official preparing for the upcoming flu season. You know that some doctors prescribe antibiotics for common ailments such as colds and viral infections that produce flu-like symptoms, whether or not the illness is caused by a bacterial infection. Antibiotics are recommended only for bacterial infections. Because of the overuse of antibiotics, many health professionals are concerned that the medications will lose their effectiveness.

In preparation for the winter season, you are writing a public service announcement that encourages people not to take antibiotics unless they are needed for a specifically diagnosed bacterial infection. For more information about antibiotic resistance, visit the textbook web sites for Chapter 13, Health and Medicine. After reading about the campaign to promote appropriate antibiotic use, write a paragraph persuading people to protect public health by using these medications properly.

Human, Personal, and Public Service

You are working as a regional outreach director for the U.S. Peace Corps. Your job includes recruiting new volunteers by persuading them that service in the Peace Corps would help them achieve their educational, professional, and personal goals. Although most people think of the Peace Corps as an opportunity to serve others, the organization offers many benefits for volunteers. After reading about the Peace Corps programs and opportunities, compose a paragraph persuading potential volunteers to get involved, or at least learn more about the Peace Corps. To learn more, visit the textbook web sites for Chapter 13, Human, Personal, and Public Service.

Business and Marketing

Marketing involves identifying people who need what you are selling and then persuading them that your product is the best one to serve their needs. As the director of marketing for a small travel agency, you send out periodic e-mail alerts to past and potential customers, informing them about current sales and other promotions. Compose a paragraph based on the proposition that readers should plan a trip within the next six weeks. Support your proposition with arguments about airline prices, vacation hot spots, and other information. If you like, you may create details about possible vacation destinations, deals, and other information or research the Internet about vacation spots.

Science and Technology

As an Information Technology executive, you are eager for your employees to stay up to date in this fast-changing industry so your company can remain competitive. You believe that e-learning, or electronic learning, is an excellent and cost-effective way to achieve this. Because you have been studying the possibilities and effects of e-learning, you are excited about bringing these ideas to your company. You decide to write a memo to your manager, explaining the benefits that you perceive from this new approach to workplace training.

Before writing your memo, you can learn more about e-learning by visiting the textbook web site and locating the instructions for Chapter 13, Science and Technology. Once you have acquired an understanding of e-learning and its benefits, write a paragraph persuading your manager to bring this technology to your company.

Environment and Natural Resources

You work for an advocacy organization that tries to protect the country's natural resources by promoting smart growth, resource conservation, and recycling programs. Your organization recently completed a report analyzing your city's recycling programs. You learned that consumers are not taking advantage of the many excellent programs that are already in place. Your research also shows that the lack of participation is, to a large degree, a result of consumers' lack of information about the benefits of recycling.

Write a paragraph aimed at consumers that encourages them to take advantage of city recycling programs. For more information about recycling, visit the textbook web site and locate the instructions for Chapter 13, Environment and Natural Resources.

Part II Summary for Career Writing

❑ A traditional paragraph contains a topic sentence, a body, and a concluding sentence. A suitable topic sentence should state a single idea about a specific topic. Body sentences should support the main idea of a paragraph with specific evidence. A concluding sentence ties a paragraph together.

❑ Illustration is the action of giving examples to explain or clarify a point. Examples should be specific and relevant.

❑ Description means creating a clear and vivid picture in the reader's mind. A topic sentence identifies for the reader what is being described. Details should be specific and should appeal to as many senses as possible.

❑ Definition is saying what a term means. Many definitions begin by naming the general category to which the term belongs, followed by details that separate the term from others in the category. Defining by difference—telling what a term is not—is another useful technique.

❑ Comparison means writing about similarities or likenesses. Contrast means writing about differences. In a comparison or contrast paragraph, the topic sentence should introduce the two subjects to be discussed. The topic sentence should also indicate the general focus of the comparison or contrast.

❑ Classification means breaking things down into groups or categories to help the reader understand the meaning of your writing. In a classification paragraph, the topic sentence states two things: who or what you are going to classify and how you are going to classify them. Subgroups and examples are used to help define and narrow the categories

❑ There are two basic types of process paragraphs: how-to and how-it-is-done. The topic sentence of a process paragraph should establish the value of the subject.

❑ Narration means structuring events and supporting details to tell a story. The writer should choose the most significant events to form the basis of the narrative.

❑ Cause-and-effect paragraphs show what causes an event or the effect of an event. Paragraphs should be about either cause or effect, but not both. Just because two events occur near one another in time does not mean that the first event caused the second event.

❑ A persuasive paragraph attempts to convince the reader to do something or to agree with the writer's point of view. The paragraph's central proposition should be a statement that is debatable. The proposition statement should be backed up with valid arguments and evidence.

14

Planning and Organizing an Essay or a Report

IN THIS CHAPTER YOU WILL LEARN TO:

- Plan and write essays and reports.

- Structure a report.

- Narrow the topic.

- Identify a main idea.

- Introduce the topic.

- Develop and illustrate the subtopics.

Using *Essays and Reports* in Writing for Your Career

Career Path	Sample Career	Use for Essay and Report Writing	Example of Essay and Report Writing
Communication and the Arts	Commercial artist	Putting together a brochure	I specialize in graphic design for campus rock groups. My work with posters, flyers, and logos blends urban and pop art motifs. My original images make music fans take notice.
Health and Medicine	Vocational rehabilitation counselor	Recommending special accommodations	This new keyboard design has been crafted to relieve symptoms of carpal tunnel syndrome. Our proposal reviews key elements of the design. It also includes testimonials and describes rehabilitation exercises.
Human, Personal, and Public Service	Librarian	Creating a web page about search engines for students	You might think that there is a secret to using the World Wide Web as a research tool. However, you can make your web searches much easier by understanding how a search engine works.
Business and Marketing	Market research analyst	Reporting on the outcome of a focus group	Results from the focus group indicate that four out of five consumers prefer soft drinks with more fizz, less sugar, and lower caffeine levels. This report will describe each preference in detail.
Science and Technology	Software engineer	Describing the specifications of a new video game	The Bumper Boogie video game is slotted for release in the fall. However, beta testing has uncovered several technical problems. For example, levels of play do not advance properly. Also, a number of graphics are distorted. These glitches will slow down our current market plan.
Environment and Natural Resources	Soil conservationist	Preventing damage to crop land	Three procedures should reduce crop diseases. First, farmers should implement a system of crop rotation. Next, they should select disease-resistant varieties of grain. Finally, they should add nutrients to enrich the fertility of the soil.

ON THE JOB

Retirement Planning

As a financial adviser, Eric Moore enjoys working with college graduates. Primarily, he assists these clients with their long-term financial goals. Here is the text of a web page he has written on the subject of retirement.

Although financial planners disagree on many issues, there's one thing they're sure about. <u>It's never too early to start planning for retirement.</u>[1] When you're in your twenties, you have a major asset that older people lack, and that is time! The sooner you start planning, the better off you will be when you decide to retire.

With time on your side, <u>a 40-year investment can make small contributions grow into a fortune.</u>[2] <u>Consider the case of Dana.</u> On an average day, she goes through $10 in pocket change. What if Dana invested this money instead? Say she opens a money management account with $1,000. Now imagine that she adds an average of $10 dollars a day for 40 years. With interest compounded annually at 5 percent, she would earn $470,000 in 40 years!

Does retirement planning mean you must give up all of your luxuries? No, but <u>it does require commitment.</u>[3] <u>Take Jared, for example.</u> He earns a moderate income as a commercial artist. However, he's been using all of his spare money to travel. <u>Now he's thinking that he should have set aside a monthly sum toward an IRA for the past five years and traveled less.</u>[3] After all, did he *really* have to see the Taj Mahal and the Pyramids in the same year?

Now find a way to save each month! You should try to take full advantage of your employer's retirement plan. <u>Bill and Susan are a married couple in their twenties.</u>[4] They have been making only minimal contributions because they are buying a home and starting a family. They believe they can't set aside substantial money for retirement at this point. <u>In the long term, however, they would be much better off contributing 10 percent</u>[4] of their income to their retirement plans.

<u>Please contact me to discuss your investment options.</u>[5] Together we can start building a portfolio for what should be the best years of your life.

Eric has tried to make his essay informative and persuasive. If you came across his web site, would you be inspired to start saving for retirement at an early age? If so, Eric succeeded in achieving his goal.

Writing Essays and Reports

When writing **essays and reports**, you will build on the paragraph skills you learned in Chapter 4. Longer compositions are made up of a series of paragraphs, each with a different purpose. Once you know the purpose of each paragraph, you should be able to produce an effective essay or report. Usually, longer compositions are divided into three sections:

- **Introduction:** An effective introduction gains your readers' attention and states the main idea.
- **Body paragraphs:** A series of body paragraphs supports the main idea with specific evidence. This may include examples, facts, or statistics.
- **Conclusion:** The conclusion recaps the points raised in the body. It should also offer a closing thought or an observation.

Take another look at Eric Moore's web page about retirement planning. Consider the function of each paragraph.

Paragraph 1: In his introduction, Eric states his main idea. He claims it is never too early to start retirement planning.

Paragraph 2: Eric starts his first body paragraph with a topic sentence that relates to his main idea. Then he gives the example of Dana. This example supports his point about investing even small dollar amounts on a regular basis.

Paragraph 3: For his second body paragraph, Eric provides a new topic sentence about commitment. To support this point, he relates the example of Jared. This example adds force to Eric's concept of early retirement planning.

Paragraph 4: In his final body paragraph, Eric focuses on a young married couple. He uses this example to illustrate the importance of contributing to an employer's retirement plan.

Paragraph 5: Finally, Eric adds a conclusion that encourages his readers to contact him to discuss their financial future.

In this chapter, you will learn the steps needed to write longer compositions. You will discover how to form a main idea, organize your subtopics and provide supporting evidence.

SELF-ASSESSMENT 14

When I need to write longer essays and reports, I can:

	Usually	Sometimes	Never
Plan my thoughts in logical order.	❑	❑	❑
Express the difference between general ideas and specific examples.	❑	❑	❑
Think of examples that illustrate my main points.	❑	❑	❑
Judge my reader's level of knowledge about the topic.	❑	❑	❑
Sum up my concept or idea in a single sentence.	❑	❑	❑

If you checked "Sometimes" or "Never" for any of the items, this chapter will help you improve your skills. Even if you checked "Usually" in every instance, you will learn more about writing essays and reports.

Planning an Essay

Essays typically have an introduction, a body, and a conclusion. In an essay, the introduction states the main idea. The body paragraphs offer supporting evidence to back up the main idea, and the conclusion recaps the points raised in the essay. In addition, the conclusion may offer a closing remark. Here is a student essay that follows this plan.

Introduction	Are you interested in how power generators work? Do you wonder how Global Positioning System technology functions? If you answered yes to either question, you may wish to pursue a career in electronics engineering.
Body Paragraph 1	First, the employment outlook for electronics engineers is very promising. Due to consumer demand for electronic devices, job openings will grow over the next ten years.
Body Paragraph 2	Earnings are also well above the national average. According to the U.S. Department of Labor, the median income of electronics engineers is $65,000.
Body Paragraph 3	Finally, you can specialize in exciting areas. These include energy production, navigation systems, and computer hardware. Daily tasks are interesting, as electronics engineers solve a variety of technical problems.
Conclusion	If you enjoy technology, want to make a good income, and like the idea of challenging work, a career in electronics engineering may be for you.

In this example, the introduction poses two questions that are followed by the main idea. Each body paragraph then presents a different subtopic related to the main idea. The conclusion restates the subtopics and sums up the essay.

did you ever?

- Write a cover letter detailing your qualifications for a new job?

- Assist a friend with homework problems, reviewing them until he or she understood them?

- Write a letter to a local newspaper about a political issue that upset you?

As in these examples, developing a longer composition demands that you pursue a line of thought for an extended period of time. This chapter will assist you in this task.

Structuring a Report

The structure of a workplace report is similar to that of an academic essay. The introduction states the purpose of the report. Next, the body paragraphs present data. Finally, the conclusion offers a solution or makes a recommendation. Here is a report that follows this order of arrangement.

Introduction

In the past ten years, our company, New Wave Software, has carved out a 7 percent market share. Our newest client, Sci-Tech, Inc., is a major manufacturer of scientific instruments. Sci-Tech wants to purchase 50 site licenses of three of our software packages. The addition of Sci-Tech to our clientele is a top priority.

Body Paragraph 1

Sci-Tech has previewed our business presentation software, Incredi-Vision 2.0, and is satisfied with the features of this package. However, our research and development team has uncovered a major glitch. When the custom animation function is selected, the entire program freezes.

Body Paragraph 2

Sci-Tech has also expressed interest in our web-based software, Amaza-Scan 3.1. The company is impressed by the ease with which this software converts scanned documents directly into HTML. However, discussion of this software is on hold until the animation glitch in Incredi-Vision 2.0 is fixed.

Body Paragraph 3

The third software package that Sci-Tech wishes to purchase is our spreadsheet program, Easy-Tab 4.0. In this software, the save function automatically overrides earlier versions of a file. Sci-Tech would like to disable this override feature.

Conclusion

The importance of these potential sales cannot be overstated. Our development team needs to correct the problems with Incredi-Vision and Easy-Tab as soon as possible. Sci-Tech has been informed that these problems will be corrected within one month.

In this example, the introduction highlights a specific issue. Each body paragraph focuses on a separate software package, and the conclusion stresses the importance of resolving technical issues.

Narrowing Your Topic

Now that you have learned how an essay and a report should be organized, you are ready to begin developing a composition. One step to take in the prewriting stage is narrowing your topic.

When writing a workplace report, you do not need to give as much thought to narrowing the topic as when writing an academic essay. That is because a supervisor normally assigns the topic of a workplace report. For instance, you may be asked to investigate the advantages of a compressed workweek. Another assignment may be to analyze the pros and cons of downsizing a department.

If you are personally choosing a topic for your essay or report, you should take the necessary time to narrow the topic. Here are three examples of how general topics have been narrowed.

(A) General Topic	web censorship
Specific Topic	filtering software that parents can use to block web sites on their home computer
(B) General Topic	code of ethics
Specific Topic	sexual harassment violations in the workplace
(C) General Topic	school discipline
Specific Topic	adoption of a school uniform policy as a way of curbing student violence

In each of these examples, a broad topic has been compressed into a more manageable subject. In Example (A), the topic of web censorship contains too many aspects for a single report or essay. By focusing on filtering software, the writer selects a topic that is narrower. In Example (B), a discussion of a code of ethics also requires broad treatment of the topic. Focusing on one ethical issue narrows the topic. Finally, the topic of school discipline in Example (C) comprises too many forms of discipline. The school uniform policy focuses on an important, but narrower, subject.

In each case, the specific topic provides a better starting point for an essay or a report. Each topic can now be fully developed with supporting evidence that adds details and examples to help the reader understand what is being presented. For instance, with Example (A), you might discuss the features of filtering software. In Example (B), you could discuss types of violations. For Example (C), you could present different ways that school uniforms would be effective.

ACTIVITY 14.1   Consider the list of general topics below. Imagine that you have been assigned to write an essay or a report for each topic. In each case, narrow the topic to one that is more specific.

1. video games

    _____

    _____

    _____

2. pollution

    _____

    _____

    _____

3. careers

    _____

    _____

    _____

4. stereotypes

    _____

    _____

    _____

5. marriage

    _____

    _____

    _____

6. cars

    _____

    _____

    _____

Discovering Your Main Idea

As you write an academic essay or a workplace report, you should focus on a main idea, also called a thesis statement. In an academic essay, the thesis statement communicates the importance of the topic. It also can preview the body of the essay. Here is an example.

Main Idea/Thesis	Unless trained to be vicious, attack dogs make good pets in homes with children.
Preview	Besides being protective, they also can be very affectionate and loyal.

In a workplace report, the main idea states the purpose. However, there are two types of workplace reports: informative reports and analytical reports. An informative report presents information, leaving the reader to draw his or her own conclusions. An analytical report, on the other hand, examines a problem and proposes a solution. In an analytical report, the recommendation becomes the most important part. Consider the following examples from an analytical report.

Main Idea/Purpose	We set out to decide whether an on-site daycare center should be made available to company employees.
Recommendation	Due to budget constraints, an on-site daycare facility would not be feasible during this fiscal year.

As you develop your main idea, try to avoid four problems that writers frequently encounter: too vague, too complicated, too focused on facts, and too personal. An example of each problem is given below, along with a suggested correction.

(A) Too Vague	Internet newsgroups are interesting.
More Effective	Some Internet newsgroups host stimulating political debates.
(B) Too Complicated	We should begin random drug testing, extend employee breaks, and look into profit sharing.
More Effective	Random drug testing will help ensure a safer workplace.
(C) Too Factual	Thomas Jefferson died on July 4.
More Effective	Even before he became President, Thomas Jefferson played a large role in shaping U.S. democracy.

(D) Too Personal   I don't enjoy CDs that contain explicit lyrics.

More Effective   CDs with explicit lyrics are inappropriate for young listeners.

The term *interesting* in Example (A) is too general. Example (B) attempts to cover too many topics. Stating a fact, as in Example (C), leaves little room for adding information. Finally, in Example (D), the main idea needs to appeal to a wider audience than just the writer (*I*).

ACTIVITY 14.2 The following main ideas can be improved. Identify the problem and label the sentence with one of the letters below. Rewrite the sentence so it is more appropriate as the main idea for a longer composition.

V = Too Vague   C = Too Complicated   F = Too Factual   P = Too Personal

_____ 1. Online shopping requires that you input a credit card number.

_____

_____

_____ 2. Teenagers appreciate a wide variety of music.

_____

_____

_____ 3. If you're like me, you dislike manipulative advertising campaigns.

_____

_____

_____ 4. Computer hackers come in many shapes and sizes, but what motivates them is the thrill of breaking into supposedly secure systems.

_____

_____

_____ 5. I find tailgaters annoying.

_____

_____

_____ 6. In our state, proficiency tests are required to graduate from high school.

_____

_____

Introducing Your Topic

Whether you are writing an academic essay or a workplace report, your introduction should acquaint the readers with your topic. In addition, an introduction should *hook* your readers' interest so they will continue reading. Here are some common strategies for creating effective hooks.

Alarming trend: Indicate a pattern that should concern your reader. For instance, if writing an essay about baseball, you might draw attention to declining ticket sales for Major League games.

Series of questions: Use a set of questions to provide an appealing lead-in to your topic. However, try to avoid simple yes-no questions. If readers can answer no to a question, they may stop reading. For example, "Do you surf the Internet?" might not produce sufficient interest in your topic. "How many times have you clicked on an inactive link?" is a better opening question.

Quotable quote: Locate a memorable quote related to your topic. For instance, if writing an essay about friendship, you might begin with Oscar Wilde's quote "True friends stab you in the front."

Startling statistic: Locate a statistic that will impress your reader. For example, if you were writing about nicotine abuse, you might point out that 62.5 percent of the high school graduating class of 2000 had smoked.

Specific illustration: Try opening your essay or report with a scenario, short story, description, or case study. Many readers find specific information appealing.

Relevant background: Document the history of a problem or an issue. This is especially useful for starting a workplace report. For example, if you were looking into current treatments for AIDS, you might recount the development of AIDS-combating drugs since the 1980s.

Myth or misconception: Use your introduction to set the record straight on an issue. For example, perhaps your reader has an improper opinion about the challenges of single-parent households, the lifestyle of hip-hop artists, or the driving habits of newly licensed drivers.

Do not think that you must limit yourself to just one of the above methods. You can use a combination of these strategies. Once you have intrigued, or hooked, your readers, you should state your main idea.

ACTIVITY 14.3 Using the key below, identify the hook in these introductions. Then write a different hook and a short paragraph that introduces the same topic.

AT = Alarming Trend   Q = Series of Questions   QQ = Quotable Quote
SS = Startling Statistic   SI = Specific Illustration   RB = Relevant Background
MM = Myth/Misconception

_____ 1. One of the fenders is rusted out. The upholstery of the driver's seat has rips and tears. The tires squeal when I go around corners. The engine has a tendency to overheat. Still, owning my used car has many hidden rewards.

_____

_____

_____

_____ 2. Many students in public speaking classes assume that effective speakers must be entertaining. However, this is not the only characteristic that makes a speaker worth hearing. Other important aspects include friendliness, sincerity, and competence.

_____

_____

_____

_____ 3. Several species of mammals are facing extinction due to poaching. For example, populations of the Sumatran rhino, Siberian tiger, and mountain gorilla have reached critical low points. If this pattern continues, many beloved mammals will go the way of the dodo.

_____

_____

_____

_____ 4. Today more than half of U.S. homes contains a computer. More than 40 percent of U.S. households are connected to the Internet as well. Within a few years, computers may be as common as television sets.

_____

_____

_____

Developing Subtopics

Now that you have narrowed your topic and developed a main idea, you must outline your essay or report so it will be easy for the reader to understand. First, you must come up with subtopics that support your main idea. Then you need to arrange your subtopics using a clear pattern.

The Document Developement Process

An effective organizational pattern for longer compositions is topical sequence. This pattern arranges subtopics in a series that is climactic or anticlimactic.

A climactic structure builds interest in your essay or report gradually. This pattern is useful when you think that the reader will read your entire composition. In contrast, an anticlimactic structure begins with the strongest subtopic and ends with the weakest. Use this pattern when you suspect the reader may stop before the end.

Here is the outline of a climatic essay about modern art.

Hook	Why is modern art confusing to so many viewers?
Main Idea	Understanding modern art is not as difficult as it seems at first glance.
Preview	Let's consider three types of modern art.
Subtopic 1	Pop Art, such as Andy Warhol's Campbell's® soup cans, focuses on aspects of popular culture.
Subtopic 2	Cubism depicts objects from multiple perspectives, for example, the fragment portraits of Pablo Picasso.
Subtopic 3	Abstract expressionism—for instance, the drip method of Jackson Pollack—conveys the emotional state of the artist.
Conclusion	Now that you know about three types of modern art, you shouldn't dread going to a museum.

In this example, a climactic order is used. Pop Art, the easiest of the three subtopics to comprehend, is explored first. The most difficult subtopic, Abstract Expressionism, appears last. In addition, specific examples of painters have been added to illustrate each type of art. More examples will be added as the essay progresses.

ACTIVITY 14.4 Select a topic for an essay or a report and develop a main idea about the topic. Then state three subtopics that support the main idea. Decide whether the subtopics should be arranged climactically or anticlimactically.

Topic: _____

Main Idea: _____

_____

Subtopic 1: _____

_____

Subtopic 2: _____

_____

Subtopic 3: _____

_____

TECHNOLOGY CONNECTION

Using PowerPoint® as an Outlining Tool

The next time you write an essay or a report, consider using the PowerPoint slide presentation program. This software can help you organize your ideas, even if you don't give a presentation.

- Title slide: Identify the title of your presentation and give your name.

- Body slides: Show the subtitle and add bullets showing the subpoints. The subtitle normally appears at the top of the slide. This is equivalent to the subtopic of an essay or a report. Usually, there is room for three to five bullets below the subtitle. This is where you plug in supporting evidence to illustrate or explain your subtopic.

- Blank slides and chart slides: Give additional features. For example, an organizational chart can be used to indicate the breakdown of your topic into separate subtopics.

Once you finish your presentation, print an outline view of your slide show. To do this, click on the Print menu option. Select Outline View under the Print What? prompt at the bottom of the gray pop-up box. Now you can use your outline as a starting point for developing the rest of your report in more detail.

Illustrating Your Subtopics

Once you have developed several subtopics, you need to add examples for supporting evidence. Consider drawing examples from the following sources.

Personal interviews: Interviews can be conducted in person, by telephone, or via e-mail. When interviewing, take notes of quotable quotes.

Journals and magazines: Articles from professional journals are suitable for reports about business, and articles from other magazines are appropriate for less technical essays.

Personal experience and observation: Use personal experiences and observations for anecdotes and descriptions that clarify your main points.

As you write your report or essay, write the general ideas before giving specific supporting evidence. This is shown in the following series of examples.

(A) General Idea	Telecommuting is becoming more common among U.S. workers.
Specific Example	In Consuelo's job, she can work at home, using the Internet to communicate with her department.
Specific Example	Frank, a consultant with clients located around the country, holds conferences in a chat room.
(B) General Idea	Interviews that take place at restaurants require knowledge of etiquette.
Specific Example	When interviewing for a position at a restaurant, Juan waited for the interviewer to place her order first.
Specific Example	Knowing that the interviewer would pay for her meal, Robyn ordered a moderately priced dinner.
(C) General Idea	Paralegals provide invaluable assistance to attorneys.
Specific Example	Tom writes and files legal briefs for court cases.
Specific Example	Monica takes depositions of key witnesses for upcoming trials.

Developing your general ideas in sufficient detail will make your composition more reader-friendly. Specific examples help the reader to understand your ideas more fully.

ACTIVITY 14.5 For each of the following general ideas, come up with a specific example that illustrates or explains it. Use complete sentences as you develop your example. The first one has been completed for you.

1. Many self-help books provide useful information.

   A diet and exercise book I purchased a month ago helped me lose five
   pounds.

2. Some cartoonists take a humorous look at real-life situations.

   _____

   _____

3. Many advanced college courses require prerequisites.

   _____

   _____

4. A person's choice of music is a good indicator of his or her personality.

   _____

   _____

5. Weekends can be very relaxing.

   _____

   _____

6. Advances in technology can make life easier.

   _____

   _____

7. Technophobes are people who are afraid of computers.

   _____

   _____

8. Certain models of cars are purchased as status symbols.

   _____

   _____

WRITING WORKSHOP

Selecting the Right Synonym

When writing an essay or a report, you may find yourself repeating one or two key words too often. Therefore, you should examine your writing to make sure you are using a variety of synonyms for key words. Choosing the right synonym is important. A discussion of denotation and connotation will help you choose the best synonyms.

Denotation refers to the dictionary meaning of a word. Synonyms generally have the same denotation (that is why they are synonyms). However, they usually have different connotations.

Connotation refers to the emotional impact of a word. The emotions a word can call up in readers may be strong or weak, positive or negative. To be sure you use the right synonym, you must understand its connotation. Here are some examples.

fate	destiny, chance, lot, fortune

Fate often has a negative connotation. For instance, an event may seem fated to happen. The term *chance* leaves the impression of loss of control, also a negative thought. *Destiny* and *fortune* possess more positive meanings. The general term *lot*, as in *one's lot in life*, has the weakest connotation.

rise	ascend, climb, mount, soar

In this case, *rise*, as in *rise to the top*, has a positive connotation. *Soar* has an even more positive meaning, implying an effortless journey. *Mount* has a strong, and possibly negative, connotation. Consider the phrase *mount an attack*, for instance. *Climb*, a more common word, may be the weakest synonym.

Whether a synonym evokes positive or negative emotions in a reader depends on how it is used with the other words around it. That is why it is important to evaluate each word as it relates to the rest of a sentence or paragraph.

Below are lists of synonyms. Decide which synonym comes closest to matching the keyword's connotation. Which synonyms are weak or strong, positive or negative?

disease	sickness, illness, virus, disorder, bug
perform	do, carry out, execute, achieve, make
war	struggle, conflict, confrontation, battle, feud

ETHICS CONNECTION

An Honest Dilemma

Part of a manager's job involves writing performance reviews of employees. It sounds easy enough, but consider the following case.

> Jennifer, an IT manager, must conduct a performance review of Phil, one of her employees. Technically, Phil is very proficient at his job, which is to consult with clients outside of the office. However, Jennifer has received several complaints from clients. Most of these people are middle managers who do not possess Phil's level of expertise. They tell Jennifer that they are having difficulty interpreting Phil's technical jargon.
>
> Part of the performance review Jennifer must complete pertains to communication skills. The better an employee looks in a review, the greater his or her chances for promotion. Jennifer realizes that if she is to be fair, her evaluation of Phil's performance must show a need for improvement. She is afraid a low score will cause Phil to seek employment with another firm. She is also aware that he might file a lawsuit claiming discrimination of some type.

Jennifer should be honest about Phil's poor communication skills. She should not put a spin on his performance that boosts his score. However she should evaluate the final review carefully to make sure it is factual and fair, in case Phil complains or brings a lawsuit.

SUMMARY FOR WRITING DOCUMENTS

- ❑ Essays and reports are normally divided into three sections: introduction, body, and conclusion.
- ❑ An important step in planning a longer composition is to narrow or limit the topic.
- ❑ A main idea, or thesis statement, expresses the significance of an essay or a report.
- ❑ Readers appreciate an introduction that grabs their attention.
- ❑ A climactic or anticlimactic order may be used when developing and arranging subtopics.
- ❑ Specific supporting evidence should be included when illustrating a subtopic. This includes examples, observations, descriptions, and anecdotes.
- ❑ The connotation of a synonym is important. Therefore, a writer should evaluate a synonym carefully for its emotional impact on the readers.

PRACTICING YOUR SKILLS

PRACTICE 1

Cory Baum enjoys his job as a software engineer. He takes a leading role in the creation of new video games. Recently, his supervisor showed him a letter from a concerned parent. Here is just one of many complaints about the company's new video game.

When I purchased Bumper Boogie for my twelve-year-old son, I was completely misled by the Parental Guidance label. How this game escaped the censors I'll never know. If anything, Bumper Boogie should be labeled *Mature*. Even so, I wouldn't understand how a mature person could gain any sort of enjoyment from this slime. Truly, I'm afraid for the welfare of my son's moral values.

Within a week, my son was addicted to your game. His homework suffered, and he skipped Little League baseball to continue playing. I became concerned when he insulted his younger sister with a sexist term. This is something he'd never done before. He followed up this comment by being disrespectful to two of his teachers—both females. I began wondering where his negative attitude toward women was coming from. One night I decided to play a game of Bumper Boogie. The scantily clad women cheering on the beach took me aback. I became sickened to learn that you could score points by running them over with a dune buggy! The level of violence in this game is also frightening. The submachine gun play in Level Three is a threat to young, impressionable minds.

What kind of values is your game instilling in our nation's youth? A game like this isn't teaching our kids respect for the sanctity of life. I'm sure you would respond by saying that it's only a game. But it's a game to which my son was addicted within one week. Try to imagine the argument we had when I took the game away from him.

All I ask is that, as you produce video games for young people, you take a moment to consider the situation from a parent's perspective. Maybe you should become a parent yourself before you design something so unimaginative.

Purpose

1. Assess the overall persuasiveness of the parent's letter. Explain your view in a short paragraph.

_____

_____

_____

Main Idea

2. Underline the sentence that expresses the main idea of the letter. Then state the main idea in your own words.

_____

_____

Structure

3. Circle the sentences that function as subtopics. As part of class discussion or in a writing journal, comment on the structure of the letter. In what ways, if any, could the organization be improved?

Response

4. If you were Cory, how would you respond to such a letter? Outline the contents of a return letter. What would you say to this parent in your or your company's defense?

PRACTICE 2

Each of the following quotes by a famous person expresses a main idea about a specific topic. Using the same topic, develop a main idea of your own.

1. "Governments tend not to solve problems, only to rearrange them."—Ronald Reagan

_____

_____

2. "TV is chewing gum for the eyes."—Frank Lloyd Wright

_____

_____

3. "Some newspapers are fit only to line the bottom of birdcages."—Spiro T. Agnew

_____

_____

4. "Education can train, but not create, intelligence."—Edward McChesney Sait

_____

_____

5. "The ultimate mystery is one's own self."—Sammy Davis, Jr.

_____

_____

APPLYING YOUR SKILLS

Now that you have learned how to develop longer compositions, you can write an essay or a report of your own.

Selecting a Topic

Begin by selecting a general topic for your essay or report. Choose one of the topics below or another subject that interests you.

Essay Topics	Report Topics
vacation spots	employee morale
video games	downsizing
movies	file sharing
news programs	cutting-edge technology
exotic pets	computer programs
politics	investment opportunities
campus rituals	environmental impact of industry

Narrowing the Topic

After selecting a topic, try narrowing it so it can be used in depth in an essay or a report. For instance, if you selected vacation spots as your general topic, you could narrow it to a specific location. Maybe you could focus on the Bahamas or the Swiss Alps. If you chose employee morale as a workplace topic, you might narrow it to morale within a specific department. For example, you might focus on the morale of employees in sales.

Developing the Main Idea

Think about the significance of the topic for your reader. Why would the reader be interested in a report or an essay about this topic? Your answer should help you express your main idea. Whether you write an essay or a report, remember to state the main idea in your introduction.

Introducing Your Topic

Think about an original way to introduce the topic. For example, you may wish to begin by asking a series of stimulating questions. Another technique is to present a startling statistic. You may need to brainstorm several different methods. Then determine which strategy is most effective.

Developing Your Subtopics

Use the following outline to express a series of subtopics related to your main idea. Then think of supporting evidence—examples or descriptions—that illustrate or explain each subtopic. Try coming up with at least two forms of supporting evidence per subtopic.

Subtopic 1: _____

_____

Supporting Evidence: _____

_____

Subtopic 2: _____

_____

Supporting Evidence: _____

_____

Subtopic 3: _____

_____

Supporting Evidence: _____

Adding a Conclusion

Usually a conclusion recaps the subtopics of an essay or a report. In addition, a conclusion may offer a closing remark or an observation. In an essay, for instance, you might conclude with a memorable example or an interesting quotation. In a workplace report, you might recommend a course of action or propose a solution to a problem.

Revising Your Essay or Report

When you finish writing a first draft of your essay or report, use the following checklist to begin the process of revision.

- ❑ Is the topic sufficiently focused to discuss in depth?
- ❑ Is the main idea stated succinctly and clearly?
- ❑ Does the essay or report contain a clear and logical structure?
- ❑ Is the topic introduced in an original or imaginative way?
- ❑ Are there a sufficient number of subtopics?
- ❑ Do all of the subtopics relate to the main idea?
- ❑ Is enough supporting evidence presented to illustrate or explain each of the subtopics?
- ❑ Does the conclusion recap the body of your essay or report effectively, as well as provide a closing thought or recommendation?

WRITING FOR YOUR CAREER

CRITICAL THINKING

Choose one or more of the following scenarios as a starting point for an essay or a report. As you respond to a topic, you may wish to research relevant sites on the Internet. To do so, go to the web site http://humphrey.swlearning.com and locate the instructions for Chapter 14 "Writing for Your Career." Access the web sites provided for additional information.

Communication and the Arts

As a telecommunications specialist, you have been hired by your college alma mater to investigate online learning options. The college offers a wide variety of career-oriented courses. In addition, it has always prided itself on its hands-on approach to learning. Live classrooms at the school have a low professor-student ratio. On the other hand, as other area colleges offer more distance-learning courses, the administration of the school believes it must begin putting more of its courses on the Web in order to compete.

Your supervisor has asked you to design a sample web site for an online course. Select a single course and write a report that describes the web site. As you write, indicate how the web site would allow instructors to maintain a one-on-one, hands-on approach to learning.

Health and Medicine

Your job as a vocational rehabilitation counselor requires you to work with recently injured and disabled clients. Many of your clients have difficulty performing tasks when they return to the workplace. One of your clients, an interior designer named Hugh, was paralyzed from the waist down by an automobile accident. Hugh wants to continue his work, which involves assisting individual homeowners with renovations of Victorian homes.

One of Hugh's difficulties is maneuvering his wheelchair through these homes. In general, older homes have not been designed to accommodate persons with special needs. For instance, elevated front porches and winding staircases pose problems for Hugh. Use your imagination to come up with a plan of action that would enable Hugh to continue working in this profession. Write a report that details your recommendations.

Human, Personal, and Public Service

As the librarian at a school, you have noticed in the past year that students use the library less often. The majority of students prefer researching the Web on their own. Thus, the number of book and periodical checkouts is down. The administration is putting pressure on you to raise the number of students who use the library. The administration has asked you to come up with three methods of involving more students in what the library has to offer. Write a report in response to the administration's request.

Business and Marketing

Remember Eric Moore, the financial planner described at the beginning of this chapter? In an effort to broaden his clientele, Eric has decided to develop a new link to his web page. He wants to devote special attention to the financial concerns of college students. Imagine that he has hired you as an intern to develop a web page on this subject.

Drawing upon your own experiences as well as those of other students you know, write the text for a web page that addresses a financial problem that college students face. For instance, you might focus on credit card debt, college tuition, or daily living expenses. As you develop the web page, illustrate each point with specific examples and offer concrete tips.

Science and Technology

As a software engineer for Lifeworks, Inc., you have taken on a new project. Lifeworks is a software program for people interested in summarizing and presenting the results of their genealogy research. While researching competing genealogy programs, you discovered a major limitation with many of them. They assume that traditional two-parent families are the norm. They don't provide options for family trees where divorce, remarriage, and/or adoption may be part of the family's history.

Think of a new genealogy software program that provides options for special cases. Then write a report, to be submitted to your supervisor, that identifies the features of the improved program. In your report, try to describe as many different family structures as possible. Provide specific examples of each one.

Environment and Natural Resources

As a regional planner for a midsized town in Ohio, you have been working with developers to build an industrial park. The complex will include three buildings containing several major companies employing more than 300 people. The addition of the industrial park will give the town a much-needed economic boost.

Originally, the site of the complex seemed ideal. For instance, a large pond provides pleasant scenery. Surrounding fields and hills add to the scenic view. However, a rare species—a newt—recently classified as endangered, has been found near the pond. The discovery of this newt has prompted daily demonstrations by environmentalists. You are worried that television, radio, and newspaper coverage of the protests is making the proposed industrial park look bad.

You have agreed to meet with developers and environmentalists at a town meeting scheduled for next week. Now you are preparing a handout for the meeting. First, brainstorm the pros and cons of the newt issue. Try looking at the problem from the industrialists' and the environmentalists' point of view. Prepare a handout for the meeting that sums up the points of each position.

15

Writing to Illustrate

IN THIS CHAPTER YOU WILL LEARN TO:

- Write essays and reports that use strong, focused examples.

- Write effective thesis statements.

- Organize your examples in logical order.

Using *Illustrative Writing* for Your Career

Career Path	Sample Career	Use for Illustrative Writing	Example of Illustrative Writing
Communication and the Arts	Graphic artist	Explaining a design to a client	The proposed design for the series of children's books will appeal to young readers. From the opening page, the design uses bright colors to capture a child's attention.
Health and Medicine	Physical therapist	Explaining how to reduce workplace injuries	Many workplace injuries result from poor planning of the work environment. One of the greatest risks comes from heavy materials placed on high shelves.
Human, Personal, and Public Service	Paralegal	Summarizing the facts of a legal case	Facts cited in the police report establish that the auto accident was not our client's fault. First, our client's car was moving no faster than 5 miles per hour.
Business and Marketing	Restaurant owner	Preparing a business plan	SushiPronto will capitalize on well-established trends in the food services industry. According to recent surveys, for example, buyers of fast food increasingly prefer low-fat items rather than burgers and fries.
Science and Technology	Park ranger	Explaining how to prevent forest fires	As Smokey Bear has said for years, you too can prevent forest fires. Many forest blazes begin when someone leaves a campfire untended.
Environment and Natural Resources	Water safety specialist	Detailing pollution control measures	Careless actions by city residents contribute to the water pollution problem. One frequent abuse is the dumping of used motor oil into storm drains.

ON THE JOB

Emergency Medical Technician

Jamie Tyler enjoys being an emergency medical technician (EMT) because she loves the action. She and her colleagues in the county's Emergency Medical Services Department provide on-the-spot medical care for victims of traffic accidents, cardiac arrest, and other acute injuries and illnesses. Personally, in five years on the job, she has helped save more than a hundred lives.

Recently, Jamie was given a new responsibility that calls on skills she did not expect to use. As the local EMT with the highest level of expertise, she was asked to contribute to a report describing her department's mission and its goals for the future. The report will help the department get the increased funding it needs.

Jamie's first task is to draft a section explaining the types of medical services that EMTs typically provide. Everybody knows basically what EMTs do, she supposes, but few people fully understand the wide range of emergency health conditions that EMTs treat and how much they rely on specialized training and high-tech equipment. For that reason, Jamie decides to write the section in an illustrative format, giving a series of examples of an EMT's daily work.

She follows the writing process you have seen throughout this book. She brainstorms ideas, then creates an outline and a rough draft. Here is her introductory paragraph for the section (paragraph 1), followed by her first example (paragraph 2).

1

The Emergency Medical Services Department provides far more than rapid response and transport to County Hospital. Before and during an ambulance ride, patients receive intensive emergency care with the most up-to-date techniques and equipment.

2

If, for example, a patient shows symptoms of a heart attack, the EMTs will administer an immediate electrocardiogram (EKG). In each ambulance team, at least one EMT is trained to interpret the EKG results. The readings can also be transmitted electronically to emergency room staff at the hospital. If the patient's heartbeat stops or becomes erratic, the EMTs can use a portable defibrillator to administer life-saving shocks. When necessary, the EMTs also use intravenous drugs to prevent additional cardiac damage. During all such cardiac interventions, the EMTs consult by radio with cardiologists at the hospital so the care the patient receives is continuous and well coordinated.

Do you think Jamie sets out her general point clearly? Is her example paragraph effective? What might she write about in her next paragraph?

The Illustrative Essay or Report

An **illustrative essay or report** follows the same principles as the illustrative paragraphs you learned to write in Chapter 5:

- It states a main point.
- It provides examples to support that point.
- It uses appropriate transitions to lead the reader from one example to the next.

Opening Paragraph

In the excerpt from Jamie's report, can you see where the main point is stated? It is in paragraph 1. Just as an illustrative paragraph starts with a topic sentence, an illustrative essay or report begins with a paragraph that lays out the topic for the rest of the document.

Body Paragraphs

After the opening paragraph stating the main point, the following paragraphs introduce the examples that will illustrate that point. To make the organization clear to the reader, writers typically start a new paragraph for each example. Notice how Jamie starts a new paragraph (2) to describe the way EMTs treat patients with symptoms of a heart attack. Her next paragraph will focus on another example, such as stroke victims or people with head trauma.

Each example should be developed with enough detail to make it convincing. Jamie names three different procedures that EMTs perform on cardiac patients (see the underlined phrases). She also describes the radio contacts between EMTs and the hospital staff.

To connect the paragraphs, longer illustrative documents rely on the same kinds of transitions you read about in Chapter 5. Notice how Jamie uses *for example* in the opening sentence of her second paragraph, creating a transition into her first example. In her next paragraph, she can use any number of other transitional terms: *another example, also, too,* and *furthermore,* to name a few.

In this chapter, you will extend the illustration skills you have already developed so you can call on them when you write longer documents.

SELF-ASSESSMENT 15

When I need to write an essay or a report that uses examples to illustrate a point, I can:

	Usually	Sometimes	Never
State my thesis in clear and specific language.	☐	☐	☐
Think of several examples to support my thesis.	☐	☐	☐
Put my examples in a logical, effective order.	☐	☐	☐
Develop each example with appropriate details.	☐	☐	☐
Use effective transitions between paragraphs.	☐	☐	☐

If you checked "Sometimes" or "Never" for any of the items, this chapter will help you improve your skills. Even if you checked "Usually" in every instance, you will learn more about writing to illustrate.

Stating Your Thesis

In a report or an essay, the sentence stating the main point is often called a thesis statement. A thesis is any point or argument that you assert to be true. Essentially, the thesis statement plays the same role in the essay as a topic sentence plays in a paragraph. Because your thesis statement sets out the point you intend to make, you should make sure it is clear, accurate, and focused on what you want to say.

Imagine that you are an environmental scientist. You are writing a brief report about your team's inspection of a land parcel scheduled for redevelopment. You have found some problems that need to be fixed before new housing units are built. Here are three possible introductory paragraphs. Read them and decide which one you think is best. In each case, the thesis statement is underlined.

Example 1

In June 20—, EnviroSpecs, Ltd., inspected the parcel of land at 1211 Market Street to determine its suitability for construction of a condominium complex. <u>The team of three inspectors found that it would be dangerous to build condominiums on this site.</u>

Example 2

In June 20—, EnviroSpecs, Ltd., inspected the parcel of land at 1211 Market Street to determine its suitability for construction of a condominium complex. <u>The team of three inspectors found that the site presents serious health and safety risks for the construction crews and for the future occupants of the condominiums.</u>

did you ever ?

- Tell a friend you had a great time on vacation and then explain why by giving several extended examples of things you did?

- State a position about the qualifications of a certain political candidate and then back it up with examples from that candidate's record?

- Give an opinion about the abilities of a particular instructor and then support it with detailed stories of what happened in class?

In many daily situations like these, you make a statement and then use extended examples to illustrate why it is true. You can apply this same technique in your writing.

Example 3

In June 20—, EnviroSpecs, Ltd., inspected the parcel of land at 1211 Market Street to determine its suitability for construction of a condominium complex. The team of three inspectors found evidence of underground oil tanks dating from the site's previous use as a gas station. <u>Unless the remnants of these tanks are excavated and removed, they pose serious health and safety risks for the construction workers and future occupants of the residences.</u>

Example 1 makes a broad statement that building the condominiums would be dangerous. *Dangerous* is a vague and loaded word. What kind of danger? How severe? Are there ways to reduce or eliminate the risk?

Example 2 narrows the thesis statement somewhat, indicating "serious health and safety risks for the construction crews and for the future occupants of the condominiums." That example is slightly more specific about the type of danger, but some readers may still assume that you are ruling out forever the possibility of building residences on this site.

Example 3 is the best alternative because it states the environmental problem in a more specific way. It narrows down the topic of the report to risks posed by the old oil tanks, and it indicates that the problem can be solved. With a focused thesis statement like this one, your readers will know exactly what you are setting out to demonstrate.

ACTIVITY 15.1

Pretend that you work for an organization that divides employees into teams to handle specific projects. To aid in training new employees, your supervisor has asked you to write an essay describing the value of this kind of teamwork.

1. Brainstorm about the topic. Is the "value of teamwork" specific enough, or do you need to narrow it down? Think specifically about how a team can handle a project better than a single person. Is a team more diverse in its knowledge, more experienced, and more creative? Jot down answers to these questions and any other preliminary ideas that occur to you.

_____

_____

_____

_____

_____

2. Now draft an opening paragraph for the essay. Remember to include a
    thesis statement that expresses your main point.

    _____

    _____

    _____

    _____

    _____

    _____

    _____

    _____

    _____

    _____

3. Look back at the opening paragraph you just wrote. Underline your thesis
    statement. Is it specific enough? Do you see how to support it with
    examples? If not, revise the thesis statement until it meets these
    requirements.

WRITING WORKSHOP

"Scannable" Writing

In today's hectic world, people often scan documents rather than read
them in detail. This is especially true in a work setting, where many
individuals are deluged by paperwork and e-mail. If you are writing for
hurried readers, it helps to make your documents as "scannable" as
possible. In an illustrative report, you can:

- Put enough specifics in the opening paragraph for a reader to get
  the gist of your argument right away.
- Make the organization of your document obvious to a quick
  browser: for instance, an opening paragraph, three body
  paragraphs that each give one example, and a concluding
  paragraph.

For an example that follows these pointers, see the "Practicing Your Skills"
section later in this chapter.

Putting Your Examples in Order

In a large dental practice, the senior dental hygienist, Elaine, is writing a summary of the office's safety procedures. Besides satisfying insurance requirements, this document will help guide new employees. In one section, Elaine wants to make the point that the staff takes many steps to prevent the spread of germs. In her outline, she lists the following examples to use:

- We sterilize all instruments after each patient's visit.
- We wear latex gloves when examining patients.
- We clean room surfaces with a germicide after each patient's visit.
- We wash hands before examining patients.
- We don surgical masks before using tools in a patient's mouth.
- We replace torn gloves immediately.

These are good examples, but they are in no particular order. If Elaine's document followed the same sequence as this outline, readers would be confused about what happens when. It makes more sense to organize the examples by when they occur:

Organize your examples

- Procedures done before examining each patient
- Procedures done during examination of each patient
- Procedures done after seeing each patient

Ordering your examples is a key part of achieving *coherence*, which you read about in Chapter 3. Here are four common types of order.

Time Order	Earliest to latest, oldest to newest, shortest in duration to longest in duration
Space Order	Top to bottom, front to back, left to right, outside to inside, near to far
Size Order	Smallest to largest, shortest to tallest, lightest to heaviest
Order of Importance	Least important to most important, lowest rank to highest rank

The order of your examples will influence the transitional expressions you use to move from one example to the next. For instance, if you choose time order, transitional words such as *next* and *later* will be appropriate. Activities 15.2 and 15.3 will help you practice order and transitions.

ACTIVITY 15.2 Use numbers from 1 to 4 to show the correct order for each set of examples. On the line below each group, explain what kind of order you used. The first item has been completed.

1. trees and bushes in my yard

    _____1_____ oak   _____3_____ lilac

    _____4_____ azalea   _____2_____ birch

    size order: largest to smallest _____

2. positions in my company

    _____ managers   _____ clerks

    _____ president   _____ vice president

    _____

3. parts of the day that I especially enjoy

    _____ a walk after work   _____ late-night TV

    _____ breakfast   _____ lunch with friends

    _____

4. supplies used to wrap my friend's present

    _____ gift wrap   _____ box

    _____ ribbon   _____ tissue paper

    _____

ETHICS CONNECTION

Tricking the Reader with Facts

"Jason Abernathy has done a terrible job as plant manager. Since he took over, production has fallen 20 percent. Because he has taken no steps to replace aging equipment, worker injuries have risen. At the same time, he is trying to cut average wages."

Jason's performance sounds bad. But what if the entire industry is in a deep recession? Wouldn't that explain all of the facts mentioned? This scenario shows how easy it is to trick readers with a biased selection of facts. To be an ethical writer, you should support your points with examples that are not only true in themselves, but also true in the impression they give the reader.

TECHNOLOGY CONNECTION

Tools for Outlining

Once you have thought about your main point, selected your examples, and placed the examples in order, you are ready to prepare a detailed outline. Full-featured word processors such as Microsoft® Word and WordPerfect® offer helpful tools for this stage. In Word, for example, the Bullets and Numbering item on the Format menu allows you to select an outline style like this:

I. First level
   A. Second level
         (1) Third level
         (2) Third level
   B. Second level
II. First level
   A. Second level
   B. Second level

ACTIVITY 15.3

Look back at the topics and examples in Activity 15.2. For each set of examples, list three transitional expressions that would help you move from one example to the next.

1. largest, next largest, smallest _____

2. _____

3. _____

4. _____

SUMMARY FOR ILLUSTRATIVE DOCUMENTS

❑ An illustrative essay or report states a main point, provides examples to support that point, and uses transitional expressions to lead the reader from one example to the next.

❑ The sentence that establishes the main point is known as the thesis statement. It should be narrow and focused enough so it can be supported by the examples that follow.

❑ Each example should be developed with appropriate details.

❑ The examples should be arranged in a logical order, such as time order, space order, size order, or order of importance.

PRACTICING YOUR SKILLS

By now, you have a good sense of how to write an illustrative report or essay. You can sharpen your skills with additional practice. In this section, you will look at part of a report by Peter Rizzo, a paralegal at a law firm.

Peter's firm is representing a client whose business suffered extensive loss when a disgruntled employee intentionally destroyed the accounts receivable database. The client's insurance company, James Assurance Group (JAG), has refused to pay for the damage, citing a clause in the policy that says "computer system penetration" is not covered. But Peter has discovered that JAG paid similar claims in the past. In his report to the main attorney for the case, he wants to give examples of JAG's earlier practices. Below is what he has written so far. The paragraphs are numbered for reference.

1   In our client's case, JAG wants to define "computer system penetration" broadly enough to exclude any intentional damage to a computer system, no matter who caused it. Clearly, the policy is not meant to protect against viruses and hacking attacks that come from *outside* the company. The question is whether the policy covers damage from sources *within* the company—in this case, an employee. Three recent claims, all based on JAG policies with the same language as our client's policy, show that internal computer system damage should indeed be covered.

2   In a 2001 incident at Roth Tools, Inc., a frustrated sales representative cut a dozen network cables in four different offices. The repair costs included not only new cables, but also many hours of time spent searching for the exact sites of the damage. Without contesting the claim, JAG paid the entire repair bill, which totaled more than $5,000. (See the Notes section for details of this case and the two that follow.)

3   In another case from early 2004, a programmer brought in a computer virus on a CD and unleashed it on the network of Programs4U, Ltd. The virus crashed the company's system and spread to the networks of four corporate clients, who immediately canceled their contracts with Programs4U. JAG paid not only for internal system repairs, but also for lost income from the canceled contracts.

4   Finally, in a 1999 case, JAG settled a claim remarkably similar to the one filed by our client. At a nonprofit agency called Housing Solutions, an angry part-time systems engineer emptied the database that stored the names and addresses of donors. He also destroyed the backup disks. The organization calculated the loss to its fund-raising efforts at $1.5 million. After initially refusing this claim, JAG settled by paying the amount in full.

5   As these examples demonstrate, JAG's actions toward our client do not agree with the company's own record. JAG's treatment of past claims shows that damage to computer systems caused by a company's employees should be covered by the insurance policy.

The Thesis Statement

1. In paragraph 1, underline Peter's thesis statement for this section of the report. (*Hint:* It is not the first sentence.)

The Examples

2. What type of order did Peter use for his examples: time order, space order, size order, or order of importance? How does his choice relate to the old saying "Leave the best for last"?

_____

_____

Transitional Expressions

3. Two of the body paragraphs begin with transitional expressions. List the number of each paragraph and the transitional expression it uses.

_____

_____

4. One body paragraph does not begin with a transitional expression because it does not need to. What is the number of this paragraph, and why was Peter able to omit transitional words?

_____

_____

5. What transitional expression does Peter use to introduce his conclusion?

_____

APPLYING YOUR SKILLS

To put your skills to use, write an illustrative essay of your own. This section will help you build the essay by guiding you through the steps of the writing process. Use a separate sheet of paper or a word processing file. Label and save each stage of your writing.

Prewriting

(a) Begin by selecting a topic for your essay. Here are some samples:

Subject	Types of Examples to Use
my favorite author	examples of the author's writing
the wide influence of popular music	examples of how music affects other areas of popular culture
the harm that gossip causes	examples of consequences from your own experience
uses of a good education	examples of benefits people gain from their education

(b) Think about how to focus your topic. If you are writing about the harm caused by gossip, will you consider all types of harm or will you focus on a particular kind?

(c) Brainstorm examples for your chosen topic. List plenty of ideas.

(d) Sort through the examples you have listed. Choose the best ones and select the order in which to place them. Considering time order, space order, size order, and order of importance, pick the most suitable option for your needs.

(e) Write an outline for your essay.

Writing

(a) Write a draft of your opening paragraph. Remember to include a thesis statement.

(b) Write your first example paragraph. Does it clearly support your thesis statement? If not, ask yourself whether the fault lies in the example or in the thesis statement. If necessary, go back and sharpen your thesis statement before continuing.

(c) Write your remaining example paragraphs. Use appropriate transitional expressions to link the paragraphs.

(d) Before your finish the first draft, check whether it follows your outline. If the two do not match, decide where the problem is. Is your writing wandering off course, or should the outline be revised because you have come up with a better organization?

(e) Write a concluding paragraph that ties the essay together and reiterates your thesis statement. Try not to repeat the thesis statement word for word. Instead, aim for fresh language with phrasing your reader will remember.

Revising

Read through your first draft. Use the following checklist of questions to make sure you have revised thoroughly.

❏ Is your thesis statement clear and focused?

❏ Does the thesis statement relate exactly to the examples you ended up using? If not, what is at fault—the thesis or the examples?

❏ Do you have enough examples to persuade the reader that your thesis statement is true? (You should have at least three examples.)

❏ Did you allow at least one paragraph for each example?

❏ Is each example developed with enough detail to be convincing?

❏ Are the examples accurate, truthful, and not misleading to the reader?

❏ Are the examples in a logical order? Can you explain the order you used?

❏ Did you use transitional expressions where necessary to guide the reader from one example to the next?

❏ Are the organization and the transitions clear enough for a reader to grasp the major features by scanning the essay? If not, did you make your essay needlessly complicated or muddled?

❏ Does your concluding paragraph link back to the thesis statement? Does it restate your point without annoying the reader by using the same words?

When you have revised thoroughly, write a second draft. Label it *Draft 2*. Then follow the same process with your second draft. Critique and revise it thoroughly. If necessary, write a third draft.

When you believe your content and presentation are as good as you can make them, move on to the editing stage.

Editing

In this final stage, check your essay for mechanical errors. Closely examine grammar, spelling, word use, punctuation, and capitalization. If you are using a word processor, run the spell checker and grammar checker, but do your own careful proofing as well. After you have polished your writing, make a new copy in the format your instructor specifies. Proofread your essay one final time for small errors.

WRITING FOR YOUR CAREER

CRITICAL THINKING

This section presents a writing project for each of the six career pathways. Choose one that appeals to you and write an illustrative essay on the subject.

When the project description refers you to the textbook web site, go to http://humphrey.swlearning.com and click on the Links tab. Look for Chapter 15, "Writing for Your Career." There you will find direct links to helpful web references.

Communication and the Arts

As a graphic artist, you are designing a box for Pat's Pizza Pieces, a new brand of snack-size, microwavable pizza slices to be sold in the frozen food departments of grocery stores. Along with your design samples, you will send the client a short essay to explain the choices you have made. As your thesis statement, describe the effect you want the design to achieve. As your examples, show how particular details of the design contribute to that overall effect.

Begin by brainstorming about eye-catching, appealing designs for a small pizza box. Think about ways to make the box visible in a freezer case. How will your design differ from those of other brands?

Draft your thesis statement carefully so it narrows the focus to one unique quality of your design. Make sure each example supports your thesis. In your concluding paragraph, try to rouse your client's enthusiasm!

Health and Medicine

Imagine that you work as a physical therapist for a health-services company that offers rehabilitation programs for workers injured on the job. Many of your recent cases have involved carpal tunnel syndrome, a painful and sometimes disabling condition of the wrist. Your supervisor asks you to write a short report to distribute to patients and their employers, detailing preventive measures to reduce the risk for carpal tunnel injuries.

In your thesis statement, focus on the possibility of preventing injury by taking steps ahead of time. Then present specific examples of ways for employers or workers to change their behavior to minimize risk. For research on carpal tunnel syndrome, consult your local library or do a web search. See the textbook web site for helpful online resources.

Human, Personal, and Public Service

You are a park ranger in your state's park system, and you have been asked to help prepare a recruitment brochure. The purpose is to attract new people to work in the state parks. Write a thesis statement focusing on the pleasures and benefits of the work. You can use a personal tone if you wish ("why I love my job as a ranger"). Give several examples to support your claim. In your conclusion, make your readers want to join the park service!

Business and Marketing

You are opening a new "theme" restaurant that will attract customers not only with its food, but also with its overall environment. You are sure it will be a success, but you need a strong business plan to convince your bank to lend you the construction funds.

Write the section of the plan in which you describe the theme of your new restaurant and give examples of how you will carry out the idea. How will the theme affect the restaurant's design? The lighting? The food itself? The overall experience for customers?

For this activity, choose any theme you would like to see in a restaurant, but make sure you support the idea with detailed examples.

Science and Technology

As a self-employed electrician, you handle a wide variety of jobs—business and residential, large projects and small ones. Today you are writing an article about your profession for the alumni magazine of your college. You plan to make a general statement about the nature of your work and then use several examples to illustrate your point.

Brainstorm what you are going to say. Think about the work electricians do, the rewards of this profession, the skills it requires, and so on. (For background on an electrician's work, see the link provided on the textbook web site.) Narrow the topic down until you have a single, clear point you want to make about being an electrician. Then brainstorm at least three examples to use.

When you are ready, write the article. Make sure it has an introductory paragraph containing a focused thesis statement, at least three paragraphs of examples, and a concluding paragraph.

Environment and Natural Resources

You work as a water safety specialist for your city's Water Department. For the department's web site, you are writing a brief article about ways the public can help keep pollutants out of the city's water supply.

The city draws its water from the local river. Even though the water is filtered and chemically treated, traces of pollutants make their way into the drinking water that flows out of people's faucets.

Much of the pollution comes from large industry, but some is caused by local residents. Some people, for instance, dump used motor oil into storm drains, where it flows into the river. Other people overuse pesticides on slopes that drain into local creeks, which also feed the river. For research into types of water pollution caused by individuals and businesses, see the links provided on the textbook web site.

In your article, include at least three steps citizens can take to reduce water pollution. Make sure your introductory paragraph has a good thesis statement. Be convincing—persuade your readers to stop polluting!

16

Writing to Describe

IN THIS CHAPTER YOU WILL LEARN TO:

- Write an introductory descriptive paragraph.

- Describe supporting details.

- Use figurative language.

- Write a conclusion that ties paragraphs together.

Using *Description* in Writing for Your Career

Career Path	Sample Career	Use for Descriptive Writing	Example of Descriptive Writing
Communication and the Arts	Choir director	Describing the program of an upcoming concert	With a mixture of classical, contemporary, and unconventional songs, this season's performance will delight and surprise. The recent recital by Christina Avalos is a lively and spirited romp through three octaves.
Health and Medicine	Physical therapist	Documenting a patient's condition and progress	Roberto exhibits a cheerful attitude and a strong commitment to continuing the plan he has begun. The ligaments in his knee are extremely delicate, even after six weeks of strength-building physical therapy.
Human, Personal, and Public Service	Kindergarten teacher	Describing a zoo to prepare children for a visit	Have you ever seen a giraffe? A giraffe is an animal with four legs and a very long neck. Its body is light brown and is covered with dark spots.
Business and Marketing	Sales associate for a home furnishings retailer	Composing a brochure advertising living room sets	Get ready for luxury! Once you sit down on this sofa, you'll never go back to that lumpy one at home. The plush upholstery is designed specifically for maximum comfort and relaxation.
Science and Technology	Technical support associate	Describing the functions of a computer's parts while troubleshooting with a client	Your computer system is composed of many sophisticated, interdependent parts. If any of the parts break, the whole computer can be affected. The complex motherboard holds all electronic elements together and connects all of the parts of your system.
Environment and Natural Resources	Park ranger	Describing the different regions of the park to visitors	The park comprises a large number of ecosystems, each with its own set of unique characteristics and charm. In the high desert piñon forest, sagebrush provides ground cover and prevents erosion on the hillsides.

ON THE JOB

Home for Sale

As a real estate agent, Renée McBride enjoys helping families find homes. When a house is on the market, Renée prepares a detailed description for prospective buyers. She posts the description on her web site, where house hunters can preview homes before deciding which ones they want to visit. The more accurate the description, the easier it is for a buyer to know whether the house is suitable. This saves time by cutting down on unnecessary visits.

Renée is thrilled about the latest house for sale. It is a beautiful three-story Victorian with original woodwork and a functioning fireplace. Renée writes a descriptive report for her web site. First, she jots down notes about the house's most significant features. Next, she creates an outline that places those features in the most effective order. Finally, she drafts her report, filling in additional details to complete the picture. After revising and editing, she is ready to post her finished document. Here are her opening paragraphs.

They don't make them like this anymore! [1] This 4,000-square-foot Victorian home on Old Ranch Island is a three-story treasure of solid construction and old-fashioned charm. With 11-foot ceilings, rambling corridors, and enormous bay windows, this home abounds in luxurious space and light. Original woodwork and a wraparound porch give this traditional Victorian a warm and inviting feeling.

Built in 1877, the house has been remodeled twice [2], most recently in 1992. It combines modern amenities [2] with Victorian elegance: claw-footed bathtubs and high-pressure showers [2]; a huge, fully equipped kitchen [2] with a quiet, sunny breakfast nook; and central natural gas heat [2] as well as functional stone fireplaces on all three floors. Wide corridors and generous windows create cross breezes that keep this home delightfully cool throughout the summer. Set back from the road on a quiet, wooded two-acre lot, this lovely painted lady is tucked away among sweet-smelling pines and vibrant oaks in a family friendly suburban community.

Did Renée create a clear picture in her reader's mind? Did the first paragraph indicate what was being described? Did the second paragraph include specific details about one aspect of the house? If so, Renée has composed an effective beginning for her advertisement.

The Descriptive Essay or Report

In Chapter 6, you learned several techniques for writing **descriptive** paragraphs. In this chapter, you will sharpen those skills while learning to extend your paragraphs into longer descriptive passages for a report, a summary, an essay, or another document. You also will learn additional techniques for using language to create clear and vivid pictures in your readers' minds.

In her report, Renée begins by capturing her readers' attention and introducing the house that she is preparing to describe.

1. Introductory paragraph

The report starts with a brief description of the house—a 4,000 square-foot, three-story Victorian—and several other key details about the house. Renée also designs her first paragraph to make the readers want to know more. With words such as *treasure, warm,* and *inviting,* she hints at the details she will describe later in her report.

2. Details by category

In the second paragraph, Renée includes more specific details. Because she is writing a long report, she can organize her details by category and include an entire paragraph for each aspect of the house she is describing.

In this case, Renée has chosen to focus the second paragraph on the house's blend of modern amenities and elegant details. She places this information near the beginning of the paragraph because she wants to make sure people know that the house is comfortable and modern even though it is old. She is aware that modern amenities are important to people looking at older houses.

SELF-ASSESSMENT 16			
When I need to write an essay or a report that uses description to create a mental picture, I can:			
	Usually	Sometimes	Never
Introduce my topic with a paragraph that captures the reader's attention.	☐	☐	☐
Determine the details that create the picture I want.	☐	☐	☐
Organize my details into paragraphs.	☐	☐	☐
Arrange the paragraphs in an effective order.	☐	☐	☐
Write a concluding paragraph that restates the thesis in fresh language.	☐	☐	☐

If you checked "Sometimes" or "Never" for any of the items, this chapter will help you improve your descriptive writing skills. Even if you checked "Usually" in every instance, you will learn more about writing to describe.

Renée will include details about other aspects of the house in later paragraphs. Because she is writing a long report, she can organize her details into categories and devote an entire paragraph to each one. She determines the order of the paragraphs based on what details she thinks are most important and how the details contribute to the mental picture she is creating.

In this chapter, you will further develop your descriptive writing skills and learn how to use them in composing longer documents.

Introducing Your Topic

When writing an introductory descriptive paragraph for a longer document such as a summary, a report, an essay, or a proposal, you should include a topic sentence that informs your reader of what you will describe. Although the topic sentence may be placed anywhere in the paragraph, it is most commonly found at the beginning.

Imagine that you are a marketing associate at a popular ski resort. You are creating a brochure that describes the resort and promotes it to potential customers. In the first paragraph, you want to get people's attention so they will continue to read. You also want to include enough basic information to let readers know what is being described. Below is a sample paragraph that fulfills both of these functions.

 Have you had enough of the winter blues? Come to a place where winter is a time to celebrate, not hibernate! Nestled in the stunning, snow-capped Adirondack Mountains, Windy Gap Village is a delightful getaway for the entire family. World-class skiing, diverse restaurants, and charming boutiques provide something for everyone. Cozy home-style condominiums provide easy access to all of these activities and more. You'll be so busy, you'll forget all about those winter doldrums!

Do you see how the writer used a hook—a catchy phrase or image—to get the reader's attention? Depending on the purpose and intended audience, a catchy opening like this may be useful. Once the reader has been "hooked," the writer identifies the subject that is being described: Windy Gap Village. Finally, the paragraph includes basic information, such as the location and a general description. The reader can expect to find a more detailed description in the paragraphs that follow.

did you ever ?

- Attend a wedding or large party and tell a friend in detail about the location, the guests, the food, and other aspects?

- Explain to someone who has never been to your hometown the many different characteristics that make it unique?

- Find the perfect gift for a friend or family member's birthday and describe the gift in detail to someone else?

In ordinary situations like these, you describe events, places, objects, and other things with extended details.

ACTIVITY 16.1 In this activity, you will practice composing and organizing the parts of an introductory paragraph. Imagine that you are describing a character for a novel you are planning to write. You will send the description—called a character sketch—to an editor at a publishing house, along with a summary of the novel's plot. The purpose of the character sketch and plot summary is to persuade the editor to publish your novel. Therefore, the description of your character should be lively and interesting.

Editors receive many proposals every day and do not have time to read each one thoroughly. Your opening paragraph must be interesting enough that the editor will want to read the entire document.

Begin by deciding on a character to describe in your sketch. The character may be based on someone you know or a celebrity, or the character may be fictional.

1. Write the character's name on the line below.

   The novel's main character:

   _____

2. Identify three or four details about the character. These should represent a variety of categories, such as physical appearance, personality traits, personal background, and current life situation (where the character lives, what he or she does for a living, and other details).

   First characteristic: _____

   Second characteristic: _____

   Third characteristic: _____

   Additional characteristic(s): _____

   _____

   _____

3. Compose an attention-getting opener that will make the editor want to read more. The opener should be one or two brief sentences. For examples, reread the paragraphs on pages 306 and 308.

   _____

   _____

   _____

4. Next, write a sentence that introduces the character. Reread the sample paragraphs on pages 306 and 308. Note that the writers identified their topics indirectly. They did not simply say, "This house is a three-story Victorian," or "Windy Gap Village is a family-style resort." Instead, they named their topics in sentences that included interesting details about those topics. ("This 4,000-square-foot Victorian home on Old Ranch Island is a three-story treasure of solid construction and old-fashioned charm" and "Nestled in the stunning, snow-capped Adirondack Mountains, Windy Gap Village is a delightful getaway for the entire family.") Write a sentence that introduces your character in an interesting way.

_____

_____

_____

_____

5. Finally, write one to three sentences that mention the additional details you identified in item 2. You should design these sentences to further interest the readers while giving a preview of the details to be included in the upcoming essay.

_____

_____

_____

_____

6. Write your complete paragraph below. The sentences do not need to be in the same order in which you composed them above. Include transitional terms as needed to make the paragraph flow smoothly.

_____

_____

_____

_____

_____

_____

ETHICS CONNECTION

Verifying Details

When writing a document that requires a great deal of description, you might come across a situation that you do not know well enough to describe accurately. When this occurs, you might be tempted to fill in the document with descriptions you have not verified.

For example, imagine that you work for a publisher of travel guides. Part of your job is to compose brief descriptions of all hotels in a certain town. You update these descriptions every few years so the company can publish guidebooks with current information. As the deadline approaches, you realize you have missed one of the hotels. The hotel is located in a distant country, and you cannot possibly visit it now. What do you do?

You might be tempted to simply reprint the old description, hoping the hotel hasn't closed or changed significantly. Or you might search the Internet or read other guidebooks to see how other writers describe the hotel. Either of these approaches is unethical because you cannot be sure that the description is accurate and up to date. In this case, the best thing you can do is be honest. Describe the hotel as it was when you last saw it and tell your readers that the description is a few years old. They may research it further on their own.

Organizing Details

When composing long documents that describe, writers can include many details to create a clear picture in the readers' minds. To make the description effective, the details must be organized in a way that makes sense.

For example, in Activity 16.1, you composed the introduction to a character sketch. In the rest of the essay, you arranged the details about the character into several paragraphs. One paragraph might focus on the character's appearance and another on his or her personal background. Another might describe the character's personality.

Consider the following descriptive essay topic and organizing details.

Topic	my ideal vacation
First Paragraph	geographic location (Where would you take your vacation? Would you go to the mountains, the beach, the desert, or another country? Would you go to a city, small town, or wilderness area?)

Second Paragraph	activities (What would you do there? Would you lie on the beach, play sports, learn a new language, or visit museums and tourist attractions?)
Third Paragraph	food (What would you eat on your vacation?)
Fourth Paragraph	people (Who would go with you? What kind of people would you meet there?)

ACTIVITY 16.2 For each suggested topic below, list four categories of details that form the supporting paragraphs of the essay.

1. a pet I once had

First paragraph: _____

_____

_____

Second paragraph:_____

_____

_____

Third paragraph: _____

_____

_____

Fourth paragraph: _____

_____

_____

2.   my favorite movie

First paragraph: _____

_____

_____

Second paragraph:_____

_____

_____

Third paragraph: _____

_____

_____

Fourth paragraph: _____

_____

_____

TECHNOLOGY CONNECTION

Cutting and Pasting

Descriptive writing differs from illustrative and narrative writing in certain significant ways. One key difference is that the descriptive writer has greater flexibility in deciding the order in which details are presented.

When writing to describe, the order of details depends on what effect the writer wants to create in the mind of the reader. This means that during revision, a writer may move details—or even whole passages—based on the way those details need to come together to draw a clear mental picture.

Fortunately, word processing technology allows you to move sections of text with a touch of a few buttons. The steps required to do this are outlined below.

- First, highlight the text you want to move. Do this with the mouse or by pressing the <shift> key while moving the cursor with the arrows on the keyboard.

- Next, choose the Cut function. This is usually found under Edit on the toolbar. Many programs also allow you to activate Cut from the keyboard; for example, by pressing the Ctrl key and the letter *c*.

- Finally, move the cursor to the desired location and choose Paste. This can be done by choosing Paste from the drop-down Edit menu on the toolbar or by pressing Ctrl and *v*.

Because it is easy to move text from one place to another with word processing programs, writers can experiment with many different placements of descriptive details to find the most effective arrangement.

Using Figurative Language

When composing the supportive paragraphs that describe your subject in detail, you can present those details in a variety of ways. One of the ways writers vary their descriptions is by using figurative language.

In figurative language, a writer uses an image or idea to represent something else. For example, have you ever struggled with a difficult problem until you finally "saw the light"? Of course, you didn't actually see any light. The expression uses light to represent the solution to a problem. Have you ever been so busy that you ran around like a "chicken with its head cut off"? Figurative expressions create compelling visual images by comparing one experience with another. Two common types of comparisons are similes and metaphors.

A *metaphor* is any description that illustrates an idea or image by comparing it to something else. An example of a metaphor and its literal meaning follows. (*Literal* indicates that the words are intended to mean exactly what they appear to mean. Language that is not figurative is literal.)

Metaphor	She ran the first part of the marathon with no trouble, but after 15 miles, she hit a wall.
Literal Meaning	After 15 miles, she wasn't able to go any farther.

Although both sentences convey the same meaning, the first example creates a more vivid mental picture. The reader knows that the runner did not actually run into a wall, but the expression illustrates the feeling of suddenly being unable to continue.

A *simile is* a specific kind of metaphor in which the speaker or writer compares two objects or ideas by using the words *like* or *as*. Similes communicate more information and create clearer mental pictures than literal descriptions. Below are two examples of similes.

Simile	This bread is as hard as marble.
Literal Meaning	This bread is very hard.
Simile	The stars looked like confetti in the sky.
Literal Meaning	The stars were many small specks spread across the sky.

As these examples demonstrate, similes not only create more effective descriptions, but also make the writing more interesting than literal language. You probably use similes often when you speak.

Many metaphors and similes are clichés—overused expressions that have lost most of their meaning through repetition. By being more original in your comparisons, you can be a better communicator. But don't get too carried away. Your comparisons should be realistic as well as original.

A third common type of figurative language is *personification*. In personification, the writer gives human characteristics to an inanimate object. For example, a writer might say that the wind "whispered," muscles "screamed in pain," or a car "stubbornly refused to start." Like similes and metaphors, personification creates vivid mental images that convey meaning clearly, often with fewer words than a literal description.

Finally, writers often add emphasis to their descriptions by using *hyperbole*. Hyperbole means exaggeration—that a writer overstates the situation in order to make a point. For example, instead of saying the leftovers had been in the fridge for a long time, a writer might state that the leftovers appeared to have been sitting on the back shelf "since refrigeration was invented."

ACTIVITY 16.3

For each example of figurative language below, write the literal meaning on the lines provided.

1. He was drowning in sorrow after his grandmother's death.

    _____

    _____

2. The sirens screamed as the fire trucks raced through the streets.

    _____

    _____

3. I'm going to put that project on the back burner for now.

    _____

    _____

4. I'm so hungry I could eat six pizzas and still come back for dessert.

    _____

    _____

5. The truth jolted me like an electric shock.

    _____

    _____

6. A river of cars flowed down the hill and around the corner out of sight.

    _____

    _____

Now create four of your own examples of figurative language and explain their literal meanings below.

7. Figurative expression _____

_____

_____

Literal meaning _____

_____

_____

_____

8. Figurative expression _____

_____

_____

Literal meaning _____

_____

_____

9. Figurative expression _____

_____

_____

Literal meaning _____

_____

_____

10. Figurative expression_____

_____

_____

Literal meaning: _____

_____

WRITING WORKSHOP

Making Writing Concise

The best descriptive writers are able to provide details that stimulate the senses. They can almost make the reader see, hear, smell, taste, or feel what they are describing. Yet without careful attention to each word, descriptive writing can become boring in its use of adjectives and other descriptive words.

Good writing is concise. Descriptive writers work hard to eliminate words, phrases, and sentences that fail to support an important point or detail. A good way to determine whether your writing is concise is to set it aside for a day or two and then reread it with fresh eyes. Evaluate each word for its meaning and for its value in the sentence. You may be surprised at how much "thinning" you can do to improve the quality of your writing.

Look at Examples (A) and (B) to see the improvement the writer was able to make during the final draft stage of the essay.

(A) First Draft	Singer-songwriters are the very best things happening in the ever-changing world of modern-day music. My own personal opinion is that the dynamic, popular, and talented Bob Dylan got the whole movement started all the way back in the turbulent, music-loving, and exciting 1960s.
(B) Final Draft	Singer-songwriters are the best things happening in modern music. I believe that the popular and talented Bob Dylan started the movement in the turbulent 1960s.

Example (A) contains words such as *very, own personal,* and *whole* that add no meaning to the writing. Example (B) expresses the same concept as Example (A), but Example (B) is easier to read because it is concise. Good writers continually review their drafts and eliminate wordiness.

Writing a Conclusion

Once you have composed an introductory paragraph and developed supporting details in the body of the document, you need to tie the essay together with a brief conclusion. The conclusion should summarize the most important points and restate any details that are especially significant.

Most summaries are contained within one paragraph. However, a summary can run into a second, or even a third, paragraph if needed.

SUMMARY FOR WRITING DESCRIPTIVE DOCUMENTS

❏   A descriptive essay or report introduces a subject. Then it provides many details organized into supporting paragraphs.

❏   When appropriate, the opening paragraph should include background information or a hook to capture the reader's interest.

❏   Figurative language conveys many ideas in a few words by comparing images or ideas.

❏   The conclusion ties a descriptive essay together and summarizes the most important points and details.

PRACTICING YOUR SKILLS

Now that you understand how to construct a descriptive document, you can develop your skills with the exercises in this section.

Ed Nguyen works for a landscape design company. The company keeps detailed records of every finished design. The landscapers refer to these designs when creating new plans, suggesting ideas to new customers, and answering customers' questions about the company's staff and its landscaping experience. Ed has just completed a design for a small city park and has written the introductory paragraph of his report. Read the paragraph and answer the questions.

Lincoln Square Park occupies a single city block in a residential neighborhood on the city's north side. Because the park has been neglected for many years, it is overgrown and unappealing to neighborhood residents. Our design is intended to make the park a pleasant and accessible gathering place. The focal point of our design is a large fountain, 12 feet in diameter, with a shallow pool appropriate for children to use as a wading pool. The surrounding area consists of paved paths radiating from the fountain to the four corners of the park. The paths are lined with inviting wooden benches and surrounded by well-tended grass. A variety of native trees provides shade and contributes to the pleasant atmosphere. Along the edges of the park, flower beds are planted with an assortment of flowering plants.

Introducing Your Topic

1. Unlike some of the sample introductory paragraphs you read earlier in this chapter, Ed's paragraph does not include a catchy opening phrase or hook. Why do you think Ed chose not to include an attention-getting opener?

_____

_____

_____

_____

_____

_____

2. Instead of using a hook, Ed begins his introductory paragraph with a few sentences about the park. Because his intended audience includes people who are not familiar with the park, he included this information as a background for the description of the park. In Ed's paragraph, underline the sentences he wrote to provide background information for his readers.

Writing to Describe

3. In addition to the background information, Ed mentions several things about the park that he will describe in more detail in the supporting paragraphs of his report. Based on the details Ed mentioned in the introduction, list three things about the park that you expect him to describe in more detail in the upcoming paragraphs. An example has been provided.

Example: <u>fountain</u>

_____

_____

_____

Organizing Details

4. Each of the items of the park that you identified above can be described in a full paragraph with additional details. Choose one of your items and refine it with at least three details Ed could include in a paragraph about that item. You may invent the details. For example, if you chose "fountain," your suggested details might be "10 feet high," "built of stone," and "water flows from the top into the shallow pool below."

Item chosen: _____

First supporting detail: _____

Second supporting detail: _____

Third supporting detail: _____

Using Figurative Language

To create vivid pictures in his readers' minds, Ed sometimes uses metaphors and similes in his descriptive documents. In this exercise, you will choose a detail that describes one aspect of the park and create a metaphor or simile that compares that object to something else.

For example, if the detail you chose was "water flows from the top," your metaphor could be "Water flows from the top, forming a watery canopy that extends from the peak of the fountain to the pool below." In this example, the writer compares the flow of water to a canopy to create a vivid mental image.

5. Selected detail: _____

6. Figurative description: _____

_____

APPLYING YOUR SKILLS

In this section, you can practice writing a descriptive essay of your own. Label and save each draft.

Prewriting

(a) Begin by choosing a topic for your essay. Here are some suggestions:

- A person you know well or a character in a favorite book
- A place you like to visit

(b) Brainstorm a list of details that describe your topic clearly and vividly.

(c) Organize your details into categories that will become full paragraphs.

(d) Decide on an appropriate order for your paragraphs and list the order.

Writing

Compose an introduction with an attention-getting opener or a bit of background information. Include details that you will describe in supporting paragraphs.

Next, write a paragraph about each group of details. For each paragraph, add three additional points not given in the introduction. Use figurative language so your descriptions will create interesting pictures in the reader's mind.

Finally, tie your essay together with a concluding paragraph. Restate a few of the most important points and reinforce the impression you want to make on readers.

Revising

Read through your first draft. Use the checklist below to help you revise thoroughly.

❑ Does your introductory paragraph clearly state the subject of your essay?

❑ Does the introductory paragraph contain additional details that will be described further in the essay?

❑ Are the additional details described further in supporting paragraphs?

❑ Do you use at least one example of figurative language?

❑ Is your language clear, specific, and straightforward?

❑ Do you use your own words and avoid clichés?

❑ Does the concluding paragraph tie the essay together?

Editing

Write a second draft. Check your work carefully for mechanical errors. When you have finished editing, make a final copy. Proofread the final draft one last time.

WRITING FOR YOUR CAREER

This section presents suggested writing projects for the six career pathways. Read through the suggestions, choose one that appeals to you, and write a descriptive essay on the subject When the project description refers you to the textbook web site, go to http://humphrey.swlearning.com, click on the Links tab, and look for Chapter 16, "Writing for Your Career."

Communication and the Arts

You are a music critic for your college newspaper in a major city. Choose a recently released CD that you would like to review and write an essay describing the CD in detail. You may choose to organize your paragraphs by song, by artist, by songwriter, by characteristics of the music (vocals, lyrics, percussion, changes since the band's last album), or in any other way that makes sense to you. Make sure your descriptions appeal to your readers' sense of hearing. They should be able to almost "hear" the songs just from reading your words.

Health and Medicine

As a pediatric physical therapist in a large medical center, you meet many children who have suffered serious injuries. Often, they and their parents are struggling to overcome the injuries and return to a more normal life. Developing close relationships with these children is one of your favorite parts of the job. Recently, you have been particularly impressed by the courage and determination of a child who suffered a spinal cord injury and learned to walk again in spite of tremendous odds. You believe this child's story would be an inspiration to others who have sustained similar injuries. Write an essay that you will submit to the local newspaper. In it, describe the child, emphasizing the personality traits that made this success story possible.

Human, Personal, and Public Service

You have been working for several years as a personal shopper at a large suburban department store. You enjoy getting to know each of your clients personally so you can become familiar with each client's taste, body type, lifestyle, favorite colors, price range, and other characteristics that affect his or her clothing purchases. Now you are training a new employee who will assume these duties for you, and you want to give the trainee a chance to practice the necessary skills before actually meeting with clients. From your notes, you type a report describing one of your clients in detail. Write the report you will give to your trainee. You may base the report on a celebrity, someone you admire for his or her taste in clothes, a family member, or a friend. After reading your report, the new employee should be able to form a mental image of the client.

Business and Marketing

You are the catalog director for a popular mail-order gift company that specializes in handmade crafts by local artisans. As the holiday season approaches, you prepare for the busiest time of year with a special catalog that introduces many new items. The catalog opens with an essay that describes this year's selection and highlights the most exciting products. Compose this introductory essay around gift items that appeal to you.

Science and Technology

As a marine biologist, you specialize in the study of coral reefs. Because of your concern that these wonders of nature may be endangered, you want to educate the public about the fascinating coral reefs and their importance to the marine ecosystem. You compose an essay describing coral reefs and send it to a popular magazine for publication. Visit the textbook web site and access the links for Chapter 19, Science and Technology. You will find background information about coral reefs that can help you write a descriptive essay.

Environment and Natural Resources

As a park ranger at Bandolier National Monument in New Mexico, you often give tours of the ancient cliff dwellings of the Anasazi people who once lived on the land that is now the park. While thousands of visitors enjoy these tours every year, many more people interested in the cliff dwellings are not able to see them in person. Your supervisor asks you to write a descriptive essay about the cliff dwellings. It will be posted on the park's web site so people everywhere can enjoy reading about them. For information, visit the textbook web site for Chapter 16, Environment and Natural Resources. Access the links provided and read about Bandolier National Monument. This information will help you write a description of the cliff dwellings.

17

Writing to Define

IN THIS CHAPTER YOU WILL LEARN TO:

- **Understand denotation and connotation.**

- **Use examples and narrative for writing extended definitions.**

- **Adapt definitions to your audience and purpose.**

Using *Definition Writing* for Your Career

Career Path	Sample Career	Use for Definition Writing	Example of Definition Writing
Communication and the Arts	Fabric artist	Explaining an artistic technique	Appliqué requires cutting pieces from one fabric and sewing them to the surface of another. In quilting, appliqué involves. . . .
Health and Medicine	Nurse practitioner	Explaining a medical practice	Wellness counseling means giving patients advice for improving their overall health. It focuses not only on diagnosed illnesses, but also on fitness and general lifestyle.
Human, Personal, and Public Service	Reading specialist	Clarifying an instructional method or program	Reading Recovery is a tutorial program for first graders. Each student receives 30 minutes of individualized instruction each day.
Business and Marketing	Educational video distributor	Defining a series of videos	Geo Giants video series teaches geography to middle schoolers. Through adventure stories, the series helps motivate students to learn about new places and people.
Science and Technology	Construction engineer	Explaining a construction technique or device	Aggregate comprises a mixture of sand and stone. Combined with a cement material, it forms concrete.
Environment and Natural Resources	Seismologist	Defining a term related to earthquakes	A fault occurs when the earth's crust fractures and is displaced. At a fault line, two portions of crust are shifting position with respect to one another. If this movement occurs suddenly, it produces an earthquake.

325

ON THE JOB

Motorized Scooters

Melinda Amaro heads a team of product specialists for the Baldridge Sporting Goods chain. Noticing the recent popularity of motorized scooters, the firm's vice president has asked the team to evaluate whether Baldridge stores should stock these items.

Early in her research, Melinda realizes that the label "scooter" covers a wide variety of products. Some are tiny contraptions that fold up as small as a vacuum cleaner. Others are larger and heavier, with seats and headlights.

She decides to research and write a two- or three-page explanation of motorized scooters as a guide. Initially, she plans to circulate this document among the team members to get their comments and reactions. Later, her pages can be incorporated into the team's final report to the vice president.

Melinda realizes that her task is one of *definition*. Essentially, she is setting out to answer the question "What is a motorized scooter?" To do so, she calls on all of the techniques she has learned about writing definitions. After researching, brainstorming, and outlining, she begins her document in the following way. (Numbers and underlining have been added for later reference.)

> Motorized scooters, as the term is used today, are <u>small, two-wheeled, single-person transportation devices</u>.[1] They can be powered by <u>batteries or by gasoline engines</u>.[2] <u>Compared to motorbikes and mopeds</u>, they are smaller, lighter, and slower. Generally, they <u>weigh less than 50 pounds and reach a top speed of no more than 25 miles per hour</u>.[3] <u>Most motorized scooters also lack seats</u>.[4] The rider stands the same way he or she would on a child's push scooter. Because of the motorized scooters' small size and limited power—not to mention the lack of lights and turn signals on the least expensive models—many states do not yet recognize them as motor vehicles. For that reason, their use on roadways is often illegal.
>
> One example of a popular motorized scooter is the ZipMotor 240. The battery holds enough charge to take the rider 5 miles at about 12 miles per hour. Weighing only 35 pounds, with a handlebar that folds flat, the ZipMotor can be carried on a bus or train as luggage. Though the platform where the rider stands is narrow, it is covered with slip-resistant matting, and the handlebar can be adjusted for any height up to 6 feet 3 inches.

Do you think this is an effective start for Melinda's definition? What do you think the next paragraph will be about?

The Definition Essay or Report

In Chapter 7, you learned to write definition paragraphs. To define a term, a paragraph is often all you need. Sometimes, however, a term is so complex or has so many possible meanings that you must write an extended definition of it, as Melinda did for the motorized scooter. This kind of definition may take up an entire essay or report, or at least a major section.

In an extended definition, you can deal with a term's connotations as well as its denotation. **Denotation** is the basic, literal meaning. A **connotation** is what the term suggests or implies beyond the literal meaning. A foreigner traveling in the United States might think the words *house* and *home* are synonyms. But when someone says *home,* the person usually means a place where he or she feels a sense of belonging or security—a connotation that the word *house* does not suggest. When you understand a word's connotations, you know what it means in practice.

An extended definition may use any or all of the techniques you read about in Chapter 7:

- Definition with one or more synonyms
- Definition by category and details
- Definition by difference (saying what the term does *not* mean)

Often there is no quick synonym available, as you can see in the excerpt from Melinda's report. No one other term closely matches *motorized scooter.* But Melinda does use definition by difference when she contrasts scooters with motorbikes and mopeds (see the double-underlined phrase). She also uses definition by category and details. That is, she places scooters in the category of "small, two-wheeled, single-person transportation devices" (number 1) and quickly adds specific details (numbers 2–4).

To extend her definition further, Melinda begins to give examples. Her second paragraph focuses on one particular scooter, the ZipMotor, and her next paragraph will discuss another example. Examples are one technique for writing extended definitions. In this chapter, you will also learn how to use short narratives and anecdotes to expand a definition.

SELF-ASSESSMENT 17

When I need to write an essay or report that defines a term in detail, I can:

	Usually	Sometimes	Never
Explain the term's connotations.	☐	☐	☐
Use examples to illustrate the term's meaning.	☐	☐	☐
Develop each example with vivid details.	☐	☐	☐
Use a narrative or an anecdote to explain the term.	☐	☐	☐
Write a concluding paragraph focusing on important points.	☐	☐	☐

If you checked "Sometimes" or "Never" for any of the items, this chapter will help you improve your skills. Even if you checked "Usually" in every instance, you will learn more about writing definition essays and reports.

Thesis, Audience, and Purpose

As you learned in earlier chapters, your first paragraph in an essay or a report should include your thesis statement, which presents the main point you are going to make. In a definition essay, the thesis statement introduces the term you intend to explain and gives a short, basic definition.

Imagine a fabric artist with an upcoming gallery exhibition. She is writing a handout to explain her technique to the gallery visitors. Here is her opening paragraph:

> *Appliqué* is a French term that literally means "applied," and in quilting it refers to a particular way of applying design elements. The elements are cut out of separate pieces of fabric and then sewn on to the top layer of the quilt. In my work, I often use appliqué for the central medallion as well as for surrounding floral images.

In this paragraph, the first sentence is the thesis statement. It begins by defining *appliqué* with a synonym, "applied." Then it puts the term in a category—a "way of applying design elements." The following sentence begins to distinguish appliqué from other methods of applying designs. Later paragraphs will extend the definition further by giving more details and examples.

Notice, too, how this paragraph takes the artist's audience and purpose into account. From earlier chapters, you know that audience and purpose influence everything a person writes. Here the artist knows that many people who come to the gallery already understand appliqué, but some visitors may not be familiar with the term. Since the artist's purpose is to expand her reputation and market—and, she hopes, sell a lot of quilts!—she makes the definition accessible to everyone. Her tone is not condescending, though. She does not want to offend the experts, so she moves quickly from the basics of appliqué to talk about its use in her own work.

did you ever?

- Tell a classmate that you believe in "fair grading" and then, at your classmate's prompting, explain in detail what you mean by that term?

- Mention a cultural event or celebration to someone from a different culture and then shed light on the subject by describing the event in detail?

- Say that you like a certain type of music and then spell out how you define that category?

In daily episodes like these, you give an extended definition to explain your use of a term. You will find the same technique valuable in writing essays and reports.

ACTIVITY 17.1 Pretend that you work as a curriculum planner for a job training institute. The institute gets much of its funding from charitable foundations. For the literature distributed to these agencies, you have been asked to explain how the institute's courses build students' work ethic. Your first task is to define *work ethic* in a relevant way.

1. Begin by brainstorming about your topic. What concepts do you associate with *work ethic?* Are there any synonyms? On the following lines, jot down answers to these questions and any other ideas that occur to you.

   _____

   _____

   _____

   _____

   _____

2. What can you say about your audience? What exactly is your purpose?

   _____

   _____

   _____

   _____

   _____

3. Now draft an opening paragraph. Remember to include a thesis statement that provides a basic definition.

   _____

   _____

   _____

   _____

   _____

   _____

   _____

   _____

   _____

   _____

   _____

   _____

Develop with Examples

After your opening paragraph, one effective way to extend your definition is by supplying examples. Remember what you learned about good examples in Chapter 5. Your examples should be *specific* rather than vague, directly *relevant* to the topic, and *supportive* of the main point you want to make. Also remember from Chapter 15 that examples should be placed in some logical order, such as time order, space order, or size order.

Look at the following catalog copy written by Isaac Roberts, who works for a distributor of educational videos:

The Excel Ants series is a collection of half-hour animated videos on character-building topics, designed for children from kindergarten through fifth grade. The brightly colored ant characters and state-of-the art animation win young viewers' rapt attention. Since the first of these videos appeared 11 years ago, the series has won numerous honors, including the 2004 Character Is Elementary Award.

Putting an essay together

A favorite with kindergartners is the program *Best Friends,* in which young Bernie Ant suspects that his friend Beatrice is telling stories about him behind his back. Bernie's resentment builds up until he bursts out with accusations that bewilder poor Beatrice. Through this incident, Bernie and Beatrice learn a great deal about trust and friendship.

For children in the third and fourth grades, *Ant Eek* has been a great success. In this program, Bernie meets his great-great-aunt Eek for the first time. Not accustomed to young people, Aunt Eek is appalled by Bernie's clothing, hairstyle, and language. In turn, he dismisses her as stupid and obnoxious. Eventually, however, old and young come to terms as they learn to appreciate each other's perspectives.

Notice how Isaac's thesis statement—his first sentence—supplies a basic definition of the series. The rest of the first paragraph expands on that general definition, and the next two paragraphs present examples of specific programs. Notice, too, that Isaac has established an order for his examples, beginning with a program for kindergartners and moving on to one for higher grades.

ACTIVITY 17.2 As the service manager for a car dealer, you are writing a handout to encourage customers to do regular maintenance on their cars. Here is your thesis statement: "Car maintenance refers to routine procedures needed to keep your car in tiptop running order."

1. On the lines below, list several examples you might use to develop this thesis statement. One has been listed for you.

   changing the oil regularly _____

   _____

   _____

   _____

2. Look back over the examples you have written. Circle the strongest ones—the ones that will best help you make your case. Then decide how to place these examples in order. On the lines below, rewrite your examples in order and explain why you chose this particular sequence.

   _____

   _____

   _____

   _____

   _____

ETHICS CONNECTION

Is Ignorance an Excuse?

Say that your supervisor asks you to prepare a brief report. Part of the task involves defining technical terms. In a hurry, you do some checking online, but you find the terms confusing. You make partial sense of them and bluff your way through the rest. The next week your supervisor complains that you got some key definitions wrong. How much are you to blame?

The English writer Samuel Johnson once wrote that "Ignorance, when it is voluntary, is criminal." In conversation, he also declared, "It is more from carelessness about truth than from intentional lying that there is so much falsehood in the world." In other words, an ethical writer tries very hard not to make mistakes out of ignorance because ignorance is not an excuse.

Develop with Narrative

Instead of examples, you can often develop a definition by using narrative—telling a story or an anecdote that demonstrates what the term means. You learned the basic principles of narrative in Chapter 11, and you can combine them with what you know about writing definitions.

The following paragraphs were written by a nurse practitioner to explain her clinic's wellness counseling. She defines the term by telling a story.

Wellness counseling, as we use the term at Applied Health Ltd., means giving patients advice aimed at avoiding problems in the future. Often we help patients identify ways to modify their lifestyle to maximize their health and energy.

Last week I counseled a patient who had a recent history of leg and foot problems—arthritis in his knees, soreness in his feet, and a pinched nerve in one ankle. When I pointed out that he was more than a hundred pounds overweight, he said, "Yeah, but that's not why I came here."

"But," I said, "don't you think your weight has something to do with the stress on your limbs?"

"I've always been heavy," he responded. "I just turned forty, and until lately, I never had leg or foot trouble."

"Yes," I said, "but the problem builds up over time, you know? And you've never been forty years old before."

Eventually he conceded that losing weight would help reduce the pain in his legs and feet. We began talking about his diet, and we found multiple ways he could reduce fat intake. Then we went on to discuss an exercise program to help him lose weight and keep his arthritis under control.

WRITING WORKSHOP

Identifying People

Besides defining terms, your workplace writing may involve identifying people. Imagine that your team is negotiating a major deal with J. B. Miller, Inc. For a report on the company, you need to write a page about the president, J. B. Miller. The task is essentially the same as definition. You want to answer the questions "Who exactly is this J. B. Miller? What are her important qualities?" Therefore, your approach can take the same form as a definition essay. Begin with a general statement about Ms. Miller and support it with details and examples.

ACTIVITY 17.3 A holiday is approaching, and a new friend of yours from a different culture does not understand the customs associated with it. You can define the holiday for her by telling a story about your own experiences. For the sake of this activity, pick a custom associated with a holiday such as Thanksgiving, the Fourth of July, Cinco de Mayo, or another special event your family celebrates. A custom connected with Thanksgiving, for instance, might be "Thanksgiving turkey dinner." Use an anecdote to tell your friend what the custom is about.

1. On the lines below, make notes about anecdotes you might use.

_____

_____

_____

_____

_____

2. Choose your best anecdote and write a short narrative definition. Begin with a thesis statement that supplies a general definition for your term. Then expand on your meaning with the anecdote you have chosen.

_____

_____

_____

_____

_____

_____

_____

_____

_____

_____

_____

_____

_____

_____

_____

TECHNOLOGY CONNECTION

Online Reference Tools

- To explore the connotations of a word, try looking it up in *Bartlett's Familiar Quotations*, which is available online. *Bartlett's* will show you how other people have used the word over the years.

- When you need to identify a well-known person, you can use web pages that offer short biographies.

The textbook web site will link you to a number of these resources. Go to http://humphrey.swlearning.com and find the instructions for the Technology Connection in Chapter 17.

The Concluding Paragraph

Like other kinds of essays, a definition essay or report should end with a concluding paragraph that wraps up what you have said and reinforces your main point. Look at this definition written by a reading specialist and think about how you would write a concluding paragraph.

Miscue analysis is a method for diagnosing a student's reading problems so teachers can focus instruction on the areas where a student needs the most help. The basic method is simple: The student reads aloud, and the reading specialist makes a record of miscues—instances when what the child says does not match the print. Later, by studying patterns in the miscues, the reading teacher can figure out why the student is having trouble.

Last week I worked with a third grader named Mark. He read me a book about firefighters, their trucks, and their hoses. Clearly, he knew what the story was about, but three times he said *horse* instead of *hose*. In other cases, too, he substituted a word with a similar spelling that made no sense in the context: *fame* instead of *flame* and *trunk* in place of *truck*. The pattern showed that Mark paid a lot of attention to sounding out words but needed to become more aware of context and meaning. We worked with him on strategies for word prediction—guessing what a word *should* be on the basis of its context.

Here is one possible way to conclude the definition.

Thus, as you can see, miscue analysis is a helpful method for diagnosing reading problems. It allows teachers to focus on a student's precise needs.

This paragraph is dull, and it merely repeats language from the opening paragraph. If you have spent two or more paragraphs defining a term, you do not need to redefine it in your conclusion. Here is a better ending.

> Other students struggle as much as Mark does, but for different reasons. Some pay a lot of attention to context, but forget to sound out the words. Some leave out words. Whatever the problem, miscue analysis helps the teacher pinpoint the source and then design instruction to meet the student's needs.

Do you see how this paragraph reinforces the meaning without duplicating the definition? In Activity 17.4, you will try writing a similar conclusion.

ACTIVITY 17.4 Turn back to the paragraphs on wellness counseling written by the nurse practitioner (in the section "Develop with Narrative"). Write a good concluding paragraph that reinforces the point without repeating the definition.

_____

_____

_____

_____

_____

_____

_____

_____

_____

_____

SUMMARY FOR DEFINITION DOCUMENTS

❑ A definition essay or report defines a term at some length, including the connotations and the denotation.

❑ The thesis statement provides a short, basic definition.

❑ The body paragraphs develop the thesis statement, often by giving examples or using narrative.

❑ The concluding paragraph reiterates the essential point without repeating it word for word.

PRACTICING YOUR SKILLS

Naomi Rose is a seismologist, a scientist who studies earthquakes. The local government agency responsible for construction codes has asked her to write a report on earthquake dangers in the region. In the following section, Naomi defines a key term, *intensity*.

Read this section and think about how it demonstrates the techniques you have learned in this chapter. The paragraphs are numbered for reference.

1   What does the word *intensity* mean when applied to an earthquake? In simple terms, intensity is the amount of surface shaking in a particular location. More exactly, it is a measure of the earthquake's effects on people, buildings, and the land itself.

2   Intensity is not the same as magnitude, which refers to the amount of energy released at the source of the earthquake. For any given earthquake, the magnitude is a fixed amount of energy. Intensity, in contrast, is not fixed; it changes depending on location. Close to the source, the intensity is likely to be high. Farther away, the intensity will be lower. Intensity at any point is also influenced by the type of soil and other features of local geology. To describe intensity, scientists use a scale ranging from I to XII.

3   As an example, consider the 1985 earthquake in Mexico. In magnitude, this was a major quake, measuring 8.1 on the Richter scale. Since the center was 300 miles away from Mexico City, the capital might have suffered little damage—except that parts of the city were built on a soil-filled basin. The basin increased the vibrations, raising the intensity to level XII. At least 8,000 people died, and property damage was estimated at $4 billion. Many buildings, large and small, collapsed.

4   At middle intensity levels, damage to property is much less extensive. At level VII, for instance, well-constructed buildings show practically no damage, though poorly built structures may crumble. One step down, at level VI, no major structural damage occurs in any type of building. And at level V, events resemble the recent experience of a

gentleman in southern California. Feeling the floor quiver and seeing dishes fall off a shelf, he remembered the advice to stand in a doorway. He opened his back door just in time to have the contents of his swimming pool wash over him and flood his carpet.

5   At the lowest intensity levels, I and II, most people do not even notice an earthquake. A very minor earthquake close by could produce level I or II intensity, as could a major earthquake far away.

6   In the bottom portion of the range, then, the intensity scale relates to the way an earthquake is "felt." At its highest levels, the scale takes structural and environmental damage into account. The scale is always a measure of the surface effect at one specific place.

Thesis and Audience

1. Underline the basic definition of *intensity* that serves as Naomi's thesis statement.

2. What level of expertise about earthquakes does Naomi assume her audience possesses? Give the level a number from 1 (no knowledge about earthquakes whatsoever) to 5 (expert).

Denotation and Connotation

3. "Level XII intensity is really bad." Does that sentence state a denotation or a connotation of the term *intensity*?

Definition Techniques

4. What technique does Naomi use for most of her definition?

5. Circle the paragraph where Naomi uses definition by difference.

6. Put an asterisk (*) by the paragraph that incorporates narrative.

The Structure

7. In what order does Naomi discuss her examples? Describe the order she has chosen.

APPLYING YOUR SKILLS

Now you are ready to write a definition essay of your own. This section will guide you through the steps of the writing process. Use a separate sheet of paper or a word processing file. Label and save each stage of the essay.

Prewriting

(a) Begin by selecting a term that you will define in your essay. Here are some possible choices:

city	loneliness
suburb	contentment
railroad	neighborhood

(b) Think about your audience. Will you be writing to define the term for your friends and classmates? For someone from a foreign land?

(c) Brainstorm ideas that will help you explain the term to your target audience. List key phrases and concepts. Consider the term's denotation and its possible connotations. List synonyms.

(d) Consider how you would place the term in a category and how the term differs from other members of that category.

(e) Do you know any good stories you can use to illustrate the term for your audience? Make notes to remind yourself about relevant anecdotes.

(f) Once you have an assortment of ideas, think about how to focus your essay. How will you state the term's basic meaning? How will you expand on that statement in ways your audience will understand?

(g) Select your best material. Which ideas relate most directly to what you want to say? Which synonyms are most useful? Which stories will give your essay some punch? After you choose the material, decide how to order it.

(h) Write an outline for your essay.

Writing

(a) Write a draft of your opening paragraph. Include a thesis statement that supplies a simple definition. As you work, consult handy reference tools, such as a dictionary, a thesaurus, and a volume of quotations.

(b) Write your body paragraphs, using as many definition techniques as appropriate. Try to make your paragraphs flow naturally from one to the next. You may want to review what you learned about transitions in Chapters 5, 15, and elsewhere.

(c) If you find your writing is deviating from your outline, decide whether to rework your paragraphs or change your outline.

(d) Write your concluding paragraph. Try to reinforce the essence of your definition without repeating yourself in a boring way.

Revising

Read through your first draft. Use the following checklist of questions to make sure you have revised thoroughly.

❑ Does your thesis statement give a clear, short definition of the term? Is this definition accurate as far as it goes?

❑ As a whole, does your essay cover the term's connotations as well as its denotation? Will your reader understand what the term means in actual use?

❑ Is the language appropriate for your audience? Is it sometimes too abstract and formal or too slangy?

❑ Have you used any applicable synonyms? Upon close examination, are they good synonyms?

❑ Have you used definition by difference when you can?

❑ Do your examples have enough detail to be meaningful?

❑ Are your examples arranged in a logical order? Could you explain this order if you were asked about it?

❑ Did you include any relevant anecdotes?

❑ Is your concluding paragraph forceful and memorable? Does it review your essential point without annoying the reader by using exactly the same words?

When you have revised thoroughly, write a second draft. Label it *Draft 2*. Then follow the same process with your second draft. Critique and revise it thoroughly. If necessary, write a third draft.

When you believe your content and presentation are as good as you can make them, go on to the editing stage.

Editing

Check your essay for mechanical errors. Examine grammar, spelling, word use, punctuation, and capitalization. If you are working on a word processor, run the spell checker and grammar checker, but do not let these tools take the place of careful proofreading.

After you have polished your writing, make a new copy in the format your instructor specifies. Proof your essay one final time for the small errors that are easy to miss when you are thinking about larger matters.

This section presents a writing project for each of the six career pathways. Choose one that appeals to you and use your new skills to write a definition essay on the subject.

WRITING FOR YOUR CAREER

CRITICAL THINKING

When the project description refers you to the textbook web site, go to http://humphrey.swlearning.com and click on the Links tab. Look for Chapter 17, "Writing for Your Career." There you will find links to helpful web references.

Communication and the Arts

Imagine that you are a musician creating arrangements for your group's upcoming CD. You decide you would like to use an unusual instrument in the background—for instance, a theremin.

Members of your band are doubtful, and some of them have never heard of this instrument. Of course, you will send them sample CDs to listen to, but you also need to help them understand the instrument in more detail. Write a letter to your group defining the instrument you want to use.

If you decide to write about theremins (which are strange and interesting instruments!), you can find information by doing a web search with that term. The textbook web site offers a link to one useful source.

Health and Medicine

You work overseas for a medical clinic named after Jonas Salk. Many of the clinic's patients have never heard of Dr. Salk, so your supervisor asks you to write a short biography to include in a pamphlet. Approach this task as a definition essay. Answer the question "Who was Jonas Salk?"

You will find many books and articles about Dr. Salk in a library. The textbook web site will direct you to the Salk Institute. You can also use the online biographical resources mentioned in the Technology Connection.

Human, Personal, and Public Service

The elementary school where you teach is developing a special program to identify and correct children's reading problems at an early age. As part of the project, you and three other teachers have formed a team to propose ways for teachers and parents to work together more closely.

Part of the task involves getting the right information to parents—helping them learn about various reading deficiencies. Much of the available material, though, is dry, technical, and scary. It makes a young child who struggles to recognize words sound like a person with a terrible disease. You decide to prepare your own fact sheets to distribute to parents.

For one fact sheet, write a definition of the term *dyslexia*. For your research, consult books, encyclopedias, and reliable web sites (see the textbook web site for a starting point). Then use several paragraphs to explain what the word does and does not mean.

Business and Marketing

Your advertising company specializes in television advertising, and your clients are happy with your work. Sometimes, though, you have communication problems because clients do not understand many of the terms common in the advertising industry. You decide to prepare a glossary booklet to hand out to them.

Pick an advertising term that needs more than one paragraph to define and write the definition for your booklet. Use a search engine and enter each keyword to find the definition. Here are some suggestions:

- spot—60-second, 30-second, 10-second
- make good
- target audience

Make your definition as practical and simple as possible.

Science and Technology

Your chemistry research company runs an internship program that gives college students the chance to work as lab assistants during the summer. Most of the applicants for the internship positions are young men. "Why aren't we getting more women?" your supervisor, Jeannette, asks. You answer that a lot of women avoid chemistry and other "hard" sciences because they think they are not talented in those fields. Jeannette retorts, "Then we need an outreach program. Can you work on that?"

You decide to construct a page for the company's web site to emphasize the scientific role of women, both in your own lab and in the sciences as a whole. As part of this page, you will include profiles of famous women scientists.

Pick one woman scientist and write a short biography in the form of a definition essay. Here are three suggestions: Annie Jump Cannon, Marie Curie, and Maria Goeppert Mayer. To start your research, look at the biographical resources listed on the textbook web site.

Environment and Natural Resources

Pretend that you are Naomi Rose, the seismologist described in the "Practicing Your Skills" section. You have written your definition of *intensity*. Now define *magnitude, Richter scale,* or a similar term in a report. You will find excellent resources at the National Earthquake Information Center (NEIC). See the direct link to the NEIC on the textbook web site.

18

Writing to Compare and Contrast

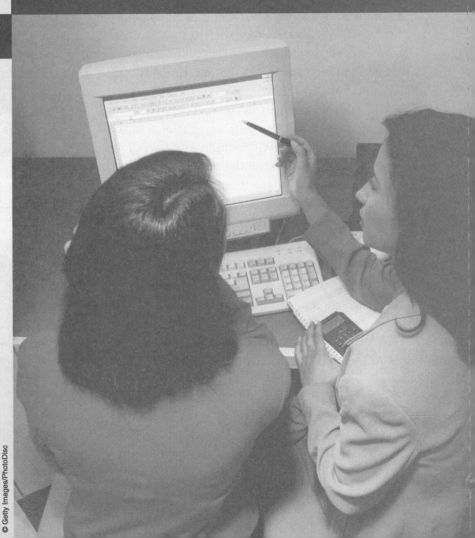

IN THIS CHAPTER YOU WILL LEARN TO:

- Structure documents based on comparison, contrast, or both.

- Write a strong thesis statement for a comparison or contrast essay.

- Use analogy, a special type of comparison.

Using *Comparison and Contrast Writing* for Your Career

Career Path	Sample Career	Use for Comparison-Contrast Writing	Example of Comparison-Contrast Writing
Communication and the Arts	Set designer	Comparing two set designs	Abner's design and Belucci's proposal both make extensive use of movable panels. Both designs also feature screens for video projections.
Health and Medicine	Chiropractor	Comparing and contrasting chiropractic with other forms of treatment	Chiropractors and licensed massage therapists both engage in manual manipulation of the spine and limbs. Their training, however, is quite different.
Human, Personal, and Public Service	Volunteer coordinator	Contrasting two volunteer opportunities	The Meadowbrook Youth Center has two different volunteer opportunities. One opening is for a math tutor to work one-on-one with an eighth grader. The second position involves assisting the office staff with a fund-raising campaign.
Business and Marketing	Benefits analyst for a labor union	Comparing and contrasting two insurance plans	The DynaHealth plan offers full hospitalization coverage, as does Health Choices. Health Choices, however, falls short in its coverage of prescription medicines.
Science and Technology	Ergonomics expert	Comparing and contrasting two computer accessories	The mouse bridge and mouse wrist rest both reduce strain on the wrist and help prevent carpal tunnel injury. The bridge saves the most space, but it requires sacrificing access to part of the keyboard.
Environment and Natural Resources	Oceanographer	Comparing or contrasting the effects of two oil spills	The *Exxon Valdez* accident, although it spilled fewer gallons, caused more environmental damage than the earlier *Amoco Cadiz* disaster.

343

ON THE JOB

Senior Citizens

Tamara Sams, a volunteer coordinator for the Chamber of Commerce, works as a liaison between corporations and charitable agencies. The charities tell her when they need volunteers. She then recruits employees of local corporations to donate their time.

Today Tamara is writing the e-mail newsletter that she sends to everyone who has shown an interest in volunteer work. She wants to mention two new openings. Both involve working with senior citizens, but Tamara sees that the tasks are quite different. In her newsletter, she decides to present these projects in the form of a comparison-contrast essay. Notice the contrasts she brings out, especially the ones marked with corresponding numbers (1, 2, 3).

In this week's summary of openings, you will find two exciting new opportunities to become involved with senior citizens. Elmview ElderCare and Langton Social Services Center need a total of eight volunteers. If you value the contributions that seniors make to our community, check out these listings. Both agencies want people not for paperwork, but for face-to-face activities. The types of activity, though, are very different.

Elmview has requested three people to assist with recreational therapy. This means helping to lead a class of 10 to 15 residents as they engage in arts and crafts, dance, drama, or song. Here you will be working alongside a licensed recreational therapist. The residents who take part are lively and remarkably creative. Be prepared to sing and dance yourself. If you can draw or paint and show someone else how to do it, bring your talents with you! This position will be a great deal of fun.

The Langton Center needs five people to help with the Square Meals Program. Volunteers deliver full, nutritious, and tasty meals to seniors who live alone and have difficulty shopping and cooking for themselves. Usually, this is a one-on-one activity, and it involves much more than handing out food. Volunteers are encouraged to sit and talk with the clients they visit. Whatever their disabilities, these seniors have much to offer, and as you trade life stories, deep friendships can develop.

Tamara makes both opportunities sound rewarding. Do you think she does a good job of conveying the contrasts?

The Basic Structure

Tamara's newsletter shows how the **comparison-contrast** approach can help you structure an entire document. You can do an extended comparison, a detailed contrast, or a combination of the two. Tamara's document is essentially a contrast essay, although she begins by mentioning similarities.

As in the other types of documents you have practiced in Chapters 15, 16, and 17, your first paragraph lays the foundation. This opening paragraph should identify the two subjects you will be comparing or contrasting, and it should include a thesis statement that presents your main idea. Tamara's first paragraph mentions the two sources of volunteer opportunities (Elmview ElderCare and Langton Social Services Center), and her thesis statement—the last sentence in the first paragraph—notes that the two agencies offer very different types of activity.

Although your thesis statement explains your point in a general way, it should not be too vague. A sentence such as "These things are similar but different" tells the reader little. Notice that Tamara's thesis statement locates the contrast in the volunteers' *activities*. This is specific enough to give the reader a clue about the content that will follow.

Like the comparison and contrast paragraphs you wrote for Chapter 8, a full document that uses comparison and contrast may follow a *point-by-point* or a *one-side-at-a-time* format. Tamara takes one side at a time, first describing one volunteer position and then switching to the other position. She makes the contrasts sharp and specific. Phrase 1 in the Elmview paragraph contrasts with Phrase 1 in the Langton paragraph. The same is true for the phrases numbered 2 and 3.

The one-side-at-a-time format is easy for the writer. If a one-side-at-a-time document continues for more than two or three pages, however, the reader may forget details about one item before reading the corresponding details about the other item. For that reason, experienced writers often use the point-by-point method for long comparisons and contrasts. Later in this chapter, you will learn about the *category-by-category* format, a variation of the point-by-point approach.

SELF-ASSESSMENT 18

When I need to write an essay or a report that uses comparison or contrast, I can:

	Usually	Sometimes	Never
Write a strong thesis statement.	❑	❑	❑
Use the one-side-at-a-time method when appropriate.	❑	❑	❑
Use the point-by-point method when appropriate.	❑	❑	❑
Weave comparison and contrast together in a long document.	❑	❑	❑
Use analogy.	❑	❑	❑

If you checked "Sometimes" or "Never" for any of the items, this chapter will help you improve your skills. Even if you checked "Usually" in every instance, you will learn more about writing comparison-contrast essays and reports.

Using the Point-by-Point Format

Because the point-by-point method is common in longer documents, this section explores it in more detail. Often the structure is simple. Each individual point of comparison or contrast serves as the topic sentence for a paragraph in the body of the document. Look at the following fact sheet written by a staff member at an arthritis clinic. The paragraphs are numbered for reference.

1   The term *arthritis* simply means inflammation of one or more joints. To make informed decisions about treatment, patients should understand the specifics of their particular form of arthritis. The two most common types, *osteoarthritis* and *rheumatoid arthritis*, differ in important ways, ranging from their causes to the age when they typically strike.

2   In its underlying cause, osteoarthritis is much better understood than the rheumatoid form. Often called "wear-and-tear" arthritis, osteoarthritis results from gradual loss of elasticity in the cartilage, the tissue that acts as a shock absorber in joints. As the cartilage stiffens, it can begin to wear away, leaving the ligaments, tendons, and bones exposed to the stresses and strains of daily movement. For rheumatoid arthritis, the cause is less clear. Many specialists believe that a hormonal change or an environmental factor, such as a virus, sets off the disease, making the patient's immune system attack the body's joints. As a result, the cartilage may wear away, as in osteoarthritis. Also, the joint lining may swell, and other organs may be affected.

3   Of the two forms, osteoarthritis is more common. It affects an estimated 20.7 million people in the United States, or 12 percent of the adult population. Rheumatoid arthritis is about one-tenth as common, occurring in 2.1 million Americans.

4   As the term *wear and tear* suggests, osteoarthritis is more closely related to advancing age. Typical cases occur in people over the age of sixty, and nearly all of us can expect to experience some degree

did you ever ?

- Discuss with a friend the similarities and differences between two musical artists?

- Contrast two items of clothing you saw in a store, detailing how they differed?

- Compare your memories of family holiday celebrations with a friend's memories?

In common situations such as these, you use extended comparison or contrast, and the same techniques can help you in writing.

of osteoarthritis if we live to a ripe old age. The rheumatoid form, in contrast, occurs most often in people between the ages of twenty and fifty, and it may even affect children. Unlike osteoarthritis, it may go into remission as the patient ages, leaving him or her free of pain for years.

5   Understanding these differences will help you monitor your symptoms and discuss treatment options with your doctor. For both forms of arthritis, the Clinic offers a wide range of treatments, from medications and exercise to surgical joint replacement. Your doctor will help you choose the options best suited for you and your lifestyle.

Look at this sample essay paragraph by paragraph.

- *Paragraph 1:* The first sentence acts as a general introduction to the topic. The second sentence indicates the purpose of this fact sheet: to help patients make informed decisions. The third sentence—the thesis statement—notes that two specific types of arthritis will be contrasted and previews the differences to be discussed.
- *Paragraph 2:* The topic sentence announces the first contrast: the causes of the two diseases. The following sentences provide supporting details.
- *Paragraph 3:* This paragraph introduces the next contrast point: how common the diseases are. Again, the topic sentence states the point, and the next two sentences provide statistics to support that point.
- *Paragraph 4:* The final contrast point—the typical age of occurrence—is stated in the topic sentence and then supported with statistics and other details.
- *Paragraph 5:* The concluding paragraph restates the main idea—that the two conditions differ and that understanding the differences will help patients manage their health and choose the best treatment.

ACTIVITY 18.1

Think about your favorite sport and pick two of your favorite players. They can be professionals, amateurs, or even friends. How would you contrast their styles and abilities? (If you do not like sports, you can choose two writers or two instructors.)

1. On the lines below, list several key differences between the two people.

(a) _____

(b) _____

(c) _____

(d) _____

(e) _____

2. Choose your three best contrasts from Question 1. List details that you could use to support these contrasts in a point-by-point format.

First contrast: _____

_____

Second contrast: _____

_____

Third contrast: _____

_____

3. Write an opening paragraph for an essay contrasting the two people.

_____

_____

_____

_____

_____

_____

_____

_____

_____

WRITING WORKSHOP

Using Subordinating Terms for Contrast

Contrast writing often uses subordinating words such as *although, even though,* and *while.* When you **subordinate** an idea, you indicate that it is less important than another idea in the same sentence.

Although chiropractors and massage therapists both manipulate the patient's back, they differ in their education and training.

The "although" clause is subordinate because, by itself, it does not make a full sentence. Here is a similar example:

Kayim studied all day, though his friend went to a movie.

Weaving Comparison and Contrast Together

In Chapter 8, you wrote single paragraphs that combined comparison and contrast. The same mixture is often appropriate for longer essays and reports. You may be analyzing two competing products or two business strategies that have similarities and differences.

When a comparison-and-contrast document becomes complicated in this way, how should you organize it? The answer is to choose the organization that best serves your purpose and that makes your ideas clear to the reader.

Say that you work in the benefits division of a labor union. The management at a local factory, where many of your union members work, wants to replace the current health insurance plan with a less expensive one. On the surface, the two plans look alike, but you believe they have big differences. In your analysis of the plans, you might begin with a one-side-at-a-time discussion of similarities, then move to a point-by-point review of the contrasts.

Advanced Micro Components wants to replace the HealthyLifePlus insurance plan with a plan called Health Choices. Although both plans cover the same medical categories, the current plan offers superior benefits.

HealthyLifePlus, the existing plan, includes coverage for hospitalization, doctors' visits, lab tests, psychiatric counseling, maternity, prescription medicines, and eyeglasses or contact lenses. Since the Health Choices plan matches up one for one in all of these areas, it seems on the surface like a good substitute. All is not as it seems, however.

Hospitalization coverage is one key difference. HealthyLifePlus allows 60 consecutive days of hospitalization for any single condition, with 100 percent reimbursement of standard hospital expenses. Health Choices covers only 45 consecutive days and limits full reimbursement to $1,000 per hospital stay. After the first $1,000, the patient pays 40 percent of the costs.

The two plans also have different approaches to prescription medicines. Under HealthyLifePlus, our members pay only $5 per prescription for generic drugs and $10 for brand names. Health Choices uses a "formulary," in other words, a list of drugs. Drugs on the list require a copay of $5, but drugs not listed cost $15. Since only 30 inexpensive drugs are included on the list, our members would be paying an extra $10 for most of their prescriptions.

In the category of vision coverage, close examination shows more hidden differences . . . .

Notice how the brief one-side-at-a-time treatment of similarities gives due weight to the likenesses, but then the document focuses on its main point, the differences, which it drives home with point-by-point analysis.

In another situation, you may want to use a different structure. Suppose you are a set designer for a local theater. You have two basic ideas for the set of a new production, and to make sure the producer understands them, you write her a comparison-contrast memo.

To accomplish the many scene changes called for in the script, I have sketched out two proposals, similar in their materials and construction but different in their techniques. For the sake of discussion, I will call them the Folding Option and the Sliding Option.

In each case, the mobile components of the set consist of five lightweight metal frames, 10 feet high by 6 feet wide, covered with painted canvas and mounted on rubber wheels. In the Sliding Option, these frames are separate, and they slide into offstage recesses when not in use. In the Folding Option, all five frames hinge together, and the stage crew folds and refolds them to create the arrangement for each scene.

The stationary components include two cloth panels, 8 feet by 8 feet, located at stage rear. These receive the video images from overhead projectors. I am assuming the projected images will form an important part of the set, so the Sliding Option places the two panels together in the center. Because of the space needed for folding the metal frames, however, the Folding Option must split the panels, placing one at stage left and one at stage right.

In terms of costs, the two options are in the same ballpark, but the Sliding Option does require extra money to create the offstage recesses . . . .

This memo combines comparison and contrast in each paragraph. It follows a *category-by-category* approach, which is essentially a version of the point-by-point format. The document sets up three categories:

- Stage components that move
- Stage components that stay in one place
- Costs

Then the memo discusses the similarities and differences between the plans in each of these categories.

ACTIVITY 18.2 Think of two of your favorite web sites. Pick two that have similar functions: for instance, two sites that sell things or two sites that offer entertainment. (If you are not a frequent user of the Web, you can choose two cars, two popular bands, or two TV shows.)

1. On the following lines, list points of comparison and contrast for the two web sites.

   Site A   **Site B**

   Similarities:

   _____   _____

   _____   _____

   _____   _____

   _____   _____

   Differences:

   _____   _____

   _____   _____

   _____   _____

   _____   _____

2. Look back over the points you have listed. Select the three that are most important and think about how to structure a comparison-contrast essay. Decide what structure you will use (all similarities first, then all differences? category by category? some other format?). Assume that your reader is a friend interested in becoming a web designer. On the lines below, write an outline for your essay.

   _____

   _____

   _____

   _____

   _____

   _____

   _____

   _____

   _____

   _____

   _____

   _____

   _____

   _____

   _____

   _____

Analogy

Chapter 8 emphasized the importance of "comparing apples with apples." That is, in a standard comparison or contrast, the two subjects must belong to the same basic category.

One special type of comparison, however, uses subjects from different categories. Using *analogy*, you explain one thing or idea by comparing it to something in a different realm. An analogy is meant to be taken figuratively, not literally. A movie reviewer might write that a romantic comedy is "as sunny and warm as a day at the beach." Obviously, the reviewer does not mean that you need to douse yourself with sunscreen before entering the movie theater. Rather, the comparison suggests that the film is pleasant, happy, and relaxing—all of those feelings associated with a day at the beach.

An effective comparison and contrast document uses a variety of components

Analogy makes your writing more vivid. It can also help you clarify an unfamiliar subject by linking it to something the reader knows well. A pharmaceutical researcher might use analogy to explain to a nonscientific audience how a drug finds its target within the body.

 The diseased cells have surface proteins with complex shapes, like jigsaw puzzle pieces. Our drug includes molecules with corresponding shapes, like matching pieces in the puzzle.

ETHICS CONNECTION

Analogy Is Not Proof

Analogies are useful for clarifying something unfamiliar, but they cannot be used as proof in an argument. Imagine that you explain the complex functions of your company by comparing it to an automobile, in which many parts function together to make the machine move. Then you go on to say, "When a car crashes, the driver is usually at fault. In our case, since the company has suffered big losses, we should blame the president." Even if the president of a company is in some ways like the driver of a car, the analogy does not prove that the president was at fault. This trick is known as *false analogy,* and ethical writers must avoid it.

TECHNOLOGY CONNECTION

Online Writing Guides

Many online writing centers provide guidance in writing comparison-and-contrast essays, and some offer interesting writing samples. A couple of especially good sites are listed on this textbook's web site. Go to http://humphrey.swlearning.com and look for the "Technology Connection" section of Chapter 18.

ACTIVITY 18.3

Think of a fairly complicated activity that you know how to do. It may be something you have learned at school or at work, or it may be a home activity.

Now imagine that you are teaching the steps in this activity to someone who has never done them before. Think about an analogy you could use to make the process clear. On the lines below, brainstorm points of comparison between the activity you are teaching and the analogy.

Activity you are explaining: _____

Step in the Activity	Analogy for That Step
_____	_____
_____	_____
_____	_____
_____	_____
_____	_____

SUMMARY FOR COMPARISON-CONTRAST DOCUMENTS

❑ Typical structures include point by point, one side at a time, and (for mixed comparison-contrast) category by category.

❑ The thesis statement gives the main idea behind the comparison or contrast.

❑ Analogy, a special kind of comparison, involves explaining something by comparing it to something in a different category.

PRACTICING YOUR SKILLS

Oceanographer Amber Jackson studies the effects of oil exploration and transportation on the world's oceans. She works as a consultant for private oil companies as well as for government agencies. Recently she was asked to write a short essay about oil spills for a web site sponsored by her state's Department of Natural Resources. Read her essay and think about how it demonstrates the techniques you have learned in this chapter.

1   When Americans think of major oil spills, they usually focus on the disaster involving the tanker *Exxon Valdez* in Alaska in 1989. Eleven years earlier, however, the *Amoco Cadiz* created an even larger spill off the coast of France. Looking at the two incidents together can help us understand the dimensions of the problem.

2   Both accidents occurred because the ship ran aground, and in both cases, a quicker reaction by the ship's officers might have prevented some of the spillage. In the *Exxon Valdez* case, 10.9 million gallons of crude oil leaked into the waters of Prince William Sound. If that amount sounds incredible, the *Amoco Cadiz* spill is even more astonishing. Because of severe weather, the *Cadiz* broke apart on the rocks, losing its entire cargo of more than 68 million gallons.

3   The slick from the *Amoco Cadiz*, 18 miles wide and 80 miles long, eventually polluted about 200 miles of the French coastline. The oil from the *Exxon Valdez*, though less than one-sixth the amount, spread to more than 1,100 miles of coastline in Alaska. Why did the *Valdez*'s spill drift so far? Experts give many reasons, including the effects of a storm shortly after the accident and the remoteness of the location, which slowed efforts to bring in cleanup crews.

4   The oil companies and government agencies used many techniques to contain the spills, some more effective than others. Booms were laid on the water to try to contain the oil. These were useful in protecting the Bay of Morlaix in France and fish hatcheries in Alaska, but in most areas, the booms accomplished little. Skimmers helped suck the oil from the water surface, but they often clogged, especially when the oil mixed with seaweed or other debris. Bioremediation efforts included applying chemicals to beaches to boost the action of natural bacteria that break down petrochemicals. This technique is like fertilizing a lawn to stimulate the grass. Ultimately, though, both cleanup campaigns required a great deal of manual work—picking up oily debris, raking sand, and washing rocks.

5   In spite of the intense efforts to contain and repair the damage, huge numbers of animals died. In France, nearly 20,000 dead birds were found, and 9,000 tons of oysters perished from the *Amoco Cadiz* accident. These are shocking numbers, but again the statistics pale by

comparison with the smaller spill in Alaska, where the oil from the *Exxon Valdez* wiped out 350,000–400,000 birds, 3,500–5,500 sea otters, and other assorted wildlife.

6   Together these tragedies suggest two basic facts about oil spills. First, it is not the sheer size of the spill that matters so much as other circumstances, such as location and weather conditions. Second, in spite of advances in technology, humans remain much better at spilling oil into water than at getting it out, and for this reason, society's dependence on oil continues to threaten the environment.

Structure of the Essay

1. Amber's essay contains both comparison and contrast. Which do you think it emphasizes more?

   _____

2. Would you say Amber uses a one-side-at-a-time, point-by-point, or category-by-category format?

   _____

3. What is Amber's thesis statement? Write it below. (*Hint:* The sentence does not specifically mention comparison or contrast.)

   _____

   _____

Use of Analogy

4. Copy the one sentence with an analogy and explain why Amber used analogy in this particular instance.

   _____

   _____

   _____

Conclusion

5. In her concluding paragraph, Amber derives "two basic facts" from her discussion. Do these follow from her comparisons, from her contrasts, or from both? Explain.

   _____

   _____

   _____

   _____

   _____

APPLYING YOUR SKILLS

Are you ready to write your own comparison-contrast essay? This section will guide you through the steps. Use a separate sheet of paper or a word processing file. Label and save each stage of your essay for convenient reference.

Prewriting

(a) Begin by choosing the subjects you will compare or contrast. Here are some possibilities:

two fast-food chains	traveling by car, traveling by airplane
American cars, European cars	your outlook in high school, your outlook now
pleasure, true happiness	the atmosphere at a professional sports game, the atmosphere at a high school game

(b) Are your chosen subjects more similar than different or vice versa? Think about whether your two subjects should be compared, contrasted, or both. Also think about the overall message you want to convey to your reader. What is the main idea of your essay? What do you especially want the reader to remember?

(c) Brainstorm individual points of comparison or contrast that will help you convey your message. Make a list of similarities and/or differences.

(d) Review your list. Select the best points of comparison or contrast. Try to think of analogies you can use to explain difficult ideas or to make your writing more vivid.

(e) Decide on the basic format of your essay: point by point? one side at a time? category by category? Will you use one format for similarities and another for differences? If you have both similarities and differences, which will you discuss first? Choose a format that will help you convey your message.

(f) Write an outline for your essay. Look it over. If it seems awkward or unfocused, revise it. For an essay that involves similarities and differences, you may need two or three outlines before you find the right one. Do not be discouraged— professional writers go through the same process.

Writing

(a) Write a draft of your opening paragraph. State the subjects you intend to compare or contrast. Include a thesis statement that presents the main idea of your essay.

(b) Write your body paragraphs following the format you planned. Use creative analogies when appropriate, but remember that they can only help explain a point, not prove it. Try to use some subordinating words, such as *although* and *while*, to keep your sentences varied and interesting.

(c) If you find your outline is not working as well as you had hoped, revise it as you write. No matter how careful your advance planning, the actual writing may lead you in a different direction than you imagined. That is acceptable, but you do not want to wander wherever the pen or keyboard happens to take you. Think about how your new ideas fit into your original framework and revise your outline accordingly.

(d) Write your concluding paragraph. Try to sum up and restate your main idea in fresh language that the reader will remember.

Revising

Read through your first draft. Use the following checklist of questions to make sure you have revised thoroughly.

❏ Does your opening paragraph clearly identify the two subjects you will be comparing and/or contrasting?

❏ Does your opening paragraph include a thesis statement that expresses the main idea of your essay?

❏ Does the body of your essay have a clear and logical structure? Will the reader feel as though he or she is being guided along in one direction? If the reader will get confused or disoriented, your structure needs more work.

❏ Do you support your comparisons and contrasts with sufficient detail?

❏ Have you used analogies to make your writing vivid and to help explain unfamiliar ideas?

❏ Is your concluding paragraph strong? Does it restate your main idea in fresh, memorable language?

Revision is the time to be severe with yourself. If you have any doubts about the way a sentence or paragraph sounds, work on it.

When you have revised thoroughly, write a second draft. Label it *Draft 2*. Then follow the same process with your second draft. Critique and revise it thoroughly. If necessary, write a third draft.

When you believe your content and presentation are as good as you can make them, go on to the editing stage.

Editing

Carefully review your grammar, spelling, word use, punctuation, and capitalization. Run the spell and grammar checker on your word processor.

When your writing is fully polished, make a new copy in the format your instructor specifies. Then proofread your essay one final time for the tiny, annoying errors that are likely to slip by in earlier stages.

WRITING FOR YOUR CAREER

CRITICAL THINKING

This section presents a writing project for each of the six career pathways. Choose one that appeals to you and write an essay that uses comparison, contrast, or a combination of the two.

When the project description refers you to the textbook web site, go to http://humphrey.swlearning.com and look for the "Writing for Your Career" section of Chapter 18. There you will find direct links to helpful web references.

Communication and the Arts

Your company publishes electronic reference books on various subjects in the arts. For instance, you have a complete *Encyclopedia of Jazz*, a *Dictionary of Films* (with listings for individual films as well as biographies of directors), and a *Handbook of American Literature*. Each of these volumes comes on a compact disc that can be accessed on any computer with a CD drive.

Unfortunately, the company's salespeople are finding that many customers prefer a printed format and are reluctant to order books on CDs. To help the sales representatives, you are writing a flyer for them to distribute to customers.

In your flyer, you want to explain why your electronic reference books are superior, at least in some respects, to old-fashioned print versions. Draw on your own experience with books and CDs to set up strong contrasts between the two formats. You do not need to make books look bad (after all, this is a book!), but you do want to convince people that reference sources on CDs are even more useful.

Hint: Think of how people use reference books. Ask yourself these questions:

- How does a user search for a name or concept in a book and on a CD? Which is more convenient for this purpose?
- What about cross-references from one entry to another? For instance, the entry on Alfred Hitchcock in the film encyclopedia would mention other entries for his individual films. In which format would these cross-references be easier to use?

Health and Medicine

Ames Hospital has a large Cardiovascular Clinic that treats hundreds of patients a year. Many patients with coronary artery disease require angioplasty or traditional bypass surgery. As a nurse in the surgical unit, you have been asked to write a brochure that explains these two procedures to patients. You want to discuss not only how the procedures are performed, but also the recovery time, the expected results, and so on.

Write an essay that compares and contrasts angioplasty and bypass surgery. You can find information at a local library. The Web also has a variety of sites that discuss these procedures. You can locate many sites with a search engine. You can also use the textbook web site, which provides some direct links to get you started.

Human, Personal, and Public Service

As a media specialist for your school district, you help teachers and administrators evaluate educational software. Often this requires comparing and contrasting features of different software packages. For instance, when a new reading program becomes available for third and fourth graders, you compare and contrast it with one that the district's teachers are already using.

For this project, pick two educational software packages and write a review that compares and contrasts them. If possible, choose ones that you have used yourself.

For research, you can find a number of online sites that provide good software reviews. Enter *software reviews* in a search engine or begin at one of the sites listed on the textbook web site.

Business and Marketing

You supervise the food displays for a chain of grocery stores. This past week when the chain was offering a low price on Spritzlee Seltzer, you noticed that some store managers placed the Spritzlee bottles on a special low table near the entrance doors. Other managers created a Spritzlee display at the end of the aisle where the seltzer is usually located.

You decide to write a memo to all managers to compare and contrast the effects of these two placements. For instance, which one is more likely to attract customers who are looking for seltzer? Which is more likely to attract customers who do not normally drink seltzer but might buy some at a special price?

For this writing project, draw on your own experience in grocery stores. Your purpose is to advise store managers about when to use each type of display.

Science and Technology

You have become involved in ergonomics evaluations for your company. *Ergonomics* is the study of ways to design furniture and equipment to reduce users' discomfort, fatigue, and health problems and to increase efficiency and productivity. Whenever your company sets up a new office or remodels an old one, your ideas come into play.

Write a short essay comparing and contrasting two similar types of furniture or equipment in terms of their ergonomic benefits and drawbacks. For example, you might compare laptop computers to desktop models or "executive" chairs with armrests to "task" chairs without armrests.

Environment and Natural Resources

The new Woodlands Nature Center features a variety of wildlife, including abundant dragonflies and damselflies around the pond. Because you work as an entomologist (an expert on insects), you have been asked to write a handout for visitors, explaining the similarities and differences between dragonflies and damselflies. Your short essay should be no more than five paragraphs. (*Research hint:* Both types of insect belong to the order called Odonata.)

19

Writing to Classify

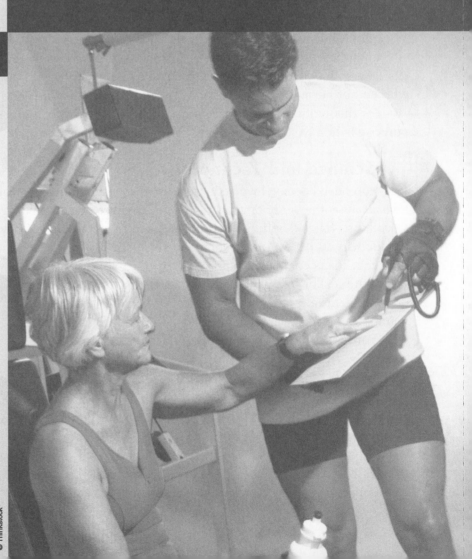

© Thinkstock

IN THIS CHAPTER YOU WILL LEARN TO:

- **Expand classification paragraphs into longer documents.**

- **Sort materials by an organizing principle.**

- **Develop categories that include descriptions and examples.**

- **Use transitions to guide readers.**

Using *Classification* in Writing for Your Career

Career Path	Sample Career	Use for Classification Writing	Example of Writing for Classification
Communication and the Arts	Music retailer	Reporting on music sales	Most sales come from three kinds of music: rock, country, and rythm and blues. Rock music accounts for nearly 60 percent of our gross sales. Of that, 67 percent is classic rock, 31 percent is modern rock, and 2 percent is disco.
Health and Medicine	Fitness coach	Writing an article about adopting a healthy lifestyle	A healthy lifestyle includes three primary components: diet, exercise, and medical checkups. This article will explore these important aspects of good health.
Human, Personal, and Public Service	Human resources director	Describing jobs at his company	Getz-Edgehill, Inc., has three categories of employees: full-time, part-time, and probationary. Full-time employees work at least 35 hours per week.
Business and Marketing	Entrepreneur	Telling prospective investors why her new line of medical products will be successful	We plan to service three categories of physicians who treat children: pediatricians, family medicine practitioners, and internists. In the past, these physicians were forced to improvise surgical techniques with tools designed for adult patients. Our products are specially designed for procedures performed on children.
Science and Technology	Project leader	Explaining why a project took longer than was expected	Several reasons account for the project delay: First, the site engineering team was held up by the installation crew's slow progress. Unfortunately, the installation crew was hindered by the bad weather. Also, materials arrived later than had been promised.
Environment and Natural Resources	Nature trail tour guide	Warning hikers about the dangers of eating the local mushrooms	In this region, you see three colors of dangerous puffball mushrooms: white, tan, and yellow. The interior of a white puffball is solid white at first, gradually turning yellow, then brown as the mushroom ages. Later, the interior changes to a mass of dark, powdery spores.

ON THE JOB

Family Camping

Cathy Crossman is the sporting goods manager at Auker's Department Store. An avid camper, Cathy likes to get away on weekends and enjoys nature and sleeping under the stars.

Recently, Cathy's supervisor asked her to write an article about camping for the store's employee newsletter. Knowing that most of her coworkers are not camping enthusiasts and that they know little about the subject, Cathy decides to begin the article with a brief description of the most popular kinds of camping. She does that so all of her readers will understand exactly what she means by "camping."

In her article, Cathy describes three different kinds of camping and she discusses the benefits of each. Here is how she begins.

There are three ways that my family goes camping: roughing it on foot [1] with backpacks, camping out of our car [2], and camping in a trailer or camper [3] at a campground. Each way has its own rewards.

For me, roughing it by foot is the most fun. We pick a trail, plan and pack what we need in our backpacks, and set off on a journey. In recent years, I have backpacked along the Appalachian Trail, in the Shenandoah Valley, and in several state parks.

Camping out of our car is an inexpensive and efficient way to travel. Last summer we drove cross-country, sleeping in tents at campgrounds. It was a wonderful way to see the United States.

Traveling by camper or trailer is another exciting way for the whole family to camp together. Trailers come in all sizes and with a variety of amenities such as kitchens, bathrooms, and showers.

If you are interested in camping, I can help you find the right style, the right equipment, and the best place to start your camping adventure. Stop by the sporting goods department. I will be happy to talk with you about your outdoor interests and your camping budget.

Do you see how Cathy uses classification to convey her message? In this chapter, you will learn to expand a classification paragraph into an essay, a letter, a memo, a report, or another longer form of writing. Classification makes the writer's point clear by organizing people, places, or things (sometimes called items or objects) into categories.

Understanding Classification

In writing, **classification** means organizing people, places, or things into categories that will make a document more effective. You may want to review Chapter 9 about classification paragraphs for a quick refresher of basic guidelines for classification.

This chapter will expand on Chapter 9 by using classification techniques in longer pieces such as essays, summaries, instructions, and other forms of writing.

When writing for classification:

- Decide how you will organize items into categories.
- Make sure you select the appropriate categories.
- Provide relevant descriptions and examples of the categories.

Cathy's essay about camping follows these guidelines. The outline she prepared is shown below. Review the outline and compare it to her essay. Did she organize her camping classification into categories that made her writing easy to understand?

Main point

There are three ways to enjoy camping: by foot, by car, and by a motorized camper or trailer.

1. By foot
   - Picking
   - Planning
   - Packing

2. By car
   - Inexpensive way to travel
   - Efficient
   - Sleeping in tents or campgrounds

3. By camper or trailer
   - Family-oriented
   - Several sizes
   - Conveniences of home

As you can see from the outline, Cathy selected one organizing principle: ways to go camping. Then she described each method and provided a few supporting details so her readers would have no trouble following her thoughts. Even if the readers know nothing about camping, they will be able to understand Cathy's writing.

SELF-ASSESSMENT 19

When I want to organize items into useful categories, I can:

	Usually	Sometimes	Never
State an organizing principle.	❑	❑	❑
Choose categories that my readers will understand.	❑	❑	❑
Provide relevant examples and descriptions.	❑	❑	❑
Recognize when my categories are not parallel.	❑	❑	❑
Use transitional expressions to move from one example to the next.	❑	❑	❑

If you checked "Sometimes" or "Never" for any of the items, this chapter will help you improve your writing skills. Even if you checked "Usually" in every instance, you will learn more about classifying topics to organize your thinking.

The Organizing Principle

The organizing principle is how you sort your material into groups or categories. In the example, Cathy sorted methods of camping. She chose that principle because she knew most of her readers were unfamiliar with camping. She communicated effectively by identifying three types of camping and by supplying relevant descriptions and supporting details of each.

What if she had selected a different organizing principle, such as the kinds of food that campers eat, the types of wild berries that she has seen while backpacking, or the wildlife that hikers observe on the trail? Those are all reasonable ways to sort camping information, but they probably are not the best ways to introduce camping to people who do not understand it.

Remember, before you write, ask yourself: Who are your readers, and what is your purpose in writing? Cathy's readers are her fellow employees who do not camp and know very little about camping. Her organizing principle is "ways to camp" and should lead to her topic sentence. Compare the two topic sentences below to see if you agree that Example (B) is the best topic sentence for Cathy's classification.

(A) Weak

My family loves camping, and we do it every chance we get. Last summer we traveled cross-country in a camper.

(B) Good

There are three ways that my family goes camping: roughing it on foot with backpacks, camping out of our car, and camping in a trailer at a campground. Each way has its own rewards.

did you ever?

- Collect coins, dolls, books, or other items and arrange your collection by denomination, brand, author, or some other organizing principle?

- Review a list of award nominations for movies? You may have enjoyed searching through the "best actor" category to see if your favorite star was nominated.

- Navigate your way around a supermarket by reading the signs at the top of each aisle. You might have seen "Canned fruit," "Pasta," and "Paper goods."

All of these everyday examples involve classifying items into categories. Using this technique in your writing will help you improve your writing style.

ACTIVITY 19.1 For each of the following subjects, write a classification paragraph that states an organizing principle and adds one or two descriptions or details. The first example has been completed for you.

1. how to do laundry

Sort dirty clothes into three piles: dark colors, light colors, and whites. Wash dark and light colors in warm water, and wash whites in hot water. If you wash a pair of blue jeans and a white shirt together, the shirt may turn blue.

2. products and services offered by your local bank

_____

_____

_____

_____

_____

_____

3. methods that employees or students use to organize their desks

_____

_____

_____

_____

_____

_____

_____

4. three different jobs at a phone company

_____

_____

_____

_____

_____

WRITING WORKSHOP

Avoid Run-on Sentences

In any writing or editing you do, the grammar must be correct. A common mistake that beginning writers make is allowing run-on sentences to clutter their writing.

When a writer crams too many ideas into one sentence, the sentence rambles from one point to another, confusing the reader and weakening the writing. The reader must pick the sentence apart and decide what was meant by each point. In today's fast-paced world, few readers are willing to take the time to do that. Review the following examples.

Run-on Sentence	On Friday mornings, I usually pick up doughnuts for the staff on my way to work, but last week I wasn't able to do it because I promised to drive my nephew to day care, and I would have been late to work if I had stopped for doughnuts.
Effective Sentence	On Friday mornings, I usually pick up doughnuts for the staff. Last week, however, I had promised to drive my nephew to his daycare center. Had I done both errands, I would have been late for work.

In the run-on sentence, the writer used 49 words. By eliminating some words in the effective example and dividing the remaining words into three sentences, the writer's message is clearer and easier to read.

Writing Descriptions

After identifying your organizing principle, you will establish the categories into which you will sort your items and provide interesting, relevant descriptions. These descriptions should include examples and supporting details about your categories that help get your point across to the readers. On the following page are topic sentences followed by descriptive examples.

Example A

MK Brand Dog Food comes in three sizes: 10-pound, 25-pound, and 50-pound bags. The two larger sizes cost less per pound, and the bags have built-in handles for an easy grip. However, the 10-pound bag is the company's biggest seller.

Example B

Engineers are classified by grade: entry-level, mid-level, or senior-level. Entry-level engineers have less than two years of professional experience. Mid-level engineers have two to five years of experience. Finally, senior engineers have at least six years of experience. An engineer's pay depends on his or her grade.

ACTIVITY 19.2 Write descriptions for each of the categories in the following topic sentences. Include examples and supporting details that help deliver a message to the reader. Write your descriptions on the blank lines below. Use additional paper if necessary.

1. Where I live, I can listen to three kinds of radio stations: country, rock, and oldies.

   _____

   _____

   _____

   _____

2. My sister Maria is allergic to three things: shellfish, cantaloupe, and peanuts.

   _____

   _____

   _____

   _____

3. Three kinds of parking permits are available where I go to school: weekday, weeknight, and full week.

   _____

   _____

   _____

   _____

Parallel, Relevant Writing

Some classification writing confuses readers because the categories are not parallel to one another or because the descriptions or examples provided are vague or irrelevant. Review the categories in the example of classification writing below.

Organizing Principle	Apartments are categorized by size.
(A) Poor Example	M&G Management offers three residential units: one-bedroom units, 2,000-square-foot units, and four-bedroom suites.
(B) Good Example	M&G Management offers three residential units: one-bedroom units, two-bedroom units, and four-bedroom suites.

Example (A) may be true, but it is confusing. "One-bedroom units," "2,000-square-foot units," and "four-bedroom suites" are not parallel to one another. Each is a logical category; but when you read the sentence, you may be confused because "2,000 square foot units" is different from the other categories that list the number of bedrooms. In Example (B), the comparison is clearer because the units are classified by number of bedrooms.

Another problem occurs in classification when an example is too vague to be helpful. Look at the following examples.

Organizing Principle	Tenants have a range of rental budgets.
(A) Vague Example	Some can spend a lot of money, while others can spend only a little money.
(B) Better Example	Some have just $500 a month to spend. Others can afford to pay up to $1,000. Still others can afford $2,000 a month.

The vague example provides no helpful information. If tenants have a range of rental budgets, obviously some will have a lot to spend while others will have only a little. To communicate effectively, the writer may need to do some research on tenants' budgets. If the writer is unable to come up with specific examples, he or she may need to find different categories.

Remember, when writing for classification, your descriptions, supporting details, and examples should be relevant to your classifications. As a rule, categories and descriptions should be:

- Supportive of the organizing principle. For example, if you say you will classify cars by style, categories should include "coupe," "sedan," "sports car," and "minivan," not "pre-owned," "new," and "showroom model."

- Parallel to one another. Categories have to match. For example, you would not classify automobiles by writing "Three types of cars: convertibles, big cars, and fast cars." You could say "Three types of cars are: compact, midsize, and large".
- Relevant to your subject. In writing for classification, you should define your categories, select examples, and provide descriptions that are relevant to your subject.

Classifying is a way of organzing

For example, if you are classifying canned soup by the size of the can, you should not describe the health benefits of soup. Instead, save that topic for another writing assignment.

ETHICS CONNECTION

The Ethics of Copy and Paste

Imagine that you are asked to write a section of your company's web site—say, a few paragraphs about customer service. You are curious to see how others have tackled the same project, so you visit a competitor's web site. After all, there is no value in reinventing the wheel. Here is a sentence you like that you found on the web site.

> Our customer service professionals rank among the industry's best trained. Each representative completes three weeks of training in computer operations, communications, and telephone skills.

Is it ethical for you to copy (remove) material directly from your competitor's web site and paste (add) it directly into your web site?

The answer is an emphatic "No"—not even if what you are saying is true. Reviewing your competitor's web site is an excellent idea. Use the competitor's material to make an outline of the essential points you want to cover and think of it as a standard that you can top! However, it is unethical to copy and paste the competitor's work.

ACTIVITY 19.3 In each of the numbered items, the organizing principle is followed by descriptions or examples that are supposed to support that principle. In every case, one selection is not as good as the others. Identify the weak selection and use one of the following abbreviations to indicate why it is weak. The first item has been completed for you.

U = Unparallel   I = Irrelevant   N = Not supportive

1. My Uncle Ken owned a pet store that specialized in tropical fish.

   _____ My favorites were the neon tetras because of the way they swam in a school.

   _____ Most were freshwater fish, but Uncle Ken had quite a few saltwater varieties.

   _____ Goldfish were the most popular, of which there were about 40 varieties in stock.

   ____I____ Ken's son Sandy worked there on weekends.

2. Book Time Bookstore specializes in children's books.

   _____ If you are looking for children's books, Book Time has a great variety.

   _____ It has more illustrated fairy tales in stock than I've seen anywhere else.

   _____ The books are arranged by age group.

   _____ I cannot remember who the tenant was before the bookstore.

3. Antonio and his family visited Collage Art Gallery because they enjoy modern art, especially late-nineteenth through mid-twentieth century.

   _____ Cezanne is Andrew's favorite painter from that period.

   _____ They were impressed by the polite museum staff.

   _____ Beth and Delena compared Matisse's nudes to Modigliani's.

   _____ The tour concentrated on the birth of impressionism at the beginning of that period.

4. Stella is an attorney who practices several areas of law.

   _____ About 20 percent of Stella's practice involves commercial real estate sales.

   _____ Half of her practice involves wills and estates.

   _____ Stella is a member of the Virginia Real Estate Brokers Association, the National Realtors Society, and the Virginia State Bar.

   _____ The remainder of her practice is made up of divorce law.

TECHNOLOGY CONNECTION

Saving Your Drafts

In the workplace, you may find yourself deleting sentences and paragraphs that do not convey the desired message. For example, what happens when your supervisor reads your draft, decides your message is not correct, and puts you on a different track? Should you discard the first draft and start over?

Sometimes information that appears irrelevant to one draft is essential to a future draft. That is why smart writers who use word processors keep all drafts of their work. Saving your drafts requires a little bit of computer memory combined with old-fashioned organizational skills.

Here are a few tips for organizing your word processing drafts.

- Create a new word processing folder for each writing project. For example, if you are asked to write job descriptions for a sales department, label a Word folder *Sales Job Descriptions.*

- Name and number each draft of the project. *salesperson 1* is one way to name and number the first draft of a salesperson's job description. Similarly, *salesvp1* is how you might name and number the first draft of the vice president of sales job description.

- When you begin a second draft for the description of the Vice President of Sales position, simply open *salesvp1.* Then select Save As and rename the new draft *salesvp2.* This way you will have a record of each draft.

- Print the filename in the header or footer of a document when working with multiple drafts. You will know from glancing at the header or footer which draft is circulating for feedback.

A method for naming and saving documents is essential in an age when multiple drafts are circulating electronically. When your readers comment about your writing, you want to be certain that you are talking about the same document.

By getting in the habit of naming, numbering, and saving your drafts, you may be able to avoid countless hours of rewriting and frantic searches for the compelling phrase, statistic, or recollection that you deleted two revisions ago.

Making Transitions

In Chapter 9, *transition* was defined as a movement from one point or subject to another. In a classification paragraph, transitional expressions signal this type of movement. In a classification essay, memo, or letter, transitional sentences guide the reader from one group of categories to the next. The examples below are from an employee handbook. They are about how one specific business is organized. The first paragraph ends with a transitional sentence signaling a new organizing principle in the next paragraph.

 The Weisberg Group has six directors, one for each department: Mr. Halpin is director of operations, Dr. Wu is director of technology, Mr. Ephram is director of finance, Ms. Romero is director of human resources, Ms. Cheshire is director of creative services, and Mr. Baldwin is director of marketing. *Together these six individuals oversee most of the company's day-to-day operations.*

The company's day-to-day operations involve developing new customers, servicing existing customers, and managing more than 200 employees in three locations.

Notice how the transitional sentence helps the writer move from one set of categories (directors) to another (day-to-day operations). In the following example, transitional words and expressions help the first paragraph flow and introduce the next topic for classification.

The Weisberg Group's Creative Services Department has four levels of employees: creative director, art director, designer, and copywriter. First, let us review what a creative director does. The creative director is an executive who works with clients to develop concepts. The creative director reports to the president of the company. Next on the organizational chart, the art director manages projects from conception through completion. The art director reports to the creative director. The designers develop the look of every web site, brochure, and advertisement. Finally, the copywriters write the text. These individuals work together as a team, creating award-winning materials for the company and its clients.

The Weisberg Group's client list is extensive. The company represents small, midsized, and large manufacturers.

Readability is improved when your paragraphs flow naturally from one to another. Easy readability is a goal every writer should seek.

ACTIVITY 19.4 Improve the clarity and flow of the brief essay below by inserting transitional sentences; reclassifying the information; breaking down the writing into additional paragraphs; or rewriting vague, unsupportive, or irrelevant descriptions and examples.

Cooking fried chicken requires the right equipment. An example of the right equipment is a cast iron skillet or a stainless steel pressure cooker. Some of the equipment is essential, and some is simply nice to have. Some of this equipment includes tools. Other required equipment includes appliances such as a fan and a gas stove with a high flame.

A cast iron skillet or a pressure cooker and a pair of metal tongs are essential. You do not need a meat thermometer, a big metal spoon, a metal rack with slats for drainage, and an apron, but these items may come in handy. You need specialized metal tools with long handles for frying your chicken. Tongs and a spatula are examples of these tools. I own tools for frying, broiling, roasting, steaming, braising, and baking. My grandmother gave me a cast iron skillet. I love it.

Fried chicken should be cooked in a well-ventilated space. You should have a good fan in your kitchen. Otherwise, your entire home may smell like fried chicken. You and your guests may love the smell of fried chicken, but not when the smell is in your sofa.

I bought some of my cookware, I received some as gifts, and I inherited some from people who didn't want theirs.

SUMMARY FOR WRITING CLASSIFICATION DOCUMENTS

❏ Classification means organizing people, places, or things into categories to make complex information easy to understand.

❏ The way a writer chooses to organize categories is known as the organizing principle.

❏ Categories and descriptions of categories should be parallel, relevant, and supportive of the organizing principle.

❏ Transitional words, phrases, and sentences help the writing flow and enable the reader to move easily from category to category.

Practicing Your Skills

Now that you understand how to write for classification, try these applications.

Practice 1

This essay classifies television programs by type (such as dramas, situation comedies, news shows, reality shows, documentaries, games shows, and made-for-television movies) and describes audiences that are attracted to each kind of program.

Our survey of students found that they enjoy three prime kinds of television programming. In general, they watch sitcoms, sports, and reality television.

First, let us examine the types of students who are most likely to watch sitcoms. These students are predominantly women, and our survey indicates that they tend to be active. In many cases, these women gather together socially at an appointed time to watch their favorite shows. This social activity is similar to how sports fans gather to watch television broadcasts of their favorite games.

Sports fans tend to watch televised games in groups. This audience is mostly male. Additionally, many of these fans are student athletes who excel at sports. Finally, reality television viewers tend to watch alone or in small groups. This audience is split evenly between men and women and is the hardest to define exactly.

The Organizing Principle

1. Find the organizing principle of this essay about television programming and underline it.

The Categories

2. What are the categories in the paragraph? Place the number 1, 2, etc. above each category.

3. Does the writer provide appropriate examples for each category? Circle the examples.

Transitions

4. Are the transitions clear and helpful? Place a bracket around each phrase or sentence that is a transition from one example to the next.

PRACTICE 2

Here is part of a classification essay written by Megan Lawson, an interface designer for a software development company. Interface designers design the screens that computer users see when they access software or visit a web site. An interface designer's job is to make it easy for people to navigate their way through the messages and buttons they see on their computer screens.

Megan is explaining the different ways that her test subjects process the graphic information presented to them on a computer monitor. The test subjects are students from a local school. Their responses can help Megan and her team design more user-friendly interfaces.

 First, we needed to devise an appropriate strategy for selecting test subjects. Test subjects were chosen based on the following criteria: interest in technology, availability, skill level, and basic intelligence test score. Our goal was to test people of average intelligence, a variety of skill levels, and a moderate interest in technology.

After selecting our test subjects, we divided them into three groups. Each group had an even mix of beginners, intermediate users, and advanced users of all ages and both genders.

We tested three different ways of processing visual information. We asked one group of test subjects to view the images from left to right, as though they were reading text on a page. We asked the second group to view the images from the top of their computer monitor to the bottom, as though they were reading a list. Finally, we asked the third group to view the images from the center out, as though they were looking at a graphic design or a puzzle.

We tested the subjects' recall after three hours. Interestingly, most of those (71 percent) who viewed the images from left to right performed at least 15 percent better than the others. Those who viewed the images in a top-down style scored second best. Of that group, 65 percent outperformed the center-out group by at least 10 percent. Lastly, those who viewed the images from the center out retained the least when tested. For example, about one-third of this group scored less than 50 percent on the retention test. By contrast, only 10 percent of the other two groups scored less than 50 percent.

Initially, I arrived at a theory to explain this phenomenon. In their daily lives, people are accustomed to reading from left to right. In our test, the task of reading from left to right required less effort than did the task of reading from top to bottom or of reading from center out. Not surprisingly, the more accustomed the students were to a processing method, the better they retained the information delivered by that method.

The Organizing Principle

1. Underline the organizing principle of Megan Lawson's classification essay to show how she sorted her topic.

The Categories

2. Circle the categories, then answer the following questions about the categories.

   - How do the categories support the organizing principle?
   - Are the categories parallel to one another?
   - Are examples and descriptions provided?

The Transitions

3. Circle the words, phrases, and sentences that Megan used to create a transition from one group of categories to the next. Megan's essay has many facts and numbers. How do the transitions lead to a better understanding of the meaning of the facts and numbers? How do the classifications help the essay flow betters?

The Descriptions and Examples

4. Underline sections where Megan describes her categories.

5. Explain how the examples help you understand the categories.

_____

_____

_____

_____

_____

_____

_____

APPLYING YOUR SKILLS

Now you are ready to write your own classification essay of at least three paragraphs. Don't forget to name, number, and save each draft.

Prewriting

(a) Begin by selecting a subject. Here are some samples.

Subject	Types of Examples to Use
Musical Preferences	Imagine that you are marooned on a desert island and you only have ten CDs with you. What would they be and why?
Supervisors	There are many kinds of supervisors. Describe a few types.
Students	Write an essay about the different groups of students at the school you attend.

(b) After you select your topic, brainstorm. Write ideas for organizing principles, categories examples, and descriptions. Next, weed out categories that are not parallel, that are confusing, or that do not support the organizing principle.

(c) When you know your organizing principle, your categories, and the descriptions and examples you want to provide, write an outline. Are you certain that the categories will support your organizing principle? Do the examples and descriptions make sense?

(d) Construct a simple outline for your paragraph.

Writing

Now write a draft. Use a precise organizing principle, relevant examples, and appropriate transitions.

Revising

Read your first draft and revise as needed to make your writing clear. Use the checklist to help with revision. Check for errors.

❑   Is the organizing principle stated clearly?
❑   Do the categories support the organizing principle?
❑   Are helpful transistions included?
❑   Do the examples lead to a better understanding of the categories?

Editing

When you are satisfied with your essay, proofread it one final time. Some writers like to give the final draft a different name from the previous drafts.

WRITING FOR YOUR CAREER

This section presents a writing project for each of the six career pathways. Choose one that appeals to you and use your new skills to write a three- or four-paragraph essay on the subject.

When the project description refers to the textbook web site, go to http://humphrey.swlearning.com and click on the Links tab. Look for Chapter 19, "Writing for Your Career." There you will find direct links to helpful web references.

Communication and the Arts

Pretend that you are in charge of tour guides at a museum dedicated to rock music. Write an introductory letter to newly hired tour guides that describes several of the museum's upcoming exhibitions. These exhibitions could be classified by era ('60s music, disco), by subgenre of music (female groups, funk, grunge), by artist (The Beatles, the Talking Heads, Led Zeppelin) or by other organizing principles. If you need help, go to the textbook web site and locate the links for Chapter 19, Communication and the Arts.

Health and Medicine

You are applying to a school that trains veterinary technicians. As a vet tech, your job will include assisting the veterinarian, performing procedures, and working with animals. In addition, you will help owners understand how to provide their pets with the best care and medical treatment. The application procedure at the school requires you to write an essay on one of several topics related to animals. You have chosen "Animals I Like" as your topic. Write an essay that classifies the animals you like. Include plenty of categories and supporting examples.

Human, Personal, and Public Service

In the criminal justice system, crimes are classified by a variety of organizing principles. Some crimes are status offenses. Status offenses are committed by juveniles. Truancy is a status offense, for example. In many, though not all cities, curfew laws are status offenses as well. Other crimes are classified by their degree of severity. For example, first-degree murder is a more severe crime than car theft. Write a report about crime in the area where you live. You may find it helpful to contact a local newspaper or television station that features a "police report." If you need some help online, go to the textbook web site and locate the links for Chapter 19, Human, Personal, and Public Service.

Business and Marketing

You recently opened a career counseling service. Your goal is to help people identify interesting careers and training opportunities. Write a brochure that describes several career areas in which you helped applicants land a job, for example, business, health, or science. Discuss the characteristics of people who are best suited for each of the careers you discuss. For example, what are some personal characteristics people need for a career in medicine? What are the characteristics people need for sales? What are the characteristics they need for management? If you want help, go to the textbook web site and locate the links for Chapter 19, Business and Marketing.

Science and Technology

Write a classification essay about the engineering profession. What does a biochemical engineer, a structural engineer, a mechanical engineer, a civil engineer, or another type of specialized engineer do in his or her job each day? Clearly support your classifications so readers will fully understand each type of engineering job. Be sure to include precise and relevant examples for each engineering discipline. If you are not familiar with engineering and need some help online, go to the textbook web site. Once there, locate the links for Chapter 19, Science and Technology.

Environment and Natural Resources

As you start your writing, begin with this organizing principle: There are three main kinds of parks: national, state, and local. Write a classification essay that supports this organizing principle. Carefully develop descriptions or examples that will help your readers understand the differences in these three types of parks. After reading your essay, they should be able to describe each type of park to another individual. If you need some help online, go to the textbook web site and locate the instructions for Chapter 19, Environment and Natural Resources.

20

Writing to Explain a Process

IN THIS CHAPTER YOU WILL LEARN TO:

- Write longer documents that explain a process.

- Develop a purpose and specify a topic for a process explanation.

- Target an audience for a process explanation.

- Establish the rationale of a process.

- Organize and describe a process in detail.

Explaining a *Process* in Writing for Your Career

Career Path	Sample Career	Use for Process Writing	Example of Process Writing
Communication and the Arts	Public relations consultant for a diamond seller	Developing a brochure for customers that describes how diamonds are made	The diamond you end up selecting for an engagement ring began its life 100 miles underground millions of years ago. Subjected to incredible pressures and temperatures deep in the earth's crust, carbon atoms bonded together to form a lattice-shaped crystal—a diamond.
Health and Medicine	Audiologist at an elementary school	Preparing a pamphlet for parents that describes screening for hearing loss	A conventional audiometry technique is used to measure your child's hearing. Screening procedures can detect hearing loss greater than 20 decibels. The procedure requires a child to raise his or her hand after a specific tone is heard.
Human, Personal, and Public Service	Travel agent	Explaining new airport check-in procedures	New FAA rules have become harsher. Passengers now must arrive at least one hour prior to their departure time. Only one carry-on bag per passenger is permitted. Besides baggage screeners, security officers also may question and search passengers.
Business and Marketing	Business executive	Describing how long-distance meetings can be conducted using a webcam	To reduce travel expenses, a webcam can be used for business meetings between branch offices. The main requirement is that each person attending must have a digital camera. The camera attaches to a computer using a dedicated card or parallel port. A film of the meeting can be stored as a file to be reviewed at a later date.
Science and Technology	Astrophysicist	Explaining to planetarium guests how a black hole is formed	A black hole forms when a massive star dies. As the star runs out of fuel, pressure forces it to cave in, which compresses its center. Once the center becomes superheated, gases are heaved into space as a brilliant supernova. Then the center becomes even denser. Eventually the core traps light within its pull.
Environment and Natural Resources	Geologist	Explaining in a park brochure how a natural bridge occurred	Zane Natural Bridge began as a sandstone cave resembling an amphitheater. The top of the cliff became cemented in place with iron and silica. Eventually the lower layer of the cliff crumbled, leaving a large gap.

ON THE JOB

Speak Up

Communication consultant Cordell Burke enjoys giving training seminars to businesspeople on the art of public speaking. He has discovered that many executives, although they are excellent leaders, dread giving speeches. Cordell's purpose is to show his audience that there is nothing magical about creating an effective speech. He has prepared the following handout to explain how skillful speakers prepare speeches.

> When Woodrow Wilson was asked how long it would take him to prepare a 10-minute speech[1], he replied, "Two weeks." When asked about a two-hour speech, he stated, "I'm ready now." As Wilson's remark suggests, preparing a short speech requires considerable effort. Experienced speakers know that dividing their work into stages is a crucial part of the speech-making process.
>
> **Narrowing a topic**[2,4]: The first step professional speakers take is to narrow the topic to fit the time frame. For example, a speaker invited by a Scout troop to give a 20-minute speech on a recent trip to Alaska[3] will focus on a single part of the trip. Instead of discussing the plane flight, hotel accommodations, and the Exxon oil spill, the speaker may concentrate on a visit to Denali National Park.
>
> **Analyzing the audience**[2,4]: Adapting a message to meet the needs of the audience is another important step. To be successful, a speaker must learn about the primary audience's characteristics. These include factors such as age, income, and level of education. Then the speaker can develop a central purpose. For instance, when speaking about Alaska[3] to a Scout troop, a speaker may focus on outdoor adventures. When speaking to retirees about the same topic, a speaker may discuss vacation packages and cruises.
>
> **Rehearsing**[2,4]: Even professional speakers rehearse and rehearse and rehearse. A common rehearsal method is to practice in front of a mirror. Another method involves asking a group of friends to form a mock audience. In this way, a speaker can continue to make minor adjustments to the speech based on feedback.
>
> Overall[5], the more a speaker prepares and practices, the more confident he or she will feel when the time comes to give an actual speech. Remember, it can take up to two weeks of preparation[5] to speak for just ten minutes.

Cordell divided his handout topic into a series of stages to make the speech-making process more understandable. In this chapter, like Cordell, you will learn to write longer documents that explain a process in depth.

Describing a Process

When joining a company, you must master a variety of **processes**. For instance, you may need to learn how the company produces its goods and services or markets its products. You also should learn how the company delivers products to customers and how your department operates. You may be given manuals with process explanations that describe how something works or functions or how something is done or made.

As part of your work, you may be asked to write a process explanation. If so, your document will be longer than the process paragraphs you wrote in Chapter 10 because you will need to go into more detail than you did when you developed a process paragraph. However, many of the same principles apply to both paragraphs and longer documents.

Take another look at Cordell's handout about the steps involved in preparing a speech. What techniques does he apply to create a process explanation for a long document?

SELF-ASSESSMENT 20

When I need to explain a process, I can:

	Usually	Sometimes	Never
Tell my reader why it is important to learn the stages of the process.	❑	❑	❑
Provide clear understanding by defining all technical terms involved in the process.	❑	❑	❑
Add interesting expanded examples that show the process in action.	❑	❑	❑
Organize my writing to clearly describe how the process unfolds in stages.	❑	❑	❑
Use graphic aids, such as a flowchart, to diagram a process.	❑	❑	❑

If you checked "Sometimes" or "Never" for any of the items, this chapter will help you improve your skills. Even if you checked "Usually" in every instance, you will learn more about explaining a process.

1. **Introduction:** Cordell uses a hook in the form of a story about former President Wilson to grab the attention of his readers and to establish the significance of his topic.

2. **Series of Steps:** He subdivides his topic into three main steps. Each step is clearly defined and illustrated.

3. **Extended Example:** His example of the Alaska speech is a thread that ties the paragraphs together. Using the same example in more than one step of the process will keep his readers interested and focused.

4. **Subheads:** To emphasize his points, Cordell uses boldface type for the main steps and uses subheads that are parallel in structure: *narrowing*, *analyzing*, and *rehearsing*.

5. **Conclusion:** As a way of bringing his document to a close, Cordell notes the importance of preparation and practice.

Now that you have analyzed Cordell's approach to his process topic, you are ready to consider techniques for developing a process document.

Developing a Purpose

Process explanations come in two varieties: instructional and informational. Each method describes a series of steps. However, each process conveys a different purpose. An instructional (or how-to) process explanation describes how the reader can perform a task. Here are examples of process topics that require a set of instructions.

Instructional Topics	how to change the oil in a forklift
	how to create a spreadsheet using Excel®
	how to operate a hot-air balloon

In contrast, an informational (or how-it-is-done) process deepens your audience's understanding about a subject. Your explanation should give the readers a good idea of how something occurs or how something is made, but it should not give directions on how to actually do or make the thing. Process explanations describe the series of steps that a process takes. This chapter focuses on informational processes.

Here are examples of process topics that are informational in nature.

Informational Topics	how NASCAR drivers negotiate turns
	how electricity is generated from coal-burning plants
	how the ozone layer screens out UV rays

As you can see, you would not expect your reader to perform any of the above processes. In the case of naturally occurring phenomenon, it would be impossible for your reader to do so!

did you ever?

- Explain to a new employee how an aspect of a company functions, such as how a conveyor system transports crates through a warehouse?

- Discuss with someone how an expert performs a certain task—for instance, how a realtor determines the value of a home or a film critic rates movies?

- Describe to a friend how a new piece of sports equipment, such as a titanium golf club, improves athletic performance?

Each of these situations involves going into sufficient detail through a series of steps. In this chapter, you will learn how to develop a detailed explanation of a lengthy process.

Specifying a Process Topic

Informational process topics are divided into three categories based on the performer of the process. First, a process may be performed by a human. Second, a process may be technological, something that is done by a machine or device. Third, a process may occur naturally. In this case, the performer may be thought of as nature or the universe at large.

Here are examples of each type of performer.

Human Performer	how magicians perform tricks
	how air traffic controllers assist pilots
	how Olympic sites are selected
Technological Performer	how chess computers make moves
	how floppy disk drives read data
	how sonar detects underwater objects
Natural Performer	how coral reefs form
	how some animals blend in with the environment
	how volcanoes erupt

ACTIVITY 20.1 List two topics for each of the following categories of process topics. Use the examples discussed above as models for your topics. Be as specific as possible.

1. human performer

   _____

   _____

2. technological performer

   _____

   _____

3. natural performer

   _____

   _____

Targeting an Audience

When developing a process explanation, you should think about the needs of your audience. Usually the audience for a process explanation is made up of readers who would truly benefit by learning about the process—the primary audience. They have an interest in the topic because the process concerns them professionally or personally. Here are examples of process topics and the typical primary audience for each.

Process Topic	Primary Audience
how a capacitor works	engineering students
how radar detectors function	new State Highway Patrol officers
how agents select film scripts	new screenwriters
how e-books are scanned	college librarians
how a pizza oven functions	restaurant owners

Keep in mind, however, that a secondary audience also may read your process explanation. These secondary readers may simply take pleasure in learning about a topic.

ACTIVITY 20.2 For each of the topics below, think of a primary audience that would have a special interest in the process. Describe the primary audience for each topic as specifically as possible.

1. How anti-shoplifting devices prevent thefts of store merchandise

   _____

2. How night-vision goggles allow a person to see objects in the dark

   _____

3. How car seats keep young children from being injured in accidents

   _____

4. How hypnotists get subjects to recall hidden memories

   _____

5. How low-fat diets combat high cholesterol

   _____

Providing a Rationale

When instructors give assignments, they explain the importance of the lesson. They realize that students want to know how an assignment is going to improve their skills or add to their knowledge of a subject. Similarly, when explaining a process, you should present the main idea that expresses the importance, or rationale, for the process.

In a workplace report about a process, a rationale should explain how the process benefits the company. The reader wants to know how the process saves time, cuts cost, or improves productivity. Likewise, in an essay, a rationale states how a process benefits the reader. Most readers appreciate knowing the value of a process in addition to learning how a process takes place.

Here are examples of process topics and their rationales. Each example has been taken from the introductory paragraph of a process document.

Topic	how euchre is played
Rationale	A popular card game on many campuses, euchre is easy and fun to play.
Topic	how an electronic card reader monitors attendance
Rationale	The new electronic attendance procedure ensures accuracy and fairness.
Topic	how a manual transmission works
Rationale	An owner's knowing the ins and outs of a manual transmission can prolong the life of a clutch.

ACTIVITY 20.3 For each subject given, write a main idea that expresses a rationale. Overall, a rationale should clearly express to the reader the biggest benefit of understanding the process. Be sure to form complete sentences. If you are unfamiliar with a topic, use your imagination or conduct outside research.

1. How television advertising is used by car manufacturers

_____

_____

2. How a baby learns to crawl

_____

_____

3. How health professionals treat patients suffering from sports injuries

_____

_____

4. How clothing stores attract customers

_____

_____

5. How football teams score points

_____

_____

6. How computer users create documents

_____

_____

7. How prospective employees prepare resumes

_____

_____

8. How cooks prepare French fries

_____

_____

9. How automatic drip coffeemakers work

_____

_____

10. How seeing-eye dogs are trained

_____

_____

Explaining a Process in Detail

How much detail should you go into when explaining a process? If describing the rules of baseball, do you need to state that the infield is in the shape of a diamond? Or can you begin with a discussion of pinch-hitting? Your decision will depend on the knowledge level of your audience.

When writing process documents of more than a paragraph or two, you need to add extra details that help the readers understand the process. In addition to describing each step of a process, you also may define terms, create analogies or comparisons, add examples, and provide background information.

Here are sentences from an essay explaining how medical ultrasound works to check on a baby in its mother's womb. Notice how extra information is provided to fully describe the first step of the process.

Step of Process	When a technician uses a probe, an ultrasound transmits high-frequency sound waves into a pregnant woman's abdomen.
Definition of Term	A transducer probe is the instrument used to send and receive the sound waves.
Analogy or Comparison	The transducer probe records the echoes of the sound waves as they bounce off the fetus in the same way a person hears echoes in a canyon.
Detail	Transducer probes come in a variety of shapes and sizes.
Background	The transducer probe uses a principle of electricity discovered in 1880.

ACTIVITY 20.4   For each of the process topics given, one step of the process is provided. Invent an analogy or a comparison that will enhance a reader's understanding.

1. How the Space Shuttle releases satellites into orbit
    Step of process: A long robotic arm lifts satellites out of the payload bay.

    Analogy: <u>The robotic arm is similar to the kind used on assembly</u>
    <u>lines in manufacturing.</u>

2. How a cell phone works
    Step of process: Radio waves are sent and received by a thin metallic antenna.

    Analogy: _____

    _____

3. How a Japanese rock garden is created
    Step of process: A gardener begins by carefully selecting and placing large rocks in a visually pleasing formation that will serve as the foundation of the garden.

    Analogy: _____

    _____

4. How a professional bowler throws a hook ball
    Step of process: As a bowler releases the ball, he or she puts a spin on it.

    Analogy: _____

    _____

5. How perfume is manufactured
    Step of process: Dozens of potential ingredients of a perfume—from jasmine to rose petals to lemon slices—are selected.

    Analogy: _____

    _____

ETHICS CONNECTION

Taking Shortcuts

When hiking through a park, you see a sign that states, "Keep on the trail." However, you decide to take a shortcut to the bottom of a hill. You have just taken an unethical action.

With a process explanation, writers must be careful not to take unethical shortcuts. What is a writer's ethical obligation when explaining the following processes?

A strength and conditioning coach recommends anabolic steroids instead of difficult physical training and exercise as a shortcut to building muscle strength.

Fast-food employees skip sanitary procedures while preparing sandwiches, resulting in the spread of a disease to customers.

Can you think of other processes—perhaps in your place of work—that employees shorten by taking shortcuts? Are these shortcuts ethical or unethical? Explain.

Organizing a Process Document

Most process documents are arranged in chronological order. When writing about a complicated process, you may need to group together any related substeps. For example, an audiologist wishes to explain to parents how the ear works. To simplify her explanation, she divides her topic into three steps: outer ear, middle ear, and inner ear. Then she adds substeps to clarify the process that takes place in each part of the ear.

Step 1	Outer ear channels sound to the eardrum.
Substeps	a. Outside rim of ear (auricle) captures sound.
	b. Ear canal sends sound to eardrum.
Step 2	Middle ear processes and amplifies sound waves.
Substeps	a. Eardrum seals in an air-filled chamber containing three small bones (ossicles).
	b. These bones include a hammer attached to the eardrum, an anvil, and a stirrup.
	c. Hammer, anvil, and stirrup transmit sound to the inner ear.
Step 3	Inner ear sends sound waves to the brain.
Substeps	a. A tube resembling a snail's shell (choclea) absorbs sound.
	b. Hairlike cells within cochlea vibrate, turning sound into nerve impulses.
	c. Auditory nerve carries impulse to brain.

When writing a process explanation, you should devote a paragraph to each separate step. In the above example, three paragraphs will be needed, one describing each part of the ear.

To move your reader forward, use transitional words and expressions. If you wish to indicate a series, use these transitions: *first, second, then, next, subsequently, in addition, at this point,* and *finally.*

If you wish to describe the outcome of a process, you can use transitions that indicate results, such as *therefore, thus, consequently,* and *as a result.*

If an analogy or a comparison is used, take advantage of one of the following transitions: *similarly, likewise, in comparison,* or *not only . . . but also.*

ACTIVITY 20.5   Think of a process topic about a subject of your choice. Then brainstorm the series of substeps involved. Group the series into three main steps. Using the outline below, describe the process in detail.

Step 1: _____

      a. _____

      b. _____

      c. _____

Step 2: _____

      a. _____

      b. _____

      c. _____

Step 3: _____

      a. _____

      b. _____

      c. _____

TECHNOLOGY CONNECTION

Adding Diagrams

Diagrams or charts are often used with process explanations. These visual aids give the reader a snapshot of a process in action. For diagrams, you need software that provides basic tools, such as shapes and lines. Microsoft Visio® provides chart templates such as:

- Flowchart: indicates the pathway of a process, including substeps

- Map: shows directions in terms of physical locations

- Organization chart: breaks down a whole unit into component parts

This type of software also may categorize diagrams by occupational field, such as geography, medicine, network design, and mechanical engineering.

WRITING WORKSHOP

Statements versus Commands

A process explanation uses a series of statements to describe how something occurs.

> A cell phone *transmits* radio signals that are picked up and processed by nearby cellular towers. Each tower, or receiver, *covers* a specific geographical area known as a cell. The receiver *sends* an identity signal back to the cell phone. The cell phone *uses* the receiver to connect to a wider network.

In contrast, a set of instructions issues a series of commands to the reader. Consider the following instructions designed to teach the reader how to use a cell phone.

> To operate a cell phone, simply *press* the "on" button that provides power from the battery. Then *check* the display, which should indicate the strength of the radio signal and the amount of battery power that is remaining. Next, *make* your call using the touchtone buttons.

SUMMARY FOR WRITING PROCESS DOCUMENTS

❑ Process explanations come in two forms: instructional and informational.

❑ Informational process explanations describe how something is done or made.

❑ Processes may be performed by human, technological, or natural performers.

❑ The primary audience of a process explanation has a vested interest in the topic.

❑ The main idea or rationale explains the importance or value of a process.

PRACTICING YOUR SKILLS

PRACTICE 1

Here is a pamphlet distributed by a car manufacturer describing how electric cars function.

 Can you imagine someday driving an electric car down the highway? What kind of driving experience would this be? With the development of hybrid cars and hydrogen fuel cells, electric cars may become as common as the gas-powered vehicles of today. The way an electric car operates is actually quite simple in both theory and practice.

The starting point of an electric car is its battery. The main reason that electric cars have not "taken off" is that current technology burdens these cars with heavy, bulky batteries with limited capacity. At this time, the battery lasts only 50 miles before it needs to be recharged. This takes us to the second stage of the electric car process.

The charging system of an electric car battery can be as ordinary as a household outlet. Anywhere an outlet is found, the battery can easily be recharged. In the future, more sophisticated charging systems may become available, delivering electricity more quickly to the battery. The battery then can be monitored for damage, as well.

After the battery is charged, a device called a controller provides electric current to the motor. An accelerator linked to a pair of resistors tells the controller how much power to deliver. This is similar to the way a gas pedal works in gas-powered cars.

The final step in the process is the motor. The motor runs on either AC or DC current, ranging from 96 to 240 volts. An electric motor makes a muffler, catalytic converter, tailpipe, and gas tank unnecessary.

Overall, an electric car is environmentally friendly, emitting less pollution than gas-powered vehicles. Already, electric motors are commonly used in forklifts and monorails. It may only be a matter of years until drivers pull their cars up to service stations to "pump" electricity instead of gas.

Main Idea

1. Underline the sentence you believe states the rationale or main idea of this selection.

2. If you were to write about this topic, would your rationale be the same or different? In either case, rewrite the rationale or main idea in your own words.

_____

_____

_____

Steps of the Process

3. Place a numeral (1–4) above each sentence that explains how an electric car operates.

Transitions

4. Circle the transitions that are used in the selection.

Extra Information

5. Underline the sentences that provide extra information about the process without actually specifying a step. Write a *T*, *E*, *A*, or *B* above the sentences to signify whether each sentence defines a *term*, adds an *example*, creates an *analogy*, or gives *background* information.

PRACTICE 2

The following process explanation is part of a park brochure.

Natural bridges are engineering feats produced by nature. These monuments can reach 100 feet in length and can arch more than 50 feet high. Most natural bridges are formed from 300-million-year-old sandstone. Usually, a thin waterfall—sometimes a trickle—falls from the upper lip of a cliff. Here the sandstone becomes cemented in place with iron and silica, minerals that resist the natural process of erosion. The lower layers, or strata, are not as tightly sealed, and the waterfall eventually hollows out a recess cave, much like an amphitheater, beneath the upper layer of rock. In some cases, a stream finds its way into a seam or crack in the layer behind the top lip of the cliff. When this occurs, the rock behind the fracture begins to collapse. Over time, a hole begins to form. Further erosion by the stream continues to widen the hole until the upper layer—still cemented in place—comes to resemble a bridge.

Main Idea

1. Underline the sentence that states the main idea.

2. Using the same topic, write a main idea of your own that would provide readers with a rationale for learning about this process. _____

_____

Additional Information

3. Jot down two questions of your own.

a. _____

b. _____

APPLYING YOUR SKILLS

As you develop a process explanation, keep in mind the following steps of the writing process.

Choosing a Topic

When choosing a topic, select a process that is somewhat extensive and requires a detailed explanation. In a workplace setting, a topic would most likely be assigned to you. In the classroom, your instructor also may designate a topic. For now, consider one of the following topics:

- How a retail clerk sells goods
- How web pages are designed
- How classes are chosen in school
- How computers are selected for purchase
- How a mountain bike works
- How text messaging works on cell phones
- How a restaurant is "closed" at night
- How notes are taken during a meeting
- How a VCR is programmed
- How an automatic shift operates in a car
- How sports injuries are diagnosed

As you select a process topic, remember that processes are performed by one of the following agents: human, technological, or natural.

Prewriting

1. Now that you have selected a topic, consider the needs of your intended readers. If you are writing for a general audience, you must cover each step in detail.

2. Write down as many ideas about the process as occur to you. At this stage, it is better to go overboard with information than to come up short on information later.

3. Consider adding extra information about the process. You may need to define terms, supply background, add examples, or invent analogies.

4. Read over your brainstorming notes several times before developing an outline. Try anticipating the kinds of questions your readers might have about the process. Have you left anything out?

Outlining the Process

Create an outline of your process explanation. Begin by listing the steps of the process in chronological order. Then group related steps into larger units or stages.

Developing a Rationale

Now that you have outlined a series of steps, work on phrasing the main idea or rationale of your explanation. The rationale should briefly express the value of the process. Give your readers a strong reason why they should want to understand the process.

Writing a First Draft

When writing a workplace report, follow the guidelines of your company or organization. For instance, you may be required to present the steps of a process in an ordered list. Such a list will make your first draft appear very structured. If writing an essay, create a new paragraph for each major step of the process. In either case, be sure to create a series of statements rather than commands, as commands signify that instructions are to be followed.

Adding a Conclusion

The conclusion of a workplace report may be a matter of simple courtesy. In it, you typically will ask your readers to contact you with any questions they still have after reading about the process you described. On the other hand, the conclusion of an essay should recap the important stages of the process. You also may offer the readers additional resources for learning more about the process.

Revising Your Document

If you have time, set your first draft aside for a day or two. When you come back to it, you will be able to evaluate it objectively. Use the following checklist to revise your process explanation.

- ❏ Have you clearly specified the process topic?
- ❏ Does your introduction express a rationale for the reader to learn about the process?
- ❏ Have you divided the process into logical steps?
- ❏ If necessary, have you pointed out substeps involved in each step of the process?
- ❏ Have you gone into sufficient detail with each step of the process?
- ❏ If appropriate, have you added extra information about the process, such as examples, background information, definitions, or analogies?
- ❏ Have you used a series of statements to identify each step of the process?
- ❏ Are there any awkward sentences or phrases that can be smoothed out?
- ❏ Can you add transitions to improve the flow of your writing?
- ❏ Have you checked your work for mistakes in punctuation and grammar?

Editing and Proofreading

Use a spell and grammar checker to assist with proofreading your document. This is the time for making final changes in the wording and phrasing of your process explanation.

WRITING FOR YOUR CAREER

CRITICAL THINKING

Write a process explanation in response to one of the following scenarios. Keep in mind the techniques presented in this chapter for developing an effective process explanation. For a given topic, you may wish to research relevant Internet sites. To do so, go to the textbook web site: http://humphrey.swlearning.com. Locate the instructions for Chapter 20, "Writing for Your Career." Then access the web sites provided for additional information.

Communication and the Arts

Imagine that you are the editor of a monthly newspaper about recent fads at school. Normally you hand out assignments and edit the work of your staff writers. This time, however, you decide that you would like to contribute an article about a campus fad. Select a fad that involves a process. The purpose of your article should be to enhance your readers' understanding of the process. As you develop your article, identify the series of steps involved in the fad. For instance, if writing about rollerblading or paintball, describe what a participant must do from start to finish in order to derive maximum enjoyment. For information on fads, go to the textbook web site and access the links for Chapter 20, Communication and the Arts.

Health and Medicine

As an audiologist in the pediatric center of a large hospital, you diagnose a variety of hearing disorders in children. Using acoustical instruments, such as a speech audiometer, you conduct tests on children to determine the cause and severity of their hearing problems. Then you prescribe a course of treatment for each patient suffering from hearing loss. Using library or Internet resources, research one of the following topics connected with the audiologist's care: (a) how the ear processes sound, (b) how hearing aids work, (c) how patients are screened for hearing loss, or (d) how a cochlear implant operates. Write a report that explains the process. To learn more about the topics, visit the textbook web sites for Chapter 20, Health and Medicine.

Human, Personal, and Public Service

Pretend that you are a travel agent who arranges cruises to Alaska, Hawaii, and a number of Pacific islands. Write a process explanation of one of the following topics to be included in a travel brochure: (a) how glaciers form, (b) how volcanoes erupt, or (c) how archipelagos are created. Whichever process topic you select, make sure you discuss the series of steps involved. Go into sufficient detail so an average reader would benefit from the material. You will probably need to use Internet or library resources to make your process explanation complete. In this case, the performer of the process is natural, so you will be working with time scales that involve thousands or millions of years. Dividing the topic into discrete stages may be a challenge! For information on the topics, visit the textbook web sites for Chapter 20, Human, Personal, and Public Service.

Business and Marketing

You have been elected to serve as the communication director of the small business club at your school. The president of the club wishes to present a series of lectures about specific local entrepreneurs, explaining how they got their start in business. She has assigned you the task of writing the handouts to be distributed at each presentation. Each handout should explain how the entrepreneur created a company, an organization, or a business. To begin, select an entrepreneur who interests you. If you have difficulty thinking of someone, choose a person from the following list. Then write an explanation of his or her achievement. Make sure that you focus on the series of steps that the entrepreneur took to reach his or her goal. For more information about entrepreneurs, visit the textbook web site for Chapter 20, Business and Marketing.

- Elizabeth Arden—formed a cosmetics empire
- Walt Disney—pioneered animated movies for children
- Henry Ford—developed the car industry
- Ray Kroc—created McDonald's fast-food chain
- Akio Marita—cofounded Sony Corporation

Science and Technology

Archaeologists study and interpret ancient cultures. Their excavations uncover artifacts that add to the public's understanding of prehistory. One subject that usually generates a great deal of debate is the Egyptian pyramids at Giza. As an archaeologist, you wish to write an article for a general audience explaining a theory about how the pyramids were built. Most likely, you will need to do outside research on this topic. Once you have completed your research, explain in as much detail as possible the entire step-by-step process of how the pyramids were constructed. To learn more about the pyramids, visit the textbook web sites for Chapter 20, Science and Technology.

Environment and Natural Resources

You are a cave scientist, or speologist, employed by your state. One part of your job is to increase visitors' knowledge and appreciation of these underground palaces. No matter how often they are lectured, tourists often damage the caverns. For one thing, they cannot resist touching the stalactites and stalagmites. Serious acts of vandalism also have occurred. In fact, a couple of stalactites have been chipped away with a hammer. Graffiti has also been spray-painted on the walls of one of the more popular caverns.

To counter such damage, you decide to post an explanation to the park service web site of the slow process of cave formation. In your explanation, you attempt to give park visitors a complete understanding of this natural process and how their actions can harm the caves. For more information on cave formation, visit the textbook web sites for Chapter 20, Environment and Natural Resources.

Narration: Writing to Tell a Story

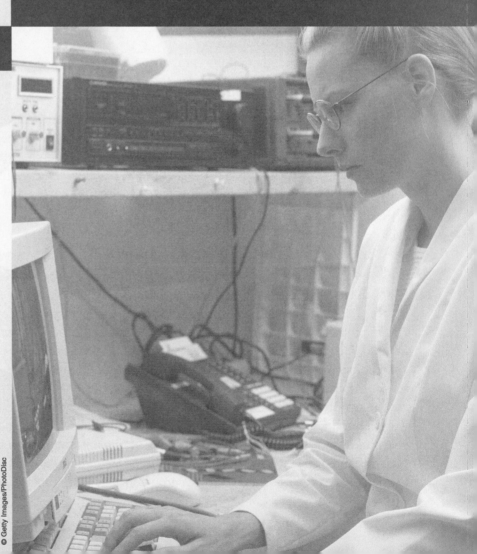

IN THIS CHAPTER YOU WILL LEARN TO:

- **Identify the main elements of a narrative.**

- **Organize the narrative with a beginning, a middle, and an end.**

- **Outline the narrative.**

- **Write a compelling and strong conclusion.**

Using *Narration* in Writing for Your Career

Career Path	Sample Career	Use for Narrative Writing	Example of Narrative Writing
Communication and the Arts	Radio talk-show host	Introducing a guest	Sallie Mae Hanson was born in Athens, Georgia, in 1957. As a child, she loved painting and drawing. As a teenager, she enrolled in the Athens High School for the Arts.
Health and Medicine	Pharmaceutical researcher	Describing the development of a life-saving drug	For years nobody believed that malaria was treatable. But scientists in our laboratory were determined to find a cure. Kevin Arrington was the first scientist to test the new chemical compound on laboratory mice.
Human, Personal, and Public Service	Campaign manager for a city council candidate	Telling the story of the candidate's successful crusade to improve local water standards	For many years, Tyrone Wallace worked with a local citizens' group to pressure the city government into providing cleaner drinking water. Citing high levels of lead poisoning among children, he demonstrated that poor water quality was hurting city residents.
Business and Marketing	Bakery owner	Describing the bakery's history to customers	My grandparents arrived in this city from the Ukraine in 1943. They had nothing. But after many years of working hard and saving, they collected enough money to buy a small storefront on Allen Street.
Science and Technology	Automotive engineer	Relating new developments in automobile brake technology	New twin-disc brake technology first appeared in 2002, and engineers expect it to be installed on most vehicles by 2006. Over the past several years, passenger vehicles have become larger and heavier, resulting in the need for more powerful brakes.
Environment and Natural Resources	Forester	Describing the process of ecological succession in a poplar forest	Raspberry bushes, which thrive on bright sunlight, spread throughout the forest floor. The bushes protect the poplar seedlings from harsh sunlight. Later the seedlings grow to their full height and provide a canopy that shades many other species in the forest.

On the Job

Toxic Waste

Jasmine Anand is an investigative reporter for a local public television station. For the past few weeks, she has been researching a story about a factory that is dumping toxic waste into the nearby Pentridge River. Her investigation revealed that the factory has a long history of evading pollution-control laws. In tracing the history of the Pentridge River, she also discovered the many ways the people used the river over the centuries. In addition, she learned the history of manufacturing in her town and the way the town's economy evolved over time.

The station will devote a 20-minute segment to Jasmine's story. Because she has so much information, she must be selective about which facts she broadcasts. First, she narrows the focus of her story. She decides to center on the factory's dumping of wastes and to include some information about the river and the town as supporting details. Second, she makes an outline that shows exactly what information she will include and its order of presentation. She designates a clear beginning, middle, and end for her narrative. Third, she chooses the additional details she will include to make the story interesting to her audience. Finally, after her organization takes shape, she begins to write an introductory paragraph.

> The Pentridge River begins as several small creeks[1] that wind down the mountain to form the rolling waterway that plunges through our town's center. Hundreds of years ago, Native-American farmers settled[1] along the river's banks and irrigated their crops with its waters. Later European industrialists harnessed the water's energy[1] for their textile mills. Today the river remains a vital part of our economy. However, it no longer carries the pure water that once gave life to an agricultural community[1]. Even the fish struggle to survive in today's Pentridge. How did this situation come about?
>
> The story begins with the construction of The Benton Paper Factory in 1956[2]. At first, the town's inhabitants were delighted at the prospect of the factory providing hundreds of new jobs[2] located within minutes of their homes. In fact, Benton did bring prosperity to a community that had recently suffered from the decline of the textile industry[2].

Do these paragraphs tell you what to expect from the remainder of the narrative? If so, Jasmine has written an effective opening for her essay. In this chapter, you will learn to write a narrative essay.

The Narrative Essay or Report

In Chapter 11, you learned how to **narrate** the major events of a story in paragraph form. Often, however, you will need to tell stories with greater complexity and detail than a paragraph allows. This chapter about narrative essays and reports will help you write these longer documents.

In Jasmine's investigation, she uncovered a large amount of information related to her original question about how the Pentridge River became polluted. When she sat down to write her story, she had to select the most important information to include. In addition, she had to structure the information so the story had a clear beginning, middle, and end. Further, she needed to introduce her narrative with an opening paragraph that informed listeners about her topic. Finally, she had to compose the essay by following her outline and presenting the story in an interesting way.

To organize the information, Jasmine began creating an outline that showed the basic elements of her story. Her outline below shows the introductory points (1) and (2) she made in the scenario on the previous page. She will continue the story by writing the middle and the end (3) and (4).

1. Introduction

- Describe the river's history
- Show that the river has not always been polluted
- Pique listeners' curiosity about changes in the river and town

2. Beginning of story

- Paper factory built in 1956
- New jobs created
- Town's population stabilizes and economy strengthens

3. Middle of story

- Owners secretly begin dumping toxic by-products
- Fish die; some children get sick
- Public questions mysterious illnesses

4. End of story

- Studies show link between illness and factory chemicals
- Citizens demand that the factory owners clean up the river

SELF-ASSESSMENT 21

When I write a narrative essay or report, I can:

	Usually	Sometimes	Never
Select and organize significant events.	❏	❏	❏
Identify a beginning, a middle, and an end.	❏	❏	❏
Choose appropriate supporting details.	❏	❏	❏
Include an introduction with background information.	❏	❏	❏
Include multiple perspectives.	❏	❏	❏

If you checked "Sometimes" or "Never" for any of the items, this chapter will help you improve your skills in writing narrative essays and reports. Even if you checked "Usually" in every instance, you will learn more about writing paragraphs that tell stories.

Once she has created an outline, Jasmine has her story's structure in place. When she begins writing, she includes additional details to add depth to her narrative. Because of the length of her essay, she is able to devote an entire paragraph to her introduction and several paragraphs to the body of the story.

Beginning, Middle, and End

In real life, events occur spontaneously with no recognizable pattern. Only when human beings communicate with one another are those events shaped into stories with a structure. To make sure that readers follow the structure, writers organize their thoughts with clear beginnings, middles, and ends. This way, the narrative reads like a story, rather than a list of sequential events.

When thinking about the beginning, middle, and end of a narrative, writers do not always start with what happened first, second, third, and so on. They identify a logical place to begin, and they introduce their story at that point. Next, they develop the narrative with several events that move the story along. This forms the body of the story and contains most of the significant events. Finally, the story, which can take the form of an essay, a report, a letter, or another piece, concludes with an ending that satisfies readers by tying up loose ends and resolving any outstanding conflicts.

For example, imagine that you are a sales representative writing a report about a meeting with a client. Below is a list of the events of the meeting.

- I arrived early and waited 20 minutes.
- The client came out to meet me, and we chatted briefly before heading to the conference room.
- I presented the details of our proposal.
- The client asked several questions, and I answered them easily.
- We agreed on the terms of the sale.
- On my way out, I was stuck in the elevator for 15 minutes.

When writing the report, you do not need to include all of these details. The logical beginning of the narrative is the start of the meeting, not your arrival at the client's office. The middle of the story is the presentation of the proposal and the client's questions. The agreement at the end of the meeting makes an appropriate conclusion. Each of these events should be described in detail in the report.

As you learned in Chapter 11, words that show sequence can form smooth transitions between events. These transitional words include *first, secondly, next, finally, afterwards, before, later, subsequently, previously,* and others.

did you ever?

- Write a book report in which you described the book's plot in detail?

- Return from vacation and tell your friends how you spent your time?

- Tell a joke that involved a detailed description of several events?

You organize sequences of events whenever you tell a story. In this chapter, you will learn to use these skills to write narrative essays.

ACTIVITY 21.1 The paragraph below appears as a list of sequential events. To turn it into a logical and meaningful narrative, the writer must identify the events that are important and decide where the story begins and ends. Read the paragraph and find a logical beginning and end. Then identify the middle—the action that moves the narrative from its beginning to its end. Write the beginning, middle, and end on the lines below.

> I got up this morning. Then I made breakfast. After breakfast, I took the dog for a walk around the block. During the walk, I ran into a former coworker whom I hadn't seen in two years. She said she left her former company last year and is currently working for an Internet-based design firm. I mentioned that I am hoping to find a new job, and she said her firm is hiring. We exchanged phone numbers and agreed to get in touch about a possible job for me. After we said good-bye, I continued on my walk and stopped at the corner store for some dish detergent before I returned home. When I got there, I paid some bills and then cleaned the kitchen. Later I ran some errands.

Beginning: _____

_____

_____

_____

_____

_____

Middle: _____

_____

_____

_____

_____

_____

End: _____

_____

_____

_____

_____

_____

Outlining the Narrative

When composing long narratives, writers can include more events and develop them in greater detail than they can with a single paragraph. Still, writers must select events carefully to keep the narrative focused and coherent. Once the beginning, middle, and end of the narrative have been identified, the writer chooses details that will add depth to the story.

Imagine that you work for a local Community Development Corporation and that you must prepare quarterly reports to send to the CDC's funders. The purpose of your narrative is to describe the CDC's activities over the past three months and to demonstrate that resources have been used effectively. First, you select the events that best illustrate your progress. The outline below lists events that you could include in your report.

I.   CDC staff produced a map of neighborhood businesses to document the services available to residents.

II. CDC staff surveyed business owners about the state of their businesses and their perceived needs.

III. Staff members helped create a business council to bring together locally based owners to brainstorm collectively about business-enhancing strategies.

If you were writing a narrative paragraph, each of these events would be mentioned briefly, in addition to a few supporting details. But in a narrative essay, each major event requires one or more paragraphs. To construct the paragraphs, the writer breaks down each major event into component parts.

For example, several steps are involved in mapping the neighborhood businesses. These steps would be described chronologically to form a paragraph or two about the production of the map.

Here is an example of how the steps and supporting details might be outlined.

I.   CDC staff produced a map of neighborhood businesses to document the services available to residents.
A.   Staff members divided the neighborhood into sectors.
B.   Each staff member was assigned one sector to explore.
C.   Within the assigned sectors, staff members met with different business owners and recorded basic information about active businesses.
D.   Together the staff created a map showing all active businesses in the neighborhood.

When composing the essay, the writer should describe these events in a paragraph by using transitional phrases, varied sentence structure, and other techniques to make the writing flow smoothly.

ACTIVITY 21.2 For each outline below, fill in three points for the major event listed. Use your imagination to create the supporting details. The first outline, based on the example from the previous page, has been partially filled in for you.

First outline: CDC quarterly report to funders

I.   CDC staff mapped neighborhood businesses.

    A. Divided neighborhood into sectors _____

    B. Documented active businesses within each sector _____

    C. Together created map to show locations of all local businesses _____

II. CDC staff surveyed business owners

    A. Enlisted support of key business owners to help design survey _____

    B. _____

    C. _____

III. Staff organized neighborhood business council

    A. _____

    B. _____

    C. _____

Second outline: Biography of an author for the introduction to a book

I.   Luis Montoya grew up on a farm in southern California.

    A. _____

    B. _____

    C. _____

II. Luis read and wrote profusely as a teenager.

    A. _____

    B. _____

    C. _____

III. In his early twenties, he traveled throughout the United States and made a living at a variety of odd jobs while writing in his spare time.

    A. _____

    B. _____

    C. _____

Third outline: Summary of a movie plot

I.   Seven teenagers spend the night together at a cabin in the woods.

A. _____

B. _____

C. _____

II. Throughout the night, the characters hear strange noises and see strange happenings.

A. _____

B. _____

C. _____

III. The characters discover that the cabin is haunted, and they escape through the woods in the middle of the night.

A. _____

B. _____

C. _____

ETHICS CONNECTION

Telling All Sides of the Story

When telling a story, writers choose which events to highlight and which to leave out. They must be careful, though, to present their narratives so that they represent different viewpoints fairly.

For example, if a journalist reports on a traffic accident, she should interview the drivers of both vehicles, a disinterested bystander who witnessed the crash, and a police officer. Since each person has seen the situation differently, she will not represent the story accurately if she tells the story from only one driver's perspective. A story told from only one point of view would bias the readers.

When writing a narrative essay, think about how the events that you describe might be interpreted differently by different people. Be balanced in your narrative.

Introducing the Narrative

After outlining your narrative, you should construct an introductory paragraph. Sometimes, especially in works of fiction, the introduction consists of a character description. In other cases, the introduction provides historical background, as in the Pentridge River example, or other information that prepares the reader for the story.

Imagine that you are a marine biologist documenting the effects of the El Niño weather pattern on sea lion populations off the California coast. You might choose to relate the events chronologically in the form of a narrative. Before beginning the narrative, you should provide your readers with background information about the sea lions, about El Niño, and about your study. Your introduction might look like this.

> Once every several years the world experiences the phenomenon known as El Niño. El Niño is a warming of waters in the Pacific Ocean off the coasts of Ecuador and Peru. This warming disrupts normal weather patterns throughout much of the world. Because the changes in weather affect fish migrations, sea lions are vulnerable to losing their food supply. For 12 years, a group of researchers from Santa Monica University studied the sea lions and their reactions to El Niño.

Once the opening paragraph has introduced the topic and provided background information, the writer can relate the events of the narrative.

TECHNOLOGY CONNECTION

Searching for Text

Most word processing programs have a search function that allows you to locate any word or phrase in your document. This feature is useful for writers who want to change a certain detail consistently throughout a document. You also may use this feature when you want to locate something you said earlier in the text; for example, how you described a certain character.

To search for text, click on the Edit menu and select Search or Find. In the box, key the word or phrase you wish to locate. If you want to change the word or phrase, key the replacement in the Replace box. The software will replace the old word with the new word throughout the document.

ACTIVITY 21.3   Below is the outline for a narrative essay. The writer has identified the beginning, middle, and end of the story and has added details for each section. Based on the outline, write an opening paragraph to introduce the narrative. Then write the second paragraph of the essay based on the details provided. Use additional paper as needed.

I.   Benjamin moved to Omaha in March.

   A. He stayed with friends for the first couple of weeks.

   B. He found his own apartment downtown.

   C. The job search was long and frustrating.

II. Benjamin found a job as a customer relations assistant at a local bank.

   A. The position would allow him to gain experience in the field of customer relations.

   B. He enjoyed the atmosphere of the small locally owned bank.

   C. He quickly showed that he was very skilled at this kind of work.

III. Last week he was promoted to customer relations manager.

   A. The position came with a significant raise.

   B. Benjamin now has a lot more responsibility.

   C. He enjoys his new job and expects to stay at the bank for several years.

Introduction:

_____

_____

_____

_____

_____

_____

Second paragraph:

_____

_____

_____

_____

_____

_____

WRITING WORKSHOP

Showing Dialogue

Often, narrative writing calls for the use of dialogue—spoken interactions between characters. Writers indicate dialogue by placing quotation marks around the words a character speaks. For example, if you write that you told your friend you would meet him at five o'clock, you could indicate that in either of the following ways:

> "I'll meet you at five o'clock," I told my friend.

> I told my friend, "I'll meet you at five o'clock."

Notice the commas after *five o'clock* in the first example and after *friend* in the second example. Except when a question mark or an exclamation point is needed, a comma separates the speaker's words from the rest of the sentence.

If you look at a book or story that contains dialogue, you will notice that the writer begins a new paragraph every time a different person speaks. So a conversation that goes back and forth would look like this:

> "What time will I see you?" he asked.

> "I'll meet you at five o'clock," I replied.

> "That's too early!" he exclaimed.

> "I know, but we have to get an early start to avoid traffic."

> "How about six?"

> "I guess that would be okay. See you then."

In this example, the writer used tag words such as *he asked* and *I replied* to identify the speakers in the first three paragraphs. The writer stopped tagging the dialogue after the first few sentences. Because there are only two speakers, readers can easily figure out who is speaking in each of the last three sentences.

Note that when writing dialogue, the writer includes the punctuation inside the quotation marks. For example, in the above conversation, the question mark in the first sentence and the comma in the second sentence both appear inside the quotation marks.

Writing the Conclusion

The concluding paragraph ties together the main ideas of the essay, restates any important points, and leaves the reader with a sense of completion. The conclusion is an opportunity to create a lasting impression.

In a narrative essay, the concluding paragraph is based on the logical event to end the narrative. You have already learned how to identify the beginning, middle, and end of the story, and you have added details to describe each event in greater depth. To write the conclusion, you will compose a paragraph in which you describe the final event of your narrative using the details you have identified.

For example, the concluding paragraph of the narrative described in Activity 21.3 might look like this:

> Last week Benjamin was promoted to customer relations manager. Because this position carries greater responsibility than his previous position, it came with a significant raise. Benjamin is very satisfied with his new job and expects to stay with the bank for several years. All of his hard work and risk taking have paid off.

ACTIVITY 21.4   Write a concluding paragraph for one of the scenarios you outlined in Activity 21.2.

_____

_____

_____

_____

_____

SUMMARY FOR WRITING NARRATIVE DOCUMENTS

❑   Narrative reports and essays tell stories with detail and complexity.

❑   The writer begins by identifying the narrative's major events. These events should show a clear beginning, middle, and end.

❑   The writer creates an outline by identifying the component parts of each major event.

❑   The essay reflects multiple points of view.

❑   An introductory paragraph includes historical background or other information that provides an appropriate backdrop for the narrative.

PRACTICING YOUR SKILLS

As the owner of a small-scale dairy farm, Owen Yungen sees his job as producing high-quality milk and yogurt as well as making connections between urban residents and the rural communities that produce their food. Every weekend he travels to a farmer's market in the city, where he answers questions about his farm, his cows, and his philosophy of agriculture. Because he cannot meet every customer, Owen decides to create a pamphlet to place in stores that sell his products. The pamphlet begins with a detailed history of Owen's farm.

I grew up in the country and spent much of my childhood exploring the woods when I wasn't helping with chores on my parents' farm. I never doubted that I would grow up to run a farm of my own. Although farming is hard work, I wouldn't want to do anything else. Food is life, and in today's fast-paced world, most of us are profoundly disconnected from the systems that produce the food we eat. My life's work is to nurture those connections and to care for the land that is the source of our nourishment. I worked hard for several years to save enough money for a down payment on a farm. In 1987, I bought 200 acres of land and a small farmhouse that had been built 100 years earlier. Starting with just 30 head of cattle, I began selling milk to stores within the community. The milk sold well, but the population was too small to provide an adequate market. Because I knew I would have a difficult time persuading grocery stores in larger towns to stock my milk, I had to persuade people that my product was truly better than the highly processed milk they were used to purchasing. So I set up a booth at the county fair and gave out free samples.

Outlining the Narrative

1. Based on what you know about Owen's purpose and the focus of his essay, identify three major events that might be discussed in the next three paragraphs.

I. _____

_____

II. _____

_____

III. _____

_____

2. For one of the events you listed above, identify three points to develop in greater detail.

Event: _____

A. _____

B. _____

C. _____

3. Based on the events and points you outlined above, compose a paragraph relating those events in narrative form. This paragraph will form part of the body, or middle, of the essay.

_____

_____

_____

_____

_____

_____

_____

_____

4. In the first paragraph, Owen told the beginning of his story. The events you outlined above will form the middle, or body, of his narrative. The end of the story will consist of a conclusion that ties the pieces of the story together and leaves the reader with a sense of completion. Based on your outline, write the concluding paragraph of Owen's essay.

_____

_____

_____

_____

_____

_____

_____

_____

_____

APPLYING YOUR SKILLS

Now use the skills you learned in this chapter to write your own narrative essay.

Prewriting

(a) First, choose a subject for your narrative. Here are several suggestions:

- A mistake I made and the lesson I learned from it
- An experience that changed me
- A favorite family story or a personal story about my childhood

(b) Second, list the major events that shape your story. Make sure your story has a clear beginning, middle, and end.

(c) For each major event, identify several points to develop in further detail.

(d) Compose an engaging introductory paragraph that sets up your narrative.

Writing

Now write the first draft of your essay. Include plenty of supporting details.

Revising

Use the following checklist to help you revise thoroughly.

- ❑ Does the narrative include several main events?

- ❑ Does the narrative show a clear beginning, middle, and end?

- ❑ Are there enough supporting details to make the paragraphs clear, coherent, and interesting?

- ❑ Is there an opening paragraph that introduces the narrative with appropriate background information?

- ❑ Is the story told from a balanced perspective? Does it include more than one point of view where appropriate?

- ❑ Is there a concluding paragraph that creates a sense of completion?

When you have revised thoroughly, write a second draft. If you believe your content and presentation are as good as you can make them, go on to the editing stage.

Editing

Check your essay for mechanical errors. Closely examine grammar, spelling, word use, punctuation, and capitalization. When you have finished editing your work, proofread the final draft one last time

WRITING FOR YOUR CAREER

Below are suggested writing projects for each of the six career pathways. Choose one that appeals to you and use your new skills to write a narrative essay on the subject. When the project description refers you to the textbook web site, go to http://humphrey.swlearning.com and look for Chapter 21, Writing for Your Career. There you will find direct links to helpful web references.

Communication and the Arts

Imagine that you are a radio talk-show host. You host a daily call-in show that profiles artists, musicians, writers, and other public figures. Usually you begin the show by introducing your guest with a brief biographical essay. You use this essay to relate the significant events and accomplishments of his or her life. At the same time, you want to make the guest appear interesting and human to the audience. Choose a public figure you would like to interview and write a brief biographical essay of that person. When writing the essay, choose appropriate events to form the beginning, middle, and end of the narrative. Include details to add depth and interest to each event you have chosen.

Health and Medicine

As a school nurse at an elementary school, part of your job is to teach children about the importance of good nutrition, good sleeping habits, appropriate hygiene, and regular exercise. To attract and maintain the children's interest, you decide to tell them a story that illustrates these points. Using cartoon characters, animals, people, or other characters, compose a brief story about how your characters became happier and healthier through use of the habits described above. For suggestions, visit the textbook web site and locate the instructions for Chapter 21, Health and Medicine. You may use the information provided to compose your story.

Human, Personal, and Public Service

As the campaign manager for a local city council candidate, you want to present your candidate as an experienced and knowledgeable citizen who knows the city well and cares about it deeply. Because the candidate has lived in the city for several decades and has been very active in city politics, you have many stories to tell. You compose a narrative describing one or more of your candidate's accomplishments in the city. Choose a local politician whom you admire (or create a fictional candidate) and write a narrative describing the person's accomplishments that make him or her a strong candidate for city council.

Business and Marketing

As a commercial florist, you enjoy telling stories about the joy that flowers bring to people who receive them as gifts. You believe that flowers are a perfect gift for any occasion, and you have seen flowers make many people happy. Telling these stories to potential customers encourages them to buy flowers for their loved ones. Compose a story about someone who received flowers and the difference the gift made in his or her life. You may tell a true story or create a fictional one.

Science and Technology

As an automotive mechanic, you are fascinated by the history of the automobile. To share your expertise, you write an essay about automobile history and send it to a local paper for publication. For information, go to the textbook web site and locate the instructions for Chapter 21, Science and Technology. Access the web site provided, locate one or more sections about automobile history, and read the material. This information will provide background to help you write your essay.

Environment and Natural Resources

Today most people take for granted that their government provides mechanisms for regulating food safety. But this was not always the case. Food-safety laws in the United States came about only after a long and difficult struggle. As a food-safety expert at your state's food and agriculture department, you must know the background of the laws that regulate food quality. To learn about the history of these laws, you need to do research on the Internet. You can begin your research by going to the textbook web site and locating the instructions for Chapter 21, Environment and Natural Resources. Access the web site provided and use the information to help you write your essay.

22

Cause and Effect: Writing That Explains Results and Reasons

IN THIS CHAPTER YOU WILL LEARN TO:

- Distinguish between cause and effect.

- Identify the central issue or event.

- Develop relevant cause-and-effect examples.

- Write a cause-and-effect document.

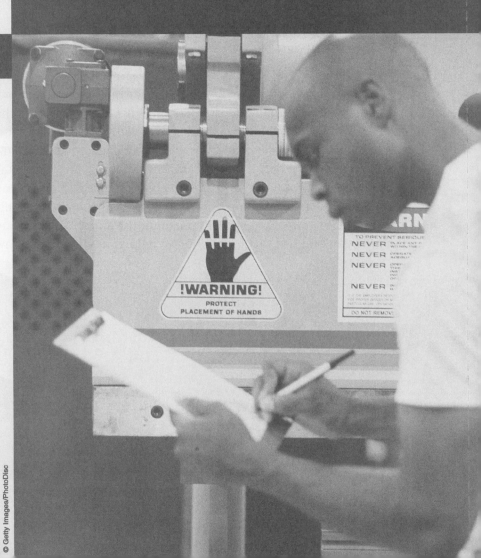

Cause and *Effect* in Writing for Your Career

Career Path	Sample Career	Use for Cause-and-Effect Writing	Example of Cause-and-Effect Writing
Communication and the Arts	Club disc jockey	Describing the music she spins	Music has amazing effects on people. It changes their moods; it makes them want to dance; and it helps them understand one another better.
Health and Medicine	Psychotherapist	Observing a patient's behavior	Jada's self-destructive behavior is the result of the abuse she endured as a child. Her substance abuse, relationship issues, and work-related problems come from the inadequacies she feels. She does not trust authority figures because she was abused by two authority figures—a teacher and a foster parent—when she was young and vulnerable.
Human, Personal, and Public Service	Truant officer	Explaining why a student must report for after-school detention	So far, Ryan has missed 21 days of school this year, and 3 of them were unexcused. These unexcused absences are the reason for Ryan's after-school detention. Also, due to these unexcused absences, Ryan is behind in his assignments and must make them up after school.
Business and Marketing	Residential landlord	Reporting on a problem rental property	Presently we have no prospective renters for the residential property at 212 Old Forest Road. The lack of interest in this property is a direct result of a developer converting several old factories only four blocks away into condominiums. The condominiums are more spacious than the Old Forest Road property, and the asking price is substantially less.
Science and Technology	Safety inspector	Designing a fire drill procedure	When the alarm is triggered, it causes the safety doors at the north end of the building to close. For that reason, occupants must evacuate through the emergency exits. After all employees exit, supervisors are required to do a head count to see that everyone is present.
Environment and Natural Resources	Meteorologist	Explaining the effect of weather conditions	Lower-than-average precipitation last winter produced a drought this spring. Because of this lack of rain, crops are stunted and lakes are low.

ON THE JOB

The Lie

As a script reader for a small theater, Harry Polis reads several new plays each week. Harry and several other individuals are the theater's "first-tier" readers. When Harry likes a script, he forwards it to the theater's literary manager, Bruce Graeber. Bruce, the "second-tier" reader, submits his choices to the artistic director, Lisa Litman. Lisa makes the final determinations about which plays the theater will present. Here is a summary of one of the plays Harry liked. The play is about the causes and effects of telling a lie.

"Anatomy of a Lie" by William Larson is a short play about how telling a lie can cause the breakdown of a relationship. The play has three characters: Jay is a successful businessman, Danielle is Jay's 13-year-old daughter, and Sharon is a family friend. The action centers on a lie that Jay tells to Danielle.

We learn that Jay has been unable to summon the courage to tell Danielle that her mother is dying from terminal cancer. Instead, he has lied to Danielle about her mother's condition. Furthermore, while he has shared some information about his wife's disease with Sharon, he has led her to believe that the illness is not terminal.

Act One explores what causes Jay to tell a lie to his daughter. We learn that experiences from Jay's childhood have taught him to lie when faced with difficult circumstances. His parents lied to him so often that he thinks lying is a natural behavior for a parent. He does not understand the harm in it.

Act Two probes the results of Jay's deceit. When Danielle learns the truth, she erupts in anger. She shouts at her father in indignation. She believes that her father has betrayed her and that she will never be able to trust him again. She also believes that her father has cheated her out of valuable time she could have spent with her dying mother. Jay's relationship with Sharon is damaged too, and Sharon no longer supports him as a friend. He is consumed with self-doubt regarding his behavior.

Did Harry do a good job of explaining the causes and effects of the character's dishonesty? If so, his readers will understand the play's message. In this chapter, you will learn how to write cause-and-effect essays so your readers understand the reasons for and outcomes of an issue or event.

Understanding Cause and Effect

In Chapter 12, you learned about **cause-and-effect** paragraphs. Now you will expand on that lesson and learn how to write an essay, a report, a letter, a memo, or another longer form of writing that explains the reasons for or the results of an issue or an event.

You have already learned that in cause-and-effect writing:

- A cause is what makes an issue or event occur, and an effect is what happens as the result of an issue or event.
- The thesis statement of a cause-and-effect document informs readers whether the document will be about cause or effect or both.
- Detailed examples of causes and effects help readers understand more about the writer's main idea.

Harry began his analysis of the play entitled "Anatomy of a Lie" with an outline. Based on the script, he saw a clear connection between the central issue, also called the main event (the lie a father told his daughter), and the consequences (effects) of the event. He also understood what caused Jay to lie to his daughter. Harry liked the play because it demonstrated why people behave the way they do. Below are notes that Harry jotted down before he wrote his essay. Can you see how this outline helped him write a thorough, well-constructed cause-and-effect essay?

1. **Central issue:** Danielle learns that Jay has been lying to her about her mother's condition: Jay has been telling his daughter that her mother will get better when she actually has a terminal illness.

2. **Cause of the main issue:** Jay's childhood was filled with lies his parents told him. He had no other model of parental behavior that would have taught him to communicate honestly with his daughter.

3. **Effect of main issue:** Danielle, who has been lied to by her father, feels betrayed and realizes that she may never be able to trust him again. Sharon no longer supports Jay.

SELF-ASSESSMENT 22

When I need to write for cause and effect, I can:

	Usually	Sometimes	Never
Distinguish between causes of an event and effects of an event.	❏	❏	❏
Identify the main event.	❏	❏	❏
Write clear, understandable examples of cause and effect.	❏	❏	❏
Conclude with a strong, logical recommendation or opinion.	❏	❏	❏

If you checked "Sometimes" or "Never" for any of the items, this chapter will help you improve your skills in writing cause-and-effect essays. Even if you checked "Usually" in every instance, you will learn more about how to write about cause and effect.

As you can see from this outline, Harry identified the central issue in the play as well as the causes and effects of the main issue. Now he is ready to write the remainder of his cause-and-effect summary of the play.

The Central Issue or Main Event

When you write for cause and effect, you describe the causes or the effects of something. Most cause-and effect-essays are about one main thing—called the central issue or main event.

The explanation of the central issue is the thesis statement. (In a paragraph, this statement is known as the topic sentence.) For example, a manager may be asked to write a memo explaining why sales are down, why people are quitting the company, or why customers are leaving. Each of these examples is an issue, and its description would be covered in a separate memo. If all of the topics were to be covered in the same memo, the issue would be broader—for example, why the company is facing financial difficulties. Each issue may have more than one cause or effect.

Read the following paragraph from a report written by a middle school principal about a new bullying policy. As you will see, the issue is the implementation of the policy, and it has had a number of effects.

 This year the school has instituted a new bullying policy. As a result, we have seen a dramatic reduction in bullying in the hallways and public areas of the building. By this time last year, 89 incidents had been reported. This year, as of today, only 17 instances have been reported. The enforcement of the policy has had several other effects in the school. For one thing, bullies know that there are serious consequences for bullying, so they are less likely to engage in it. Also, the victims feel protected. These students are happier, and, overall, they seem to be performing better in school than in previous years.

In the paragraph, the principal explores the results of implementing a new policy. He links events such as the policy, the reduction in bullying, and better performing students to *the cause*. His thesis statement reads as follows: *We have seen a dramatic reduction in bullying.* Using clear examples, relevant supporting details, transitional expressions, and a strong conclusion, he will prove that his thesis statement is true.

did you ever?

- Consider the effect of sleep deprivation on your ability to concentrate?

- Tell a customer why an item he special-ordered has not yet arrived at the store?

- Write an e-mail to a manager explaining what caused you to miss a meeting?

All of these situations involve common cause-and-effect events. With a little practice, you can apply cause-and-effect thinking to your writing.

ACTIVITY 22.1 For each of the subjects in the following list, write a thesis statement that explains a central issue. Follow up with one or two examples of the causes or effects of the central issue. The first item has been completed for you. The issue is in **bold**, and the effects are <u>underlined.</u>

1. how studying in a group improves grades

   <u>My experiences in school have shown me that there is strength in</u> <u>numbers.</u> My friends and I have gotten fantastic results from **studying** **together as a group** instead of individually. The positive effects of group study include <u>improved grades</u> and a <u>deeper understanding of</u> <u>the subject matter.</u>

2. how a good manager produces results

   _____

   _____

   _____

3. how a company-wide dress code affects morale

   _____

   _____

   _____

4. why I was absent from work yesterday

   _____

   _____

   _____

5. why a salary freeze for one year is necessary

   _____

   _____

   _____

6. how high employee turnover affects productivity

   _____

   _____

   _____

WRITING WORKSHOP

Avoiding Weak Cause-and-Effect Writing

Good writing shows the connection between central issues and their causes or effects. When writing for cause and effect, think through an event carefully to establish its relationship to causes and effects. Ask yourself whether the relationship will be clear to readers. Consider the examples below.

(A) Weak	My employer started a new attendance policy. Anyone who misses three days of work without an excuse gets fired. No one likes the new policy, and some people have quit because our employer doesn't trust us.
(B) Strong	My employer's new attendance policy has caused people to quit. Because people don't believe they are trusted, their morale is down. When morale is low, people are more likely to quit.
(C) Weak	I had good teachers, and my grades were good. I wouldn't have had good grades were it not for my teachers. My teachers cared.
(D) Strong	My grades were good because I had good teachers. My teachers spent extra time with me when I needed help and arranged tutoring when I had trouble learning.

In Examples (B) and (D), the thesis statement describes the event and tells whether the paragraph will be about cause or effect. Both of these samples are followed up with relevant supporting details. In Examples (A) and (C), however, the relationship between the event and the cause and effect is unclear.

Adding Relevant Examples

Earlier you learned that after identifying the central issue and writing the thesis statement, you should include examples and supporting details to help make your point. When writing for cause and effect, be sure to choose examples that strengthen your thesis statement.

For example, imagine that you are the property manager at a busy professional building in your town. The building's owners have asked you to write a memo about why tenants are leaving. Your memo will be about cause, not effect. It should include clear examples that describe why tenants are leaving.

> High rents and low service levels are the main causes of tenant turnover in our professional building. Seventy-five percent of the city's office buildings reduced their rents this year, but we raised ours. Half a dozen tenants told me this is why they left us this year when their leases were up for renewal.
>
> In addition, last May about a quarter of our building's maintenance staff was laid off, and now we lack the human resources to provide good maintenance services. The Howell Building, two blocks away, promises a one-day turnaround for service calls. Unfortunately, we can't compete with them in providing maintenance service.

Can you see how this memo shows cause and effect by using clear, concise examples? The main event in this example is high tenant turnover in a professional building. The memo examines the causes of the main event and provides strong supporting examples and details to help the reader understand the main point.

Now read the memo written another way. How does it differ from the first version?

> A half dozen tenants left us when their leases were up for renewal, which I said in a previous memo was going to happen. If we want to stop tenants from leaving, we should rethink our rent structure and lower the fees. We also should realize how important maintenance service is and provide faster service when tenants request a maintenance call.
>
> Last May about a quarter of our building's maintenance staff was laid off, even though I warned everyone that this was a bad idea. The maintenance staff is overworked. The Howell Building, two blocks away, promises a one-day turnaround for service calls. We cannot offer that level of service. How can we compete with the Howell Building?

In this example, the writer failed to stick to the cause-and-effect structure, resulting in a harsh memo that casts blame instead of showing causes. Which of the examples do you think is more effective?

ACTIVITY 22.2 Write one or two details after each of the following thesis statements. Make sure your details are relevant to the cause or the effect that is required (in parenthesis). The first one has been completed for you.

1. When the power went out in our office, it had disastrous effects. (effect)

   Two meetings were postponed, which meant that two deadlines had to be pushed back. The rescheduling interfered with several projects.

2. Last year's layoffs led to hardship for many of the employees who remained with the company. (effect)

   _____

   _____

   _____

3. John's negative attitude was the sole reason for her discharge from the organization. (cause)

   _____

   _____

   _____

4. The band's success resulted in personal problems for the musicians. (effect)

   _____

   _____

   _____

5. Failure to eat a healthy breakfast can lead to health problems. (cause)

   _____

   _____

   _____

6. When the computer system crashed, it affected productivity. (effect)

   _____

   _____

   _____

Organizing a Cause-and-Effect Essay

When writing for cause and effect, you must choose the correct order of the causes or effects that you describe. In most cause-and-effect essays, the causes or effects are presented in *time order* or by *order of importance*. There are four ways to order the events:

Beginning to end	Most important to least important
End to beginning	Least important to most important

Assume that you are a quality assurance engineer for a home appliance manufacturer. Your job is to test kitchen equipment for safety, efficiency, and function.

Imagine that you are writing a letter to a parts supplier after discovering a problem with an oven. In the letter, you examine the effects of a structural error in the thermostat housing that causes the oven to overheat. This creates a serious safety problem. The same structural error in the thermostat housing causes the inside oven light to stay on when the oven door is closed. This does not create a safety problem, but it is an annoyance to cooks.

In your letter, you should describe the more serious effect (an overheated oven) before you describe the less serious effect (the light staying on).

The oven does not work because of a structural flaw in the thermostat housing. Because of the flaw, the oven overheats when it is set to 350 degrees or higher. Also, the same structural flaw in the thermostat housing causes the inside light to remain on even when the oven door is closed. For the oven to work properly, the thermostat housing needs to be about a quarter of an inch shorter than it is currently.

Choosing the right order for causes or effects is important, though sometimes difficult.

The events in this letter are ordered from most important to least important. Note the use of the word *Also*—a transitional word signaling that another effect is about to be described.

Now imagine that you are writing an e-mail to your manager at the home appliance manufacturing company. You need to explain that you were unable to complete your quality assurance testing because the parts arrived damaged. The main event is your inability to perform the test, and you are writing the e-mail about the cause of that event. In this situation, you will present the causes in time order because you want to explain why something did not happen on time. Note the transitions—*Then* and *Finally*—that signal time sequence to the reader.

> Unfortunately, the testing did not occur on schedule because the parts arrived damaged. When I discovered the damaged parts, I telephoned and e-mailed the supplier, but he took two days to get back to me. Then shipping the new parts took another two days. Finally, almost a full day was needed to prepare for the testing.

What about ordering cause-and-effect writing in reverse—from the least important to the most important or from the end to the beginning? The type of order you use is mostly a matter of style and personal choice. As you go through the process of rewriting an essay, you may want to experiment with the order of events to see which way flows better and will have the biggest impact on your reader. For example, here is a paragraph that goes in reverse order—from the least important to the most important.

> The oven does not work because of a structural flaw in the thermostat housing. On account of the flaw, the inside light stays on even when the oven door is closed. However, there's a more serious consequence to the flaw: The oven overheats when it is set to 350 degrees or higher.

Here is the time sequence explained from most important to least important.

> Unfortunately, the testing did not occur on schedule because several of the parts I ordered arrived damaged. It took almost a full day to prepare for the testing after the parts arrived. It took a day to get new parts after I realized the first ones were damaged. Before that, it took the supplier two days to return my call.

The time sequence is less clear in this example when it is reversed from least important to most important. There may be times, however, when you find reversing the sequence to be more appropriate. For example, if you were explaining the effects of learning to swim, you might begin with an example of your saving a person's life because of your skill and then work backward to your days as a beginning swimmer.

ACTIVITY 22.3 Poor workplace communication can result in missed opportunities and stalled careers. Can you imagine a situation where poor communication might cause an employee to miss an opportunity?

Write an explanation of the central issue in the communication you imagine and of the effects it could have. For example, the effects of forgetting to check your voice mail could include missed meetings, canceled appointments, unhappy customers, and disappointed colleagues. Choose one of the four organizational patterns discussed on page 427 and write your cause-and-effect description. Write the description a second time in the opposite order. Which method is more appropriate for your essay?

1. beginning to end

_____

_____

_____

_____

2. end to beginning

_____

_____

_____

_____

3. most important to least important

_____

_____

_____

_____

4. least important to most important

_____

_____

_____

_____

_____

TECHNOLOGY CONNECTION

Add Cause and Effect to Your Resume

Most job seekers keep their resume on their computer's hard drive, and more employers are asking job candidates to submit their resumes electronically. This process helps companies eliminate overuse of paper; it spares job candidates the expense of postage and printing; and it delivers the resume in just a few seconds. Storing your resume electronically means you can easily tweak it so it is tailored to specific jobs for which you apply. Also, you can rewrite your resume to make its presentation stronger.

Before you send your next resume, take a few minutes to update it for cause and effect. How do you add cause and effect to your resume? When you list your accomplishments, show the *effects* of your efforts. For example, "I improved customer service" sounds okay, but here is an improvement that emphasizes cause and effect: "I improved customer response time by an average of 30 seconds per call, which resulted in an excellent rating on customer surveys." As you can see, the revised version links the writer's initiative with a positive outcome. It shows both the cause and the effect.

Each time you learn a new skill or gain experience in a job, go to your stored document and update it to show the effect of your efforts. Giving frequent attention to your resume will ensure that you don't forget any of the important information.

The Concluding Paragraph

In writing for cause and effect, the concluding paragraph is your opportunity to tie everything together—to show that the causes or effects that you described explain the main event.

Suppose that you are a dietician who is employed by a school district. You have observed that when children arrive at school without eating breakfast, they tend to perform worse than children who have eaten breakfast. You sit down to write a report to the school board. In your report, you will describe the effects of hunger on school performance. Here is a possible thesis statement: *Hunger causes students to learn at a slower pace.*

You may go on to describe several effects of hunger in school children, such as higher absenteeism, more detentions, and lower grades. After providing a suitable number of detailed examples, you will reach a conclusion:

> Considering these facts, I recommend a breakfast program because no child should have to attend school hungry.

ACTIVITY 22.4 Go back to Activity 22.1 and select one of the sample thesis statements with supporting details and relevant examples. Develop one or two middle paragraphs that show either causes or effects. Then write a concluding paragraph that includes a recommendation or a conclusion. Use a separate sheet of paper if you need more space.

_____

_____

_____

_____

_____

_____

_____

_____

_____

_____

_____

_____

ETHICS CONNECTION

Cause, Effect, and Truth in Writing

Cause and effect can be tricky. Suppose that you are a department store manager and your supervisor has asked you to write a report summarizing an investigation of a recent break-in at a company-owned warehouse. The investigation resulted in a number of findings. First, your assistant manager failed to set the alarm on the night of the break-in. Also, the burglars—who were caught by the police—could not be linked to your assistant manager in any way. In fact, the burglars admitted that they had been prepared to dismantle the alarm system but were happy to find that it had not been set.

If you know that the two events (the alarm not being turned on and the burglary occurring) were coincidental and not causally related, you have an ethical obligation to say so in your report—even if the assistant manager is a poor employee who your supervisor has wanted to dismiss.

Cause-and-effect techniques can be used to tell the truth or to mislead readers. Unless you are writing fiction, you should stick to the truth.

WRITING WORKSHOP

Less Is More: Cutting Unnecessary Words

Really, little, rather, quite, very, and a host of other words can impede the flow of otherwise strong cause-and-effect writing. Sometimes in early drafts, writers feel the need to modify nouns and verbs with unnecessary adjectives and adverbs. Consider the following sentence:

> When students come to school feeling really hungry, it can have quite a bad effect on their overall performance.

There are a number of unnecessary words and phrases in that sentence. It could be rewritten this way:

> Hunger causes students to learn at a slower pace.

The second version is about 50 percent shorter than the first, but it is stronger. Good writers know that rewriting involves reviewing each draft to eliminate any words that bog down a sentence, using only those that enhance a noun or verb.

SUMMARY FOR WRITING CAUSE-AND-EFFECT DOCUMENTS

❑   Writing for cause and effect involves explaining the reasons for or the results of a central issue or main event.

❑   A cause is what makes an event occur, and an effect is what happens as the result of an event.

❑   Most causes and effects are organized by time order or by order of importance.

❑   When writing for cause and effect, be sure that the events you describe are related by a cause. Just because Event A occurred before Event B does not mean that A caused B to occur.

❑   The concluding paragraph is your opportunity to tie everything together.

PRACTICING YOUR SKILLS

Construct a cause-and-effect essay about the causes or the effects of a mechanical or technical malfunction. For example, you could write about what caused the damage to your car (another car sideswiped it) or about the effects of the damage to your car (it's too dented to drive). You could write about what caused your computer to crash (a virus, for example) or about the effects of the crash (you lost a lot of work and you turned in a paper late). If you need additional space, use a separate sheet of paper.

1. First, develop a thesis statement about the central issue. For example, *The purpose of this essay is to persuade you that you should not penalize me for submitting my paper late because of a computer crash.* This tells the reader that the essay is about cause.

_____

_____

_____

2. Next, write one or two paragraphs explaining the causes or the effects of the central issue. For example, *When my computer crashed, I lost a lot of data that was on the hard drive. Even after the drive was restored, I lost several days of work.*

_____

_____

_____

_____

_____

_____

_____

_____

3. Finally, write a concluding paragraph that summarizes what you just wrote and that reinforces your message. For example, *Now that you understand the reasons why my paper was late, I hope you will agree to extend the deadline in my case.*

_____

_____

_____

APPLYING YOUR SKILLS

Now you can write a cause-and-effect essay on your own. Remember to name, number, and save each stage of your writing.

Prewriting

(a) Select a general subject for your essay. Here are some samples from which to choose:

Subject	Examples of Cause and Effect
popular music	How politics affect music
physical fitness	The positive effects of exercise
commitment	How financial success is one result of hard work
company policy	Donald got fired because he arrived late to his job too many times

(b) After deciding on your topic, brainstorm about it. Write down ideas for thesis statements. What do you want to communicate about your topic? What is the main issue? Jot down possible examples and supporting details. Let your ideas flow. This is not the time to edit. You can go back and do that later.

(c) When you have a list of ideas for examples and supporting details, decide the order in which you will present them. Use two or three relevant and specific examples or details in each paragraph.

(d) Construct a simple outline for your essay in a form like this:

Thesis Statement _____

_____

PARAGRAPH 1 _____

_____

PARAGRAPH 2 _____

_____

PARAGRAPH 3 _____

_____

PARAGRAPH 4 (CONCLUDING PARAGRAPH) _____

_____

Writing

Now write the first draft of your essay. Remember, you should use appropriate transitional words and expressions to show a time sequence or an order of importance, to signal that you are planning to describe a new cause or effect, or to help your essay flow.

Revising

Read your first draft. Use the following checklist of questions to make sure you have revised thoroughly.

- ❑   Is the thesis statement strong enough so that the rest of the essay can support it?
- ❑   Do you clearly identify a main issue?
- ❑   Are the topic sentences in all paragraphs about the cause of a central issue or about the effect of an event?
- ❑   Does the essay use *because, accounted for, was the result of, was caused by, was the reason for,* or similar words to show cause and effect?
- ❑   Are the examples clear and relevant?
- ❑   Is the writing strong enough to show a relationship between the cause and the effects? Remember, just because Event B happens after Event A does not mean that A caused B. If a relationship exists, are you showing it clearly?
- ❑   Did you choose a good order of causes or effects in all of your paragraphs? Try reversing the order or switching from order of importance to time sequence in some paragraphs. Then read your paragraph aloud to see which order makes the most sense.
- ❑   Does the concluding paragraph do a good job of tying things together, expressing your opinion, or making a recommendation?

When you think you have revised your essay thoroughly, write a second draft. Then follow the same process with your second draft. Critique and revise the essay thoroughly.

If possible, put the second draft away overnight. Then return to your essay the next day. With fresh eyes, look for small, easily overlooked spelling mistakes and keying errors that might have slipped by when you were concentrating on more important matters of substance and style.

After you have corrected the errors, write a third draft if necessary.

Editing

In this final stage, check one final time for errors in grammar, spelling, word use, punctuation, and capitalization. Eliminate words, phrases, and even entire sentences that are unnecessary.

After you have polished your writing, make a new copy in the format your instructor specifies.

WRITING FOR YOUR CAREER

CRITICAL THINKING

This section presents a writing project for each of the six career pathways. Choose one that appeals to you and use your new skills to write a cause-and-effect essay on the subject.

When the project description refers you to the textbook web site, go to http://humphrey.swlearning.com and click on the Links tab. Look for Chapter 22, "Writing for Your Career" and the helpful web references.

Communication and the Arts

You are the communications director for a nonprofit community development organization. Write a memo that describes the effects of losing two major donors. Was the organization forced to lay off staff? Did it cut back its activities? Will it have to move to a smaller office?

Begin by establishing a cause-and-effect thesis statement. Then show how one cause or effect led to another and another and another, all of which support your thesis. Remember to include examples, details, transitional expressions, and a concluding paragraph.

To complete this exercise, you may need to do some Internet research on community development organizations. For information that will help you with this assignment, go to the textbook web site for Chapter 22, Communication and the Arts.

Health and Medicine

You are a psychologist who has been asked to write a case study of a young man who arrived at your clinic with a crippling, irrational fear of birds. His phobia has left him a virtual prisoner in his own home for the past five years.

If you need help understanding phobias, visit the textbook web site and locate the instructions for Chapter 22, Health and Medicine. In your case study, write about the causes of phobias. From the numerous theories put forth by mental health experts about the reasons for phobias, select one that makes sense to you and develop your case study based on that theory. Use your imagination to develop the details and examples.

Human, Personal, and Public Service

Pretend that you are a police officer at the scene of a two-car traffic accident. After making certain no one is hurt, you interview the drivers of both vehicles as well as two witnesses.

Write a report that explains how the accident occurred. In your thesis statement, suggest who or what caused the accident. In subsequent paragraphs, describe the causes in detail so the reader will have a good understanding of how the accident occurred.

Business and Marketing

Many business leaders have said that failure is often a better teacher than success. Have you ever been part of a failed business venture of any type? Perhaps, for example, you were unable to sell your quota of items in a fund-raising project for your school. What did you learn? Would you take the risk again? If so, what would you do differently the next time?

Write an essay about what caused an unsuccessful venture. Use an example from your own experience or write about a business you know, perhaps one owned by a friend or a relative.

Tell the business's story. What caused the failure? Examine the causes and follow up with relevant examples and supporting details. Use transitional words and expressions and include a strong concluding paragraph.

Science and Technology

Write an essay that describes the effects the Internet has had on your chosen career path. For example, the Internet has had a powerful effect on law enforcement because federal databases can now be accessed online. The Internet has had a big effect on manufacturing because companies can get up-to-date inventory information online. They also can use the Internet to exchange information with customers quickly. What effects has the Internet had on your preferred industry?

Environment and Natural Resources

Imagine that you work for a community organization that promotes recycling and alternative energy sources such as solar and wind power as an alternative to pollution-emitting sources. Write an essay about the main causes of air or water pollution. You may want to write about factories and automobiles, or your research may lead you to other major causes of pollution. Conclude your essay with recommendations on how to improve the environment. For information about the environment, visit the textbook web site and locate the links for Chapter 22, Environment and Natural Resources.

23

Writing to Persuade: Longer Documents

IN THIS CHAPTER YOU WILL LEARN TO:

- Persuade readers to do something.

- Prioritize your arguments.

- Utilize persuasive techniques and strategies.

- Write persuasive essays and reports.

Using *Persuasion* in Writing for Your Career

Career Path	Sample Career	Use for Persuasive Writing	Example of Persuasive Writing
Communication and the Arts	Newspaper columnist	Expressing your view on an issue	Politicians should not be allowed to accept money from individuals or private interests to fund their campaigns. If campaigns were funded publicly, politicians would no longer be beholden to special interests.
Health and Medicine	Chiropractor	Promoting preventive medicine through healthy lifestyles	Americans spend billions of dollars on medicines, surgery, and doctor visits. If you take better care of yourself, you can avoid many health problems.
Human, Personal, and Public Service	High school guidance counselor	Explaining to students the benefits of a college education	As my mother used to tell me, education is the one thing that cannot be taken away from you. If you want to earn a higher average starting salary, make sure you graduate.
Business and Marketing	Manager of a new restaurant	Promoting the restaurant to potential clients	You haven't experienced Middle Eastern food until you've been to Casablanca! Come try our affordable prices and vegetarian options. Bring the children too. We have something for everyone.
Science and Technology	Anesthesiologist	Explaining to patients the importance of avoiding food and drink for several hours before surgery	Anesthesia is somewhat risky, but you can reduce your risk if you consume no food or drink for at least 12 hours before surgery. There are several reasons for avoiding food and drink. First, anesthesia causes vomiting in some patients.
Environment and Natural Resources	Landscape architect	Persuading a client to use native plants	Native plants are well adapted to our environment and require less maintenance than introduced species. By sowing sage grass in our climate, you will use 78 percent less water than with Kentucky bluegrass.

ON THE JOB

Advertising Campaign

Anthony Garcia works for a small advertising firm. Although his job demands a lot of time and hard work, he enjoys using his creative talents. Recently, the firm signed a contract with a drink bottler to develop an advertising campaign for Mega Surge, an energy beverage. Anthony has an idea about how to approach the project.

He discusses his idea with his manager, who asks him to write a proposal. In the proposal, Anthony is to outline his suggestions and explain why they would be effective in advertising Mega Surge. Soon the advertising team will meet to review proposals from members. Each team member will present ideas and make a case for them.

As the first step in writing his persuasive essay, or proposal, Anthony brainstorms his plan and makes a list of the advantages, or arguments. Next, he reflects on his audience—the other members of the advertising team—and decides which of his arguments will appeal to them most. After choosing his major arguments, he outlines his essay and chooses details to back up the arguments. Finally, he composes a first draft. His first two paragraphs are shown below.

Walking down the sports drinks aisle in a supermarket is overwhelming. Who could imagine so many different varieties? How can our customers choose just one from the dozens of tempting, brightly colored drink alternatives? The answer: They can't choose. They must associate Mega Surge¹ with something positive and be drawn to our¹ product instinctively. We want them to be able to make a quick¹ decision without having to remember facts. The way we do this is through the following common and successful¹ advertising technique.

We project images of active people² of all ages doing exciting² and adventurous things while drinking Mega Surge. We start with rock climbing in Utah and end with ocean sailing in Florida, thereby² placing our product in different geographic regions. Picture a beautiful Utah rock face with an unspoiled desert in the background. The climber, alone in the mountains, takes a refreshing sip of Mega Surge and shouts with excitement! Then we flash to a handsome sailboat riding the waves as friends laugh and relax in the sun, each one holding a can of Mega Surge.

Does Anthony's introduction convince you that his idea is good? Do you think he has a plan that will sell drinks? If so, his writing is effective. In this chapter, you will learn strategies to help you write persuasive essays and reports.

The Persuasive Essay or Report

In Chapter 13, you learned techniques for **persuading** readers to do something or to adopt your viewpoint. In this chapter, you will further develop those skills. Then you will apply them to longer documents such as reports, letters, and proposals.

In the On the Job example, Anthony wants to persuade his coworkers to follow his suggestions for an advertising campaign. He has two objectives: to describe his ideas clearly and to demonstrate to his coworkers why the ideas will work. To describe his suggestions, he will use the descriptive writing techniques you studied in Chapters 6 and 16. To convince his coworkers to agree with him, he will identify the benefits, organize the information carefully, and back up his arguments with appropriate details.

Anthony begins by identifying the advantages of his advertising scheme. Next, he selects the arguments that will appeal the most to his intended audience. Finally, he outlines his essay and backs up each argument with several details. His outline is below. The items listed in Nos. 1 and 2 of the outline are matched to the underlined items in the scenario.

1. **Form positive association in customers' minds**

   - Customers will be drawn to the product instinctively.
   - There will be no need for customers to remember specific facts about the product.
   - This is a common and successful advertising technique.

2. **Appeal to a wide audience**

   - Most people crave adventure and excitement.
   - The campaign is appropriate for all ages and geographic regions.

This outline will be Anthony's guide as he composes his essay. After introducing the essay with a few attention-getting sentences, he will develop each argument using the details he listed above. He may decide to add one or two arguments such as *create easy-to-produce ads* and provide several details to support the argument. To make his arguments most effective, he will emphasize his coworkers' own interests. Finally, he will conclude with a paragraph that reviews and restates his most powerful arguments.

SELF-ASSESSMENT 23

When I write a persuasive essay or report, I can:

	Usually	Sometimes	Never
Select the most persuasive arguments.	❑	❑	❑
Choose arguments that interest my audience.	❑	❑	❑
Support my arguments with evidence and details.	❑	❑	❑
Organize my arguments effectively.	❑	❑	❑
Apply appropriate techniques of persuasion.	❑	❑	❑

If you checked "Sometimes" or "Never" for any of the items, this chapter will help you improve your skills. Even if you checked "Usually" in every instance, you will learn more about writing to persuade.

Prioritizing Your Arguments

The opening paragraph of a persuasive essay must contain a thesis statement that clearly gives the central proposition and the writer's opinion. In a persuasive essay, a writer develops several reasons why the readers should agree with the central proposition, or idea.

The effectiveness of the essay depends to a large degree on presenting the arguments in a logical order. Sometimes writers follow the thesis statement with their strongest argument. Other times they save the best argument for last. Both strategies are acceptable. The one you choose will depend on the purpose and audience of each essay.

The best way to determine the appropriate order of arguments is to put yourself in the readers' position. What are their greatest concerns, interests, and values? In Anthony's example, he knows that the first priority of his coworkers is a successful advertising campaign. Therefore, he begins by emphasizing how his ideas will encourage buyers to choose Mega Surge.

Now imagine that you have started a small home-improvement business. The business entails doing odd jobs around your customers' homes—from painting to carpentry to minor repairs. To get started, you must persuade potential investors to lend you money to buy equipment. Here are the reasons, or arguments, you have decided to highlight in your essay:

- I intend to pay generous dividends to investors.
- The initial investment is small.
- Based on my business plan, I expect to turn a profit quickly. I should be able to pay back the initial investment within two years.

Before making an outline, you must prioritize your arguments. Put yourself in the reader's position. If you were asked to invest in a business, what would be your primary interest? What would make you want to invest?

In this case, investors would probably be most concerned about whether the business can survive and turn a profit. After all, if the business fails, it does not matter how generous the dividends would have been. Furthermore, the size of the investment alone is not a strong enough argument to get the reader hooked. Therefore, the argument that emphasizes the strong business plan is likely to be most effective.

did you ever?

- Write a cover letter explaining why you were the best candidate for a job?

- Make a case for your political viewpoint by backing up your position?

- Give a friend reasons why taking a vacation with you is a good idea?

You use persuasion every day. In this chapter, you will learn to apply your persuasive skills in essay writing.

ACTIVITY 23.1 Each item below describes a situation that calls for a persuasive essay. Several arguments are given. In each case, identify the audience and consider the readers' concerns and interests. Then name the argument you think is most effective. Explain your reasons.

1. As a clinical psychologist, you believe that employer health insurance should cover the costs of psychological counseling for employees. To persuade others of your view, you write a letter to be published in a journal for practicing psychologists. Your proposition is that psychologists should work together to advocate for coverage of psychological counseling.

Arguments:

- Treating mental health problems early prevents more severe problems later. Therefore, employees would be healthier and more productive if their company's insurance covered psychological counseling.
- If all insurance carriers covered counseling, they could bargain for "bulk" discounts from practitioners that would help keep costs down.
- Offering insurance coverage for counseling services would result in people recognizing that counseling is a serious part of maintaining good health. This would reduce some of the stigma attached to those who seek help from psychological practitioners.

Audience: _____

Most important argument: _____

_____

_____

Reasons: _____

_____

_____

_____

2. You are a lawyer whose client, a car manufacturer, is being sued by a customer because a tire blew on her two-year-old car, causing an accident. You are planning your presentation to the jury. You plan to argue that the car manufacturer cannot be held liable for car accidents. The jury is a diverse group of people representing the population of your city.

Arguments:

- Drivers are responsible for maintaining their tires. Car manufacturers cannot be held responsible for crashes caused by worn tires.

- If car manufacturers had to pay damages for accidents caused by worn tires, they would charge more for their cars, and most people would be unable to afford a car.
- Driving will never be perfectly safe, and manufacturers cannot predict every possible risk factor involved in driving.

Audience: _____

Most important argument: _____

_____

_____

Reasons: _____

_____

_____

_____

3. As a digital audio engineer, you develop technologies that improve the quality and availability of audio recordings. Some people argue that these technologies should be restricted because they make it possible for consumers to pirate copyrighted recordings. You believe that people should have access to the newest technology as long as artists receive fair compensation for their work. In an article for a newspaper, you argue that antipiracy laws should not interfere with consumers' rights to access the music.

Arguments:

- Audio technology should benefit everyone. Consumers' access should not be restricted because a small percentage of people will use the technology in illegal or unethical ways.
- New audio technologies create enormous possibilities for artists who want to reach broad audiences through the Internet. Restricting audio technology would interfere with artists' freedom of expression.
- Limiting access to new technologies would discourage engineers from developing new capabilities. This would hurt everyone since we all benefit from improvements in technology.

Audience: _____

Most important argument: _____

_____

_____

Reasons: _____

_____

_____

_____

ETHICS CONNECTION

Persuasion versus Propaganda

Persuasion is the art of using logic and evidence to influence others. Sometimes, especially in advertising and political campaigns, writers go beyond logic and evidence to try to change people's minds by manipulating their emotions. This unethical means of persuasion is known as propaganda.

Propagandists use many techniques to try to sway others' views. Common techniques include name-calling, repetition, and glittering generalities. In name-calling, writers attack their competition by using labels instead of presenting evidence. For example, an unethical politician might say, "My opponent is a liar and a fool." This attack is designed to anger or frighten readers so they turn against the other candidate. The statement does not include factual information. In contrast, ethical writers give their readers rational reasons to demonstrate why they should vote for one candidate instead of another.

A second propaganda technique is repetition. This means a writer repeats the same statement often to implant it in the readers' minds. Like name-calling, repetition is an unacceptable substitute for evidence. Writers who use this technique expect that readers who hear the same statement often enough will think it is true, even without any evidence to back it up.

Glittering generalities are statements that make vague claims without any specifics or facts. For example, a politician might say, "You should vote for me because I stand up for people's rights." While this statement may not be intended to deceive, it is meaningless without any explanation of which rights the candidate supports and what he or she has done to support them.

A good persuasive writer makes specific arguments that can be backed up by evidence. This ensures that the writing follows ethical guidelines.

Supporting Your Arguments

In the body of a persuasive essay, each paragraph consists of one argument that addresses the central proposition and detailed evidence to support that argument. The evidence should be factual and verifiable. In other words, the writer should be able to show that the evidence comes from reliable sources. This helps establish credibility, as discussed in Chapter 13.

Imagine that you are writing an essay arguing that fuel efficiency standards on cars should be raised. You have generated a list of arguments, selected the best ones, and prioritized them according to your goals. Now you need to present the evidence.

Your first argument is that increasing fuel efficiency would reduce air pollution. To support this argument, you must present the readers with several facts about air pollution. You also should discuss the relationship between clean air and lower rates of fuel use. Below are the facts you have assembled:

- Passenger cars and light trucks together account for a large percentage of all air pollution in the United States.
- Air pollution from cars causes high levels of smog in many cities. This leads to health problems for those living in urban areas.
- The number of cars on the road is growing all the time, so reducing the amount of fuel each car uses is essential to controlling air quality in our country.

Next, you must develop these facts into a paragraph. The writing style should be similar to that of an illustrative paragraph, which you studied in Chapter 5. First, you write your thesis statement—increasing fuel efficiency would reduce air pollution—then follow it with the supporting evidence. You should use transitional phrases so the paragraph reads smoothly.

For each argument, you should follow a similar process of locating supporting evidence and developing it into a complete paragraph. Finding factual evidence usually involves research. When conducting research, make certain that your facts come from reliable sources.

Finally, to establish credibility, you must identify your sources of information. By citing authoritative sources, you show that the information is reliable. For example, if one of the facts above came from the Environmental Protection Agency, you could include that information in the paragraph. The sentence might look like this:

> According to the Environmental Protection Agency, air pollution from cars and trucks leads to many health problems for people living in large cities.

In Chapter 13, you learned about various techniques writers use to support their propositions. In addition to citing authoritative sources, these techniques include stating factual evidence, addressing opposing arguments, and establishing credibility. You will use the same strategies when writing persuasive essays and reports.

ACTIVITY 23.2 Each item below presents a central proposition and a supporting argument. The central proposition is the thesis statement. The argument is one of the writer's reasons why the reader should agree with the thesis statement. For each argument, list three facts that support it. You will need to invent information as these are fictional cases.

1. Central proposition: You should take advantage of our new long-distance calling plan.

   Argument: If you make more than four long-distance calls per month, this plan will save you a lot of money compared to your current plan.

   Supporting facts:

   a. _____

   _____

   _____

   b. _____

   _____

   _____

   c. _____

   _____

   _____

2. Central proposition: Local businesses should advertise in the town's weekly newspaper.

   Argument: Advertising in the *Westtown Journal* will greatly increase your business with local residents.

   Supporting facts:

   a. _____

   _____

   _____

   b. _____

   _____

   _____

   c. _____

   _____

   _____

3. Central proposition: I am a highly qualified candidate for this job.

   Argument: I have extensive experience in this field.

   Supporting facts:

   a. _____

   _____

   _____

   b. _____

   _____

   _____

   c. _____

   _____

   _____

4. Central proposition: You should support more funding for local schools.

   Argument: More school funding would improve student performance.

   Supporting facts:

   a. _____

   _____

   b. _____

   _____

   c. _____

   _____

5. Central proposition: This city needs better public transportation.

   Argument: Investing in commuter trains stimulates local economies.

   Supporting facts:

   a. _____

   _____

   _____

   b. _____

   _____

   _____

   c. _____

   _____

Persuasive Strategies

In addition to presenting factual arguments, writers use other techniques to encourage readers to see a particular viewpoint: appealing to shared values, appealing to common sense, refuting potential counterarguments, predicting outcomes, and using examples/anecdotes. These techniques, combined with factual evidence, can enhance the effectiveness of a persuasive essay.

Shared Values

When appealing to shared values, writers emphasize values or philosophies that are specific to the target audience, including religious, cultural, and political ideals.

In other cases, writers appeal to more universal values, such as fairness, honesty, and courage. If arguing for changes in taxation, a writer might appeal to fairness by showing that a different tax system would be fairer to citizens.

Common Sense/ Rhetorical Question

To appeal to common sense, writers present their argument as if it is the most—or the only—reasonable position. For example, a writer might ask a rhetorical question to suggest that a position's correctness should be obvious to readers.

A rhetorical question is one that intends to make a point. Its purpose is not to get an answer. An example of a rhetorical question is this: Don't you think it's about time the city repaved this road? The intention is to suggest that repaving the road now is a matter of common sense.

Refuting Counterarguments

Refuting potential counterarguments is a powerful persuasive strategy. It requires writers to anticipate what readers with an opposing view might say and then to argue against that position. This technique allows writers to make their point before readers have an opportunity to think about the opposite side.

For example, if attempting to persuade someone to switch banks, you might make the following statement: "All banks may seem alike, but once you see the benefits we offer, you'll want to join us!" In this way, you strengthen your argument by showing that you recognize other views and can address them.

Predicting Outcomes

Predicting possible outcomes is a powerful strategy. A politician might try to get voters' support by predicting that her opponent will overspend and put the city into bankruptcy.

Examples/Anecdotes

Writers may use examples and anecdotes to support their strategy. An anecdote is a brief story that makes a point. For example, imagine that you are arguing that college tuition should be lowered so everyone can have the same educational advantages. You might give examples of students who were unable to afford tuition. You could also tell an anecdote about someone who experienced extreme hardship because of the high cost of tuition.

TECHNOLOGY CONNECTION

"Undo" Mistakes

Often, word processors allow writers to work so quickly that they make careless mistakes in typing and/or editing. Fortunately, these mistakes are easy to fix if your word processor has an Undo function—as long as you catch the mistake right away. To use the Undo function, go to the Edit menu on the toolbar and select Undo from the drop-down menu. The program will automatically erase the last change you made, whether you deleted, pasted, changed the font, or used another command. By continuing to select Undo, you can erase the last several keyboard actions.

ACTIVITY 23.3   For each of the arguments made in Activity 23.2, use one of the persuasive strategies to make a case for the argument. Additional arguments are also given for you to identify a strategy.

1. If you make more than four long-distance calls per month, this plan will save you a lot of money compared to your current plan.

    Strategy: <u>common sense/rhetorical question</u>

    Argument: <u>Do you really want to continue paying high long-distance</u>

    <u>rates when you could be paying much less?</u>

2. Advertising in the *Westtown Journal* will greatly increase your business with local residents.

    Strategy: _____

    _____

    Argument: _____

    _____

    _____

    _____

    _____

3. I have extensive experience in this field.

    Strategy: _____

    _____

    Argument: _____

    _____

    _____

    _____

    _____

4. More school funding would improve student performance.

    Strategy: _____

    _____

    Argument: _____

    _____

    _____

    _____

    _____

5. Argument: Investing in commuter trains stimulates local economies.

Strategy: _____

_____

Argument: _____

_____

_____

_____

6. I deserve a raise based on the quality of my work.

Strategy: _____

_____

Argument: _____

_____

_____

_____

_____

7. Ergonomically supportive chairs and desks can prevent a lot of computer-related injuries.

Strategy: _____

_____

Argument: _____

_____

_____

_____

_____

8. Hiring a financial planner could help assure yourself of a financially secure retirement.

Strategy: _____

_____

Argument: _____

_____

_____

_____

WRITING WORKSHOP

Citing Sources

In the "Supporting Your Arguments" section, you saw how, within the body of an essay, a writer might cite the source of his or her information for an argument. Depending on the type of document, writers may cite sources in other ways. For example, they often use footnotes or endnotes.

To create a footnote or an endnote, place the cursor at the point in the essay where you are including information from the cited source. On the toolbar, click Insert, then Reference. From the pull-down menu, select Footnote. The word processor will provide a choice of footnotes or endnotes. (In some programs, you click on Footnote first, instead of Reference.)

The example below demonstrates how a writer could use a superscript—a raised number—to identify a footnote in the text of an essay. Notice that the matching superscript at the bottom of this page gives the complete citation for the example, a web site from the U.S. Department of Agriculture. This is a citation that readers will view as reliable.

Footnotes are listed at the bottom of a page. A few lines of space come between the end of the essay and the footnote.

> Calcium can be found in surprising places. For example, one-fourth of a mango contains over 40 percent of the recommended daily allowance for young children.[1]

Endnotes are similar to footnotes. However, all information about endnotes sources is placed in a list at the end of the document. Writers use endnotes and footnotes when they need to provide detailed information about their sources but do not want to interrupt the flow of the essay. Many writers believe that endnotes are less of an interruption than footnotes because of their placement at the end of an essay or a document.

[1]USDA, "What Foods Are Good Sources of Vitamin A, Vitamin C, Calcium, and Iron?" http://www.fns.usda.gov/tn/Resources/appendb.pdf.

SUMMARY FOR WRITING PERSUASIVE DOCUMENTS

❑ Persuasive essays argue for a point of view or try to persuade the reader to do something specific.

❑ Persuasive essays state a central proposition that is supported by arguments.

❑ Arguments should be prioritized based on the reader's interests and concerns.

❑ Each paragraph consists of one argument.

❑ Arguments are based on factual evidence.

❑ Persuasive strategies can strengthen a writer's position.

❑ Popular persuasive strategies include appealing to shared values, appealing to common sense, refuting counterarguments, predicting outcomes, and using examples and anecdotes.

PRACTICING YOUR SKILLS

As the fund-raising director for a small nonprofit center that provides homeless services, Gina Gorzyca tries to persuade individuals and institutions to donate money to support the center's operations. To convince them that the center will make good use of their gifts, she must clearly demonstrate in a letter that the center has done effective work in the past and that it has clear and well-thought-out plans for the future. The information about its activities will form the body of her persuasive letter, or essay, which she will send to past and potential donors. The introduction will state her thesis, or proposition, clearly. It also will capture the readers' interest and provide background information about the organization. The introductory paragraph appears below.

Are you aware that children are the fastest-growing segment of the homeless population? Researchers estimate that the average age of a homeless person in the United States is nine years. That means millions of children are growing up without the resources they require to become healthy, happy, and productive adults. Here at the Safe Child Foundation, we are dedicated to providing support to children and families in our community who face temporary or chronic lack of housing. Our goal is to provide short-term shelter and long-term support so families can become self-sufficient and children can stay with their loved ones. To continue helping these people, we need your help.

The introduction includes basic facts designed to make readers aware of the problem the center faces. It also describes the center's approach and shows that its efforts are intended to have long-term effects. Finally, it states the central proposition: Readers should donate money to the foundation. The next several paragraphs will consist of arguments designed to persuade readers that they should donate money. Each argument will be supported by evidence.

Prioritizing the Arguments

1. Before she composes the body of her letter, Gina makes a list of arguments that support her central proposition. When making the list, she considers her audience—people and organizations that have expressed an interest in helping homeless children—and takes their concerns and interests into account. Here is her list of arguments.

   - Spending money to support homeless children saves money by preventing worse problems in the future.
   - By donating money, you will bring hope and comfort to a child's life.

- Because our organization is efficient, we have low overhead. Over 85 percent of our funds go toward our programs for children.
- Because we focus on empowering people and helping them continue their success, your gift will have a positive, long-term effect.

 Based on your understanding of the intended audience, which argument do you think is most effective and therefore should be placed prominently in Gina's essay? Explain the reasons for your choice.

Most effective argument: _____

Reasons: _____

_____

Supporting Your Arguments

2. Gina must provide several facts to back up her arguments. Each argument, along with the supporting evidence, will become a paragraph in the body of her essay. Providing evidence often requires research. Use the Internet or other sources of information to find several facts that support the following argument: Spending money to support homeless children saves money by preventing worse problems in the future.

_____

_____

_____

_____

Using Persuasive Strategies

3. In addition to her factual evidence, Gina will use persuasive strategies to make her essay more effective. Choose one of the arguments from number 1 and construct an argument using one of the strategies described in this chapter.

- Appealing to shared values
- Appealing to common sense
- Refuting counterarguments
- Predicting outcomes
- Giving examples or telling anecdotes

_____

_____

_____

_____

APPLYING YOUR SKILLS

Now you can use all of the skills you learned in this chapter to write your own persuasive essay. Follow the stages of the writing process used throughout the book.

Prewriting

(a) First, choose a proposition for your essay. Here are some suggestions:

- All colleges and universities should be tuition-free.
- You (the reader) should move to my city or town.
- Children should be raised with strict discipline.

(b) Second, identify the audience for your essay and jot down your ideas about the reader's interests and concerns.

(c) Next, develop and prioritize your arguments. Identify the most effective argument. Rank the other arguments in declining order of importance.

(d) For each argument, list several facts or pieces of evidence that back it up. This will probably require some research. Cite your reliable sources.

(e) Consider the persuasive techniques discussed in this chapter. Choose two of your arguments and develop them using two of the techniques described.

Writing

Now write a draft that includes introductory and concluding paragraphs.

Revising

Read and revise your draft by referring to the following checklist.

❑ Does the introductory paragraph state your central proposition clearly?

❑ Do your arguments appeal to the reader's interests? Are they factual and specific? Are they prioritized effectively?

❑ Do you provide detailed evidence to support your arguments?

❑ Does your evidence come from reliable sources?

❑ Did you use persuasive strategies effectively?

Now write a second draft and revise it thoroughly. Try to get another opinion.

Editing

In this final stage, check your essay for mechanical errors. Closely examine grammar, spelling, word use, punctuation, and capitalization.

When you have finished editing your work, make a final copy in the format your instructor specifies. Proofread the final draft one last time.

WRITING FOR YOUR CAREER

CRITICAL THINKING

From the six career pathways below, choose a project. Use the skills you learned in this chapter to write a persuasive essay. For information that can help with your research, visit the textbook web site at http://humphrey.swlearning.com and locate the instructions for Chapter 23, Writing for Your Career.

Communication and the Arts

Imagine that you are a newspaper columnist in your town. Every week you publish a column expressing your views on important national, regional, or local issues. Collect a few newspapers and find an article, a letter, or an opinion piece that especially interests you—or choose an issue about which you feel strongly. Write a column in which you state your view in the form of a proposition. Back up your proposition with arguments based on evidence. Log on to a search engine such as Google.com, Yahoo.com, or MSN.com and research information to support your arguments.

Health and Medicine

As a chiropractor, you believe that disease prevention is the most powerful medicine. You encourage patients of all ages to eat well, sleep well, exercise regularly, stop smoking, and avoid stress. Write a persuasive essay in which you argue that if people took better care of their daily health, they could cut down significantly on medications and doctor visits. In essence, they could prevent illness before it started. Use some of the persuasive strategies from this chapter to make your points.

Human, Personal, and Public Service

Assume that you are a high school guidance counselor whose primary responsibility is to counsel students about their post-high school options. You help young people apply to college, search and apply for jobs, and make important decisions about their future. Because you have seen many young people rush through these decisions, you work hard to persuade students to spend a significant amount of time and energy evaluating their goals, strengths, and values, and then plan accordingly. Write an article for the school paper in which you state a central proposition and make a thesis statement. Support your thesis statement with powerful arguments. Cite all of your sources so readers will recognize that the material is reliable and that you are a credible writer.

Business and Marketing

Working in the marketing department of a large software company gives you plenty of opportunity to persuade potential clients that your company's software products can make their lives easier. Based on software that has helped you, write an essay to persuade others that they should take advantage of the same software. Consider the concerns and questions of the readers. Give reasons why they should use the software you recommend. For help with the research, go to the textbook web site and locate the links for Chapter 23, Business and Marketing.

Science and Technology

Genetic engineering is a technique used by scientists to change the characteristics of certain species. This technique is performed by splicing genes from one living thing onto the DNA of another. For example, by implanting the gene of a cold-water fish into a tomato, scientists can develop a tomato that withstands cold weather without freezing. Many people are excited about this technology, while others have doubts about its safety. Some think that any food containing genetically modified (GMO) ingredients should be labeled to indicate their GMO content. The companies that produce these foods believe that the labels would only frighten customers and should not be required. Write an essay in which you argue for or against requiring GMO foods to be labeled. You may need to do some research to find factual evidence to support your arguments. To obtain research for your essay, go to the textbook web site and locate the links for Chapter 23, Science and Technology.

Environment and Natural Resources

As a scientist who works for your state's water department, your job involves protecting the safety and reliability of your state's water supply. An important part of your job is to educate the public about the importance of water conservation. Write a persuasive essay in which you argue that individual consumers can and must contribute to the long-term health of the water supply by monitoring the consumption of water in their homes. Research regarding water supplies can be located at the textbook web site. Locate the links for Chapter 23, Environment and Natural Resources.

24

Summaries of Long Documents

IN THIS CHAPTER YOU WILL LEARN TO:

- Summarize articles, reports, and other longer documents.

- Write a thesis statement for a summary.

- Identify and describe key points for summaries.

- Develop useful executive summaries.

Using *Summaries* in Writing for Your Career

Career Path	Sample Career	Use for Summary Writing	Example of Summary Writing
Communication and the Arts	Manager of communications	Highlighting a nonprofit organization's track record in a summary of its annual report	In short, the Community Development Council has championed seven construction projects, created 165 new jobs, and invigorated an impoverished neighborhood. The lives of individuals and the community will be enhanced by the Council's efforts.
Health and Medicine	Nurse	Summarizing a physician's orders	Dr. Forman's orders for a change to a healthier lifestyle include several points. Begin a high fiber/low fat diet, develop and follow an exercise regimen, quit smoking, and make another appointment to see Dr. Forman in six months.
Human, Personal, and Public Service	Career counselor	Summarizing a magazine article	In her article, Juanita Gomez discusses three styles of professional resumes—chronological, functional, and combined. She compares the three styles and explains how job seekers should decide which style is right for them.
Business and Marketing	Paralegal	Summarizing a witness's testimony	During her two-hour deposition, Ms. Shapp testified that she was in her home on the night of May 14 and that she did not hear any sounds coming from the apartment next door. Upon further questioning, she indicated that she had spoken to the defendant on the phone at about 7 p.m. on May 14.
Science and Technology	Software manager	Condensing a client's lengthy letter about a computer problem	Dennis Santangelo is unable to connect to the network and the Internet about 50 percent of the time. According to his complaint, his computer is slower now than before. Also, Mr. Santangelo is receiving numerous "low systems resources" messages, but we cannot figure out why.
Environment and Natural Resources	Park planner	Summarizing rules for parking motorized vehicles	Here is a breakdown of how we charge for parking cars on the grounds of the arboretum: Members may park for free. Single-day visitors may purchase a parking permit for $10.00. Extended-stay visitors may purchase three-day permits for $6.00 per day. Violators are subject to a $100 fine and a towing fee.

461

ON THE JOB

Retaining the Knowledge

As an assistant in the human resources department at the Hoeber Department Store, Norma Weiser is responsible for editing the monthly newsletter. The newsletter is designed to boost employee morale, reinforce the corporate mission, and keep employees up to date on management trends. Employees look forward to receiving the newsletter, and Norma is dedicated to providing interesting and important articles.

Norma subscribes to several management magazines. Each month she reads the magazines, identifies articles she thinks will be of interest to Hoeber employees, and summarizes three or four of them for her readers.

Below is Norma's summary of a three-page article she read. The article featured several ways to ensure that employees who leave an organization don't take their knowledge with them until they have passed it on to other employees.

<u>HR should get more involved in knowledge retention,</u>[1] according to the article "Retaining the Knowledge" by <u>experts from the Institute for Strategic Change. This think</u>[2]<u> tank of economists, management consultants, and business leaders suggests that companies follow three steps to retain knowledge within the company. First, locate </u>[3]<u>where the knowledge is kept—perhaps it is stored in the heads of a few key employees. Start a system for tracking the person who has the most critical knowledge. Second, pass down </u>[4]<u>the knowledge.</u> <u>One step you can</u> take is to <u>begin a mentoring program where long-time employees share their knowledge with new hires.</u> Also, you can follow up by training everyone who should have access to the knowledge. <u>Keeping retirees around is also</u>[5]<u> important. For example, offer consulting opportunities, part-time employment, and mentoring opportunities.</u>

Employees leave companies for many reasons, but their departure should not cripple an organization. <u>If the company is vulnerable to surprise departures, start a knowledge retention program now.</u>[6] Months—sometimes years—of training are needed to replace knowledgeable employees who leave without passing on their knowledge to their replacements.

Norma condensed a long magazine article into the summary above. Do you understand the point of the longer article? Is the writing clear? Did Norma give credit for the ideas to the appropriate source? In this chapter, you will learn how to summarize long pieces of writing into shorter ones by reducing complex information into easy-to-understand main points.

Understanding Summaries

A **summary** is a condensed version of a chapter, an article, a speech, or another piece of writing. While, by definition, a summary is shorter than the original work, it is not simply a pared-down version. Instead, it is a discussion *in your own words* of the key points of the original work. In the summary, you should maintain the integrity of the original document by making sure you do not distort the views, ideas, or attitudes contained in the original.

An effective summary includes these elements.

- The author, title, and source of the original work
- A thesis statement that says what will be summarized
- A brief description of the original work
- Key points that sum up the original work
- Final recommendations, opinions, or conclusions.

Can you see how Norma's summary in On the Job follows this model? Compare them below to the numbered examples.

1. **Thesis statement**
   Because too much information leaves the company when employees quit, retire, or are fired, Human Resources should get more involved in knowledge retention.

2. **Description of the longer text**
   The Institute for Strategic Change published a list of recommendations to help companies retain the knowledge that employees have in their heads.

   Key points

3. Track what employees know about the key business operations.

4. Start mentoring programs, conduct exit interviews, and develop other methods of learning what people know.

5. Keep retirees on by hiring them for part-time work or as consultants.

   Final recommendation

6. If too much company knowledge is concentrated in the heads of just a few employees, you could be in trouble if those key employees leave. That is why you should start a knowledge retention plan as soon as possible.

SELF-ASSESSMENT 24

When I need to summarize long writing into a shorter document, I can:

	Usually	Sometimes	Never
State the main point of the original material.	❑	❑	❑
Tell the point in my own words, not just excerpt the original.	❑	❑	❑
Eliminate unnecessary details to help condense the writing.	❑	❑	❑
Stay on track and not get diverted by themes that diverge from the main point.	❑	❑	❑
Make recommendations or draw conclusions.	❑	❑	❑

If you checked "Sometimes" or "Never" for any of the items, this chapter will help you improve your summary writing techniques. Even if you checked "Usually" in every instance, you will learn more about writing effective summaries.

The Thesis Statement

As you learned in Chapters 4 and 14, a thesis statement should state one main point. The thesis statement should be focused enough that the rest of the writing can support, prove, or develop that point.

The thesis statement of a summary should tell the reader what will be summarized. That may sound obvious, but remember that an article or a report may make many points, some being more important than others. For a summary, the thesis statement should identify, in just one or two sentences, what the overall longer document is about. Look at the thesis statements below and compare the "good" statement with the other two.

(A) Too Generalized	An article said that HR should get more involved in knowledge retention.
(B) Too Specific	HR should start a mentoring program, a plan for keeping retirees around, and a formal system for tracking knowledge.
(C) Good	HR should get more involved in knowledge retention, according to the Institute for Strategic Change.

Example (C) is the best of the three alternatives because it references the original material (the article), it states one main point, and it tells the reader what will be summarized. Example (C) suggests what will come next: Readers can expect to learn more about what human resource departments should do to protect their companies when key employees leave the firm.

did you ever?

- Read a review of a movie in a newspaper or magazine or on the Internet to help you decide whether to see the movie?

- Write a book report that condensed a novel into two or three pages containing a description of the story's main characters, key points, plot, and relevant themes?

- Describe in a two- or three-minute condensed version an hour-long speech you attended?

All of these situations involve summarizing, a technique that can help you write clear and concise condensations. With a little practice, you will be able to write informative summaries that others find helpful.

ACTIVITY 24.1 For each of the following subjects, write a concise thesis statement that will introduce key points to be used in a summary of the topic. The first item has been completed for you.

1. my favorite movie

   In *The Music Man*, Professor Harold Hill, a con man, teaches himself
   and all of River City, Iowa, a lesson in humanity.

2. the dress code at my school

   _____

   _____

   _____

   _____

3. the vacation policy at my job

   _____

   _____

   _____

4. the last chapter I read in this book

   _____

   _____

   _____

5. a recent episode of my favorite television show

   _____

   _____

   _____

   _____

6. a book I read recently

   _____

   _____

   _____

   _____

WRITING WORKSHOP

Eliminating Examples, Details, and Quotes

In summarizing, knowing what to eliminate is as important as knowing what to include. Here is a paragraph and its one-sentence summary from a business article.

Paragraph	A married couple sold their small business to a third party. Both stayed on—he as vice president, she as bookkeeper. They were instructed by the new owner to pay bills only as the owner directed. When the couple realized that taxes weren't being paid, they notified the IRS. The new owner fired them.
Summary	A businessman fired two employees who formerly owned the business because they reported him to the IRS.

The summary omitted the employees' marital status and titles and the events leading up to the discovery. Here is the next paragraph and summary sentence.

Paragraph	The IRS went after all three. The couple paid its share of the assessment, then went to court for a refund. The court ruled that the couple had been responsible for ensuring that taxes were paid—even though the new owner had instructed them not to pay. However, since the couple hadn't willfully failed to pay the taxes, they showed a good-faith effort. The judge ruled, "You are due a refund because you did all you could to ensure that the taxes were paid."
Summary	In the end, the judge made the business owner pay the taxes and said the former owners were not liable.

Here the summary sentence eliminates details about the IRS and what the judge said. Put the two sentences together to determine whether they tell the essentials of the article.

Including the Key Points

How do you know which points to include and which points to exclude in your summaries? The first step is to read and then reread the original material or your own notes about the original material. When you fully understand the original's meaning, you should have no trouble distinguishing the relevant points from the less relevant points.

If the point isn't a key point, delete it.

Each point should support, develop, or prove the thesis statement. If a point does not contribute to the main idea, it should be cut from the summary. An irrelevant point can take the reader off in an unwanted direction, causing distraction and confusion.

A student's thesis statement and key points written to summarize a business course are given below. Do you see anything wrong with the student's key points?

Thesis Statement	Professor Katin's lectures cover three of the most important elements of management: communication, commitment, and character.
Key Points	(A) Writing, speaking, and listening are the three most essential communication skills for a manager.
	(B) Managers who are committed to their profession, ethical in their conduct, and hard-working are positive role models for employees.
	(C) Managers who are of good character are often better parents and attend more school activities with their children.

Example (C) does not develop the thesis statement. The thesis statement says that character is an important part of management, not parenting. In other words, Example (C) is off the topic. In Examples (A) and (B), the key points state why communication and commitment are important. They support the thesis statement, and they describe the course. Therefore, they should go into the summary.

Taking Notes for Summaries

Identifying key points in an article, a report, or another work can be a challenge. Therefore, finding a systematic way of taking notes is extremely important. Try this simple rule-of-thumb method.

- When condensing a business document, write one sentence per paragraph that sums up the paragraph.
- When condensing a book, write one sentence per chapter.
- When summarizing a movie or a lecture, write one sentence for every three to five minutes of material.

After you read the sentences together, you should see a summary begin to form. Some sentences may need to be rearranged, eliminated, or rewritten, but with additional organization of the sentences, you will have the summary you need.

The organizational pattern you use for your summary will depend on the type of article, report, or other work you are summarizing. Three patterns for organizing a summary are: chronological, order of importance, and topical. Here are examples of when each organizational pattern might be used.

Chronological	Notes for a summary of a book on the Civil War would likely be organized chronologically, according to the years battles were fought or other events occurred.
Order of Importance	A report about the challenges a company will face in the future might be summarized according to the importance of the challenges. Raising cash to keep technology current might come first, followed by locating outstanding job applicants and purchasing a new building for the manufacturing division.
Topical	A government report of a major health scare, such as "Mad Cow Disease," might be summarized according to topics: discovery of the problem, health risks to cows and to humans, and methods of stopping the disease.

Paragraphs from an article on how to cut prescription drug costs are shown on the next page. A student assigned to summarize the article wrote one sentence per paragraph as a start for the summary. The student's sentences are in blue. When you read the sentences in blue, you should see a summary of the essay begin to form. The next step is to arrange the key points—in blue—into an organized summary.

Prescription Drug Costs in the United States

In *Human Resources Update,* the newsletter of the Barnum Company, Irv Ragen and Shamith Hampler wrote on one of the most important issues facing employers and employees today: rising health care costs.

Irv Ragen and Shamith Hampler wrote about rising health care costs in Barnum Company's monthly newsletter.

Prescription drugs are the country's number one health care expense. However, there is good news: You can show employees easy methods of reducing prescription drug costs. When you say, "Sorry, but you're going to have to pay more this year," you also should add, "But here's how you can offset the additional costs—and probably save some money!"

Health care costs are going up every year, but companies can teach employees how to save money on prescription drugs.

Employers expect health care spending to soar 15 percent next year. But the maximum additional costs that firms say they can handle is only 10 percent. The resulting gap will more than triple the average worker's health care costs over the next five years—that is, if cost shifting alone continues to be the employers' primary means of cost containment. The two strategies given below can help employees cut costs. So get the word out during meetings and new employee orientations and in memos, on bulletin boards, and via e-mail.

Two strategies for reducing costs are available.

Pick up the phone. We called four drug stores within a three-mile radius and asked the cost of a prescription for Vicodin®, regular strength, 30 pills. Interestingly, the prices ranged from $23 to $35—a difference of about 30 percent. It took less than ten minutes to call four pharmacies. Encourage employees to compare prices and to go with the best deal.

Price shop: Different pharmacies charge different prices for the same medicine.

Split pills. Many prescription drugs are available in bigger doses for less money. Lipitor® is the same price for all strengths. A patient can save up to $100 a month by purchasing a larger strength and cutting the pill in half.

Patients can save up to $100 a month by buying pills in bigger doses and splitting them.

Now read the student's summary, organized according to paragraph topics.

Summary of the article "Prescription Drug Costs in the United States"

In the company newsletter, Irv Ragen and Shamith Hampler wrote about rising health care costs. Employers may not be able to control rising health care costs, but they can tell employees how to save money on prescription drugs. Price shopping and pill splitting are two ways employees can reduce the cost of prescription drugs. Employers should share these strategies with employees.

ACTIVITY 24.2 After each paragraph below, which is excerpted from "Glimpses of Great Masters at Home—Beethoven," by Arthur S. Garbett, write—in your own words—one sentence that summarizes the entire paragraph.

1. Beethoven suffered a three-fold loneliness: he was unmarried; he was deaf; he was a genius. The first deprived him of the loving sympathy he so much needed; the second, of social intercourse and of the music that was the breath of his life; and the third set him apart from all mankind. Beethoven had many friends. They were kind to him, helped him when he was troubled, and provided him with financial assistance. Beethoven felt the lack of a real companion keenly; he needed someone to play David to his Jonathan. "I have no real friend," he wrote to Bettina Brentano. "I must live alone. But I know that God is nearer to me than to many in my art, and I commune with Him fearlessly."

   _____

   _____

2. To speak of the "home life" of this lonely, homeless genius seems strange. Save when he visited such friends as Count Licknowsky or Prince Lobkowitz, save for his brief glint of home life with the Breunings in Bonn, after his mother died, his whole life was spent in Vienna, in one dreary attic after another. Occasionally the monotony was broken by a visit to the country in search of health; but mostly he wandered from one lodging to another; and, from the many descriptions given by those who visited him, one gathers always the same impression of bare walls, scanty furniture, scattered papers, a piano or two and a few other musical instruments, clothes lying where they fell and a general atmosphere of indifference to material things.

   _____

   _____

3. Before deafness interfered, he was sociably included; and his genius as a pianist made him welcome in princely houses, where otherwise his bluff speech and open rudeness might have denied him admittance. As silence closed about him, however, he locked his doors to all save his intimates, and even to them at times. Schindler, Ries, Moscheles, Carl Czerny, Lobkowitz, Rasoumowsky, and other persistent friends, however, kept in touch with him constantly, and were wise enough to regard his outbursts of passionate irritability as merely pathological symptoms, the consequence of a mighty spirit forced to take shelter in a frail, inadequate body. In return they were privileged to watch the unfolding of his ever-growing genius.

   _____

   _____

ETHICS CONNECTION

Say It *Your* Way

When condensing long documents, it is important to summarize in your own words. At the same time, a summary should reflect the original author's intent, not your personal opinions. A summary is a condensed version, not an editorial analysis.

Some writers use word processing applications to copy an excerpt from one source (often on the Internet) and paste it into their own work. Excerpting is acceptable when the source of the excerpt is identified, but keep in mind that excerpting is not summarizing.

Sometimes writers excerpt from the original material, change a few words, swap a pronoun or two, and call it their own. That is not summarizing either; it is plagiarizing. Plagiarism is unethical. In business and publishing, plagiarizing may result in civil penalties and other court judgments (not to mention professional disgrace).

Transitions

In summaries, transitional words, phrases, and sentences help guide the reader from one key point to the next. Below is a summary of the article about saving money on prescription medicines. It appears two ways: Example (A) has no transitions; Example (B) has three transitions.

Example A
Health care costs are on the rise, but people can save money on prescription drugs. Price shopping and pill splitting are two ways to save money when purchasing prescription drugs. Employers should communicate these strategies to employees.

Example B
Health care costs are on the rise, but people can save money on prescription drugs. *For example,* price shopping and pill splitting are two ways to save money when purchasing prescription drugs. *Many employees are getting hit with higher premiums. Therefore,* employers should communicate these strategies to employees.

Do you see how the transitional word, phrase, and sentence help the summary flow by giving direction to the reader? Remember, summaries should be concise. Therefore, you don't want to overuse transitions. You should, however, include a few transitional words that make the reading easier by moving the reader from point to point.

WRITING WORKSHOP

Executive Summaries

Business reports and proposals often begin with an executive summary—a one-page (or less) summary of the document. An executive summary allows busy senior managers to digest the meaning of a report or proposal in minutes without having to read the entire document. In most summaries, a writer condenses another writer's longer work. In an executive summary, however, it is your own writing that you condense. Although the executive summary appears at the top of the report or proposal, it should be written last. Here is an example of an executive summary for a report about a computer-based training system.

> The Shelly System is the latest in computer-based training. Proponents of the system claim it can be used to train customer service representatives faster and more thoroughly than ever before. This report will focus on its implementation at Parker Products, Inc. Included in this report are before-and-after test scores, testimonials by students and instructors, technical specifications, and prices for the software

ACTIVITY 24.3 Below is a summary of an investor's meeting held at a Florida retreat. The summary lacks transitional words, phrases, or sentences, and the key points read like a list. Rewrite the summary to direct the reader from one event to the next.

The investor's meeting last week consisted of six guest speakers and several seminars about technology. Troy Raheem talked first. His presentation was about next year's marketing initiatives, which should cost less than last year's while reaching more people. Drew Black talked after that. His presentation was about next year's enhanced distribution model, which will enable the company to surpass its competitors in fast delivery. Dorothy DeMeo talked last. Her presentation was about how a new category management system will enable the company to process three times the amount of orders in half the time. She says we will have fewer errors. Rachel Trueblood talked about next year's financial picture, which looks rosy. Everyone liked hearing what she had to say because finances will affect the overall success of our company.

Each department presented a seminar to educate investors on what the company is doing to outsell its competitors. Marketing's presentation was on Internet marketing. Operation's presentation was on supply chain management software. Technology's presentation was on data management. Finance's presentation was on important changes in the tax laws that will affect the company.

_____

_____

_____

_____

_____

_____

_____

_____

_____

_____

_____

_____

_____

_____

_____

_____

_____

_____

_____

_____

_____

_____

_____

_____

_____

_____

_____

TECHNOLOGY CONNECTION

Keeping E-mail Summaries "Above the Fold"

In the world of business, people are frequently asked to summarize a meeting, a conference, or another event in an e-mail. Here is a simple guideline for writing a summary in an e-mail or on a web page: Write it so the reader does not need to scroll down to read what you wrote. Instead, try to make your summary fit into the space that is within view when the reader is looking at the computer monitor.

"Above the fold" is an expression that comes from the newspaper industry. Long ago, editors discovered that the stories included on the top half of the page—the stories above where the newspaper was folded in half—were the stories that attracted the most readers. More recently, computer usability experts realized that the same holds true for e-mail and for web site users. Research shows that most online readers pay closer attention to the content that appears at the top of the e-mail—"above the fold"—than to the content "below the fold." Sometimes readers simply stop reading when they get to the bottom of the screen.

Over the years, numerous usability studies have shown that online readers simply prefer not to scroll down. Therefore, when you summarize something in an e-mail, try to keep your summary— or at least its most important points—"above the fold."

Of course, differences in the size of monitors, e-mail programs, and computer settings (not to mention varying lengths of original material) mean that this guideline is not an exact science. But it should help you determine a reasonable length for your e-mail and web page summaries.

SUMMARY FOR WRITING SUMMARIES

- ❑ A summary is a condensation of a chapter, an article, or another work.

- ❑ Summaries are written in the summary writer's own words but express the original writer's intent.

- ❑ A key point is a relevant part of the original material.

- ❑ In a summary, the thesis statement says what will be summarized.

- ❑ A summary writer eliminates unnecessary examples and details in favor of the original's key points.

- ❑ In summaries, transitional words, phrases, and sentences help direct the reader from key point to key point.

PRACTICING YOUR SKILLS

Now that you understand the elements of a good summary, put your knowledge to work in the following activities.

PRACTICE 1

Read this report about services from the president of an industrial janitorial service to the board of directors. Then follow the instructions at the end.

The Special Services Division (SSD) at Home Methods Associates (HMA) is staffed with expert technicians who work all day, every day, with our clients' most troublesome floors, walls, carpets, and windows. Unlike other janitorial contractors who only occasionally perform specialized work, our SSD personnel clean and polish building materials every day that others may try to tackle only once or twice a year. What's more, those small contractors can't respond with the speed or range of services that we can. With HMA as a service contractor, our clients can feel confident that every part of their building will receive the care it needs. Our Special Services Division is broken into five business groups:

Carpet Care. Our technicians are fully trained and capable of providing restorative cleaning to any type of carpeting, from broadloom to squares, from nylon to wool. We can also clean a client's delicate oriental rugs. Because carpets resoil, we strongly recommend that our clients purchase an ongoing maintenance program that provides appropriate levels of service where they are most needed. Maintenance programs are known to prolong the life and beauty of a carpeting investment and help keep the appearance of a building at a consistent level. Ongoing maintenance services are available to our clients for an annual fee.

Marble and Stone Care. HMA is one of only a few contractors in the country who is authorized by MarbleKing to provide its marble maintenance program. HMA's technicians are highly experienced in the care of expensive stones such as marble, travertine, and granite. Our company spends thousands of dollars each year in its technician training program, thus assuring clients of our company's reliability. Too often we see janitorial contractors treating these surfaces like tile, using the wrong products and methods. Stones are very different from man-made materials, and they have their own unique requirements. Proper care of these surfaces requires an understanding of how stones react to cleaning agents and when and if to apply coatings to the stones. Our methods include diamond honing and polishing, recrystallization, surface impregnation, and—when appropriate—surface sealing. Often, we can restore a stone to its original beauty and will recommend the proper maintenance to avoid costly future restorations.

Metal Maintenance. Extensive work in the city has made us familiar with the vast array of architectural metal surfaces in our clients' buildings. Our technicians clean, restore, and coat a full range of metals, including aluminum, brass, bronze, and stainless steel. They can remove scratches and years of oxidation from the metal, polish it to look like new, and apply a protective coating that will make any building's metal look as beautiful as when it was first installed. No other janitorial contractor in this market has the capability to provide this service with its own in-house technicians. Furthermore, no other metal maintenance contractor can begin to provide the range of services that we offer.

Specialty Cleaning. Our SSD technicians are called on frequently to perform a wide variety of services that include stripping and refinishing vinyl tile; construction cleanup; pressure washing; and cleaning of ceiling tiles, window blinds, and light fixtures. We welcome the challenge of cleaning unusual finishes and investigate carefully to determine the most appropriate cleaning methods for imported or unique finishes that require special care. If something needs cleaning, we've got the experience to do it! From floor to ceiling, our staff has tackled every kind of job you can imagine. Our technicians are professionals, working quickly to the customer's complete satisfaction.

Disaster Preparedness and Recovery. All too often, pipes break, sprinkler heads go off, roofs leak, or plumbing systems go awry. A building manager's worst nightmare, a fire, may leave his or her tenants in a frustrating and vulnerable position! As soon as we receive a call over our toll-free telephone line, we respond with trained professionals. Our crews can remove the water from a client's building, dry it, and get the client back in business fast! There is no other local contractor who offers this level of response and professionalism. Clients will not suffer through the anxiety of having one or two janitors desperately trying to remove thousands of gallons of potentially contaminated water with a shop vacuum. Our crews are prepared and equipped with high-capacity water-moving equipment, pumps, and an impressive array of dehumidifiers and air handlers. They will clean all affected surfaces, remove odors, and restore your building's finish to the best possible condition. Should a disaster occur, HMA will help you through this difficult time with experienced crisis management.

The Thesis Statement

1. Find the thesis statement and underline it.

The Key Points

2. Identify and circle one key point per paragraph.

3. Write one sentence to sum up each paragraph.

_____

_____

_____

_____

_____

_____

_____

_____

_____

4. Arrange the sentences into a summary.

_____

_____

_____

_____

_____

_____

_____

_____

_____

_____

_____

5. Include transitions to help the reader get from one key point to the next.

The Conclusion

6. Underline the original work's conclusion.

7. Add a conclusion to your summary. Remember, you should reach the original writer's conclusion, not your own.

_____

_____

_____

_____

_____

PRACTICE 2

Here is an article about managing employees. After you read it, follow the instructions at the bottom of the article.

A growing number of firms are testing candidates to gauge their personality types and predict who's right for a job. If you, like many employers, are considering using personality testing on job candidates, keep in mind that experts caution that not every test is effective. They say firms should take special care to match the appropriate test to the traits they seek in employees. For example, if you are measuring attitude, make sure the test includes several questions that address items related to attitude, including traits such as cooperation and sense of responsibility. Additionally, employers should remember to use these tests alongside the interview process—not as a substitute for it.

Soon after one retailer began testing its sales associates for personality traits and placing the associates with specific accounts that would profit from these traits, the organization reported a 15.4 percent increase in sales per hour. At the same time, turnover dropped 18 percent, and the time it took to make a decision about whether to hire a specific associate was reduced from several days to just 24 hours.

If you're considering introducing this kind of testing, you will find many options available. You should work closely with your supplier to ensure that you select the right testing program for your business's needs.

The Thesis Statement

1. Find the thesis statement and underline it.

The Key Points

2. Identify and circle one key point per paragraph.

3. Write one sentence to sum up each paragraph.

_____

_____

_____

_____

_____

_____

4. Add transitions to help the reader get from one key point to the next.

5. Arrange the sentences into a summary.

_____

_____

_____

_____

_____

_____

_____

_____

_____

Conclusion

6. Underline the original work's conclusion.

7. Add a conclusion to your summary. Remember, you should reach the original writer's conclusion, not your own.

_____

_____

_____

_____

_____

_____

_____

_____

_____

_____

_____

_____

_____

_____

_____

_____

APPLYING YOUR SKILLS

Now go to your Data CD, Chapter 24, Summaries, and select the article about employment law to summarize. You will work through the stages of the writing process. Save each stage of your writing so you can observe your progress.

Prewriting

First, select an essay from your data CD. Read and reread the original material until you understand it thoroughly.

Next, develop a thesis statement that sums up the essay in one or two sentences. Then identify one key point in each paragraph and develop that point into one sentence. Finally, construct a simple outline for your summary in a form like this:

THESIS STATEMENT _____

_____

_____

_____

KEY POINT 1 _____

_____

_____

_____

KEY POINT 2 _____

_____

_____

_____

KEY POINT 3 _____

_____

_____

_____

CONCLUSION _____

_____

_____

_____

Writing

Write your summary by arranging the key point sentences. Use transitions to move from one key point to the next.

_____

_____

_____

_____

_____

_____

_____

_____

_____

_____

_____

_____

Revising

Read through your first draft. Use the following checklist to help you revise the draft.

❏ Does the thesis statement say what will be summarized?

❏ Is the summary written in your own words?

❏ Are the key points relevant and specific?

❏ Are the transitions smooth so a reader understands where each point begins and ends?

❏ Does the writing flow from one point to the next?

Write a second and, perhaps, a third draft. When you believe your summary is as good as you can make it, begin editing.

Editing

Check your paragraph for mechanical errors. When you are satisfied that all grammar, punctuation, and spelling are correct, make a final copy.

WRITING FOR YOUR CAREER

CRITICAL THINKING

Choose a writing project from one of the six career pathways and use your new skills to write a summary of the topic. When the project description refers you to a web site, go to http://humphrey.swlearning.com and click on the Links tab. Look for Chapter 24, "Writing for Your Career."

Communication and the Arts

Imagine that you are applying for a job as an assistant editor at a publishing company. If hired, one of your responsibilities will be to read stories and novels that writers submit to the publisher. Your job will not be to recommend manuscripts but to read and condense them into one-page summaries. You may have to read one or two manuscripts a week. Your interviewers want to test your skills. Therefore, as part of the interview process you have been asked to write a summary of *The Hounds of the Baskervilles* by Arthur Conan Doyle. You will find the entire manuscript online by going to the textbook web site and locating the link for Chapter 24, Communication and the Arts. Remember, your summary should stick to the plot and should not include your opinions about the manuscript.

Health and Medicine

You are a registered nurse at a community hospital. Lately you have observed that when physicians give patients a great deal of information about lowering cholesterol, the patients sometimes become overwhelmed and confused about how to care for themselves. You decide to visit the American Heart Association web site, read a lengthy article about avoiding heart attacks, and summarize it so patients have an overview of lifestyle changes they can consider. Go to the textbook web site and locate the instructions for Chapter 24, Health and Medicine. You will find a link to the American Heart Association's web site, which has numerous articles about healthy living. You should select one, read it, and write a summary for your patients.

Human, Personal, and Public Service

As the manager of a local crisis center, you are compiling information for a brochure about coping with everyday stress. One section of the brochure will be directed at people who serve as caregivers to family or friends who are living with chronic illnesses. On your Data CD, you will find an article about caregiver stress from the U.S. Department of Human Services. Read and reread the article. Then summarize it in two or three short paragraphs.

Business and Marketing

You are an administrative assistant who works for the CEO of a small manufacturing company. Every Tuesday at noon, your supervisor invites a few key employees to an informational lunch meeting. At these meetings, each department head gives a presentation on his or her particular area of expertise. Your responsibility is to take notes. Today the vice president of finance talks about budgeting. For this assignment, go to your Data CD and locate the article called "What Is a Budget?" Read and reread the article and summarize it in one paragraph.

Science and Technology

You are a research assistant at a biotechnology company. Last night you read an article in a scientific journal and thought your colleagues would find it interesting. Your department hosts a weekly lunch meeting where employees are encouraged to share useful information. You decide to write a summary of the article and distribute copies to your colleagues. For this assignment, you may read any scientific article you wish on the *Popular Science* web site and summarize it in one page or less. You can find the *Popular Science* web site by visiting the textbook web site and locating the link for Chapter 24, Science and Technology.

Environment and Natural Resources

As a teaching assistant at a high school, you are helping to prepare a curriculum about the environment. Your assignment is to read what the Environmental Protection Agency (EPA) includes on its web site about global warming and the climate. Next, you should summarize what you read in one page or less. You will find the EPA's web site by visiting the textbook web site and locating the link for Chapter 24, Environment and Natural Resources.

Reports and Proposals

IN THIS CHAPTER YOU WILL LEARN TO:

- **Identify the differences between proposals and reports.**

- **State a position.**

- **Develop facts and details.**

- **Write a report or persuasive proposal.**

Writing *Reports* and *Proposals* for Your Career

Career Path	Sample Career	Use for Reports or Proposals	Example of Report or Proposal
Communication and the Arts	Fund-raising assistant at a charitable organization	Reporting on the results of a local fund-raising campaign	Taro Warren and Ally Tores canvassed the entire north side of town and distributed 1,000 flyers. Eighty people from the north side attended the fund-raiser, and fifteen of them made a $50 contribution.
Health and Medicine	Health club manager	Proposing the purchase of new exercise equipment	Investing in the L39 System makes good sense. In a survey, our members said they are willing to pay a higher membership fee if we upgrade our exercise equipment. They also said they will leave if we do not add state-of-the-art equipment.
Human, Personal, and Public Service	Resident adviser at a residential treatment facility	Filing an incident report	Mary Ann left again last night. When I confronted her this morning, she denied it. After I showed her the surveillance video, she admitted leaving. I issued her a written warning, and she took a drug test.
Business and Marketing	Production manager	Proposing to hire new employees	Based on the demand for our product, our production capabilities, and our past performance, I believe we should add two assembly workers to each shift next quarter.
Science and Technology	Quality assurance inspector	Documenting test results	We tested the new web site by simulating thousands of hits. The web servers and the backup system worked perfectly. The test was successful, and we are confident that the site is stable.
Environment and Natural Resources	Municipal parks administrator	Proposing a summer youth job program	This proposal describes why the jobs program will be successful. Unemployment is expected to drop among youths this summer. Crime rates should drop in areas serviced by the program, and participants should be eager to continue clean-up efforts part-time during the school year.

ON THE JOB

Difficult Conversations

Eli Kass works as a marketing manager for Baker Recreational Gear. One of his responsibilities is to write a monthly newsletter to customers. The newsletter includes articles about the sporting goods industry and helpful stories about management practices. Sometimes, after attending a management seminar, Eli writes about one or two speakers who made a big impression on him. Below is Eli's report on a talk given by management consultant and author Shea O'Neill, Ph.D.

In his presentation *Having Difficult Conversations with Employees and Coworkers*[2] given at the Technical Manager's Conference in Atlanta, management consultant Shea O'Neill stated that most workplace lawsuits occur because managers don't communicate well with employees. He provided step-by-step instructions for handling difficult conversations about an employee's performance, personal habits, or work ethic. Dr. O'Neill, a professor of business[3] management at Bradford University, found in a study that at least 60 percent[1] of employment-related lawsuits are the result of poor communication between managers and employees. Moreover, O'Neill suggests that many of these lawsuits are avoidable. For example, during annual performance[4] reviews, most managers say they are too embarrassed to tell low-performing workers how they are really doing. "You're performance is fine," they say, when the worker's performance actually needs improvement. O'Neill's research shows that managers are like everybody else: They don't want to hurt other people's[5] feelings. While this sentiment may reduce stress for both managers and employees, it is shortsighted, according to O'Neill. When an employer fires an employee who has been told all along that he or she is doing a good job, that employee feels angry. As O'Neill says, "Employees[6] do not sue because they get fired. They sue because they are bitter." Good communication can change that.

Eli summarized the key points of the seminar in his report. Is his report clear and interesting? Does it include a source, supporting details, and a conclusion? After this chapter, you will know how to write effective, factual reports and compelling, persuasive proposals.

Understanding Reports and Proposals

A **report** is a reaction to an event, a person, a place, or a thing. A description of what happens when industrial chemicals are mixed is a *lab report*. A description of a business, including its yearly financial statement, is an *annual report*. A term paper for a class is a *research report*. A history of events leading to job disciplinary action is *an incident report*. A written reaction to a book is a *book report*. A documentation of worksite events is a *field report*. Reports should include a thesis statement and facts and details that support the thesis statement.

A **proposal** is a persuasive report. In business, a proposal is typically a request for money, resources, or approval. Proposals rely on facts and examples that support the author's request.

Essentially, report writers want to explain events, and proposal writers want to call their readers to action. Effective reports and proposals include:

- A strong thesis statement describing the main point or need.
- A summary of the event being reported or the need being discussed.
- Appropriate references that verify the writer's statements.
- Supporting data such as facts, examples, reasons, and answers to objections.
- Final conclusions, recommendations, opinions, or requests.

Can you see how Eli's report includes all of the above?

1. Thesis:

Most workplace lawsuits occur because managers don't know how to communicate well.

2. Source:

A management conference.

3. Supporting fact:

The speaker is a professor of business.

4. Example:

When giving performance reviews, many managers are too embarrassed to tell people how they are really doing.

5. Detail:

Managers don't want to hurt other people's feelings.

6. Conclusion:

People don't sue because they get fired; they sue because they are bitter. Good communication can change that.

Stating a Position

Report and proposal writers give their position or main point in a thesis statement of one or two sentences, usually near the beginning of the report or proposal. The thesis statement for a proposal should say what the writer wants.

Imagine that you are the customer service manager for a retail chain and that you believe customer service representatives should be permitted to work overtime in order to handle customer calls during the holiday season. You decide to write a proposal to your supervisor requesting overtime for your staff. The main point of your proposal is that high service levels cannot be maintained during the four-week holiday shopping season unless your staff works more than the usual 40-hour week. Look at this example.

 Proposal

The maximum number of calls a customer service representative can handle is 25 per hour. Based on last year's business, we expect 2,500 calls a day during this holiday season. Our CSRs can handle that volume only if every person works 15 hours overtime per week.

In a report, the thesis statement is a brief summary of the topic. It sends a signal to the reader: "Here, in a nutshell, is what this report is about." Read this example.

Report

Last holiday season our customer service fell to unacceptable levels. This report explores the reasons for our Customer Service's shortcomings. The report will conclude with a number of recommendations about how to rectify the problem this year.

did you ever?

- Write a "newsy" letter to friends and relatives during the holiday season?

- Write a report to document an incident that occurred on the job or at school?

- Make a written request for additional resources to complete a job on time?

These activities involve reports and proposals. With practice, you will be able to write reports and proposals that get your main idea across.

ACTIVITY 25.1 For each of the subjects below, write a concise thesis statement that gives your position or summarizes your main point for a report or proposal (as identified in parenthesis). The first item has been completed for you.

1. a software update (proposal)

   If we upgrade now, we will stay ahead of our competition.

   _____

   _____

2. hiring an assistant to help a busy sales department (proposal)

   _____

   _____

   _____

3. the last book you read (book report)

   _____

   _____

   _____

4. an employee who is suspended for three days due to unexcused absences (incident report)

   _____

   _____

   _____

5. a solution to a traffic problem (proposal)

   _____

   _____

   _____

6. an explanation of why $500 was spent on a company's softball team (budget report)

   _____

   _____

   _____

WRITING WORKSHOP

Conducting Web Research for a Report

Many people are familiar with Internet search engines such as Yahoo! and Google. Today these powerful tools connect more people to more data on more topics than at any other time in history. If you have access to the Internet at home or at a library, you can search for information for reports and proposals by typing keywords into a search engine. Say that you work for a company that wants to purchase a new automated payroll system. All that remains is for you to select a vendor to sell you the system and to service and support it. Your manager asks you to write a report on the top three automated payroll solutions.

A search using the keywords *automated payroll solutions* leads to about 130,000 web links. By browsing the top few links, you get an idea of who the major vendors are. If you search using just the keyword *payroll,* you will find many trade organizations and other sources of information about payroll. Connecting keywords with a + will help you narrow your search by turning up only results with the string of words that you enter. If you type in the keywords *automated + payroll + solutions + Atlanta*, you will find sites related specifically to automated payroll solutions in Atlanta.

Be creative in coming up with keywords. Use the brainstorming techniques you learned earlier in this book. Here are some other keywords you might use to research automated payroll solutions:

- *pay systems*
- *payroll software*
- *compensation*
- *pay solutions*
- *salary software*

Remember, just because you see something on the Web does not mean it is a verified fact. The Internet is a valuable research tool, but you should think of it as no more than a good start. To write your report on payroll vendors, for instance, you will probably need to make a few telephone calls, interview the vendors, and ask them to verify the facts you found on the Web. Your local or school library contains journals and magazines for additional research. During the entire process, take accurate notes and keep a list of relevant web sites so you can access them again.

Including Facts and Details in a Report

In school, a student may be assigned to write a report about a book, an article, a television program, or a movie. This kind of report is known as a reaction paper because it is the writer's reaction to an event. In the business world, managers may be asked to write reports that summarize events and make recommendations. These reports are also reaction papers. In reaction papers, writers use facts or logical arguments to back up their opinions.

While a report may be a personal reaction to an event, the details and examples should be rooted in fact. That is why you should conduct research using the Internet or other resources such as journals and encyclopedias when you write reports and proposals.

If someone were assigned to write a book report, he or she might begin with a brief summary of the book, followed by an explanation of his or her reaction to it. For example:

> The book *Walk the Walk* (Biz21 Publishing, 2004), by Carl Blum, is a guide for executives who want to lead by setting a good example. I think this book is excellent because it provides easy-to-follow steps for being a leader. It describes how to bring out the best in yourself and everyone around you. It also discourages intimidation techniques, such as instilling fear in employees. I tried a few of the techniques described in the book—and they work. I believe managers could benefit from reading *Walk the Walk*.

Can you see how the writer summarized the book, provided a proper reference (the author, the publisher, and the year of publication), stated a thesis, and gave factual details to support the thesis?

Suppose the writer had merely stated that the book was excellent, but hadn't added the supporting facts. The opening paragraph would not have been as strong.

> The book *Walk the Walk* (Biz21 Publishing, 2004), by Carl Blum, is a guide for business executives who want to lead by setting a good example, not by instilling fear among their workers. I think this book is excellent, and if you read it, you'll agree.

In the first example, the writer's personal experience and the relevant details support the statement that *Walk the Walk* is a good book. In the second example, the writer simply tells the readers what their opinions will be ("… and if you read it, you'll agree."). The writer provides no factual details or examples to entice the reader to read the book. This approach is weak because readers need to be persuaded that a book is worth reading. To do this, the writer should try to think like the reader and choose words that are appealing and interesting.

ACTIVITY 25.2   For each of the following thesis statements, write one or two factual examples or supporting details. Use actual facts, not just your personal opinions. You may need to conduct some research so your examples and details are based on fact. The first example has been completed for you.

1. The United States is as diverse in its seasonal changes as it is in its people. The country has many climates and a wide range of temperatures.

    According to the Weather Facts web site, the highest recorded

    temperature in the United States was 134° F / 56.7° C, in Death

    Valley, California, on July 10, 1913. The lowest recorded temperature

    in the United States was -79.8° F / -62.1° C, in Prospect Creek,

    Alaska, on January 23, 1971.

2. Stock market experts generally agree that when stock prices go up, bond prices go down. For that reason, many investors hedge their investments by buying both stocks and bonds.

    _____

    _____

    _____

    _____

3. Certified public accountants are highly trained professionals. A CPA must complete a series of exams and gain practical experience before becoming certified.

    _____

    _____

    _____

    _____

4. Here at Green Bell Productions, we spend so much money on commercial photocopying that we should build our own copy center. An in-house copy center would improve our efficiency and bottom line.

    _____

    _____

    _____

    _____

Documenting Events for a Report

Many reports are written to document the facts leading to a main event. Frequently, though not always, a report of this type is part of a disciplinary record, or it is documentation of an unusual event that needs to be shared with others in an organization. Often, it is prepared for a legal file. This kind of report is known as an incident report.

In health care facilities, counseling centers, schools, and other institutions, incident reports are used to document behavior. In industry, incident reports are written to explain events and to identify who is accountable.

Imagine that you are vice president at a small software company. When one of your programmers is injured entering the building, you require him to get medical attention at a hospital and to obtain a report from the doctor. Next, you write an incident report for the company's files and include the time of the accident, the actions taken to obtain medical care for the programmer, and the extent of his injuries. The incident report will go into the programmer's personnel file. If he files a lawsuit against the company claiming that he was injured because of the company's negligence, the incident report will prove to a judge that the company acted in an appropriate manner.

An example of a similar report is shown below. Note the clear, relevant facts that the writer documented to prove that the hotel took the appropriate action.

Donna Rubio was dismissed because she falsified expense reports. Outside auditors found that Donna had been billing the company for personal use of her automobile for several months. Further inquiry revealed that she had billed the company for more than $400 in personal items such as clothing and cosmetics.

Thorough research is essential for building a solid base of factual information for your proposal or report.

In the past, employees have been fired for less serious violations of the company's policies. In fact, company records show that within the last five years, two other employees were dismissed for lesser offenses.

In this case, the employee admits that she understood the policy but willfully violated it. Donna's misuse of funds, falsification of records, and misleading answers to the auditors' initial questions left us with no alternative but to terminate her employment.

The factual details in this report support the writer's thesis statement regarding why the employee was terminated. If the report is used as evidence in a lawsuit, the facts will be clear to readers.

When writing an incident report, supporting details should be verifiable facts that are relevant to the main point of the report. An incident report may not require the same kind of research as a reaction paper. Instead of finding factual details on the Internet or in a book, you will need to interview witnesses, reconstruct the incident, and describe step by step what led up to the incident. Your summary should state the final outcome of the incident, how the incident was resolved, and whether it was resolved satisfactorily.

In an incident report, factual details should be:

- Relevant to the thesis (or main point).
- Clear to the reader.
- Accurate in the assertion of facts, figures, and direct quotes.

ETHICS CONNECTION

Avoiding One of Plagiarism's Gray Areas

You already know that it is unethical to "lift" someone else's writing word for word and try to pass it off as your own. There are, however, gray areas involving plagiarism that may come up when you write reports. You should carefully evaluate all of your final documents to make sure you do not stray beyond the gray areas into lifting someone else's writing.

What if you use someone's ideas, but not their exact words, to support your thesis? Must you credit the person, or can you sometimes ignore a citation? Can you just state the theory and hope that no one will ask you where it came from?

The answer to this question is, "No." When you paraphrase someone else's ideas to support your thesis, you should give that person credit. For example, film director Alfred Hitchcock once said that a camera shot of a character's hand moving up a stairway banister creates suspense for an audience. If you were writing a reaction paper about a suspenseful movie, you might want to use the Hitchcock example to describe how the director achieves a sense of suspense on film. In this case, you should cite Alfred Hitchcock in your paper as the source of your information.

Which of the following sentences carries more authority?

- "It is well known that a shot of a character's hand inching up a banister creates suspense."

- "As director Alfred Hitchcock once observed, a shot of a character's hand inching up a banister creates suspense."

ACTIVITY 25.3

In this activity, you will develop an incident report based on a main event and a set of facts. Some of the facts will be useful to you, and others will not. Your job is to select the appropriate facts and construct a report. You should end your report with a conclusion that is drawn from the facts and that supports the thesis statement or main point.

Imagine that you manage a group of analysts at a financial services firm. An analyst, Fred, has been reporting to work late every day, and now he is to be disciplined. You are to write an incident report documenting the events that led up to Fred's three-day suspension.

Write an incident report explaining the events that led to Fred's suspension. Use only the facts that support the main idea: Fred was suspended because he violated his employer's policy.

Main Event	Fred received a three-day suspension for violating the company's attendance policy.
Fact	Fred was over an hour late to work on three occasions last month.
Fact	The corporate attendance policy is stated on page 16 of the Employee Handbook.
Fact	Fred received a written warning each time he was late.
Fact	Fred won "Employee of the Month" twice last year.
Fact	I showed Fred the company's attendance policy and asked him to sign a letter stating that he understood it.
Fact	Last year Fred's coworker was late three times, but in her case, we chose not to discipline her because we thought she might sue us.

_____

_____

_____

_____

_____

_____

_____

TECHNOLOGY CONNECTION

A Picture (and a Good Caption) Is Worth a Thousand Words

Today it is easier than ever to include eye-catching graphs and charts in reports and proposals. A pie chart or a bar graph can add an extra dimension to your report or proposal when it is presented and introduced properly. Graphs *show* instead of merely *tell*. In the sample bar graph below, the big difference between one group of survey respondents and the other two groups can be seen at a glance.

Most graphs that are included in a report or a proposal require an explanation so readers understand how the graph is related to the text. Often, the explanation is included in a *caption*, written above or below the graph. The caption should summarize the graph's relevance to the writer's point.

Many popular home-computing programs include simple tools for creating graphs and charts. With a little practice, you can add important visuals to reports and proposals.

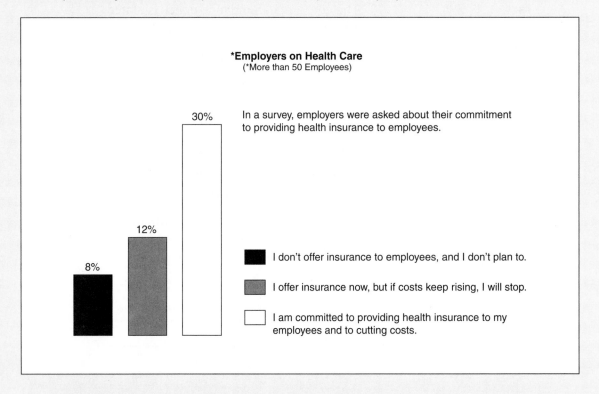

*Employers on Health Care
(*More than 50 Employees)

30%

In a survey, employers were asked about their commitment to providing health insurance to employees.

12%

8%

■ I don't offer insurance to employees, and I don't plan to.

▨ I offer insurance now, but if costs keep rising, I will stop.

□ I am committed to providing health insurance to my employees and to cutting costs.

Considering the steep rise in health care costs, you'd think that most employers would be itching to get out of the health care business altogether. But you'd be wrong. Only 8 percent of employers surveyed are dissatisfied with health care. The vast majority wants to be involved. Employers are willing to pay a reasonable share of the costs, and they want to provide employees with information and resources about health care.

Writing a Persuasive Proposal

There are two basic types of proposals: solicited and unsolicited. Solicited proposals are the kind that someone asks you to write. For example, suppose you mention to your manager that you have ideas about how to improve your company's efficiency. If your manager is interested, he or she may ask you to write a proposal in which you outline your best ideas.

On the other hand, you might draft an unsolicited proposal that explains your ideas about the company's inefficiencies and offers a solution.

Remember, a proposal is a persuasive report. It is a call to action. As a proposal writer, you are asking someone for something. When you write a proposal, your readers may be skeptical about your request. That is why at least some of the factual details you choose to convey should counter the reader's objections. For example, if you are proposing a bigger budget for your department, you may expect the reader to object by saying, "I'm not sure this is worth the investment."

When you write a proposal, brainstorm all objections your readers may have to your idea, and counter the objections in advance with well-researched facts. For the above objection, you should clearly explain in the proposal what items the increased budget will cover and why the items are important.

Most proposals are a response to a problem or a challenge, and the proposal writer is offering a solution. Below is a section from an unsolicited business proposal. This proposal is trying to convince investors to put money into specialized veterinary equipment for puppies. Can you see how it contains a thesis statement—or challenge—along with factual details to support the writer's main point?

    G&O, Inc., is dedicated to producing a full line of veterinary surgery tools for puppies. While many large companies manufacture veterinary surgical tools for adult dogs, none are dedicated solely to the specialized needs and equipment requirements of the $20 million puppy market.

    Veterinary surgery on puppies is increasing every day: More and more procedures are performed each year by a growing number of practitioners. However, the lack of puppy-specific devices causes veterinarians to improvise by adapting adult animal equipment to the special requirements of younger animals. The improvisation can be time-consuming—and potentially risky. Many procedures could be performed on puppies faster and more safely if the tools were designed especially for them.

    G&O, Inc., is dedicated to making devices in all areas of the veterinary field. Initially, the company will introduce six products. By producing devices with clear advantages over current product offerings, G&O, Inc., is assured success in this lucrative and fast-growing arena. Each G&O, Inc., product eliminates one or more steps in a procedure, saving both time and money.

By using a combination of direct marketing, specialized educational tools, and compatible designs, G&O, Inc., intends not only to serve the veterinary surgical community, but also to enhance the market by developing tools that will enable veterinarians to perform more procedures on their patients.

To serve and maintain the direction of G&O, Inc., a board of distinguished leaders in the field of veterinary medicine has been assembled: Hector Luna, DVM, Timothy Banski, DVM, and Nina O'Kalyn, DVM, Ph.D. These industry leaders and product pioneers will provide G&O, Inc., with guidance, product ideas, and market credibility.

ACTIVITY 25.4

Now it is time for you to develop a proposal. When you write a proposal, your goal is to get the reader to do something—approve a project, support an idea, or grant a request.

Using the business challenge and facts below, write a brief *solicited* proposal to your supervisor in which you request new employees for your department that assembles and distributes industrial cleaning equipment. Before you write, consider the objections management may have to your plan and make sure your proposal addresses those objections.

Write the proposal based on the facts. Remember, you do not need to incorporate all of the facts—just those that are relevant to your proposal. You may need to perform some research for this activity. For help, visit the U.S. Department of Labor's Bureau of Labor Statistics web site at **www.bls.gov.**

Challenge	Demand for our products has exceeded the supply. Two independent analysts agree with our own assessment that in order to keep up with demand for sweepers, buckets, and mops, we should hire three new assembly workers.
Fact	Currently each worker averages five hours of overtime per week. Hiring three new workers will eliminate overtime.
Fact	Some workers like to work overtime, and other workers don't.
Fact	Eliminating overtime will save the company thousands of dollars each year.
Fact	Money saved on overtime can be spent on other things. Extra money is important for any company.
Fact	All assemblers are hourly workers and must earn time and one-half for any hours over 40 that they work per week.

Fact	We could conduct a study to decide whether hourly workers or salaried workers are most cost effective for the types of jobs we offer.
Fact	If we hire, train, and start new assembly workers within the next two months, we will meet demand by the end of this year.
Fact	Research has shown that, at present, our workers are performing at maximum capacity.
Fact	I surveyed our employees, and about 70 percent of them told me that they feel "burned out" from working extra hours.
Fact	All new hires must be approved by the Vice President of Operations.

_____

_____

_____

_____

_____

_____

_____

_____

_____

_____

_____

_____

_____

_____

_____

_____

_____

_____

WRITING WORKSHOP

Persuasive Transitional Expressions for Proposals

In earlier chapters, you learned how transitional words, phrases, and sentences help a writer move from one example to the next. Persuasive transitional expressions help connect a report's main point or a proposal's need to the supporting facts. Examples of persuasive transitional words and phrases include these:

- therefore
- as you can see
- as clearly shown
- logically
- realistically
- you can see how
- obviously
- the conclusion is
- to our advantage
- it stands to reason
- this implies a course of action
- research indicates
- as a result
- I encourage you to
- the evidence points to
- basic experience suggests
- reliable experts agree

These expressions all connect a thesis to its supporting facts. Consider how the persuasive transitional words and expressions below (in italics) help convince readers that the writer is making a good proposal.

Our Human Resources Department surveyed employees and found that most workers (70%) rank health benefits as their number one concern. Interestingly, most of those surveyed (64%) said they do not have a good understanding of their medical benefits. *The statistics point to a course of action:* We should do a better job of communicating our medical benefits. *As our research shows,* employees don't know what excellent benefits they have. *It stands to reason* that we should invest in better communication, not better benefits.

SUMMARY FOR WRITING
PROPOSALS AND REPORTS

- ❑ A report is a reaction to an event, a place, a person, or a thing.

- ❑ A proposal is a persuasive report—a call-to-action for the readers.

- ❑ Reports and proposals begin with a clear thesis statement.

- ❑ Some reports document events leading up to a main event; others react to an event.

- ❑ Reports contain relevant, factual details that develop a thesis.

- ❑ Ethical writing means properly citing your sources and referencing other people's ideas instead of claiming them as your own.

- ❑ Proposals contain relevant, factual details that support a proposed solution to a business challenge.

- ❑ A good proposal anticipates and counters readers' objections.

- ❑ Research for reports and proposals should be fair, objective, and thorough.

PRACTICING YOUR SKILLS

Now that you understand the elements of a good report or proposal, apply your knowledge in the following activities.

PRACTICE 1

A reporter who focuses on payroll and compensation wrote this report.

 Many employees are unaware of the worth of their total compensation package. According to a recent study conducted by Watson-Witney Consulting, one of the best ways to improve morale and retention is to let workers know what they're really worth to you. According to the study, employees who know what their total compensation is stay with their employers almost twice as long as those who do not.

Here's an idea to help employees understand their total compensation: Prepare "Total Compensation Statements" that detail base pay, overtime or merit pay; the cost of vacation time, personal days and sick days; the cost of company-sponsored health plans, retirement and other benefits; and the cost of any legally mandated benefits.

The Watson-Witney study showed that employees who may be thinking of leaving often have a change of heart after they see how much their employer invests in them. At the very least, they may compare your package of compensation with others and learn to value their job more.

The Main Point

1. What is the writer's main point? Underline it.

Examples and Details

2. What facts does the writer use to support the main point or thesis? Circle them.

The Conclusion

3. Does the writer reach a conclusion at the end of the summary? Is the conclusion supported by fact? What is the conclusion?

_____

_____

_____

_____

PRACTICE 2

Here is part of a solicited proposal in which an events coordinator requests additional money for a major fund-raising event. Read the proposal and note the business challenge, the factual details, the examples, and the conclusion.

This year's "Stars Ahoy" fund-raising event should be held in a bigger building. A bigger hall will cost approximately $2,400 more than the Styler Center, but it can accommodate 200 more people. Presently we are looking at an overflow crowd, and we are receiving four to six calls a day about the event. It is reasonable to conclude that we could fill the larger hall. Even by conservative estimates, we will be able to raise about $25,000 more by renting the bigger hall.

"Stars Ahoy" has become a highly respected event in this region, and our company gains a high level of recognition for coordinating the activities. As we plan future events, we should recognize that additional funding might become necessary. As this year's estimates suggest, the additional funding should result in more revenue.

This would not be the first time a charity event was "upgraded" to a bigger venue and a bigger budget. Our conservative financial projections are based on similar events in Los Angeles, Chicago, and Boston. In each of these places, the fundraiser netted more in the larger space than it did in the smaller space. Research, history, and expert financial projections all point to one solution—we need to raise more money this year than we did last year. The solution is to move this year's event to a bigger venue. I hope that you agree and will decide to increase this year's budget.

The Main Point

1. What is the challenge?

_____

_____

2. Four factual details are given. What are they?

_____

_____

_____

_____

The Flow

3. Circle a transitional word, expression, and sentence.

4. Does the proposal flow? Is the proposal easy to read? What techniques did the writer use to achieve flow and readability?

_____

_____

_____

_____

_____

_____

_____

The Conclusion

5. How does the writer tie up the details at the end?

_____

_____

_____

_____

_____

_____

_____

6. Does the proposal close with a strong conclusion? What makes the conclusion strong?

_____

_____

_____

_____

_____

_____

_____

7. Is there a clear call to action? What is it?

_____

_____

_____

_____

APPLYING YOUR SKILLS

Now write a report or proposal of your own. Save each draft of your writing.

Prewriting

(a) Begin by selecting a topic for your report or proposal. Here are some samples.

Subject	Types of Material
Community	Write a report about a community service project in your town or city.
Business	Propose a salary raise for yourself.
Education	Write an incident report explaining a two-day suspension for fighting in school.
Culinary Arts	Review a restaurant that you like.

(b) Complete research, write a topic sentence, identify points, and make an outline.

Topic Sentence _____

EXAMPLE OR DETAIL 1 _____

EXAMPLE OR DETAIL 2 _____

EXAMPLE OR DETAIL 3 _____

CONCLUSION _____

Writing

Word your thesis precisely and develop each factual detail and example clearly. Add transitional words, phrases, and sentences. Write a concluding paragraph that restates your thesis, makes a recommendation, or states an opinion. Make sure your facts are relevant and name your sources of information.

Revising

Read through your first draft. The following checklist can help you make revisions.

- ❏ Do you adequately describe the business challenge?
- ❏ Do factual details support your proposed solution to the business challenge?
- ❏ Does the proposal address objections you anticipate your readers to have?
- ❏ Is your research balanced, fair, and thorough? Do you cite your sources?

Editing

Check and proofread your work. Make a new copy and proofread again.

WRITING FOR YOUR CAREER

CRITICAL THINKING

Choose a project from below that appeals to you and write a report or proposal. When the project description refers to the textbook web site, go to http://humphrey.swlearning.com and look for Chapter 25, "Writing for Your Career."

Communication and the Arts

You are assistant manager at a museum gift shop. Your supervisor asks you to compare attendance records to gift shop visits. The goal is to identify the types of exhibits that attract the most people to the gift shop. If museum management knows in advance which exhibits will draw the most gift shop customers, it can do a better job ordering inventory and scheduling employees during peak hours.

Write a report that compares visitors to two or more different kinds of museum exhibits. Identify the events and the types of items visitors purchase. Show how the buying habits of customers differ when they attend different types of exhibits; for example, a display of famous paintings versus a display of medieval armor. For this report, you do not need to conduct research. Instead, estimate the numbers of visitors based on your own thinking or your experience in museums.

Health and Medicine

Assume that you are a business manager for a medical practice. One of your challenges is handling complaints from angry patients who wait up to an hour before getting in to see their doctor. Your office has an obvious scheduling problem, and you must fix it. Currently the average wait is almost 40 minutes. You believe that if the practice hired one more physician, wait time would be cut to a reasonable 12 minutes. Also, with additional staff, the practice could expand its hours of operation. Write a proposal suggesting an additional physician to the head of the practice. Be aware that this managing physician is not in a spending mood. Your proposal should be designed to overcome her objections.

Human, Personal, and Public Service

Imagine that you are a teacher at a public high school with a diverse student population. In recent months, there have been a number of complaints about racial prejudice, religious intolerance, and sexual harassment on campus. You know about educational programs that help students achieve understanding and tolerance. After performing some research, you decide to make a proposal to your principal. In your proposal, you want to convince your principal that students and teachers at your school would benefit from a program that teaches tolerance. For Internet help with this topic, go to the textbook web site and look for Chapter 25, Human, Personal, and Public Service.

Business and Marketing

You are the manager of customer service for a retail catalog company. Your company's board of directors is considering outsourcing the company's customer service functions to another firm that has a large automated customer service department. This would mean the loss of about 25 customer service jobs. You believe the jobs should remain in-house. Write a proposal for continuing your customer service department just the way it is, not outsourcing the jobs to another company. Suggest that your company should invest in state-of-the-art customer service software. (You should end your proposal with this recommendation.) For information on the Internet about automated customer service solutions, go to the textbook web site and look for Chapter 25, Business and Marketing.

Science and Technology

Write a report about the planet Mars. Start with a clear thesis statement. What do you want to say about the Red Planet? Have you spotted it in the night sky? Do you think men and women will travel to it one day? Base your assertions on facts about Mars. You can find plenty of online help by visiting the textbook web site for Chapter 25, Science and Technology.

Environment and Natural Resources

Write your personal response to a newspaper, magazine, or Internet article about the environment. Express your opinion at the beginning of your report and include a summary of the article. Use appropriate examples and supporting details to prove your point. Include transitional words, phrases, sentences—even paragraphs, if necessary—to help you move from example to example, to help your writing flow, and to reinforce your main point.

Part III Summary for Career Writing

❏ Essays and reports are normally divided into three sections: introduction, body, and conclusion.

❏ Specific supporting evidence should be included when illustrating a subtopic of an essay or report. This includes examples, observations, descriptions, and anecdotes arranged in logical order.

❏ An illustrative essay or report states a main point, provides examples to support that point, and uses transitional expressions to lead the reader from one example to the next. The examples should be arranged in a logical order, such as time order, space order, size order, or order of importance.

❏ A descriptive essay or report introduces a subject. It provides many details organized into supporting paragraphs. When appropriate, the opening paragraph should include background information or a hook to capture the reader's interest. The conclusion ties a descriptive essay together and summarizes the most important points and details.

❏ A definition essay or report defines a term at some length, including both the connotations and the denotation. The body paragraphs develop the thesis statement, often by giving examples or using narrative.

❏ Typical structures for compare and contrast essays and reports include point by point, one side at a time, and category by category. Analogy, a special kind of comparison, involves explaining something by comparing it to something in a different category.

❏ Classification essays and reports organize people, places, or things into categories to make complex information easy to understand. Categories and descriptions of categories should be parallel, relevant, and supportive of the organizing principle.

❏ Process explanations come in two forms: instructional and informational. Informational process explanations describe how something is done or made. Instructional process explanations describe how to do something.

❏ Narrative reports and essays tell stories with detail and complexity. The writer begins by identifying the narrative's major events. These events should show a clear beginning, middle, and end. The essay reflects multiple points of view.

❏ Writing for cause and effect involves describing either the reasons for or the results of a central issue or event. A cause is what makes an event occur, and an effect is what happens as the result of an event.

❏ Persuasive essays argue for a point of view or try to persuade the reader to do something specific. Arguments should be prioritized based on the reader's interests and concerns and on factual evidence.

❏ A summary is a condensation of a chapter, an article, or another work. Summaries are written in the summary writer's own words, but express the original writer's intent.

❏ A report is a reaction to an event, a place, a person, or a thing. A proposal is a persuasive report—a "call-to-action" for the readers. Research for reports and proposals should be fair, objective, and thorough. Ethical writing means properly

Writer's Handbook

THE SENTENCE: Where It All Starts

A basic **sentence** tells one thing that happens or describes the way something or someone is. A basic sentence expresses a single, complete thought.

Example A	*The technicians enjoyed their work retreat.*
Example B	*Promptness counts.*
Example C	*Alex prepared the annual report.*
Example D	*Carlota mailed the proposal.*

The two basic elements, or **parts**, of a sentence are the **subject** and the **verb**.

The *subject* is who or what the sentence is about.

The *verb* is what happens.

Look at Example A above.

*The **technicians enjoyed** their work retreat.*

Ask yourself these questions about the example:

Who or what is the sentence about (the subject)? It is about the *technicians*.

What happened (the verb)? They *enjoyed* their work retreat.

Technicians is the subject, and *enjoyed* is the verb.

Now look at the remaining examples and ask the same questions.

Promptness counts.

The sentence is about *promptness*, and *counts* is what happens. *Promptness* is the subject, and *counts* is the verb.

***Alex prepared** the annual report.*

Who or what is the sentence about? It is about *Alex*. What happened? He *prepared* something, the annual report. The subject is *Alex*, and the verb is *prepared*.

***Carlota mailed** the proposal.*

Who or what is the sentence about? It is about *Carlota*. What happened? She *mailed* something, the proposal. The subject is *Carlota*, and the verb is *proposal*.

DO IT YOURSELF

Circle the subject and the verb in these sentences.

1. Logan brought a coworker with him.

2. Claire changed the cartridge.

3. Los Amigos has the best buffet.

4. This trail needs a new sign.

5. Mareshia made the arrangements.

6. The store opens next week.

Some sentences need more words *to complete the action* or *to tell something about the subject*. The word or phrase that completes the action is called the **object.** The object completes the action or tells something about the subject in a sentence.

Look at these examples that show an object.

Example A

*Logan brought a **coworker.***

Brought is what happened, so it is the verb. But *Logan brought* doesn't make sense. It is not a complete thought. What Logan brought is a *coworker.* *Coworker* is the object of this sentence because it tells something about what the subject did.

Example B

*Claire changed the **cartridge.***

What did Claire change? Claire changed the cartridge. *Cartridge* is the object.

Example C

*__Los Amigos__ has the best **buffet.***

This sentence describes something about the subject, *Los Amigos.* By itself, *Los Amigos has* is not a complete thought. What it has is *the best buffet. The* best *buffet* is the object of the sentence.

Basic Building Blocks of the Sentence

We	respect	customers.
Subject	**Verb**	**Object**
Who or what	What happens	Completes what happens or
the sentence is about	in the sentence	describes something about
		the subject in the sentence

DO IT YOURSELF

Circle the **subject**, **verb**, and **object** in each of these sentences. Mark them S, V, or O.

HINT: Don't worry about the extra words. Concentrate on those words you believe are the subject, verb, and object.

Example:

Aruba is a popular destination.

(Aruba) (is)   a popular   (destination.)
  S   V   O

1. I just finished the book.

2. The water quality tested better this time.

3. Jerry is the top candidate.

4. The box contains a copier.

5. Cooper is her last name.

Sentences can become longer and more complex in different ways.

>They can have more than one *subject* or more than one *verb*.

>They can *say more than one thing* about a subject as long as the thoughts are linked in the right way.

These example sentences have more than one subject:

>*Dion* and *Marilyn* are the top candidates.

>*Aerobics* and *weight training* are essential to fitness.

>*Apples* and *oranges* are fruits.

>*Telephones* and *pagers* are useful.

>*Desks* and *cabinets* need keys.

These example sentences have more than one verb:

>The glasses *fell* and *broke*.

>Tammy *folded* and *stamped* the brochures.

>The children *ran* and *played*.

>The copier *jammed* and *stopped*.

>The customer *talked* and *laughed*.

These example sentences combine more than one thought about a subject:

>I just *finished* the book, and it was very *good*.

>Aruba is a *popular* destination *in spite* of the heat.

>The water quality *tested better* this time, but it must be *closely monitored*.

>The sofa is *old*, and the *fabric is fading* on its cushions.

>Sandals are *nice* in summer, but they *get sandy* when worn on the beach.

As you move through the sections of this handbook, you will become confident in writing sentences that express what you mean to say in a way that is clear to your readers.

Sentence Fragments

You know that a sentence expresses a complete thought. If a sentence does not express a complete thought, it is called a **sentence fragment**. It can be missing the **subject**, the **verb**, or the **object**. When you are talking, you may speak in sentence fragments, as shown in Example A.

Example A

"Where are you going?"
"To the lab."

Instead of answering *"I am going to the lab,"* you may simply say *"To the lab."* This is a sentence fragment because it has no subject, *I,* and no verb, *am going.*

When writing, all sentences must be complete. That way, they are clear to the reader. Here are some examples of sentence fragments:

Example B

The last thing we need. Another screwdriver.

Good service reps remember the primary goal. To answer the client's question.

The soil sample that was just collected.

Look at the first sentence more closely. What is missing? How can the sentence be made complete?

The last thing we need. Another screwdriver.
         S?   O?

There are two nouns, *thing* and *screwdriver,* in these related sentence fragments, but there is no verb. The word *need* is a verb, but it is part of a phrase describing *thing.* You don't know what *the last thing* is. The second sentence fragment, *Another screwdriver,* also has a noun, but no verb. When you link the two sentences with a verb, they become one complete sentence:

*The last thing we need **is** another screwdriver.*

Now take a look at the second example.

Good service reps remember the primary goal. To answer the
         S   V   O   V

client's question.
         O

In this example, the first sentence is complete. It has a subject, *service rep;* a verb, *remember;* and an object, *goal.* But the next related group of words is a sentence fragment. It has a verb form, *to answer,* and an object, *question,* but no subject. Linking this sentence to the first one with a verb makes one complete sentence:

> Good service reps remember the primary goal **is** to answer the client's question.

You also can link the two sentences with a colon (:). The colon signals that an additional descriptive phrase is coming up.

> Good service reps remember the primary goal: to answer the client's question.

Look at the next example.

> The soil sample that was just collected.
>   S

Sample is the subject. *Was* could be a verb; but because it is in a phrase starting with *that,* it is part of a phrase describing, or modifying, *sample.* This sentence fragment is unclear. You could rewrite it by taking out *that.*

> The soil sample was just collected.

With this rewrite, *was* becomes the verb. More information could be given by adding another verb and an object:

> The soil **sample** that was just collected **will be enough**.

Now the sentence has a subject, *sample;* a verb phrase, *will be;* and an object, *enough.*

Words to Remember

Some words tell you that a modifying phrase is about to begin. Since these modifying phrases sometimes include a verb, make sure the main sentence also includes a verb. By themselves, these modifying phrases would be sentence fragments.

after	*after we came back*	**that**	*that was just collected*
because	*because you did so well*	**when**	*when the results come in*
if	*if nothing goes wrong*	**which**	*which they brought*
since	*since the room is free*	**while**	*while the computers were down*

DO IT YOURSELF

Write a complete sentence using each of the sentence fragments below.

HINT: With the first three examples, you can make a complete sentence by linking the fragment and the related sentence. Do this by replacing the period (.) with a comma (,) or by removing the period. Don't forget to change the first letter of the new phrase to lowercase (from As to as, for example).

1. Jane will start filling shelves. As soon as the next shipment arrives.

   _____

2. He seems much more energetic. Since he lost 20 pounds.

   _____

   _____

3. We can still meet the deadline. If we work quickly.

   _____

   _____

Write a complete sentence using the sentence fragments below.

HINT: Figure out what is missing from each fragment: a verb, a subject, or both. Then add words that will make a complete sentence.

3. The last thing we need.

   _____

   _____

4. My best friend.

   _____

   _____

5. Casablanca, which is a classic movie.

   _____

   _____

6. The best tool belt available.

   _____

   _____

7. On a boat to the Caribbean

   _____

Run-on Sentences

A **run-on sentence** happens when more than one thought "runs together" in a sentence without being linked in the right way. There may be no punctuation between the thoughts, or a comma may be used. (For related information, go to page 565, Linking Ideas.)

Examples

Noah's parents came in yesterday we discussed hearing aids for him.

It rained all day, we did not go to the beach.

The sales figures reveal an opportunity we should take advantage of this.

Look at the first example. The sentence expresses two complete thoughts, each with its own subject, verb, and object.

Noah's parents came in yesterday.   We discussed hearing aids for him.
     S   V   S   V   O

Sentences like this can be linked into one sentence in a number of ways:

- By adding a comma and the word *and* or another linking word

*Noah's parents came in yesterday, **and** we discussed hearing aids for him.*

- By adding a semicolon (;)

Noah's parents came in yesterday; we discussed hearing aids for him.

(Note: Use a semicolon only when each phrase could be a complete sentence.)

- By adding a comma between the thoughts and a modifying word at the beginning

***When** Noah's parents came in yesterday, we discussed hearing aids for him.*

In the second sentence, the two thoughts are already separated by a comma.

It rained all day, we did not go to the beach.
S V   S V   O

But this is not enough. To link it in the right way, use one of the linking strategies:

*It rained all day, **and** we did not go to the beach.*

*It rained all day, **so** we did not go to the beach.*

It rained all day; we did not go to the beach.

***Because** it rained all day, we did not go to the beach.*

In the third example, the two thoughts slide together confusingly:

The sales figures reveal an opportunity we should take advantage of this.
S   V   O   S   V   O

They can be linked into one sentence using one of the three strategies:

*The sales figures reveal an opportunity, **so** we should take advantage of this.*

*The sales figures reveal an opportunity, **and** we should take advantage of this.*

The sales figures reveal an opportunity; we should take advantage of this.

DO IT YOURSELF

Rewrite the following run-on sentences so they are well-linked, complete sentences.

HINT: Find where the two phrases meet and make the change there.

1. (Sookie is doing the storyboards)(she says they will be finished by 5 p.m.)

   _____

   _____

2. Be careful shifting into fourth gear the transmission is acting up.

   _____

   _____

3. Paul kept his voice down, the baby was sleeping.

   _____

   _____

4. The sopranos are practicing they have almost memorized their parts.

   _____

   _____

5. Flowers are blooming it is spring.

   _____

   _____

6. My head aches I may be getting a cold.

   _____

NOUNS

A **noun** is a word that names a person, a place, a thing, or an idea. A noun can be used as the *subject* of a sentence (what the subject is about) or as the *object* of the sentence (who or what receives the action in the sentence).

A noun can be:	To find a noun:
a person *Kendra, Allen Iverson, Dr. Juarez* a place *supply room, Denver, downtown* a thing *pencil, hot pack, mango* an idea *persistence, freedom, usefulness*	A noun answers the question *Who* or *What*. For example: "What are you looking at?" *Those flowers, the specs, my watch* "Who is that?" *My friend, our supervisor, Toby*

Proper and Common Nouns

A noun can be **proper** or **common**. A **proper** noun is the name for a specific person or place, such as Kendra or Denver. A proper noun begins with an uppercase letter. In addition to names, proper nouns include holidays, months, days, religions, and nationalities (Thanksgiving, November, Thursday, Methodist, Indonesian, Native American).

A **common** noun is the word for a person, a place, a thing, or an idea, but it is not the name of a specific one. Examples of common nouns in the box above include *pencil, supply room,* and *freedom*. Most nouns are common nouns.

Compound Nouns

A noun can be made up of more than one word. Then it is a **compound** noun. Many compound nouns are made up of two words side by side. Others are combined into one word, and some are hyphenated. Here are some examples of compound nouns:

waiting area	*handshake*	*light-year*
loan application	*cleanup*	*father-in-law*
community watch	*breakthrough*	*by-product*
physical therapist	*thunderstorm*	

To determine whether a compound noun is one word, two words, or hyphenated, look it up in the dictionary.

Singular and Plural Nouns

Nouns can be **singular** or **plural.** A singular noun refers to one thing.
A plural noun refers to more than one thing. (Note: Refer to Section 13
on spelling to learn more about the spelling of nouns.)

Most nouns can be made plural simply by adding an *s* at the end.

manual	*manuals*
component	*components*
exercise	*exercises*
boy	*boys*

If a noun ends with a *y*, it can usually be made plural by changing the *y* to *ie*
and adding an *s*.

category	*categories*
candy	*candies*
folly	*follies*
hobby	*hobbies*

If a noun ends in *ey*, it can be made plural by adding an *s*.

alley	*alleys*
monkey	*monkeys*
key	*keys*
galley	*galleys*

Nouns that end in certain sounds, such as *s*, *sh*, *ch*, or *x*, can be made plural
by adding *es*. They are spelled the way they are pronounced.

petri dish	*petri dishes*
tax	*taxes*
branch	*branches*
catch	*catches*

Some nouns that end in *f* or *fe* become plural by adding *ves*.

knife	*knives*
sheaf	*sheaves*
half	*halves*

Some plural nouns are irregular and must be memorized.

foot	*feet*
child	*children*
person	*people*

DO IT YOURSELF

Rewrite these singular nouns as plural nouns.

1. firearm _____   6. assembly _____

2. wish _____   7. house call _____

3. turkey _____   8. dress _____

4. intake form _____   9. strategy _____

5. factory _____   10. life _____

In each sentence below, find the singular noun that should be plural and change it to the correct plural form.

HINT: Words such as *more, many, most, three, four,* and other numbers tell you that the noun they modify should be plural.

11. The new project manager will oversee three project line.

_____

_____

12. Too many employee have been coming in late.

_____

_____

13. The tree lost most of its leaf in the thunderstorm.

_____

_____

14. Both of his elbow need to be bandaged.

_____

_____

15. Our retriever had four puppy last week.

_____

_____

VERBS

The **verb** tells what the subject does or is, or it tells what is happening to the subject. The verb provides the *action* in the sentence. Without a verb, the sentence is not complete.

Verbs, by changing a little, give information about who is performing the action, when it is being performed, and other things.

Watch how these verbs change depending on who is performing the action:

I	*direct*	I	*look*	I	*cause*
You	*direct*	You	*look*	You	*cause*
She	*directs*	Clark	*looks*	The economy	*causes*
We	*direct*	We	*look*	We	*cause*
They	*direct*	Clients	*look*	These factors	*cause*

Note that the only change in most verbs involves adding an *s* when the verb's action is done by a *he, she,* or *it.* (This is called third-person singular; see box.)

Just as a noun can be singular (*about one thing*) or plural (*about more than one thing*), verbs also can be singular or plural.

Look at the first verb example above (*direct* or *directs*):

> **She** directs

This form refers to a singular subject. *She* is a singular subject.

> **We** direct, *they direct*

This form is correct for plural subjects. *We* is a plural subject.

> *I direct, You direct*

The verb also is correct for first-and second-person singular. *I* is a first-person singular subject, and *you* is a second-person singular subject.

Person

If you write …	Grammatically speaking, it is …
I	First person
You	Second person
He/she/it	Third-person singular
We	First-person plural
They	Third-person plural

Making Verb and Subject Agree

The form of the subject and verb in a sentence should match, or **agree**.

If the **subject** is **singular**, or about one thing, the **verb** should be **singular**. If the **subject** is **plural**, or about more than one thing, the **verb** should be **plural**.

If the subject is *third person* (*he, she, it, they*), the *verb* should be *third person*. If the subject is *first person* (*I*), the *verb* should be *first person*.

Examples

Amanda directs the reading program.

one person   singular verb

Amanda and *directs* are both singular, and both are third person.

The bears walk through the campsite at night.

plural subject   plural verb

Bears and *walk* are both plural, and both are third-person.

When a sentence gets longer or more complex, the basic parts still need to *agree*. A word or phrase may come between the subject and the verb, and that can cause confusion about which word is the subject. You can check subject-verb *agreement* by separating the subject and verb from the modifying phrases and comparing them. The examples below show words that come between the subject and the verb.

Examples

The delay in the shipment of bricks are holding up the job.

The delay (in the shipment of bricks) are holding up the job.

singular noun   plural verb

HINT: The *bricks* in the modifying phrase makes the phrase sound plural, but the real subject is *delay*. Try not to let words that end in *s* confuse you. The correct verb form is as follows:

*The delay in the shipment of bricks **is** holding up the job.*

DO IT YOURSELF

Rewrite each sentences so the subject and verb agree.

HINT: Place parentheses around the modifying phrase that comes between the subject and verb. This will make it easy to match the subject with the verb.

1. Proper maintenance (of vehicles) are crucial.

   _____

2. Brad, along with his friends, are coming to the park.

   _____

3. All of the students, including Keisha, is benefiting from the new unit.

   _____

4. The birds, especially the one flying in front, is headed south for winter.

   _____

In the following sentences, the subject comes after the verb. Find the subject first; then make sure the verb agrees with it. Write the correct verb if one is needed.

5. On the table is all of the cutting tools for our next project.

   _____

6. There is still many questions to be decided.

   _____

7. It is the cake that you smell.

   _____

8. In my yard is all of the leaves.

   _____

9. They are the proposals that you want.

   _____

10. In my lawn chairs is the leaves that have to be removed.

   _____

Active and Passive Voice

Verbs also can be **active** or **passive**.

When the *subject* in the sentence *does something*, the verb is active.

Example A   Subject does something

*The art **therapist attends** treatment team meetings.*

***Nick opened** the envelope.*

When something *is done to the subject* in the sentence, the verb is passive.

Example B   **When something is done to the subject**

*The boiler **tank was** fabricated using the heavier gauge steel.*

*The **office is** cleaned every night.*

HINT: In the passive voice, you will see a form of the verb *to be* (*is, was, have been, will be*) as part of the verb phrase. This is sometimes called a *helping verb*.

Here are two versions of the same sentence. One is written in the active voice, and the other is written in the passive voice.

Active	*The art therapist saw her new patients today.*
Passive	*The new patients were seen by the art therapist today.*
Active	*We will complete the vocational assessments by Friday.*
Passive	*The vocational assessments will be completed by Friday.*

Writing in the active voice makes your sentences more direct and gives them stronger impact. Sometimes, though, it makes more sense to write in the passive voice. This puts more emphasis on the action than on the subject.

Example C

The swimming pool was emptied before we arrived.

Two tellers were hired last week.

The accounting team was meeting with senior management.

Elderly patients were waiting for their physicians.

Hair stylists were attending a convention.

DO IT YOURSELF

Change these sentences from passive voice to active voice or from active voice to passive voice. Then read the old and new versions. Which sounds better? Put a check mark by the one you prefer.

HINT: This change will involve moving the subject and object. If the subject is first, changing voice will mean putting the object first, and vice versa.

1. The meeting was opened by the mayor.

   _____

   _____

2. Career day was attended by over 100 students.

   _____

   _____

3. Help will be needed to weld the final seam.

   _____

   _____

4. Our team finished the feasibility study on the new park design.

   _____

   _____

5. Bryan Flanagan's talk inspired the trainees.

   _____

   _____

6. The package was delivered by Diana.

   _____

   _____

7. The workers were upset with the change of schedule.

   _____

   _____

8. Several packages were damaged by the water leak.

   _____

   _____

Tense

Verbs also tell the time when something happens. The verb's **tense** tells the time: whether the verb's action is happening now, in the past, or in the future.

Examples

Present	*He tries.*
Past	*He tried.*
Future	*He will try.*

Other tenses also are used to describe actions that are completed in the past, present, or future. These are called *past perfect tense, present perfect tense,* and *future perfect tense. Perfect* in this sense means the action has been completed.

Example

Present perfect   *He has tried.*

He was trying, but now, in the present, his trying is completed.

Past perfect   *He had tried.*

He was trying, but sometime in the past, his trying was completed.

Future perfect   *He will have tried.*

He will try, but at some point in the future, his trying will be completed.

Another tense tells that the verb's action is still happening. It is called **progressive,** which means the action is still in progress. It involves using the verb **to be** and adding *ing* to the main verb.

Example

Present progressive	*He is trying to complete the assignment very quickly.*
Past progressive	*He was trying to complete the assignment very quickly.*
Future progressive	*He will be trying to complete the assignment very quickly.*

DO IT YOURSELF

Change the verb's tense in each sentence to the new tense indicated.

1. Past: I expected soybean prices to go up.

   Present: _____

2. Present Progressive: Nancy is writing the text labels for the watercolor show.

   Future: _____

3. Past: We drove the truck to town.

   Present progressive: _____

4. Present progressive: We are looking into the problem.

   Past progressive: _____

5. Past: Carlos found the slide projector.

   Past perfect: _____

6. Future: This couple will need a few more counseling sessions.

   Past: _____

7. Future: The sign will be replaced by Tuesday.

   Future Perfect: _____

8. Past: Ted inspected the irrigation ditch after the storm.

   Future: _____

Irregular Verbs

Most verbs in English are regular. That means they change to past tense by adding *ed* or *d*. Some verbs are **irregular.** Their past tense changes in different ways. The only ways to learn these irregular verb tenses is to memorize them or use a reference manual that lists irregular verbs. Here is a list of many of the irregular verbs you will want to know.

COMMON IRREGULAR VERBS

Present	Past	Past perfect (had …)	Present	Past	Past perfect (had …)
am, are, is	was, were	been	pay	paid	paid
become	became	become	ring	rang	rung
begin	began	begun	run	ran	run
bite	bit	bitten	see	saw	seen
bring	brought	brought	sleep	slept	slept
build	built	built	spring	sprang	sprung
buy	bought	bought	strive	strove	striven
choose	chose	chosen	swim	swam	swum
come	came	come	take	took	taken
do	did	done	teach	taught	taught
drive	drove	driven	tell	told	told
fall	fell	fallen	throw	threw	thrown
fight	fought	fought	wear	wore	worn
freeze	froze	frozen	write	wrote	written
get	got	gotten			
give	gave	given			
go	went	gone			
grow	grew	grown			
hear	heard	heard			
hold	held	held			
know	knew	known			
leave	left	left			
lend	lent	lent			
lay	laid	laid (to place)			
lie	lay	lain (to rest)			
make	made	made			

DO IT YOURSELF

Each of these sentences has an incorrect irregular verb. Write the verb in the correct form.

HINT: Figure out what tense is being used. You can check the chart of irregular verbs if you are not sure what the correct form is.

1. A new bug sprung up when we ran the software.

   _____

   _____

2. Judith's cell phone ringed in the meeting.

   _____

   _____

3. Hiram seen the new trailer sprayer being delivered.

   _____

   _____

4. This department has always strove to do its best.

   _____

   _____

5. I sleeped late because my alarm clock did not go off.

   _____

   _____

6. The drill is laying on the bench where Andre put it.

   _____

   _____

7. Grandpa had laid down for a nap.

   _____

   _____

8. Andrea begun her speech with a joke.

   _____

   _____

9. The fertilizer drum must have broke last night.

   _____

   _____

Gerunds and Participles

You've seen the *ing* form used with "to be" verbs as part of one kind of present tense, such as *Denise is going to the store*. Two other verb forms—gerunds and participles—can be made by adding *ing* to a verb. As a **gerund**, the verb can take the place of a noun in a sentence.

Examples of gerunds

Laughing is the best medicine.

Observing Mars tonight will be easy.

I admire someone who keeps exercising no matter what.

A gerund also can refer to something in the past. This is done by adding the gerund form of have, *having*, to the past tense of the verb.

Examples of gerunds

Larry left early, having talked to all of the dealers.

Having learned all of the steps, she now dances beautifully.

As a participle, the *ing* verb can act as an **adjective**, a word that modifies a noun. (More about adjectives follows on page 540.) You also can use a past tense verb as an adjective.

Examples of participles

Jackson gave Bonnie a teasing look.

The copying machine is down.

All of the children like mashed potatoes.

Infinitives

The infinitive is the verb's **basic form**. It is usually preceded by the word *to*. Think of it as the "generic" verb; it can take the role of a noun, an adjective, or an adverb (another modifying word you will learn about on page 542).

Examples

to carry	*to answer*	*to laugh*
to designate	*to handle*	*to whisper*

I always wanted to work with people.

It won't be easy to take those measurements.

To succeed is the goal we cannot forget.

PRONOUNS

Pronouns are words that replace nouns to simplify speech and writing. Pronouns allow you to write *Millie fed her dog and then took him for a walk*, instead of *Millie fed Millie's dog and then took Millie's dog for a walk*. Without thinking about the grammatical rules behind pronouns, people use pronouns every day when they talk and write. Pronouns are some of the most common and useful words.

Personal Pronouns

Personal pronouns substitute for nouns in a sentence. Different pronouns are used depending on what role the noun is performing in the sentence—whether it is the subject or object or something else.

Subjective pronouns (*I, you, he, she, it, we, they*) take the place of the subject.

> **Examples of subjective pronouns**
>
> *Hakim will finish when **he** gets back from Chicago.*
>
> *The clinic can see more patients when **it** stays open late.*
>
> *Team members get more accomplished when **they** cooperate.*

Objective pronouns (*me, you, him, her, it, us, them*) take the place of the object.

> **Examples of objective pronouns**
>
> *Darla assigned that task to **me**.*
>
> *My client asked me to go to lunch with **him**.*
>
> *Please take a look at **them** immediately.*

Possessive pronouns show ownership. They can modify a noun to show ownership (*my, your, his, her, its, our, their*), or they can take the place of a noun that belongs to someone or something (*mine, yours, his, hers, its, theirs*).

> **Examples of possessive pronouns**
>
> ***Our** projections turned out to be optimistic.*
>
> *The pleasure was all **mine**.*
>
> *That gift is **yours**.*

Reflexive pronouns *reflect* an action back to the subject. They also can be used for emphasis. Reflexive pronouns include *myself, yourself, himself, herself, itself, ourselves, yourselves, themselves.*

Examples

You and Pat must get to the hotel **yourselves**.

I will write the guidelines **myself**.

Loretta delivered the package **herself**.

The handicapped gentleman shoveled the snow himself.

Samuel and Adam, who are twins, cleaned the garage themselves.

Personal Pronouns at a Glance

Subjective (substitutes for the subject)	Objective (substitutes for the object)	Possessive (shows ownership as modifier or noun)	Reflexive (reflects action back to subject)
I	me	my, mine	myself
you	your	your, yours	yourself
he, she, it	him, her, it	his, her, hers, its	himself, herself, itself
we	us	our, ours	ourselves
you (plural)	you (plural)	your, yours (plural)	yourselves
they	them	their, theirs	themselves

Other Kinds of Pronouns

Other kinds of pronouns play different parts in sentences. They include the following:

Indefinite pronouns refer to nonspecific groups, persons, or things.

Relative pronouns take the place of a noun in a statement (clause) within the main sentence.

Interrogative pronouns introduce a question.

Demonstrative pronouns point to something or someone.

Here are examples of each of these kinds of pronouns:

Indefinite pronouns	Relative pronouns	Interrogative pronouns	Demonstrative pronouns
everybody	which	who	this
someone	who	what	that
anybody	whom	which	these
no one	whose	whatever	those
each		whoever	such
several			
whom			
both			
many			
most			
either			
some			
more			

DO IT YOURSELF

Each of these sentences needs a pronoun. Read the sentence and the clue that tells what the pronoun is substituting for or what kind of pronoun is needed. Fill in the pronoun that makes the most sense.

1. Did the judge give _____ the court calendar?
   (Marlene)

2. Make sure _____ receives a copy of this report.
   (Nathan Alicante)

3. It seems certain that _____ will attend the seminar.
   (both clients)

4. Please contact the dealers about _____ preseason orders.
   (the dealers')

5. _____ are the records we are looking for.
   (The records right here)

6. You must wash _____ thoroughly to avoid contamination.
   (reflexive pronoun for you, singular)

7. Do you still want _____ recommendation for Ms. Singer's nutritional care plan? (possessive pronoun for me)

8. If the crop protectant was not shipped yesterday, _____ will be late.
   (the crop protectant)

9. _____ logs the most orders wins this week's prize.
   (interrogative pronoun for he or she)

10. If Mr. Cortez isn't in, you can leave the package with _____ else.
    (indefinite pronoun, one person)

Making Pronouns Agree

Just as a verb must agree with the subject in a sentence, a **pronoun** must agree with the noun it refers to, called its **antecedent**.

Examples of nouns and antecedents

Victor ate lunch by himself.

Both the subject, *Victor*, and the reflexive pronoun, *himself*, are third-person singular.

The actress learned the lines by herself.

Both the subject, *actress*, and the reflexive pronoun, *herself*, are third-person singular.

I made a copy of my key for Ana.

Both the subject, *I*, and the pronoun, *my*, are first-person singular.

I ran an errand for my supervisor.

Both the subject, I, and the pronoun, my, are first-person singular.

Several members have not sent in their dues yet.

Both the subject, *members*, and the pronoun, *their*, are third-person plural.

The vegetables are showing their growth.

Both the subject, *vegetables*, and the pronoun, *their*, are third-person singular.

Don't Let These Confuse You!

Because they sound the same, these words are sometimes confused. But the meanings are different!

Possessive Pronoun	Contraction
its	it's (short for it is)
their	they're (they are)
theirs	there's (there is)
whose	who's (who is)
your	you're (you are)

Getting Who and Whom Straight

Who is the interrogative, or questioning, pronoun for a *subject*.

> Who goes first?
> S   V

> I don't know (who picked up the package).
> S   V   O

Whom is the interrogative, or questioning, pronoun for an *object*.

> Whom will be given the biggest bonus?
> O   V   S

When in doubt, turn the question around: The biggest bonus will be given to whom?

> We must find out (whom they chose).
>   O   S   V

Turning the phrase around makes it clearer: They chose whom?

Keeping Pronoun References Clear

Because a pronoun is more general than the noun for which it substitutes, it is important to make clear *to whom* or *what* the *pronoun is referring*. This becomes an issue when the subject and object are similar.

Example A

Carolyn told Alissa (she couldn't participate in the workshop).
    S   O

Does *she* refer back to Carolyn or Alissa? Both Carolyn and Alissa are feminine, so there is no way of knowing which of them couldn't participate in the workshop.

If Carolyn is the person who cannot participate, you could rewrite this sentence as follows:

Carolyn told Alissa that she herself couldn't participate in the workshop.

Or as: *Carolyn told Alissa that she, Carolyn, couldn't participate in the workshop.*

If Alissa is the person who cannot participate, you should repeat her name in the modifying phrase:

Carolyn told Alissa that Alissa couldn't participate in the workshop.

Example B

The car sideswiped a tree, and it suffered a bad scrape.
    S   O   S   O

Did the car or the tree suffer a bad scrape? Both the car and the tree are singular inanimate objects, so *it* could refer to either of them.

To rewrite this sentence clearly, you could repeat the noun or add an identifying detail that makes clear the thing to which *it* refers.

*The car sideswiped a tree, and **the car** suffered a bad scrape.*

*The car sideswiped a tree, and it suffered a bad scrape **on the door**.*

*The car sideswiped a tree, and **the tree** suffered a bad scrape.*

*The car sideswiped a tree, and **its bark** suffered a bad scrape.*

Often writers don't notice unclear pronouns until after they have read the sentence. Writers should reread what they have written as if they were readers who knew nothing about the topic.

Sometimes a pronoun is more vague than it needs to be. In the examples that follow, the pronoun does not really refer to the thing for which it seems to substitute.

Example A

On the news, they said the state budget was passed.

They refers vaguely to some people, but *news* is inanimate. You should remove the reference to *they* when rewriting this sentence:

The news report said the state budget was passed.

We heard on the news that the state budget was passed.

Example B

In this company, they have casual-dress Fridays.

They refers vaguely to some people, while *company* is a collective noun. Here are two ways to make this sentence clearer:

This company has casual-dress Fridays.

The management of this company allows casual-dress Fridays.

Common Pronoun Problems

The previous section discussed how a pronoun must agree with the noun it replaces. Not only must it **agree** in **gender** (*he* or *she*) and **number** (*he/she/it* for singular and *they* for plural), it also must **match** the **form of the noun it replaces** (subject or object).

Writers sometimes have trouble with double subjects and double objects. Remember to use a subjective pronoun to replace a subject and an objective pronoun to replace an object. The following examples are written correctly:

Examples

*Sean had breakfast with Francie and **him**.*

She and I went shopping together yesterday.

*Just between you and **me**, I don't think this is a good idea.*

A good way to determine which pronoun to use is to imagine the sentence with a single subject or object:

*Sean had breakfast with **her** (not she).*

She went shopping; I went shopping.

The third sentence in the example is a bit trickier because a person wouldn't say "between me." However, by substituting another similar word, the pattern becomes clearer: *with me, to me, about me, by me,* and so on.

DO IT YOURSELF

For each sentence, circle the correct pronoun.

HINT: When the sentence has two subjects or two objects, take away the one you know is correct. Read what is left. Does the sentence make sense?

1.   Armando invited (her/she) and me to the lecture.

2.   The trainers chose Laura and (him/he) for the presentation.

3.   (She/Her) and Mr. Bradbury would benefit from the nutrition plan.

4.   Valerie and (he/him) will share the same sales territory.

DO IT YOURSELF (CONTINUED)

These sentences follow the rule that tells you to use the subjective personal pronoun after the verb to be. Circle the correct pronoun.

5. The lead writers for the installation guide will be Ian and (me/I).

6. After one long knock and two short knocks, I know it is (he/him).

Rewrite each sentence, eliminating the vague pronoun.

7. On the weather report, they predicted a hot weekend.

_____

_____

8. In that course, they make you work hard.

_____

_____

In each sentence, the pronoun could refer to the subject or the object or to one of two objects. Decide what you want the sentence to say and rewrite it more clearly.

9. Maggie told Alicia she must bring the guitar to the next rehearsal.

_____

_____

10. Jeremy loves his dog Archie; he's learned how to sit up and beg.

_____

_____

11. He picked up the cereal and the spoon, and ate the whole thing.

_____

_____

MODIFIERS

Modifiers are words or phrases that provide additional information about a thing or an action. They help to make the meaning of a sentence more specific by describing something about the thing or action.

Here are important questions that modifiers help to answer:

> What kind is it, or what is it like?
>
> How many are there?
>
> How does it compare to something else?
>
> How is it done?

There are two main kinds of modifiers: **adjectives** and **adverbs**.

Adjectives

Adjectives modify nouns. They are usually, though not always, placed before the nouns, as shown in the examples below.

> **Examples**   **Adjectives modifying a noun**
>
> *She did a **fine** job on the report.*
>
> *The **contracted** builders for the subdivision have applied for a **conservation** easement.*

In the first example, the adjective *fine* modifies *job* and says what kind of job she did on the report.

In the second example, the adjective *contracted* tells which builders applied for an easement. The word *conservation*, which is usually a noun, is an adjective in this sentence, telling what kind of easement.

An adjective can also be used in a sentence describing something or someone. In this case, it may be placed after the noun. When placed after the noun, adjectives are sometimes harder to identify.

> **Examples**   **Adjectives describing something or someone**
>
> *The wiring job for the new information system was **hard** to do.*
>
> *The workload seems **lighter**, now that we've added two new employees.*

You can be sure these are adjectives, not objects, by changing the sentences around:

Examples **Changing the sentence around to identify an adjective.**

It was a hard wiring job.

It is a lighter workload.

If the words work as modifiers in this changed form, they are adjectives.

DO IT YOURSELF

In these sentences, add an adjective in the space provided. Be sure it modifies the noun. Use your imagination to come up with a good adjective—just be sure your sentence makes sense.

1. Next year, we are planning three_____exhibitions.

2. The storm was_____.

3. This is a _____business plan.

4. We need to add a technical writer with_____skills.

5. Do you like the_____model, or the one you have now?

6. This marketing team must solve some_____problems.

7. The conference schedule looks_____.

8. We are preparing a/an_____line for the fall.

9. I see some_____possibilities in this strategy.

10. The_____mark is clear and helps me understand the directions.

11. A_____shelf adds to my efficiency at work.

12. The_____degree leads to an opportunity for a lucrative career.

13. _____school is an exciting time for most students.

14. _____information can be obtained by surfing the Internet.

15. _____fishing is a favorite sport of many people.

Adverbs

Adverbs modify verbs. They can also modify adjectives and other adverbs. They often end in *ly: quietly, really, handily, forcefully.*

Example A

*We must work **quickly** to meet the deadline, or the schedule for the entire project must be moved back.*

In this example, the adverb *quickly* modifies the verb *work* and specifies how fast we must work.

Example B

*They waved **wildly** at the bus, but it didn't stop.*

The adverb *wildly* modifies the verb *waved*, telling how they waved at the bus.

Example C

*Greg **just** finished recording the results of the customer service survey that was mailed to 1,500 people.*

In Example C, the word *just* tells more about when Greg finished recording the results. It is an adverb, even though it does not end in "ly".

Some of the most commonly used adverbs do not end in *ly*. They include:

almost	*quite*
just	*still*
now	*very*
often	*yet*

Example D

*Are you **still** planning to attend the lecture?*

In this sentence, *still* modifies the verb phrase *are planning*. It tells that something else may affect the subject's plans.

Example E

*Her explanation was **quite** amusing.*

In this example, *quite* modifies the adjective *amusing*. It works just like an adverb with *ly*, such as *really* or *extremely* would.

DO IT YOURSELF

In these sentences, add an adverb to modify the verb, adjective, or other adverb. To get started, try to think of an *ly* word or some other adverb that makes sense. If you choose an adverb without an ly ending, that is all right.

1. You must learn to give injections_____, so patients will not suffer unnecessarily.

2. Zach drove _____back from the hospital, and he was careful to obey all traffic laws.

3. How_____did they look for the formula for the chemical solution before they found it?

4. Our team was commended for finishing the job_____.

5. Your first task is to prove that the plan is_____viable.

6. I_____see seagulls from my window.

7. Dr. Connors will be_____delayed.

8. Speak_____and carry a big stick.

9. This_____came as a complete surprise.

10. We believe you will be_____pleased with the revised guidelines.

11. This jeans style is aimed at a/an_____younger group.

12. We are expecting_____two hundred attendees at the nursing convention that will be held in Dallas.

13. An automotive repair technician must_____be prepared to deal with the public.

14. Rhonda is_____looking forward to her first job as a cosmetologist.

15. Emergency Medical Technicians work_____to take care of injured and ill patients.

16. Banks are changing their hours_____to meet customer demand for more convenient banking times.

17. Reporters are_____likely to be put in dangerous situations during times of war.

How to Spot Adjectives and Adverbs

Many **adjectives** are just simple descriptive words. Sometimes an adjective can be the same word as a noun. An adjective also can be made by adding a new ending to a noun.

Simple adjectives	Adjectives that can also be nouns
red, blue, green	dark, light
big, small, short, tall	fun
sad, happy	good, evil
nice, mean	

Adjectives made from nouns

time	timely	star	starry	rectangle	rectangular
night	nightly	tear	tearful	business	businesslike
rain	rainy	will	willful	photography	photographic

Notice that two adjectives in the list above, *timely* and *nightly*, have the *ly* ending. Even though they have an *ly* ending, they are not adverbs.

Adverbs can be formed from adjectives by adding "ly":

tearful	tearfully	narrow	narrowly
happy	happily	soft	softly
stiff	stiffly	cautious	cautiously

When the adjective already ends *in ly*, no change is necessary. Review the examples below that show both adjectives and adverbs that end in *ly*.

Example A   Adjective, modifying the noun

*We watched the **nightly** news before going to bed.*

Here *nightly* is an adjective, modifying the noun *news*.

Example B   Adverb, modifying the verb

*The guinea pigs' cage must be cleaned **nightly**.*

Here *nightly* is an adverb, modifying the verb *cleaned*.

Because adjectives and adverbs come in so many different forms, a writer must understand whether they are modifying a noun or a verb. The writer's first task is to identify how the word being modified is used in the sentence.

DO IT YOURSELF

In each of these sentences, change the adjective provided into an adverb. Underline the verb the adverb is modifying.

HINT: Changing the adjective to an adverb usually just involves adding *ly* to the end.

1. The consultants will help us make this transition _____.
   (smooth)

2. Ms. Atkins _____ appreciates your input on this.
   (great)

3. We must not move too _____, even though the deadline is close. (hasty)

4. I _____ support the final recommendation in the report.
   (strong)

5. You must insert the new component _____.
   (careful)

In these sentences, change the word provided from a noun to an adjective. This will involve adding one of the following suffixes: able, ish, ful, al, y.

6. All sales reps should dress in a _____ manner.
   (profession)

7. We assure you that the oversight was not _____.
   (intention)

8. Miranda's new glasses make her look _____.
   (book)

9. Our customers want the most _____ styles available.
   (fashion)

10. Grated lemon will make this sauce even more _____.
    (zest)

11. As we move forward, we are committed to remaining _____ to our original mission.
    (faith)

Spoken Adverbs vs. Written Adverbs

Sometimes in speaking, people drop the *ly* from the **adverb**. When writing, it is important to use the adverb correctly. Compare the *ly* words in Examples A and B.

Example A   Dropping the "ly"

Make sure the bolt fits tight.

Example B   Adding "ly" appropriately

Make sure the bolt fits tightly.

Using Common Modifiers Correctly

Some closely related pairs of adjectives and adverbs can cause confusion for writers. For example, *good* and *real* are adjectives; however, *well* and *really* are adverbs.

Adjective	Adverb
good	well

Incorrect example

The presentation went good.

Correct example

The presentation went well.

The word *good* is modifying the verb *went;* therefore, it should be an adverb, *well*.

Adjective	Adverb
real	really

Incorrect example

The new sales representative is real nice.

Correct example

The new rep is really nice.

The word *real* modifies the adjective *nice*, so it should be an adverb.

DO IT YOURSELF

Read these sentences and decide whether the correct word should be an adjective or an adverb; then circle the correct word. **HINT:** What word is it modifying? Remember that an adverb can modify an adjective or adverb as well as a verb.

1. This client's mobility has (actual/actually) improved even though he has not followed his exercise regimen.

2. The new population survey is (crucial/crucially) to our deer-management program.

3. It is going to be an (awful/awfully) long wait.

4. We were (real/really) gratified by the attendance at the community meeting.

5. The land management plan was written (hasty/hastily).

6. Cloud cover made it a (disappointing/disappointingly) night for stargazing.

7. I will be (glad/gladly) to take over Jeff's clients while he is on vacation.

8. Most of the aquatic species have rebounded (vigorous/vigorously).

9. When the library stays open late, the students will (sure, surely) appreciate it.

10. The security guard ran (quick/quickly) to check out the problem.

11. Robots operate (smooth/smoothly) if they have been manufactured correctly.

Making Comparisons with Adjectives and Adverbs

Adjectives and **adverbs** allow you to make comparisons among different people, things, or actions. Comparisons show degrees of difference, and they usually follow a pattern of *regular, more,* and *most*. Look at the patterns below:

Examples   Comparing with adjectives

Regular Form	More	Most
full	*fuller*	*fullest*
easy	*easier*	*easiest*
hard	*harder*	*hardest*
light	*lighter*	*lightest*
thin	*thinner*	*thinnest*

Examples	Comparing with adverbs	
Regular Form	**More**	**Most**
fully	*more fully*	*most fully*
easily	*more easily*	*most easily*
lightly	*more lightly*	*most lightly*

When an adjective contains more than one syllable, it usually adds the word *more* or *most* to show a comparison.

excellent	*more excellent*	*most excellent*
rapid	*more rapid*	*most rapid*
encouraging	*more encouraging*	*most encouraging*

The comparative forms of **excellent** are not **excellenter** or **excellentest**, for instance. If the adjective ends in *y*, as in **easy**, **funny**, or **happy**, it follows the usual pattern.

A few common adjectives are irregular and form an entirely different word in their *more* and *most* form.

Regular Form	**More**	**Most**
good	*better*	*best*
some, many	*more*	*most*
bad	*worse*	*worst*
little	*less*	*least*

DO IT YOURSELF

Rewrite these sentences to change the highlighted adjective or adverb to the correct word. A few other words may have to change also in order for the new sentence to make sense.

1. The asbestos levels in the basement were (higher/highest) than we expected.

    _____

2. Joe Pinella seems like a (more/most) enthusiastic candidate.

    _____

3. Danielle came up easily with the (good/best) answer.

    _____

4. We arrived earlier/earliest than anyone for the on-site inspection.

    _____

DO IT YOURSELF

Read these sentences, and then fill in the correct form of the adjective or adverb. Certain words, such as *than*, will tell you which form of the adjective or adverb is needed. Does this word indicate a usual degree, more than usual, or the most?

1. When we count inventory, it will be _____ (hard) to count the toy items than the clothes.

2. Business is the _____ (slow) on Tuesdays.

3. We must follow the guidelines _____ (careful) to avoid further mistakes.

4. Rep. Woodward's speech took the _____ (long) of all.

5. I can't imagine the cleanup going any _____ (easy) than that.

6. Sandra is the _____ (tall) basketball player.

7. She is _____ (tall) than some of the male players.

8. That is the _____ (busy) street in town.

9. Clams are the _____ (cost) seafood at this time of year.

10. Terik made the _____ (high) grade on the test.

Compound Adjectives

Two words, and sometimes more, can be joined by a hyphen to form a **compound adjective** when the adjective comes before the noun it modifies. The hyphens are needed for clarity.

Incorrect example   **Adjective not hyphenated**

We are happy to have such a well known guest.

Correct example   **Adjective hyphenated**

We are happy to have such a well-known guest.

The reader in the incorrect example might think at first that the noun is well, not guest. The hyphen makes clear that *well* is part of the modifier.

If the modifier comes after the noun, the hyphen is not needed. Review the examples below for a better understanding of modifiers that come after nouns.

Example A   **Modifier before noun**

We are happy to have such a well-known guest tonight.

Modifier after noun

We are happy that our guest tonight is so well known.

Example B   **Modifier before noun**

It will be crucial to obtain high-quality components.

Modifier after noun

It will be crucial to obtain components of high quality.

Example C   **Modifier before noun**

I cannot attend the whole three-day conference.

Modifier after noun

I cannot attend the conference all three days.

DO IT YOURSELF

Place the hyphen where it is needed in the following sentences. Think carefully about the position of the compound adjective before deciding whether to add a hyphen.

1. The report was well conceived, which added to the writer's prestige in the office.

2. The dress was well worn, but it still looked great on its owner.

3. A ten day course of antibiotics is often prescribed for sinus infections.

4. The training was scheduled as a ten day course.

5. The course ran for ten days and provided excellent training.

6. Receiving an award from your peers is a high honor.

7. A poorly run hotel will soon lose its customers.

8. My light sensitive eyes have trouble in heavy sun.

9. A four sided box may be a square or a rectangle.

Articles

A, an, and *the* make up a special group of adjectives called **articles**. These words are easy to use correctly if a few guidelines are followed.

A and *an* are indefinite articles. That means they refer to any non-specific person, thing, or action. *A* is used before a word starting with a consonant. *An* is used before a word starting with a vowel. Notice that the article can come before an adjective or before a noun.

> **Examples**   **Indefinite articles coming before consonants and vowels**

> *a folder*   *an airplane*
> *a candle*   *an error*
> *a terrific idea* *an excellent meeting*

The is the definite article. It indicates that you are referring to a specific person, thing, or action.

> **Examples**   **Definite article "the"**

> *the presentation*
> *the centerpiece*
> *the instructions*
> *the new survey*

DO IT YOURSELF

In these sentences, fill in the article that is indicated. Does the sentence make sense afterward?

1. We need to take _____ hard look at this problem.
    (indefinite article)

2. Nora will be handling _____ PowerPoint presentation.
    (definite article)

3. _____ acupressure massage will be offered on our
    (indefinite article)   Monday night schedule.

4. We want to thank all those who contributed to _____
    beta testing of this program.   (definite article)

5. The visit to Hawk Mountain will be _____ exciting
    highlight of the park tour series.   (indefinite article)

Dangling Modifiers

If a **modifying phrase** that starts a sentence does not refer directly to the subject, it is called a dangling modifier. It can create confusion as to the real subject of the sentence.

Example A   Dangling modifier

After cleaning out the cabinet, the files looked much better.
　　　V　　　　　O　　　S　　　V

Example B   Dangling modifier

Before removing uniforms, the pockets should be emptied of their contents.
　　　V　　　　O　　　　S　　　　　V

Example C   Dangling modifier

While eating dinner, the car was stolen.
　　V　　　O　　S　　　V

In the first example, the reader begins by asking, Who cleaned out the cabinet? The *files* is the subject in the main part of the sentence. But *files* cannot clean out cabinets. The subject of the modifying phrase should be clarified to remove this confusion.

> *After we cleaned out the cabinet, the files looked much better.*

Alternatively, the modifier can be a passive form that highlights the object being discussed:

> *After the cabinet was cleaned, the files looked much better.*

In the second and third examples, the reader should not have to wonder how pockets can remove uniforms or whether cars eat dinner.

> *Before anyone removes their uniform, the pockets should be emptied of their contents.*

> *While we were eating dinner, the car was stolen.*

Here's how the sentence can be rewritten and improved using a passive phrase:

Examples   Passive-verb phrase

Before uniforms are removed, the pockets should be emptied of their contents.

While dinner was being eaten, the car was stolen.

To check whether the modifier is correct, turn the phrases around. Do they make sense?

> *The pockets should be emptied of their contents before uniforms are removed.*

> *The car was stolen while dinner was being eaten.*

Another way to clear up a dangling modifier is by changing the subject of the main part of the sentence. It should match the modifying phrase.

Examples **Subject of sentence modifies the phrase**

After cleaning out the cabinet, we agreed that the files looked much better.

> (Who cleaned out the closet? *We* did.)

Before removing uniforms, you must remember to empty your pockets of their contents.

> (Who is removing uniforms? *You* are.)

While eating dinner, they heard the car had been stolen.

> (Who was eating dinner? *They* were.)

Whatever way you choose to rewrite a sentence that contains a dangling modifier, be sure that both parts match. Either they have the same subject or they each have a clearly identified subject.

DO IT YOURSELF

Rewrite these sentences to remove the confusion created by dangling modifiers. For the first four, rewrite by adding the subject to the modifying phrase.

1. Debugging the system, his persistence was rewarded.

   _____

2. Bumping into the mail cart, my papers fell all over the floor.

   _____

3. Looking for safety violations, the trash had built up too much near the door.

   _____

4. Checking the campsite, the tree had blown down.

   _____

DO IT YOURSELF (CONTINUED)

These sentences also have dangling modifiers. This time, rewrite them by putting the subject directly after the modifying phrase.

5. While watching TV, the electricity went off.

    _____

6. Rereading the report, the diagrams are out of order.

    _____

7. After fixing the air conditioning, the office is much more comfortable.

    _____

8. Turning on the computer, the screen was completely blank.

    _____

Misplaced Modifiers

Misplaced modifiers can also lead to confusion. The way to avoid this is to keep the word or phrase that serves as the modifier as close as possible to the noun it modifies.

Here are some examples of sentences with misplaced modifiers. Notice how an unintended meaning can result when the modifier is separated from the noun.

Examples   Modifier separated from the noun

Jane and I saw the new desks going to lunch.

We did not notice the signs driving so fast.

Sam put his sandwich in the fridge that he would eat later.

Judy stored the document on the hard drive that she will delete later.

Reading these sentences, the reader might think *the desks went to lunch, the signs drove fast, Sam planned to eat the fridge later,* and *Judy will delete the hard drive.* The sentences can be clarified by placing the modifying phrases nearer to the nouns.

Examples   Modifier near the noun

While going to lunch, Jane and I saw the new desks.

Because we were driving so fast, we did not notice the signs.

Wanting to eat his sandwich later, Sam put it in the fridge.

Expecting to delete the document tomorrow, Judy stored it on the hard drive.

In the last two sentences, the modifying phrases at the end could be kept, as long as they are made clear.

Sam put his sandwich in the fridge, so he could eat it later.

Some one-word modifiers can change the meaning of the sentence depending on their placement. Be sure you put them in the right place to say what you really mean.

Example A   Placement of one-word modifiers

I just finished reading that book.

I finished reading just that book.

The first sentence indicates the subject, *I*, finished reading that book very recently. The second sentence indicates the subject, *I*, finished reading that book and no others.

Example B   Placement of one-word modifiers

Dr. Henderson will only observe the second-year students.

Dr. Henderson will observe only the second-year students.

The first sentence indicates that *Dr. Henderson* will only *do one thing*, which is to *observe*. The second sentence indicates that *Dr. Henderson* will *observe only one group*, the second-year students.

Example C   Placement of one-word modifiers

The editor caught almost fifteen errors.

The editor almost caught fifteen errors.

The first sentence indicates that almost *fifteen errors were caught*. But in the second sentence, *almost* modifies *caught*. This tells the reader, probably incorrectly, that the errors were *almost caught but were not*.

DO IT YOURSELF

Read each of these sentences. Then rewrite the sentence, changing or moving the modifying word or phrase to remove the unintended meaning. You may have to change a few words to make the phrase work in its new position. You may have to "make up" a subject for the sentence.

1. The appetizers were served to the guests on napkins.

_____

2. Andrew almost finished eight layouts for the new building design.

_____

3. I spoke to the woman down the street named Gladys.

_____

4. Rudy found his dog returning home from work.

_____

5. Please do not come into the office with a runny nose and a fever.

_____

6. The candle is on the fireplace mantle burning.

_____

7. Jeff ran around the track in a jogging suit.

_____

8. Susan saw her baby drying the laundry.

_____

9. My boss instructed me doing word processing.

_____

10. Madelyn turned the corner driving fast.

_____

NONSTANDARD USAGE

Some words and expressions are not an accepted form of standard English, even though they are used in casual conversation. **Nonstandard expressions** may be colorful, but they should be left out of writing unless they are directly quoted from someone's spoken words.

Here are examples of some common nonstandard forms and ways to write them in accepted standard English.

Double Negatives

In English, the negative form of a verb should be written only once in a sentence. **Double negatives** are fairly easy to identify and correct since they sound wrong when spoken aloud. Using double negatives, either when speaking or writing, is evidence of a poor grammar background.

Incorrect Example A   Double negative

I don't never want to see that behavior again.

Both *don't* and *never* are negative forms of a verb; therefore, they should not be used in the same sentence. Note how the double negative has been eliminated in the following three examples.

Correct Example A   Single negative, three options

I don't ever want to see that behavior again.

I don't want to see that behavior again.

I never want to see that behavior again.

Incorrect Example B   Confusing double negative

Nobody isn't looking forward to the new Star Wars movie.

Both *nobody* and *isn't* (the contraction for *is not*) are negative words. The sentence should be rewritten. Note how the confusing double negative has been eliminated in the following two examples.

Correct Example B   Single negative, clear double negative

Nobody is looking forward to the new Star Wars movie.

There isn't anyone looking forward to the new Star Wars movie.

DO IT YOURSELF

Rewrite the following sentences to remove the double negatives.

1. Don't you never serve me undercooked chicken again; it gave me food poisoning the last time.

   _____

   _____

2. Nobody wasn't responsible for the accident; it just happened.

   _____

   _____

Nonstandard Verb Forms

Some **nonstandard verbs** have entered our vocabulary. While some people use these words, most readers consider the person who writes nonstandard words to be uneducated.

Ain't

You may have been told "'Ain't' ain't a word." It is a word, but it is a nonstandard contraction for "am not," "is not" or "are not" (I ain't, he ain't). The standard (correct) contractions for the negative form of **to be**, in present tense, are:

I'm not	*(I am not)*
We're not	*(We are not)*
You're not	*(You are not)*
He's not, she's not	*(He is not, she is not)*
They're not	*(They are not)*

Incorrect Example A   Correct form of "to be"

They ain't coming back to the bargaining table.

Correct Examples A   Correct form of "to be"

They're not coming back to the bargaining table.

They are not coming back to the bargaining table.

Incorrect Examples B "Ain't" used instead of correct form of "to be"

We ain't ever going to work with anyone like Willard again.

Correct Examples B   "Ain't" used instead of correct form of "to be"

We're not ever going to work with anyone like Willard again.

We're never going to work with anyone like Willard again.

We are never going to work with anyone like Willard again.

Done, Be

Done and **be** are nonstandard ways of indicating verb tense. *Done* indicates the past perfect tense of the verb *to do* and should only be used to indicate an action already finished in the past.

Incorrect Example A   Incorrect use of "done"

Tabitha done a great job organizing the closed files.

Correct Example A   Correct use of "done"

Tabitha did a great job organizing the closed files.

Tabitha has done a great job organizing the closed files.

Incorrect Example B   Incorrect use of "done"

They done closed early for the holiday.

Correct Example B   Correct use of "done"

They closed early for the holiday.

They have closed early for the holiday.

The word *be* is sometimes used in nonstandard English to substitute for *is* or *will be*.

Incorrect Example A   "Be" used instead of "is" or "will be"

Kenny be coming in a few minutes.

Correct Example A   Correct use of "is" or "will be"

Kenny will be coming in a few minutes.

Incorrect Example B   "Be" used instead of "is" or "will be"

Aliya be the best nurse on the morning shift.

Correct Example B   Correct use of "is" or "will be"

Aliya is the best nurse on the morning shift.

Incorrect Example C "Be" used instead of "is" or "will be"

We be running out of disk space after this program is installed.

Correct Examples C   Correct use of "is" or "will be"

We will be running out of disk space after this program is installed.

We will run out of disk space after this program is installed.

Do It Yourself

Rewrite these sentences using the correct, standard verb forms.

1. They ain't going to be shipping that style after December.

   _____

   _____

2. Anthony ain't doing too well with the new equipment.

   _____

   _____

3. All the supervisors done showed up for the dedication of the new building.

   _____

   _____

4. Loni be our new assistant.

   _____

   _____

5. Jon and Rosita be saving for a down payment on a house.

   _____

   _____

Non-Agreeing Verb Usage

Writers make a variety of mistakes when using verbs. The verbs in these sentences **do not agree** with their subjects.

Incorrect Example A   Verb not in agreement with subject

He don't care about finishing on time.

He is a singular subject, but *don't*, a contraction for *do not*, is the verb form for first- and second-person (I or we).

Correct Example A   Verb in agreement with subject

He doesn't care about finishing on time.

Incorrect Example B   Verb not in agreement with subject

The chairs was missing from the conference room.

Chairs is a plural subject (more than one chair), but *was* is the verb form for a singular subject.

Correct Example B   Verb in agreement with subject

The chairs were missing from the conference room.

Incorrect Example C   Verb not in agreement with subject

The package come in yesterday morning.

In this case, the modifying phrase *yesterday morning* tells that the event happened in the past. The verb should reflect this.

Correct Example C   Verb in agreement with subject

The package came in yesterday morning.

Incorrect Example D   Verb not in agreement with subject

I seen it with my own eyes.

In standard English, *seen* is part of the past perfect tense of "to see," so it should only be used in that way (I had seen, he had seen).

Correct Example D   Verb in agreement with subject

I saw it with my own eyes.

I have seen it with my own eyes.

DO IT YOURSELF

Rewrite these sentences so that the verb forms correctly match the nouns they describe and are in the correct tense.

1. Bonita don't know when the new shipment is coming in.

   _____

   _____

2. They was planning to announce the program upgrade tomorrow, but now they have to wait.

   _____

   _____

3. Leo come in while we were discussing whether to take out the loan.

   _____

   _____

4. We just seen the plans for the new branch office.

   _____

   _____

5. The sales team leader come in late to the meeting.

   _____

   _____

6. Rachel done erased three paragraphs of the report she was writing on the computer.

   _____

   _____

7. Angel seen me with the birthday present I bought him.

   _____

   _____

8. Samantha were one of the fastest readers I ever seen.

   _____

   _____

Omitted Verbs

In another kind of nonstandard verb usage, verbs or parts of verb phrases are omitted.

Incorrect Example A   Omitted verb element

Where they disappear to so quickly? This sentence seems to describe an action that has happened in the past. Adding a word or two to the verb phrase will make it clearer.

Correct Example A   All parts of verb phrase included

Where did they disappear to so quickly?

Where have they disappeared to so quickly?

Incorrect Example B   Omitted verb element

What you mean, telling us we can't meet the delegates?

In the opening phrase, the verb *mean* cannot stand by itself. It needs another verb in order to be a proper question.

Correct Example B   All parts of verb phrase included

What do you mean, telling us we can't meet the delegates?

Incorrect Example C   Omitted verb element

Devon take the orientation tour tomorrow.

The modifier *tomorrow* tells us this sentence is speaking about the future, so the helping verb *will* is missing for the future tense.

Correct Example C   All parts of verb phrase included

Devon will take the orientation tour tomorrow.

Incorrect Example D

Margarita go to the meeting for me at 10 a.m.

The modifier *10 a.m.* tells that the meeting will be held later, so the helping verb *will* is missing for the future tense.

Correct Example D

Margarita will go to the meeting for me at 10 a.m.

DO IT YOURSELF

In these sentences, circle the standard verb form.

1. We (done/have done) that assignment already.

2. Marcos (be/is) eager for a job placement.

3. Briana (give/gave) me most of the materials already.

4. They (weren't/wasn't) the ones we were expecting.

5. Tom (doesn't/don't) seem as committed to the project now.

6. They (be/will be) finished with the inventory by next Tuesday.

7. They (go/went) back home before we got here.

Rewrite these sentences, changing the verbs to standard usage. You may be able to think of more than one possible version; just write one.

8. Arthur done completed all his exercises.

   _____

9. We won't never make that mistake again.

   _____

10. The minister be done with the sermon.

    _____

11. Answering machines wasn't the best way to get clients' messages.

    _____

12. Medical assisting ain't a easy job.

    _____

13. Weren't them the same reports I turned in before?

    _____

14. Who don't know how to get to the customer's office?

    _____

15. I be out of here in a few minutes.

    _____

LINKING IDEAS

Many sentences express more than one idea. The ideas are written as one sentence because they are related. Certain words are used to **link the ideas** and show how they are related.

Coordinating Conjunctions

Some simple words can be placed between sentence clauses containing separate ideas. These words, called *coordinating conjunctions*, help to show the relationship between the ideas. Some of the most common coordinating conjunctions include these:

and	for
but	nor
or	so
yet	

Example A Coordinating conjunctions

I heard back from the Watsons, **and** *they said they want to hire us.*

The meeting is scheduled for 9 a.m., **but** *I want to be a few minutes early.*

In the first sentence, *and* shows a simple relationship between two ideas: *hearing back from the Watsons* and *they want to* hire us. A comma is used before the coordinating conjunction, *and.*

In the second sentence, *but* links two ideas that are related in a different way: *the meeting is scheduled for 9 a.m.,* but (even so) *I want to be a few minutes early.* A comma is placed before the coordinating conjunction, *but.*

These sentences are made up of two independent ideas (independent clauses). Each of them could be a sentence by itself.

Example B Ideas in separate sentences without conjunctions

I heard back from the Watsons. They said they want to hire us.

The meeting is scheduled for 9 a.m. I want to be a few minutes early.

In Example B, the independent clause from Example A has been written as a separate sentence. Therefore, the two phrases do not need to be connected by a coordinating conjunction.

Both Examples A and B are correct, and you may use your personal preference when you write sentences with independent clauses.

Starting Sentences with Conjunctions

Some grammar rules do change. In the past, it was considered unacceptable to start a sentence with a coordinating conjunction. But now, placing a coordinating conjunction at the beginning of a sentence is an accepted and effective way to emphasize an idea:

> **Example C**   **Coordinating conjunctions at the beginning of a sentence**

> We expected many complaints about the change in the company's logo. But the response was extremely positive.

> Hopes were high for Big Kahuna's new album. And they have delivered.

DO IT YOURSELF

In these sentences, circle the coordinating conjunction that makes the most sense. In a few cases, more than one might work. You may circle more than one.

1. We met with the investors, (and/but/so) they will not get back to us till Friday.

2. Rainfall was high all month, (and/so/yet) hotel occupancy rates remained strong.

3. Jesse missed the server renewal deadline, (but/and/so) we may lose our domain name.

4. The sea surface temperatures have been correlated, (for/and/nor) they are in the normal range.

5. We arrived at closing time, (and/so/but) they let us in anyway.

6. The new web design has been uploaded,(so/yet/for) you can show it to the client.

7. I've never tried this recipe, (and/but/so) it looks really good.

8. My work load has increased (and/but/so) things should lighten up soon.

Subordinating Conjunctions

In some sentences, the main idea is supported by another phrase that cannot stand on its own, even though the phrase adds information. That phrase is called a *dependent clause* or a *subordinate clause*. It is linked to the main idea with a word or phrase called a **subordinating conjunction**.

> ### Example A
>
> *They can't count the votes **until** all the polling places close.*
>
> ***When** we look back on this, we'll laugh.*
>
> ***Although** I am prepared to give the speech, I would prefer that someone else made the presentation.*
>
> *I will be more comfortable giving this invoice to the client **if** you will proofread it.*

In the first sentence, the subordinating conjunction *until* tells something that must happen to make the main idea possible (counting the votes). However, *until all the precincts come in* is not a complete idea on its own. It depends on the rest of the sentence in order to make sense.

In the second sentence, the subordinating conjunction *when* introduces information about the timing of the main idea, *we'll laugh*. However, *When we look back on this* cannot stand on its own as a sentence; it just supports the main sentence.

The third sentence uses the subordinating conjunction *although* to introduce a possibility (*Although I am prepared to give the speech*), but the rest of the sentence is required in order to make a complete thought (*I would prefer that someone else made the presentation*).

The fourth sentence uses the subordinating conjunction *if* to introduce a possible action (*if you will proofread*) that may cause a result (*I will be more comfortable*).

Do you notice another difference between the four sample sentences? There is no comma used when the subordinate clause comes after the main idea. But when the subordinate clause comes first, a comma must separate it from the main part of the sentence.

Common Subordinating Conjunctions

after	*before*	*although*	*if*	*except*
as, as if	*provided that*	*because*	*since*	
that	*when*	*though*	*whenever*	
unless	*while*	*about*	*in*	

Do It Yourself

In these sentences, choose a subordinating conjunction from the list below that makes sense, and fill it in. All the subordinating conjunctions should have been used at least once when you are done.

although	unless
as	until
before	whenever
if	whether
that	while

1. We can't expect to interest potential investors _____ the prototype is ready.

2. The train left the platform _____ I ran down the stairs.

3. The coastline will be at risk _____ the hurricane comes any closer.

4. _____ we want to grow the business, we can't hire any more employees now.

5. She said yes _____ Gary finished asking the question.

6. I need to know _____ you want the logo to appear in black and white or color.

7. _____ the shipment arrives tonight, the team won't finish in time.

8. Troy advises signing a flexible lease _____ we look for a building of our own.

9. These microbial cultures will give information on the bay's ecology _____ we can't get anywhere else.

10. _____ I have a sales committee presentation, I can't sleep the night before.

11. _____ I can prepare the final draft, I need some additional statistics.

12. The project cannot go forward _____ I receive some help.

Semicolons and Conjunctive Adverbs

Semicolons can be used to link two related independent ideas into one sentence. If you use a semicolon, each part of the sentence must be able to stand on its own.

Example A

A semicolon can link two parts of a sentence; each part must be a complete idea.

Ms. Lyons is a fine administrator; I urge you to consider her application favorably.

I appreciate your input on this matter; we will make a decision soon.

Conjunctive adverbs are a group of words that can be added after the semicolon. These words help to show the relationship between the two ideas. Some of these words are:

accordingly	*moreover*
besides	*nevertheless*
consequently	*otherwise*
for example	*still*
however	*therefore*
instead	*thus*

Whenever such a word is used after a semicolon, it must be followed by a comma.

Example B

*Our third-quarter sales predictions proved to be too high; **consequently**, we must revise the current manufacturing schedule.*

*Matt did not hire the candidate we expected; **instead**, he asked human resources to reopen the search.*

*Most nurses enjoy the in-service programs; **besides**, it offers a good chance to catch up with colleagues.*

In the first sentence, *consequently* tells the reader that the second idea is a consequence of the first idea.

In the second sentence, *instead* emphasizes that the second idea was not the one originally expected.

In the third sentence, *besides* tells the reader something additional follows that supports the first idea.

DO IT YOURSELF

Rewrite these pairs of sentences, connecting them with a semicolon.

HINT: Don't forget to change the first letter of the second sentence to lowercase.

1. Many customers have requested this color. We will be adding it to the line soon.

   _____

   _____

2. The soybean crop forecast was low last year. We expect a higher yield again this year.

   _____

   _____

3. Fares to Istanbul are at their lowest in years. Savvy travelers will take advantage of this.

   _____

   _____

Rewrite the following pairs of sentences using a semicolon followed by one of the following conjunctive adverbs. You may feel that more than one fits; just choose one.

accordingly	still	moreover	consequently
however	besides	therefore	otherwise

HINT: Don't forget to add a comma after the word you include.

4. Marc has not covered the entire territory yet. I believe he can do the job.

   _____

   _____

5. The new guidelines have arrived. All offices should be in compliance by the end of the month.

   _____

   _____

6. Response to the new account promotion has been strong. It will be continued for now.

   _____

   _____

Correlative Conjunctions

Correlative conjunctions always come in pairs. They link together two closely related parts of a sentence. Because they are being closely compared, the two parts should always be in the same form.

Here are some correlative conjunctions. Look for more on keeping these elements parallel in the next chapter.

both/and
not only/but also
neither/nor
either/or

Example A   Both/and

Sales of both the top-end and the lower-priced speakers have been steady.

Example B   Not only/but also

Not only did the painters finish early, but they also left the rooms nice and clean.

Example C   Neither/nor

Neither Emily nor her assistant has any idea where the meeting will be held.

Example D   Either/or

Either we train that puppy properly, or we find another home for it.

Misused Conjunctions

The common conjunctions *where* and *while* are often misused. *Where* should only be used to indicate place. *While* means *at the same time*, but can also mean *although*. Using a comma when *while* replaces *although* helps keep things clear.

Incorrect Examples   Where/when

I just heard where interest rates are going up.

Casual-dress Friday is where everyone wears jeans.

Correct Examples   Where/when

I just heard that interest rates are going up.

Casual-dress Friday is when everyone wears jeans.

Correct Examples   While

Beth will take the patient history while Gina preps the room.

I believe these pipes should be replaced, while Frank disagrees.

DO IT YOURSELF

In these sentences, choose the correct correlative conjunction needed in each sentence. When you are done, all the correlative conjunctions should have been used once.

> both/and
> not only/but also
> neither/nor
> either/or

1. _____ you'll go _____ I'll go, but someone must deliver the contract before 2 p.m. on Friday.

2. _____ will sales go down, _____ some staff will have to be cut if we lose the construction contract for the new government office building.

3. _____ Enrique _____ I have been assigned to the marketing team.

4. _____ Cassandra _____ Tim had any warning that customers were complaining.

Using Where and While: Rewrite the first two sentences, replacing *where* with a word that correctly conveys the meaning. Rewrite the last two sentences to correctly convey the meaning. **HINT:** Remember, the use of a comma before *while* changes its meaning: do you want it to mean *although or at the same time?*

5. The fourth Thursday of each month is where I get to report on the progress we've made in the development of the new software.

   _____

   _____

6. We heard a rumor where the job has been put on hold.

   _____

   _____

7. The overhead just keeps going up and up while Margaret says it doesn't matter.

   _____

   _____

8. This step requires you to rotate the dial while listening carefully for clicks.

   _____

   _____

PARALLELISM

Parallelism in grammar means that the different elements of writing match, or agree. You have already learned that verbs must agree with nouns and that modifiers must agree with whatever they modify.

The following sections provide some guidelines to follow for keeping all elements of a sentence parallel.

Parallel Structure

Similar elements of a sentence should be expressed in the same form. If, for example, you use several verbs, the tenses of all verbs used should match. If an element is introduced by an article (and, the, or), the article should be the same each time.

Incorrect Example A   Non-parallel verbs

A police officer pledges to preserve, to protect, and setting a good example.

In this sentence, the first two verbs are expressed in the infinitive (*to preserve, to protect*) while the third is in the present progressive (*setting*).

Correct Example A   All verbs parallel

*A police officer pledges **to preserve, to protect, and to set** a good example.*

Incorrect Example B   Non-parallel nouns

This job takes guts, humor, and being persistent.

In this sentence, three objects are listed to tell what the job takes. The first two are straightforward nouns, but the last is a gerund, made from the verb "to be."

Correct Example B   All nouns parallel

*This job **takes guts, humor and persistence.***

Incorrect Example C   Non-parallel adjectives

The copier was old, dusty, and looking run-down.

In this sentence, the third adjective should match the first form of the first two.

Correct Example C   Parallel adjectives

*The copier was **old, dusty, and run-down.***

Parallelism with the Conjunctions *and* and *or*

If a sentence has two independent clauses linked by the coordinating conjunctions *and*, *or*, or *but*, each clause must be phrased in a parallel form. Use a comma between independent clauses linked by coordinating conjunctions.

Incorrect Example A　Non-parallel elements linked by *or*

Ozzie suggests putting the sale rack by the door, or move it close to the register.

This sentence describes two suggestions by Ozzie. Both are clauses starting with a verb: *putting* and *move*. The two verbs need to be in the same tense.

Correct Example A　Parallel clauses linked by *or*

*Ozzie suggests **putting** the sale rack by the door **or moving** it close to the register.*

*Ozzie suggests that we **put** the sale rack by the door or **move** it close to the register.*

Incorrect Example B　Non-parallel elements linked by *and*

Speaking well and a neat appearance are both important.

This sentence has two subjects. The first is a noun phrase in the form of a gerund (an "ing" word): *speaking well*. The second should be phrased in the same way:

Correct Example B　Parallel elements linked by *and*

***Speaking** well and **having** a neat appearance are both important.*

Parallelism with Correlative Conjunctions

In the last chapter you learned about linking similar elements through correlative conjunctions, such as *both...and*, *either...or*, and *neither...nor*.

When using these paired conjunctions, you must remember to make exactly parallel the parts that follow the conjunctions.

Incorrect Example A　Correlative conjunctions

You must either fix the lock, or you have to replace it.

In this sentence, the elements following the words "either" and "or" are not parallel. Since the first element begins with the active verb *fix*, the second element shouldn't start with a "to be" verb.

Correct Example A   Correlative conjunctions

*You must either **fix** the lock or **replace** it.*

Incorrect Example B   Correlative conjunctions

The impact was not only positive, but it also lasted a long time.

Here the two elements that follow "not only" and "but "are not parallel. The first element to be compared, *positive*, is an adjective, while the second element is an entire independent idea.

Correct Example B   Correlative conjunctions

*The impact was **not only** positive **but also** long-lasting.*

DO IT YOURSELF

Find the two correlative conjunctions in each of these sentences. Then rewrite each one so the elements following the conjunctions are parallel. Even if both elements already start with a verb, the verb forms must match exactly. Use commas correctly.

1. We need both to increase productivity and maintain employee morale.

   _____

   _____

2. Medication is able not only to minimize reflux symptoms, but can accomplish this with only mild side effects.

   _____

   _____

3. Either I return the dress or have to get new shoes.

   _____

   _____

4. The nursing students will be responsible both for monitoring supplies and to check patients' vital signs.

   _____

   _____

DO IT YOURSELF

In these sentences, find the parallel elements. In each case, the two elements are phrased slightly differently. Rewrite one of the elements so both are truly parallel. Use commas correctly.

1. Our fitness program includes help with weight management, if you have a medical condition, and stress management.

   _____

   _____

2. A police officer is pledged to preserve, to protect and never giving up till the crime is solved.

   _____

   _____

3. You will be assisting in the marshland remediation project and help out on the French Creek cleanup as well.

   _____

   _____

4. The satellite sensors are equipped to detect mineral, gas, or the oil deposits in this area.

   _____

   _____

5. Opening a safe lock requires knowing how to drill, take impressions, and manipulating the lock mechanism.

   _____

   _____

6. Both our goals and how we design the methodology will contribute to our success.

   _____

   _____

7. We accept payments by the year or monthly.

   _____

   _____

SENTENCE VARIETY: Keeping Your Writing Lively

Career writing should be engaging as well as informative. Each sentence should motivate the reader to continue. Look at these examples of dull and lively writing.

Example A   Dull

John was short. He was not much over five feet tall. He didn't talk very much but worked very hard. He drew unusual pictures and listened to strange music. The other people in the office thought he was weird. Most people liked him, though.

Example A   Lively

John, a quiet man barely five feet tall, was known around the office as one of its hardest workers. Perhaps he said little because he was always wearing earphones and listening to music that few of his co-workers had ever heard. Despite his strange musical tastes and the odd doodles he scribbled on his notepad, nearly everyone liked him.

Example B   Dull

Something was wrong with the copy machine. It was making strange noises. It wouldn't print anything out. Then the man from the repair company came and did something to it. We are worried because it still makes some funny noises. At least it works now.

Example B   Lively

First, our copy machine made alarming noises; then it just died. We were in a tizzy because we couldn't print out anything. Fortunately, the repair man came and saved the day. Though it still makes grinding sounds, at least it turns out copies. We're keeping our fingers crossed.

In Dull Example A, each sentence starts in the same way. All are short and choppy. Look individually at three short sentences in Dull Example A.

John was short. He was not much over five feet tall. He didn't talk very much but worked very hard.

By combining the three short sentences and adding a few more words, a new, more interesting, lively sentence can be formed. Note how easily and logically the sentence flows after being rewritten.

John, a quiet man barely five feet tall, was known around the office as one of its hardest workers.

In Dull Example B, the sentence structure has a bit more variety, but it is still choppy and uninteresting.

> *Then the man from the repair company came and did something to it. We are worried because it still makes some funny noises. At least it works now.*

Adding dynamic phrases can turn a routine event into a little story. See how using people's reactions in this example makes it more dramatic.

> *Fortunately, the repair man came and saved the day. It still makes grinding sounds, but at least it turns out copies. We're keeping our fingers crossed.*

Adding Variety to Sentence Structures

To add "punch" to sentences, change their structure. You can do this in two simple ways: (1) by using introductory words, phrases, and clauses or (2) by using a combination of active and passive verbs.

Introductory Words, Phrases, and Clauses

Introductory words or short phrases help lead the reader into a sentence by giving the sentence more life or adding a change of pace. All types of words can be used to set the tone or provide the sense that something is about to happen.

However	*Although*
To begin with	*In addition to*
First	*Second*
Quietly	*Without a sound*
Finally	*Last*
When	*If*
Early in the morning	*At daybreak*

Longer introductory clauses are complete thoughts that modify the main thought. Often, long introductory clauses can stand alone as independent sentences if the introductory word is removed. However, moving a clause to the beginning of another sentence can add variety to both the language and the structure of the sentence.

Notice how introductory phrases and clauses added to the reading interest in Lively Examples A and B on the previous page and above.

> *Despite his strange musical tastes and the odd doodles he scribbled on his notepad, nearly everyone liked him.*

> *Though it still makes grinding sounds, at least it turns out copies.*

DO IT YOURSELF

Rewrite the dull sentences in the two paragraphs below by adding an introductory word, phrase, or clause.

HINT: You may find that you can use part of one sentence to introduce another sentence.

Paragraph 1: The interview went fast. I was anxious about it. The interviewer seemed interested in me. She told me to come back on Tuesday. Was I relieved.

_____

_____

_____

_____

_____

_____

_____

_____

_____

Paragraph 2: Our team leader had to go home early. He was sick. We didn't have enough to do. We sat around feeling uncomfortable. Some of us played games. Then it was time to go home.

_____

_____

_____

_____

_____

_____

_____

_____

_____

Active and Passive Verbs

Active verbs, generally, are stronger than passive verbs. However, switching between active and passive verbs can make your writing more interesting.

Active	Passive
Pete knew him	*He was known to Pete*
Glenda fixed the chair	*The chair was fixed by Glenda*
Shakespeare wrote **Hamlet**	**Hamlet** *was written by Shakespeare*

Example   Active verbs without variety

Who took my eraser? I kept it in a secret place. Only Alice *knew* about it.

Example   Passive verb used for variety

Who took my eraser? I kept it in a secret place, *known* only to Alice.

DO IT YOURSELF

In the following paragraph, change one of the sentences to the passive voice for variety.

HINT: Remember, sometimes it helps to combine sentences or parts of sentences.

We came in late. Our boss yelled at us. I can't blame her for being mad at us. The subway made us late. It never comes on time.

_____

_____

_____

_____

_____

_____

_____

Use a Broad Vocabulary

Finding a variety of different words that mean the same thing can improve your writing greatly (even if it means taking extra time to think of the exact words you want to use).

Basic word	Alternate words
big	large, massive, enormous, gargantuan
little	small, tiny, miniscule, microscopic
building	structure, edifice, skyscraper
corner	nook, cranny, angle
happy	delighted, joyous, wonderstruck
slowly	creepingly, at a snail's pace
interesting	entertaining, dramatic, breathtaking
important	historic, stupendous, earthshaking
remote	at the end of a long road, hidden behind trees
attractive	exquisite, beautiful, gorgeous

Using lively words in place of dull ones can make your writing much more interesting. Sometimes moving parts of the sentence around leaves room to say things in a more interesting way.

Example   Dull Vocabulary

I hate this pen. I'm going to buy a new pen that writes. Then my reports won't look so bad, and the boss won't complain so much.

Example   Lively Vocabulary

I despise this pen. I'm going to buy a ballpoint that flows across the paper. Then my handwritten notes will look nicer, and the boss will stop telling me he can't read them.

Example   Dull Vocabulary

The day is too long. I want to go home and get started on my hobby. I make clay statues, though many of them don't look like anything you've ever seen.

Example   Lively Vocabulary

I'm itching for work to be over so I can roll up my sleeves in my sculpture studio. My clay work is abstract. Its forms come from inside my head and don't reflect the real world.

DO IT YOURSELF

Rewrite the paragraph below using more interesting words to replace the dull or repeated ones.

Last night it rained a whole lot. The rain came down very fast and covered everything. It flooded our street; and when I came in to work, I found that it had flooded the office too. It was a mess! The water was gone by afternoon, but the messy paper was stuck to the floor. I hope it doesn't rain like that again soon.

_____

_____

_____

_____

_____

_____

_____

Keep a Clear Train of Thought

When writing, try to keep a clear line of thought that carries your reader along with you. Don't jump back and forth between different ideas or descriptions.

Example

Here is a poorly written report about a delivery problem. Notice how it jumps back and forth between thoughts.

This morning we didn't have enough copy paper and had to get more from the people down the hall in accounting. That has happened a lot lately. The people who are supposed to deliver it either forget or they are late. We have called them, but it doesn't seem to make any difference. We don't have enough pencils and pens either, but the water cooler is okay.

Some of the information in this report is useful and vital, but some of it isn't. The report does not flow clearly or logically.

Here are some of the problems with the report:

What the report says	Difficulty or confusion
"had to get more from the people down the hall in accounting"	This is not part of the problem being described.
"This has happened a lot lately."	How often?
"The people who are supposed to deliver it"	Who are they? The supplier? The office delivery persons? Name of company?
"We have called them"	To whom did you talk? What did this person say?
"We don't have enough pencils and pens either."	Is there an overall problem with all the office supplies?
"but the water cooler is OK"	This has nothing to do with what the report is discussing.

To make the situation you are describing clear in your reader's mind, you need to include all the details that are important to the problem or that make the situation special. Leave out the ones that have nothing to do with the real problem.

Here is one way the report could be rewritten, with the necessary information added and unimportant details dropped.

> *For the third time this month, we have run out of copy paper. According to Miss Hazleton, the secretary at Gigantic Paper, Inc., the problem is with the delivery firm, Overnight Supplies. Our calls to Overnight have had little effect. Though the copy paper situation is the most pressing, we have had general difficulties with Overnight deliveries being late or cancelled without explanation.*

The best writing combines all the aspects of "lively writing" that have been covered in this section.

- Variety of sentence structure

- A broad vocabulary

- Clear, logical order to your line of thought

DO IT YOURSELF

Here is a descriptive paragraph that needs some work. Rewrite it with more flair by using sentence variety, interesting words, and a smooth flow of language.

The office walls need new paint. They are cracked and scarred. The color is old and dirty. It is covered with fingerprints. Some of us would like to hang pictures. We think photographs would look nice, or flowers. Light blue would look nice, or maybe a sort of cream color. One of those Van Gogh paintings might work too. Maybe we could use different colors on different walls. You may not think that is a good idea. Nobody knows what you, our bosses, think about this. That is why we are writing this report to you. We are not trying to be difficult, but we think it is time for a change.

_____

_____

_____

_____

_____

_____

_____

_____

_____

_____

_____

_____

_____

_____

_____

_____

PUNCTUATION

It takes more than a string of words to make interesting and readable writing. You also need punctuation to help the reader see how the words work together. Without punctuation, ideas and phrases become a confusing jumble. Consider the following examples of correct and incorrect punctuation.

Incorrect Example A   Sentences strung together without punctuation

Even with extra time schedules fell behind the office was not able to function properly for at least half a day we had nothing to do.

Correct Example A   Same sentences, properly punctuated

Even with extra time, schedules fell behind. The office was not able to function properly. For at least half a day, we had nothing to do.

Incorrect Example B   A confusingly punctuated sentence

Lets all go, down to the, laundromat; where we can wash our clothes and, talk about the weather?

Correct Example B   The same sentence, properly punctuated

Let's all go down to the laundromat, where we can wash our clothes and talk about the weather.

Incorrect Example C   Incorrect meaning caused by improper punctuation

Who told the supervisor?

Correct Example C   The same sentence, properly punctuated

Who told, the supervisor?

In Incorrect Example A, you can't immediately tell whether *time* goes with *schedules* or if the *schedules fell behind the office.*

In Incorrect Example B, the commas interfere with the reading, rather than help it. Also, the question mark does not belong at the end of the sentence, as the sentence is not a question.

In Incorrect Example C, you are led to believe that the supervisor was told something, when, in fact, the supervisor may have been the person who told. Incorrect Example C is a perfectly correct sentence; however, because of improper punctuation, it does not deliver the message the reader intended.

Punctuation provides a type of road map. It tells the reader where a sentence is going and where to stop along the way.

Basic Rules of Punctuation

For everyday writing, here are some of the most common rules of punctuation. A few more complex rules will be covered at the end of this section.

Punctuation mark	Basic use
Question mark (?)	Ends a sentence that asks a question.
	How can Priscilla not like raspberries?
Period (.)	Ends most sentences that are not questions. Also used after an abbreviation.
	She thinks raspberries taste horrible.
	Oct. is the abbreviation for October.
Comma (,)	Separates similar items in a string.
	Raspberries have hard seeds, juice that stains, and a funny taste.
Semicolon (;)	Separates independent parts of a sentence.
	I disagree; I like raspberries.
Colon (:)	Sets off a new thought, example, or explanation. Introduces a classification.
	Here's what I think: You're wrong.
	The children were divided into four age groups: 5-7, 8-10, 11-13, and 14-16.
Apostrophe (')	Shows who or what something belongs to. Also marks letters left out in contractions.
	That is Priscilla's problem.
	That decision doesn't surprise me.
Exclamation mark (!)	Ends a sentence that makes an especially strong statement. Also used after a word inserted to show surprise or other strong emotion.
	Leave this office right now!
	Oh! I didn't realize you like raspberries so much.

DO IT YOURSELF

Use the rules on the previous pages to correct punctuation errors in these sentences.

1. The room was full of people dogs and cats?

   _____

2. Dorians boss isnt in today, so shes taking the day off.

   _____

3. I wish Dean wouldnt twiddle his thumbs so much because it bothers me.

   _____

4. Duff likes to spend time on his hobbies playing basketball riding his skateboard, and listening to music.

   _____

5. Petra writes clearly it shows in the way she uses correct punctuation.

   _____

6. Hanks tie looks crooked to me

   _____

7. The report Ari turned in lacked descriptions details and classifications.

   _____

8. You told me you were going to meet the proposal deadline the report was late. I'm angry.

   _____

9. Why arent you coming with me to the meeting.

   _____

10. February is the month for the Presidents Day vacation.

    _____

More Complex Rules of Punctuation: Commas and Apostrophes

Commas and apostrophes cause the most difficulty in punctuation because they can be used in several different ways. Consider the following example:

Example

*Before entering the room, Ray helped adjust his **wife**'s hat, but neither of them noticed that her hem was torn. Ray failed to see, as well, that his shoes, socks, and pants **didn't** match. They made a strange couple at the **Jones**'s house party, where all the other guests were properly dressed.*

The comma and the apostrophe have been used in several different ways in this example, governed by different rules of usage. Review the following for correct usage.

Important Rules for Commas

The comma is the most versatile punctuation mark; therefore, it has the widest range of rules for use. The following are some of the most important.

Example A   Introductory phrases

Rule: Commas are used after most introductory phrases, except single words or very short phrases, and after dependent clauses in sentences.

Before you mail a letter, be sure to put a stamp on it. Tomorrow you will be glad that you did.

Example B   Nonessential words and phrases

Rule: Commas are used to set off words and short phrases that are not essential to the meaning of the sentence.

You might be tempted, I think, to leave out a comma. I would not do that, however, if I were you.

Example C   Items in a series

Rule: Commas are used to separate all the items from each other in a series.

I brought home a bag of bananas, oranges, tangerines, and other good things to eat.

DO IT YOURSELF

Use the rules in the previous section to correct the use of commas in these sentences.

1. Whatever you plan to do make sure you come home early.

   _____

   _____

2. Please give me the file with the notes on Mrs. D'amico Mr. Fegal Ms. Ramblen and the other flu patients.

   _____

   _____

3. What happens next in my opinion is irrelevant.

   _____

   _____

Example D   Independent clauses

Rule: Commas are used to separate two long, independent parts of a compound sentence. A comma is not needed when the two parts are short and fit naturally together.

The medical article is too technical for me to read tonight, and I am too tired to keep trying. The pages are short but they are dense.

Example E   Explaining a word or clause

Rule: Commas set off parts of a sentence that explain a word, clause, or phrase or tell about it in more detail.

I brought home my paycheck, which included a raise.

Marcia is delighted by the range of choices for her desk, such as the color, the size, and the number of drawers.

I read the latest report, an enlightening description of the company's future plans.

DO IT YOURSELF

Use the previous two rules to correct the use of commas in these sentences.

1. I hardly care about replacing the lamp but I think I need a new coatrack.

    _____

    _____

2. She is happy, and she smiles a lot.

    _____

    _____

3. The home fries the best part of a hearty breakfast were cooked perfectly.

    _____

    _____

Example F   Different items in different series

Rule: When talking about different items in different series, use a semicolon to separate the items of the main series.

The things we need to order are new wastebaskets; a desk chair for Sigmund; and office supplies such as paper clips, pens, and pencils.

Example G   Natural pauses

Rule: It is sometimes helpful to use a comma to indicate a natural pause that would come if you were reading or speaking the sentence. This is not a hard-and-fast rule.

A chronological resume highlights your work, starting with your current job.

Whatever is, is right.

DO IT YOURSELF

Use all of the previous comma rules to correct these sentences.

1. Strange as it may seem we often have a meeting a seminar and a report scheduled for the same time.

   _____

   _____

2. I like Carmen because she is cheerful likes dogs cats and lizards and always has something nice to say.

   _____

   _____

3. It is strange to find right here in the middle of this sentence an extra phrase.

   _____

   _____

4. Take my word for it but don't do anything until your supervisor agrees.

   _____

   _____

5. Lars didn't know what to do next although he had brought his work sheet with him.

   _____

   _____

6. When you think about it adding commas does not take long and it makes your sentences more coherent tidy and even clever.

   _____

   _____

7. Wonderful news Juan is coming home soon.

   _____

   _____

Important Rules for Apostrophes

Apostrophes can cause confusion because they are used in different ways.

Example 1

Most of the time, Cal's desk was clean, but today it wasn't.

The apostrophe in *Cal's* shows that the desk belongs to Cal. In *wasn't*, the apostrophe shows that the letter *o* has been left out of the contraction for *was not*.

Example 2

It's a good idea to remember that the cat would rather not have its back scratched.

The first *it's* is a contraction of *it is*. The apostrophe replaces a letter that is left out when two words are joined. The second *its* is the possessive pronoun, which does not use an apostrophe. *Its* shows that the *back* belongs to (or is possessed by) the cat.

Here are some examples and rules for the use of apostrophes. Some of these were covered earlier in this section.

Example A   Singular possessive nouns

Rule: Single possessive nouns require an apostrophe plus the letter *s*, even if the noun ends in *s*.

*If you press down too hard, you will break the **pencil's** point. Failure is **success's** opposite.*

Example B   Plural possessive nouns ending in s

Rule: Plural possessive nouns that end in *s* take an apostrophe without an extra letter *s*.

*Beware of the **roses'** thorns.*

Example C   Plural possessive nouns not ending in s

Rule: Plural possessive nouns that do not end in *s* take *'s*.

*Do not sneak off with the **children's** candy.*

Example D   Possessive pronouns

Rule: Most possessive pronouns do not take an apostrophe.

*He found **his** missing false teeth.*

*That green pack of cards is **ours**.*

Example E   Plural of numbers

Rule: Do not use an apostrophe when writing the plural of numbers.

*Aunt Nellie was vigorous well into her **90s**.*

*Natasha was delighted to find **10s** and **20s** in her wallet.*

Example F   Plural of proper name

Rule: To form the plural of most proper names, add *s* without an apostrophe. If the name ends in *s*, add *es*.

*We should invite the McDonald**s** and the Jones**es** to the office party.*

Example G   Plural of hyphenated phrase

Rule: An apostrophe and *s* are added to the last word in a hyphenated phrase to form the plural.

*Never contradict the editor-in-chief**'s** opinion.*

Example H   Using "of" phrase to avoid apostrophe

Rule: When use of an apostrophe might lead to a clumsy or confusing structure, use an *of* phrase to show the possessive. (Note: This is not a hard-and-fast rule.)

*I don't like the expression on the face **of** the man in the back row.*

Example I   Missing letters in contractions

Rule: Apostrophes take the place of missing letters in contractions.

*I **can't** tell you the capital of Uzbekistan right now, but **I'll** think of it soon.*

(Note: Avoid confusing contractions and possessive pronouns that sound alike. Here are a few examples:)

Contraction (apostrophe)	Possessive pronoun (no apostrophe)
it's	*its*
they're	*their*
there's	*theirs*
who's	*whose*
you're	*your*
he's	*his*

Do It Yourself

Add (or remove) apostrophes to correct the following sentences. Remember to add *s* where required and to write the correct contraction or possessive pronoun form.

1. I think the mistake is Neds, but Im not really sure who's it is.

   _____

   _____

2. Their better off for knowing that bees's stings can cause shock.

   _____

   _____

3. Its tiresome to enter columns of 30's and 40's all day.

   _____

   _____

4. Time loses it's meaning when your working hard.

   _____

   _____

5. I think thats the boss' daughter, and she has everyones attention.

   _____

   _____

6. The reports due tomorrow, and Im not close to being finished.

   _____

   _____

7. Dont disregard your brother's in-law advice, because he was told about the deal by the Cavali's, who are the owners.

   _____

   _____

CAPITAL LETTERS

Capital letters make words stand out, but they must be used carefully. Capitalization is fairly simple to learn because it generally follows simple, logical rules. Review the following rules and examples. This is one area in which it is especially valuable to check out newspapers and magazine articles for guidance. Review each example of a rule.

Example A   **First word of a sentence**

Every job requires some writing skill.

Example B   **Names of people**

Elvis Presley and Elmer Fudd are both famous, but one is a fictitious character.

Example C   **Names of organizations and places**

The home office of State Street Bank is located in Boston, Massachusetts.

Example D   **The pronoun I**

Pilar and I both had interviews with the same company yesterday.

Example E   **A person's title when used with the name**

Mr. Bricker was a friend of President Eisenhower.

Example F   **Initials**

For the report, I read a book by H. G. Wells.

Example G   **Adjective formed from a proper name**

Our company president's background is Eastern European.

Example H   **Months, days of the week**

Solomon's birthday is Tuesday, June 4.

Example I   **Words used as names or part of a name**

My Aunt Reba is a marketing director.

Example J   **Specific periods and events of history**

The Renaissance and the Industrial Revolution helped shape the modern world.

Example K   The first letter of a compass direction when it
                 designates an actual place, but not when it simply
                 points in a direction

*I grew up in the **North** but often head south for vacations.*

Example L   The first letter of important words in the title of a
                 book, magazine, poem, or similar work

The title of the article was "Ten Ways to Succeed at Work."

Example M   Historical documents

*The **U.S. Constitution** and the **Magna Carta** are important pieces of
history.*

Example N   Names of languages, races, nationalities, and
                 religions

Americans** with an **Irish** background frequently are **Catholic.

Example O   Acronyms

***CEO** stands for Chief Executive Officer of an organization.*

DO IT YOURSELF

Place capital letters in the following sentences according to the rules
just presented.

1. personally, I prefer to visit alabama rather than mississippi.

    _____

    _____

2. on friday we loaded the truck before driving to detroit.

    _____

    _____

3. I heard about mr. Stein's daughter, erika, but I've never met her.

    _____

    _____

Do It Yourself (CONTINUED)

4. Don't you think col. Horky has a fascinating hungarian accent?

_____

_____

5. Some hispanics prefer to be called latino.

_____

_____

6. Although they are different, southern baptist and american baptist churches share some characteristics.

_____

_____

7. Many people donate money to care because they believe it is a good charity that spends its money wisely.

_____

_____

8. Moving south of the freeway brought me to the city with the name northeast, pennsylvania.

_____

_____

9. Two of my favorite movies are "star trek" (including all of the sequels) and "the x-files."

_____

_____

10. As a group, native americans treasure tradition.

_____

_____

11. The meeting will be held on wednesday, october 4.

_____

_____

Capitalization Special Cases and Exceptions

Certain special cases for capitalization stand by themselves or modify the basic rules.

Example A   **Pronouns other than I**

Rule: Although the personal pronoun *I* is always capitalized, no other pronoun is capitalized unless it begins a sentence or is part of a title.

*Did they think **I** did it, or did they blame you?*

Example B   **Personal titles that follow a name**

Rule: Personal titles that follow a name are generally not capitalized.

*The speaker was Bill Gates, **president** of Microsoft.*

*Tony Blair is the **English prime minister.***

Example C   **Articles, conjunctions, and prepositions in titles**

Rule: Do not capitalize articles, conjunctions, or prepositions in titles of articles, books, shows, institutions, movies, chapters, and so on.

*At the Arquette Library, I read **The Name of the Rose** and an article entitled "**Getting More from Life and Love.**"*

Example D   **Seasons of the year**

Rule: The names of the seasons of the year are not capitalized.

*We enjoy our trips to the lake in the **spring** and **fall.***

Example E   **General historical periods**

Rule: Do not capitalize a general period in history

*Several important events have taken place in the **modern era.***

Example F   **Name of a specific company**

Rule: Capitalize the name of a specific company or business but not a general area of business.

Companies like General Dynamics are involved in the airplane industry.

DO IT YOURSELF

Add capital or lowercase letters as needed, following the rules on the previous pages.

1. Sometimes work makes Me feel like i am on a merry-go-round that never stops, but I'm determined to keep on riding until it suits me to get off.

   _____

   _____

2. For Lacey's civil War report, she described the Summer battles.

   _____

   _____

3. I remember mr. Giles because he was President of the photography club.

   _____

   _____

4. The gloomy weather during the Winter makes me tired.

   _____

   _____

5. Federico is proud of his new title, vice president of operations, the position he has wanted since joining us three years ago.

   _____

   _____

6. The paper Peninah will give at the conference is titled "Winning Ways To Jump-Start A Career In Danger of Failing."

   _____

   _____

7. I saw the movie lord of the rings when it first came to theaters.

   _____

   _____

QUOTATION MARKS

The main use of quotation marks is to show that what you are writing is an exact copy of what was originally said or written.

| Example A | Something that was said |

Aaron said to Alexandria, "We need to get this order out as quickly as possible."

| Example B | Something that was said |

"Do we need to get this order out quickly?" Aaron asked.

| Example C | A magazine article that was written |

The purchase included three copies of the magazine article called "How to Get Orders Out Quickly."

| Example D | A poem that was written |

"The Road Not Taken" is a poem by Robert Frost, one of America's most famous poets.

The quotation in Example A repeats *exactly* what Aaron said to Alexandria. The quotation in Example B repeats an *exact* question that Aaron asked. Example C gives the *exact* title of an article, and Example D shows the *exact* title of a poem. The *exact* words in all four examples are enclosed by quotation marks.

| Example E | No exact words repeated |

Aaron said something about getting that order out as fast as possible.

| Example F | Exact article title not given |

The purchase included three magazines with an article on getting orders out fast.

| Example G | Exact poem name not given |

Robert Frost wrote a famous poem about taking different roads through the woods.

In Example E, Aaron's exact words are not repeated; instead, the speaker paraphrases his comments. In Examples F and G, neither the exact title of the article nor the exact title of the poem is given, only a general description of what it is about. Quotation marks should not be used in any of the three cases.

DO IT YOURSELF

Add or remove quotation marks as needed in the following sentences.

1. I don't know why Masami told me "I shouldn't carry out the trash."

   _____

   _____

2. To be or not to be is a famous line from Shakespeare.

   _____

   _____

3. Barb read an article about the Internet economy, so I asked her, Is it interesting?

   _____

   _____

4. Born in the USA is a popular song by Bruce Springsteen.

   _____

   _____

5. Masami said to me don't carry out the trash.

   _____

   _____

6. Barb read an article entitled Making Money on the Internet.

   _____

   _____

7. Do you have a book that tells about "talking quietly in public places"?

   _____

   _____

8. Why did my supervisor say "My report needed rewriting"?

   _____

   _____

Single and Double Quotation Marks

Sometimes people who are quoted repeat something that was said by another person. This is called a quote inside a quote and is set off by a single quotation mark inside the double quotation mark. (Note: A single quotation mark is made with the apostrophe key.)

Examples

Harriet said, "I couldn't find the kit, even though Mac told me, 'It's on the shelf.' "

"Don't tell me, 'You go first,' " said Harriett when Mac told her to walk.

What Mac said is included in what Harriet said, so it is set off by single quotation marks that fall inside the double quotation marks.

Special Cases and Punctuation

Sometimes, quotation marks are not used where they might be expected. At other times, they may be allowed for effect even when you are not directly quoting a person or written item. There is no easy way to tell the difference; however, these guidelines will help. (Note: Rarely use quotation marks in this way, as they clutter your writing.)

Example A   Titles of long works

Rule: Titles of most long works, such as books, plays, or movies, are typed in italics or underlined if handwritten. No quotation marks are used.

Janet was terrified by **Night of the Living Dead.** *On the other hand, she really enjoyed reading* **Love Story.**

Example B   Title of a report or an essay

Rule: Do not put quotation marks around the title of a report or an essay you are handing in, since you are not quoting someone else.

What I Didn't Do Last Summer *by Ira Wellberg* (a writing student)

Example C   Emphasis or humorous effect needed

Rule: A word or phrase may be put in quotation marks for emphasis.

We really **"danced around the clock"** *last night.*

It's not my place to question your **"sincerity."**

DO IT YOURSELF

Correct the use of quotation marks in these sentences.

1. Cedric didn't like the plot of the new movie Crazy over Oysters.

   _____

   _____

2. I overheard our supervisor say, "Tell Rosanne, "The order is complete," before you go home."

   _____

   _____

3. The title of the report is Getting Along with People at Work.

   _____

   _____

4. Who are you to tell me that I have an old-fashioned hairstyle?

   _____

   _____

5. Most students have been required to read Exodus in some class at school.

   _____

   _____

6. It takes one to know one is a cliché my childhood friend often used when I called her a silly name.

   _____

   _____

7. I have just finished reading The Scarlet Letter.

   _____

   _____

8. "Come with me" to the mall, my friend said.

   _____

   _____

Quotation Marks and Punctuation

Some of the rules governing the use of quotation marks and punctuation may seem unusual. Nonetheless, they are the ones followed by professionals and the ones you are expected to use in your writing. Not following these rules will make your writing look as though it came from an amateur. Review the rules and example below.

(Note: If you are reading material written by an English writer, you may notice that punctuation is used differently, with more quotation marks than is outlined in the rules below. However, the following rules should be followed strictly when writing for an American audience.)

Example A   **Pointer phrases that show who is being quoted**

Rule: Use commas to separate short *pointer* phrases such as *she said* from the quotation.

"Don't sit on the cat!" **he yelled.** *"I would never do that,"* **she exclaimed,** *"because I love cats."*

Example B   **Phrases that are a natural part of a sentence**

Rule: If the quotation is a natural part of the sentence, it should not be separated from the rest of the sentence by a comma.

I loved **"It's just a flesh wound"** *in Monty Python.*

Example C   **A quotation that comes before the end of a sentence**

Rule: When the end of a quotation comes before a pointer phrase that ends the overall sentence, put a comma after the quotation and a period at the end of the sentence. (See Example D.)

"I can't stand the heat," *whimpered Marcellus.*

"That's not my stapler," *said Lupe.*

Example D   **Sentences that end with a quotation**

Rule: Put periods *inside* the closing (or final) quotation mark when the quotation is also the ending of the sentence.

Marcellus whimpered, **"I can't stand the heat."**

Lupe said, **"That's not my stapler."**

Example E   Colons and semicolons with quotation marks

Rule: Put colons and semicolons outside the closing quotation mark.

You won't catch me saying, "Let's go to the bowling alley"; I don't like bowling.

Example F   Questions marks and exclamations marks with quotations

Rule: Put question marks and exclamation marks *inside* the closing quotation mark when they are part of the quotation. Put them *outside* the quotation mark when they are part of the remaining sentence.

Cora asked, "Which way is the water cooler?"

The quotation is also a question, so it requires a question mark.

Do you think we'll have to listen to Mr. McGruder's talk on "How to Hold a Pencil"?

The exact title of a talk is inside the quotation marks, but the title itself is not a question. The full sentence is the question, so the question mark goes after the quotation mark.

"Help! The building is on fire!" yelled Charelle.

I was so exhausted I could hardly listen to the talk "Becoming a Millionaire before Thirty"!

DO IT YOURSELF

Use the rules above to punctuate the following sentences correctly.

1. "I'll be back in just a minute." said Austin.

    _____

    _____

2. I asked 'What's the matter?' and she shouted "Go away"!

    _____

    _____

DO IT YOURSELF (CONTINUED)

3. After I sneezed, Haley said, "Bless you;" I don't think she meant it literally.

   _____

   _____

4. "There's something odd in my coffee", said Bruno

   _____

   _____

5. "Are you going to the museum with me" asked Jocelynn

   _____

   _____

6. Sanjay responded, "What time are we going to leave"

   _____

   _____

7. "Stop" yelled the traffic officer as he ran after the burglar

   _____

   _____

8. "That's so exciting, shouted Bette; "I won a free ticket to "Concert Under the Stars"

   _____

   _____

9. "What time is your job interview" Paloma asked Brendano, "and where are you going after the interview"

   _____

   _____

10. Seven employees brainstormed ideas then one person said, "it's time to settle" on one idea.

    _____

    _____

Using Ellipses

An ellipsis is a series of periods used to represent missing parts of a quotation. The ellipsis is used when the whole quotation is too long to include or when some parts of the quotation do not relate to the topic. When the ellipsis replaces the end of a quotation, it is followed by a closing quotation mark.

Example

Franz Kafka, the Czech author, wrote, "You do not need to leave your room. Remain sitting at your table and listen. . . . The world will freely offer itself to you to be unmasked."

Here are examples of two basic rules for using ellipses.

Example A Words removed from the middle of a sentence

Rule: When removing words from the middle of a quoted sentence, use three periods, with spaces before, after, and between each dot.

"Four score and seven years ago our fathers brought forth, on this continent, a new nation . . . dedicated to the proposition that all men are created equal."

Example B Words removed from the end of a sentence

Rule: When removing the end of a sentence, whole sentences, or whole paragraphs, the ellipsis should include a period and three spaced dots. The fourth period represents the end of the last sentence quoted.

"Four score and seven years ago our fathers brought forth, on this continent, a new nation. . . . Now we are engaged in a great civil war. . . ."

DO IT YOURSELF

Rewrite the following paragraph by removing the second sentence and substituting an ellipsis.

Oliver acted like a deer in the headlights when his supervisor asked a question. Unfortunately, his shyness made him appear unprepared. He's working to build his self-confidence.

_____

_____

SPELLING

Business writing is judged as much on spelling, grammar, and punctuation as on style and ideas. Yet spelling may be more difficult in English than in any other language.

You will feel more secure about the accuracy of your writing if you buy a good dictionary that provides correct spellings and word definitions. However, if spelling is a particular concern, you might want to purchase a separate spelling dictionary that not only lists common misspellings, but also guides you to the correct spelling.

English has many rules for spelling, and nearly all of them include exceptions that must be learned individually. Study the most common rules and their exceptions shown below.

Example   i before e

Rule: *i* comes before *e* except after *c*—or when sounding like *a* as in *neighbor* and *weigh*.

Exceptions to Rule: seize, weird, leisure, either

Guidelines from Word Sounds

The way a word sounds is often a clear guide to how it should be spelled. The following examples and guidelines can help you figure out spellings based on sounds. However, each guideline has many exceptions. The guidelines alone should not serve as a substitute for learning the correct spelling of specific words.

Example A   The silent e

Guideline: A silent *e* at the end of a word usually gives a long sound to the vowel that comes before the *e*. *Long* means that the vowel sound is the same as the vowel's name. For example, an *o* can sound like "oh" (long sound) or "ah" (short sound). If a word has an "oh" sound, you can safely assume that you should add an *e* at the end.

You can change **mat** *to* **mate** *by adding an* e. *You also can get* **rid** *of a* **ride** *by dropping the* e.

Example B   Words ending in f

Guideline: Most common words ending in an *f* sound are spelled with a double *f*.

We took the **skiff** *out in a stiff breeze, so Clara had to wear her* **muff.**

Example C   Words ending in k

Guideline: Many common one-syllable words that contain a short vowel and end in a *k* sound are spelled with a *ck*. Words with a double *o*, however, use only the *k*.

*Look how **black** the **crack** in the **brick** appears in the sunlight. We read about that in a **book**.*

DO IT YOURSELF

Using the examples and guidelines on the previous pages, correct the misspellings in the following sentences.

1. I can't find a way to deflat the cushion on this chair.

    _____

    _____

2. Considering the state of the economy, I'd stik with your current stok.

    _____

    _____

3. Jeremy, there's a thread hanging from your cuf.

    _____

    _____

4. The staf is delighted by the slat of candidates for the election.

    _____

    _____

5. The longe ride hom always maks me tired.

    _____

    _____

Common Rules, Exceptions, and Problem Words

This section covers three of the most important spelling rules, the exceptions to the rules, and words that cause difficulty because of their spelling. You may need to refer to this section often, as trying to remember all of the rules can lead to confusion and misspellings.

Common Rules

As noted earlier, all spelling rules in English have numerous exceptions. Only a few such examples and rules are shown here. No matter what the rule, you must learn the individual exceptions.

Example A   Suffixes following y

Rule: When a word ends in a consonant followed by *y*, change the *y* to *i* before adding a suffix. (Keep the *y* when adding the ending *ing*.) For example, *silly* becomes *sillier*.

*We're **happier** now than the **coziest**, most **easily** contented clam that ever went **hurrying** along the shore.*

*The data entry **keying** was some of the **sloppiest** work I have ever seen from a data processing specialist.*

*The **runniest** lines in the oil painting occurred at the top of the picture, where they were covered, fortunately, by the large frame.*

Exception: slyly

Example B   Suffixes after a short vowel

Rule: When the final vowel has a short sound and is followed by a consonant, usually double that consonant before adding a suffix that begins with a vowel. Two examples of suffixes that begin with vowels are *ing* and *ed*.

*I don't think I could have **netted** that fish without your help.*

*This report does not seem to be **formatted** correctly.*

***Wetting** solution is used by people who wear contact lenses.*

***Sitting** all day is hard for me to do.*

Exceptions: traveler, marvelous, busing

Example C   Suffixes after a long vowel

Rule: When a word ends in a silent *e*, drop the silent *e* before adding a suffix beginning with a vowel. Keep the *e*, however, when the suffix starts with a consonant, such as *ly*.

*We took a course in **mining**. The **timing** of the training was poorly planned.*

*I wouldn't depend **solely** on any rule to determine spelling.*

Exceptions: courageous, mileage, truly

DO IT YOURSELF

Using the previous rules, correct the spelling in the following sentences.

1. The consultant's ratting of our team was at the top of the scale.

   _____

   _____

2. Such a beautyfully written report shows that you are really triing.

   _____

   _____

3. What is the dat of the next meeting? Are we all invitted?

   _____

   _____

4. I'm bitting off more than I can chew but not deniing how much fun it is.

   _____

   _____

5. The happyest day of my life was when I met my biological father.

   _____

   _____

Words That Sound Alike

Certain words sound alike but are spelled differently and have different meanings. A few such word groups are listed below. When you are unsure of exact meanings, check your dictionary.

are	*our*	*hour*
brake	*break*	
cloths	*clothes*	
here	*hear*	
lead	*led*	
let's	*less*	
ours	*hours*	
proceed	*precede*	
rain	*rein*	*reign*
read	*red*	
stake	*steak*	
sum	*some*	
their	*there*	*they're*
theirs	*there's*	
to	*too*	*two*
way	*weigh*	
witch	*which*	
write	*right*	

Beware of spell checkers: Computer spell checkers can tell you when a word is spelled correctly. However, they cannot tell you when you have chosen the correct word. After using a spell checker, go over your spelling again by reading the document.

Example   **Errors not caught by spell checker**

I like the yellow chair butter that the green one. If it were up to me, I would all ways choose yellow.

DO IT YOURSELF

Correct the sound-alike words in the following sentences. Keep your dictionary handy.

1. They drove a steak through the vampire's heart. How much did it way?

   _____

   _____

2. They can't find the lab report that they red. Is that are problem to?

   _____

   _____

3. The subject will usually proceed the verb in a sentence.

   _____

   _____

4. Bad ethics lead him to loose his job as team leader.

   _____

   _____

5. The committee will meet hear next week for the public hearing.

   _____

   _____

6. Less all ride together to the convention.

   _____

   _____

7. They're supervisors wear having a meating about pay increases.

   _____

   _____

8. Getting the facts rite is important too a reporter.

   _____

   _____

Words Often Misspelled

The list below includes many commonly misspelled words that are likely to occur in business writing.

accommodate	*all right*	*a lot*
always	*analyze*	*calendar*
category	*changeable*	*committee*
competent	*desperate*	*develop*
eighth	*embarrass*	*exaggerate*
February	*gauge*	*guard*
harass	*irrelevant*	*judgment*
mathematics	*millennium*	*missile*
noticeable	*permissible*	*privilege*
receipt	*receive*	*recipe*
relieve	*secretary*	*seize*
surprise	*through*	*truly*
vacuum	*writing*	*yield*

Special Problem Areas

Some areas of spelling are not covered by rules. You simply must be aware of the specific (and sometimes peculiar) spellings in each case and correct them before submitting a formal document.

Advertising shortcuts

In business writing, avoid simplified spellings introduced by advertising—words such as *lite* and *thru*. If in doubt about the correctness of a spelling, refer to a dictionary.

Company names

Double-check the spelling of company names. Often they adopt odd spellings or use capitals differently to catch readers' attention—*Rite Aid, CIGNA*.

Terms used in your business

Companies or industries adopt their own spelling for terms specific to their type of business. When in doubt, look at your company's printed material. Does it use *bio-engineering* or *bioengineering*, *e-business* or *e-Business*, *archaeology* or *archeology*?

DO IT YOURSELF

Find and correct the misspellings in the sentences below.

1. Dwight said that there would be a mathmatics refresher course tonite.

   _____

   _____

2. We were truely impressed by the lab test. It is allways accurate.

   _____

   _____

3. Let's take a brake before we guage what we've learned.

   _____

   _____

4. Silvia locked the vaccum chamber and sliped into her seat.

   _____

   _____

5. Bridget's work load can't accomodate any more tasks.

   _____

   _____

6. My friend works on misseles as a part of his military assignment.

   _____

   _____

7. I was embarased when a person in the office said I harrassed her.

   _____

   _____

CHOOSING YOUR WORDS

The actual words you use in a paragraph, an essay, or another type of document can make the difference between informative, specific writing and dull, general writing. If your goal is to motivate the reader to spend time and attention on what you write, then you must choose words that are appealing. As a part of this section, you may wish to review Chapters 6 and 16 about descriptive writing.

> **Example**   **Dull, general writing**
>
> *We believe that our business is the most complete of its kind anywhere. Therefore, we propose that you sign the attached contract.*
>
> **Example**   **Lively, specific writing**
>
> *National Products has been the leading producer of quilted matting for the last five years, according to Angstrom Research. Please look over the attached contract, which meets the demands you specified at an exceptionally low price.*

The Pitfalls of Language

Although every writer develops his or her own style, certain guidelines can help in choosing language that makes the reader take your writing seriously. Lazy writing is evident by the types of common mistakes that are often apparent in a hurriedly written document.

> **Example A**   **Use precise terms**
>
> **Guideline:** Whenever possible, use precise descriptions or numbers, rather than vague terms such *about, around, kind of,* and *I guess.* Precise terms motivate the reader to continue.
>
> Precise writing is very important in business, as it can make the difference in whether a company wins an account, sells a product, receives a contract, secures new clients, or soothes the feelings of an annoyed customer.
>
> **Imprecise, general writing**
>
> *Our company can deliver the products you want when you want them.*
>
> **Precise, specific writing**
>
> *Westfield can customize any product according to your specifications and deliver it within five working days.*

Imprecise, general writing

Our seafood is delicious, and you'll go home satisfied.

Precise, specific writing

Our chefs stimulate your taste buds with savory Chilean sea bass that has been rubbed with five herbs and spices and grilled lightly over glowing embers.

Imprecise, general writing

Most school reading programs just don't work. Ours does, and we can prove it.

Precise, specific writing

Maelstrom Associates' reading program is the only one to be certified by the National Testing Guild as raising test scores for 80 percent of students.

DO IT YOURSELF

Rewrite these imprecise sentences to make them more precise. Use specific, descriptive words.

1. The passive restraint device in our automobiles helps eliminate human fatalities.

    _____

    _____

2. We serve some of the best hamburgers around.

    _____

    _____

3. Do not spill soda into the typing part of your computer.

    _____

    _____

Example B   Use the proper preposition

Guideline: Prepositions are often tricky in English. If you are unsure of which one to use, try to find a similar example as a reference.

Improper preposition: *Keva, who was in charge of purchasing, submitted the invoice **on** the new computer.*

Proper preposition: *Keva, who was in charge of purchasing, submitted the invoice **for** the new computer.*

Example C   Add variety to your language

Guideline: Don't use the same word repeatedly. Keep a thesaurus handy and find substitute words.

Poor variety: *Cliff had **worked** hard, but he had never **worked** as hard as today.*

Good variety: *Cliff had **worked** hard, but he had never **toiled** as he did today.*

DO IT YOURSELF

Rewrite these lifeless sentences to add appeal. Be aware of what prepositions you use.

1. I guess I don't much like tasteless drinks or bad food.

    _____

    _____

2. We couldn't agree with how to do the work, so we didn't do it.

    _____

    _____

3. They're pieces of paper all over the place, whole sheets of paper and even little pieces too.

    _____

    _____

Example D   Use correct terminology

Guideline: Learn the terminology from your field or business and use it accurately.

General, nonbusiness terminology: *The telephone operators don't consider themselves to be salespeople.*

Business terminology: *The call center representatives don't consider themselves to be telemarketers.*

Example E   Avoid jargon

Guideline: Even when writing a company report, use plain English wherever possible, rather than unclear or empty terms that will confuse the reader.

Unclear, empty terms: Nicole said that she anticipated the incipient negative situation.

Plain English: Nicole said that she had dealt with the problem in advance.

DO IT YOURSELF

Rewrite the following sentences, substituting clear, precise business terminology for nonbusiness terms or jargon.

1. Removing the contents of waste containers was not included in the guidelines under which I was hired.

   _____

   _____

2. The airline report indicated that not enough people had been hired to seat all of the passengers.

   _____

   _____

Sexist Language

Although it may take extra effort, you should avoid using the male or female pronoun when referring to people in general. Also avoid stereotyping jobs by gender.

Example   **Sexist**

The story was about the heroism of firemen, policemen, and mailmen.

Example   **Neutral**

The story was about the heroism of firefighters, police officers, and mail carriers.

It may be difficult to find a neutral term or a simple way to make the noun plural. In such cases, an expression such as *he or she* is permissible, but it should not be used often. A better alternative may be to use the plural pronoun *they*. However, be careful not to make the error of using a plural pronoun, such as *they*, with a singular verb.

Example   **Correct use of plural pronoun**

Firefighters, police officers, and mail carriers: They are all heroes.

Example   **Incorrect use of plural pronoun**

When someone fails the test, they can take it again.

DO IT YOURSELF

Rewrite these sentences in correct gender-neutral style.

1. To show her best, an assistant must write well.

   _____

   _____

2. If anyone reads my report, they should be satisfied with it.

   _____

   _____

Slang and Clichés

Business and other formal writing uses a somewhat different vocabulary from everyday conversation. Slang (street talk) and clichés are seldom appropriate for formal writing.

Slang

Business writing that includes slang may not be taken seriously; therefore, avoid slang in business writing as much as possible. Some words, such as *hassle* and *sitcom*, have moved from slang to more general acceptance. However, it is best to avoid such terms in business writing unless you are sure they are accepted at your workplace. You can usually find a nonslang alternative.

Slang example

We were hanging around the water cooler trading jive when the lights went kabam. The afternoon was blown, so we went back to our pads.

Business example

While we were talking at the water cooler, the lights went out without warning. Since it was impossible to do any work, we all went home.

Clichés

A cliché is an overused expression that has lost its impact from being heard or read too often. Clichés can make career writing (and the writer) look out of date.

Example with clichés

Wes came in with a box as big as a house and started raving like a lunatic at everyone. When I asked him why he was being such a crybaby, he looked at me like I had lost my marbles.

Example avoiding clichés

Wes came in carrying a massive box and began shouting insults at the employees. When I asked him why he was acting so absurdly, he stared at me with cold, fierce eyes that were intimidating.

Clichés are often harder to weed out of writing than slang. They become so much a part of your thinking that you may not recognize them. If you find yourself wondering if a particular phrase is a cliché, see if it draws an accurate picture. Is that package really "as big as a house"?

DO IT YOURSELF

Choose your words carefully to rewrite the following sentences.

1. Henry was as quiet as a mouse while studying for the science test.

   _____

   _____

2. After the merger, our company's stock price went right through the roof.

   _____

   _____

3. The formula we learned today really blew me away.

   _____

   _____

4. By this afternoon, we should see the light at the end of the tunnel.

   _____

   _____

5. The first things a guy needs to learn about when driving are the stop and go pedals.

   _____

   _____

6. The least likely functional outcome is that we will be unable to assure the level of work output.

   _____

   _____

7. Acknowledging the deficit in the impending budget acquaints us all with the restraints we face.

   _____

   _____

Index